Conrad Richter

I cannot remember ideas. They are forgotten in two or three minutes, even less. One of the constant, important functions of my life must be to set them down at once whatever the circumstance. Get it down at the moment it comes. Don't let it get away between the shelves of the library.

If your journal has only 1 line paragraphs, so much the better if they are real authentic thoughts. You inherited too much developing — theological seasonings frothy, recoiling & thinking for a new idea. A lay man is more versatile in his thoughts. A lay man in the paragraph says something different instead of saying the same thing in other words. It enriches the writing, thickens it, gives the reader a constant & humbling impression of the writer's strength & power. You think these things had less then. Set them down & crowd your paragraph with new thoughts & angles.

I thought these things at 12 o'clock midnight on the 13th.

Conrad Richter

A Writer's Life

DAVID R. JOHNSON

For Dave and Ed —
August 10, 2013

THE PENNSYLVANIA STATE UNIVERSITY PRESS
UNIVERSITY PARK, PENNSYLVANIA

Library of Congress Cataloging-in-Publication Data

Johnson, David R., 1943–
    Conrad Richter : a writer's life / David R. Johnson.
      p.   cm. — (Penn State series in the history of the book)
    Includes bibliographical references and index.
    ISBN 0-271-02097-0 (alk. paper)
    1. Richter, Conrad, 1890–1968. 2. Novelists, American—20th century—Biography.
I. Title. II. Series.

PS3535.I429 Z74 2001
813'.52—dc21
[B]

00-057132

It is the policy of The Pennsylvania State University Press to use acid-free paper for the first printing of all clothbound books. Publications on uncoated stock satisfy the minimum requirements of American National Standard for Information Sciences—Permanence of Paper for Printed Library Materials, ANSI Z39.48–1992

FRONTISPIECE: A handwritten page of Richter's journal, dated December 14, 1937. Richter's journal served as a writing record, a diary of daily happenings, and, as in this entry, a place for reflection on his writing process. Often Richter typed his journal entries.

Contents

List of Illustrations

Introduction:
River to the Sea

On March 9, 1961, Conrad Richter was surprised to receive a telephone call from his publisher, Alfred Knopf. Though friends for more than twenty years, the two men communicated primarily by letter; telephone calls from Knopf came about as frequently as visits from the publisher to the novelist's home in the small Pennsylvania town of Pine Grove. Knowing his friend, Knopf began tentatively. "I think I have good news for you," he said. In the pause that followed Richter ran through in his mind possible news that his publisher would know first—strong sales figures, a book club contract, perhaps an offer for film rights to a novel—but he was unable to guess the news Knopf had for him that day: Richter's latest novel, *The Waters of Kronos*, had been selected for the 1961 National Book Award for fiction. Almost as quickly as he understood the significance of his publisher's words, Richter grasped why Knopf had prefaced his announcement as he had. When Richter had won the Pulitzer Prize for fiction in 1951, there had been no dinners to attend, no public ceremony for the novelist to dread in advance and grit his way through. But the new prize, Richter understood, was going to be a different experience: the announcement of the National Book Awards would be a media event—and he at the center of it. He would even be expected to speak. When Richter asked if recipients always attended, Knopf was ready for the question. "Even Faulkner," he replied.[1]

Feeling "stampeded but helpless," Richter listened glumly as Knopf explained the details to him. In addition to attending the actual ceremony, Richter would be asked to join the year's other two winners, William Shirer and Randall Jarrell, in a photographing session, a news conference, and a television interview. As his publisher well knew, Conrad Richter had an unusually strong aversion to such affairs. In Pine Grove and elsewhere Richter was known to enjoy the company of others and to be good company himself: among friends, his laughter and gentle wit came effortlessly. But the novelist, who often sought out conversations with strangers, relishing the speech of ordinary people, had a dread of public events that bordered on a phobia. He habitually declined invitations to attend dinners, give lectures, grant television or radio interviews, or even attend signings at bookstores. When a circumstance like the National Book Award ceremony required his attendance, he was unable to work for days beforehand, suffering unallayable anxiety. Understanding Richter's limits, Knopf promised to get him excused from the television interview, provided his author agreed to go with him, after the awards ceremony, to the opera.[2]

On March 15, the day of the awards ceremony, Richter negotiated the photography session without incident, though he thought the photographer who insisted that he pose holding his book in front of him "asinine." But at the news conference, the first question was "Where's Mr. Richter?" for only Shirer and Jarrell were to be seen. Entering the conference room, Richter had discovered a raised platform with three chairs upon it and a microphone in front of each. Unprepared to be so conspicuous to so many eyes, he placed himself in the first row of seats, directly below Jarrell and Shirer, and he sent Knopf's head of advertising, Harding Lemay, to explain that there he would stay throughout the questions. He would not participate, but if anyone cared to approach him afterwards, he would answer questions for individuals.

Of those who did approach the author of *The Waters of Kronos*, several were critics and reviewers who had already written reviews of his work, helping to spread Richter's reputation for fine, well-crafted novels, novels set in a past Richter re-created in a distinctively simple, richly evocative style. The most widely known were his first, *The Sea of Grass*, and a trilogy of novels about a family westering into frontier Ohio, beginning with *The Trees* and ending with *The Town*, the novel that had won the Pulitzer. These novels had made him nationally prominent, his face easily recognizable from the photographs that appeared with reviews in news magazines and major newspapers. But if reporters knew the face, they did not know, and may have been surprised by, the man who received their questions. Smiling a large, generous smile, Richter listened attentively to his questioners, then answered their queries seriously and with good humor. So controlled were his replies, his voice so confidently modulated, that it was hard to imagine why, just an hour earlier, he had declined to join his fellow winners on the platform. If they asked, he would have told them, simply, as he had often told others, that speaking in public was not one of his talents. He would not have said, because it was the sort of personal information he chose to keep to himself, that since adolescence he had been struggling to overcome his intense self-consciousness in public. One reporter did ask how Richter planned to deliver his acceptance speech before a large audience. "Oh," Richter responded, "you have a surprise coming." That evening when Richter's name was announced, it was not Richter but Alfred Knopf who strode to the lectern to read the acceptance speech.[3]

Following the National Book Award ceremony, Conrad Richter kept his promise to attend the opera with Alfred Knopf, hearing Leontyne Price in *Aida*. The next day Richter skipped the television interview and returned to Pine Grove, where the seventeen completed chapters of a novel about his father's life as a country minister awaited him. And already he was gathering information for another novel, a book based on his own life, the story of a shy boy who struggled to understand his nervous sensitivity and to surmount it. When several years later Richter finally wrote the first pages of the novel he sometimes referred to as "River to the Sea," he began with a chapter entitled "The Odd One"— corrected in the heavily edited typescript to read "The Boy"—followed by this first sentence: "The boy didn't know what was wrong with him then, only that he was different from other people including his brothers and parents." Shortly thereafter he listed the three qualities of the boy's family that "especially baffled him": how easily "they could let themselves die in sleep"; how they could "welcome the company of other human creatures with their strangely disturbing presences, smells, and voices"; and "how they could go to the Golgotha of a church on Sunday, eager to join the press of other people suddenly and unaccountably subdued as if drugged."[4]

That boy was one Conrad Richter, an exceptionally sensitive child so uncomfortably out of place in his own family that he questioned whether he was even, rightly, a member of it. But as Richter himself certainly understood, from the beginning there had been another, a different Conrad Richter, one who was intensely attached to his parents and brothers, unhappy whenever his mother was not at home. This Conrad Richter took pleasure both in the idea of his patrician heritage from his mother's side—the Conrads, early settlers of Pine Grove, and the Henrys, like the Conrads a family of prominent Lutheran clergymen—and almost equal delight in the idea of his Richter ancestors, generations of shepherds from the Black Forest. From them he inherited, he believed, his love of the out-of-doors, his preference for solitude, his dislike of large crowds, and his fear of speaking in public.

A family portrait from 1894 shows Lottie and John Richter with their three sons, baby Fred in Lottie's arms, the toddler Joe leaning against his father's knee, and Connie, four years old, standing sturdily between his parents. Roundfaced and blonde, Connie looks directly into the camera, a bright, alert young boy. In his facial features one can already make out his grandfather Henry's distinctive jaw line, though young Connie's mouth is fuller than that of his angular grandfather. In a portrait with Joe, taken perhaps six months earlier, Connie especially resembles his mother. In later portraits and candid snapshots from his teenage years, Connie looks more like his father at a similar age. If there had ever been any doubt of his parentage—and there was not—the close family resemblances would have put an end to it. He was most certainly Johnny and Lottie's boy, a Conrad, Henry, and Richter. The stolid Pennsylvania Dutch of Pine Grove, Pennsylvania, would have thought it some joke on the Richters if their oldest boy Connie (they pronounced it Kunnie) had ever said out loud what he was thinking.

By his teenage years Conrad Richter had dabbled in photography enough to be able to take a whimsical double exposure of himself. In it one Conrad Richter, in suit and tie, has settled himself comfortably on the front stoop of the family's home. His legs pulled up and his hands clasped about his left knee, he smiles in good humor and frankness as he looks directly at his double. The other Conrad Richter, standing beside the porch, a foot on the first step and his arm resting on his knee, seems less attentive to the event of the photograph or to his alter ego beside him. Jacket off and tie in disarray, he looks somewhere into the distance, not unhappy but unsmiling, as if he has not yet quite taken in a comment just made by his wisecracking twin. Perhaps the different expressions were deliberate; perhaps not. Regardless, the double exposure invites a symbolic interpretation, for in his early manhood there remained at least two Conrad Richters, and the two still somewhat in conflict.

One might be named "the go getter," as he would title an early story, an outgoing young man with modern ideas with the verve to put himself forward, and plans to accomplish great things. At the top of his list was making "a little pile" of money to rescue his parents and especially his mother from the "desperate penury" of a small-town minister's salary.[5] This young man was full of plans to succeed in business and not at all shy in trying out his ideas. (Before he was twenty he would establish a wholesale lumber business and later try to market nationwide a Pennsylvania Dutch staple, pretzels; at twenty-two he invested all he could in a speculative silver mining venture, buying the shares on time.) Nor was he hesitant in introducing himself to pretty young women on trains or in writing letters to the director of the National Park Service and the president of the United States to ask for jobs, or to William Dean Howells and Jack London, among others, proposing himself as a private secretary. This Conrad Richter had a winning manner, making him a leader among his friends. If he was at times a little shy, he had a smile that was genuine and mild blue eyes (he would call them gray) that looked straight at the person he was talking to. People liked him.

It was the other Conrad Richter, however, whom Richter chose to portray first in his story of his life. This was the young man who would worry for days before an interview with one of the people to whom he had written so confidently, taking out his growing irritability on his family. This was the man who, after such an interview, would go home to write paragraphs in his personal notebooks assessing his performance, emphasizing his mistakes in what he said or should have said, ending with advice to "contain" himself, which meant bridling his inclination to what he called the three C's, confiding, confessing, and criticizing others.[6] His extreme dread of such experiences did not lessen after he gained prominence as a novelist. Once when Richter was visiting his brother Fred's family in Syracuse, New York, a newspaper reporter found out he was in town and called Fred to ask for an interview. Discovering that his brother had agreed, Richter flew into a rage that frightened Fred's two sons, and he fretted irritably until the newspaperman actually arrived. Then Richter submitted to the interview with warmth, humor, and what appeared to Fred's sons, young Fred and Eduard, to be utterly unself-conscious ease. It thoroughly puzzled them.[7]

Richter saw such behavior as the inheritance from his ancestors in the Black Forest. He was simply a peasant, unfit for celebrity or any public occupation, he occasionally reminded himself in his journal. On the publication of his second collection of short stories, *Early Americana*, Richter was surprised and pleased with the first reviews his stories received, but uneasy, too. When he heard that the review in the *New York Herald Tribune* was accompanied by a photograph of him, he commented to himself wryly, "I am a little overwhelmed with my importance," then continued his journal entry with a cautionary reminder: "I am not meant for greatness. I am a shepherd's grandson and am at peace and ease only alone with animals and nature as a shepherd. . . . Perhaps if I remember I am a kind of solitary shepherd, a quiet gentle amused shepherd even with people, I shall manage to get along. But if I ever get the notion I am clever, companionable, interesting, a conversationalist, I am hopelessly lost. It is beyond me."[8]

Less than two months later Richter found himself in a decidedly unpastoral Hollywood, a screenwriter for Metro-Goldwyn-Mayer. A photograph taken that fall, or perhaps the following fall when he was again putting in a four-month assignment screenwriting, displays the public Richter. In it he walks along a Los Angeles street, striding confidently toward the camera. Wearing a well-fitting suit of medium gray and a natty snap-brim hat, he could be a movie producer or director, or one of Hollywood's moguls. He has confidence, his appearance announces; it shows in his stride, his well-trimmed mustache, in the jaunty angle of his hat. This is a man who is going somewhere important. And in truth he was: at forty-six he had finally achieved something like the success he had been so eager to accomplish as a young man, selling a number of his stories to the *Saturday Evening Post*, which during the depression found its way into more American homes than any other magazine. That fall his first serial story, *The Sea of Grass*, appeared in the *Post*; it was later published as a novel by the prestigious publishing house of Alfred A. Knopf. And before either appeared, MGM would buy the motion picture rights to Richter's *The Sea of Grass* for $15,000—more than triple what Richter had earned in any year of his life—as a film property for its premiere stars, Spencer Tracy and Katharine Hepburn.

During Richter's first stint at screenwriting, Alfred Knopf had written to his half brother at MGM, the man in charge of the studio's 125 writers, to say that Richter had "the guts and integrity" not to be "carried away" by Hollywood.[9] This was strong—and shrewd—testimony and Edwin Knopf's own experience was to bear out his brother's estimation. In Richter's first week at MGM, Knopf had pressed him to sign a contract with a series of four options, each with a substantial increase to a final salary of $1,200 a week. When Richter declined, Edwin Knopf had walked about his office in such agitation that Richter would later ask his Hollywood agent, Gerald Adams, if he had made Knopf angry. "No, he was just amazed with you," was the agent's laughing reply. Then Adams explained to the novice Richter that he had turned down what for screenwriters was "the most sought after thing in pictures."[10]

At the time, Edwin Knopf knew comparatively little about his new writer. He may well have been even further perplexed at Richter's refusal if he had known more of the real story of Richter's writing career, a story that Richter, ever inclined to be secretive about his personal life, preferred to keep to himself. That fall Richter did offer a highly selective version of his past to Alfred Knopf, who had learned that Richter had already published three books—a collection of short stories and two nonfiction books on his theories about the evolution of human consciousness. When Knopf asked to read all three, Richter at first put his publisher off, and when Knopf pressed for copies, Richter dismissed his early writing career with characteristic understatement. He had tried writing the best stories he could and found they paid him almost no money. Thereafter he wrote stories of the ordinary commercial variety, like most in *Brothers of No Kin*, his first story collection. When his daughter as a senior in high school brought home great works of literature, he too read them, and this reading rekindled his ambition to write better stories than the pulp westerns and popular magazine stories that supported his family through the dark years of the depression. The result was that he began to write "the best fiction that was in me that would sell."[11]

Sorting out from his life a story for his publisher, Richter created a simple fable about a writer who turned from a modest livelihood to attempt a larger ambition and succeeded, a fable that he would regularly repeat in later years. Although Richter's explanation is not precisely a misrepresentation, it is a story most notable in what it leaves out. The final sentence in Richter's explanation to Knopf, a sentence seemingly itself the stuff of Hollywood, contains as much candor as any sentence in the letter: "The first better story I did in 1934 was 'Early Marriage,' and the popular short story I was doing at the time the other sold is still unfinished and put away against such a time when this sort of work may again become necessary."[12] There was indeed a pulp western Richter had put away while he sold "better" stories to George Horace Lorimer at the Curtis Publishing Company. But the story was only put away; it was not discarded. He was keeping it "against such a time when this sort of work may again become necessary." For all his sense of purposeful direction, his air of a man going places, the man striding so confidently in the photograph was not then—and would not ever be—as sure of the future as he preferred others to believe.

In a 1955 letter to a fellow writer, Frank Gruber, Richter tried out another version of his story, equally fable-like: "When people ask me the secret of writing successful stories, I say, lose all your money in the stock market, go deep into debt trying to save the stock so you can't pay the interest, have a sick wife who needs doctors and care and a kid who must go to school and be decently dressed, and have all this happen during a depression like 1929, 1930 when you can't get a job to save your soul—then by the great god Pan if you have anything in you, it'll come out. This, I suspect, is the plan of this world."[13] Again the last sentence is the most telling, an admission slipped into what otherwise seems almost bluster. In it Richter opens just a crack the window into his personal beliefs about the meaning of life. The "plan of this world" to Richter is that humans must struggle; it is only by undergoing such times as Richter's own desperate experiences in the depression, only by such acts of will as Richter's efforts to bring into submission his own nervous disposition, that people evolve into higher levels of consciousness. His first two nonfiction books were about just this idea; so too was his later book, better received but still misunderstood, *The Mountain on the Desert*.

At the end of his first four-month assignment at MGM, Richter confided in Edwin Knopf another piece of the story he had left out in his sketch to the movie executive's brother, an admission that made Richter's refusal of the contract all the more puzzling. Richter had arrived in Hollywood more than $8,500 in debt, debt that began with the stock market crash in 1929 when he lost in a single day his life's savings of $15,000. As wary of Hollywood as a shepherd's grandson would be, he agreed to work for MGM because he had no other way to clear himself and his family of so much debt. But he had no illusions; Hollywood might well turn out to be as much of a trial as the stock market crash had been—another opportunity for Richter to play his part in the plan of the world. As he remarked in his journal at the beginning of his contract, "I told Adams earlier that I should be willing to go through hell to get my debts paid and I must not be surprised if fate takes me up on it."[14]

Richter left Hollywood in late February 1937, just after *The Sea of Grass* was published by Alfred Knopf. He returned for one more contract the following year, and then he was done with Hollywood forever. From the perspective of admiring readers and fellow writers, Conrad Richter's career thereafter was a model of a certain kind of artistic behavior. His novels came out regularly, about two years apart, for the rest of his life. None would be faddish or sensational. None would treat sex or violence graphically. But each would be greeted by loyal readers—and critics—anticipating the next Conrad Richter novel. Virtually all sold at least modestly well, and several very well indeed, and all would be translated into a long list of foreign languages.

As he traveled in a triangle formed by the Southwest, Florida, and his hometown of Pine Grove, Pennsylvania, Richter carried with him his increasingly battered portable typewriter and the loose pages of whatever novel was in progress. Because his wife Harvena and he loved the high desert of New Mexico, they returned often to Albuquerque, where they had spent the hardest years of their marriage. They loved as well the richly varied seasons in the Pennsylvania hills surrounding their hometown of Pine Grove. Whether in Pennsylvania or New Mexico, no matter how engaged he might be in his writing, each day Richter took time for an afternoon ride onto the desert around Albuquerque or into the hills above Pine Grove. That time was Harvey's, whose recovery from tuberculosis left her a semi-invalid. Because winters in New Mexico and Pennsylvania were too cold for Harvena and California too far to travel by car, in Richter's last years Florida became, almost by default, their home for the coldest months each year. There they avoided the tourist attractions and crowded beaches, renting modest cottages in smaller, out-of-the-way towns.

During Florida winters Richter was less inclined to press himself on writing a novel, allowing himself more time to keep up a remarkable correspondence, answering every letter he received. Many of his correspondents were fellow writers, usually ones less well known than Richter. Having himself been helped by the kindnesses of other writers when he was struggling in Albuquerque, Richter deliberately attempted to return the favor. He was especially solicitous of writers close to home in Pine Grove, driving out to Richard Wheeler's cottage in Swope's Valley to make friends with the reclusive writer, introducing Julia Hikes, whose novels were published under her maiden name, Julia Truitt Yenni, to his agent and his publisher. When a young editor for *American Heritage* by the name of David McCullough came to interview him, Richter encouraged him to write his own books and then pressed his agent, Paul Reynolds, to take on McCullough as a client.

By 1951, the year he won the Pulitzer Prize for fiction, the appearance of a Richter novel would be a modest literary event. Each novel was reviewed in major newspapers nationwide, with news and literary magazines sending staff writers to interview him and photographers to capture his portrait for their pages. After his second novel, Richter never read the reviews of his books. Instead, he relied on his wife to read them and then select passages to read aloud to him. On one such occasion, Richter interrupted his wife after several glowing sentences of praise, saying he could not bear to hear more. Then he went out to water the lawn for several hours until the effect of those words had worn off.[15]

Although Richter belonged to P.E.N., the international writers' organization, and to the National Institute of Arts and Letters, both offering opportunities to meet and mingle with the nation's literati, he seldom could bring himself to attend the dinners and other public affairs of either, sending his daughter in his place. And just as often as not, when chance put him in the way of famous writers, Richter would avoid the meeting. When he could not, he afterwards taxed himself with being too slow, too fumbling in his conversation. When another writer complimented him in person, he could never quite believe that such praise was not extorted by the personal meeting, as if people believed that he expected such talk from them. Just after the National Book Award ceremony, Richter stepped from an elevator to be greeted by Bernard Malamud and a man who spoke about *The Waters of Kronos* in embarrassing superlatives. "I tell people about the book," he exclaimed, declaring that too few readers knew of Richter's marvelous work. The speaker was Isaac Bashevis Singer, and only in time would Richter come to believe that the writer's praise was not fulsome. Over the next several years reports would come to Richter that Singer was publicly pronouncing him "a great talent," America's best novelist. In the occasional correspondence between the two writers, Singer sometimes began his letters with the salutation "Dear Master."[16]

To those who were acquainted with Richter, this man of modest habits and unpretentious lifestyle seemed someone who had found his center, a writer who did not care for public adulation or the distractions of public appearances. His course seemed fixed on a constant star, one of his own choosing, and he navigated safely by that star despite changing currents and popular tastes. That is not to say that Conrad Richter was without his small indulgences. He bought his shirts and pajamas from Brooks Brothers, simple accommodations to luxury. In his later years he drove Cadillacs, though he always bought used ones— preferring their functional superiority and prestige but unwilling to pay full price to acquire them—and drove them long after his neighbors had traded in their Fords and Buicks for new models. But these were clearly exceptions. Like so many other Americans who had suffered through the Great Depression, Richter was close with his money. Once his nephew Bill took Richter to a discount appliance store to buy a new toaster. There Richter chose the cheapest model available, explaining to his nephew that "we only make toast at breakfast."[17] But if Richter was known by his family and neighbors to be thrifty, that was a practice for which, in the Pennsylvania Dutch country of his childhood and later years, there was no reason for rebuke. Rather, it made him simply another townsperson. He might be famous, but to the residents of Pine Grove he was still Connie, just as he had been to his mother and Aunt Lizzie long ago, in the years before the turn of the century when Pine Grove streets were paved with brick and the shade trees hung in a canopy over the sidewalks.

In his last years, Richter placed a snapshot inside the front cover of a devotional notebook he carried in his old corduroy jacket. Although around Pine Grove Richter habitually wore the jacket until Harvey threw it away to keep him from wearing it any longer, he was even in old age more attentive to what his neighbors thought of him than any of them would have guessed. The photograph inside his notebook was one of himself from the depression days in Albuquerque, a picture he evidently had not prepared himself for. In it he stands bareheaded in the outdoors, hair cropped exceptionally close and high above his ears. His collar is open, his sleeves rolled up, his pants unpressed. One arm slightly behind him, he stands with his legs apart, a man uncomfortably aware that his picture is being taken and making no attempt to look happy about the experience. The picture is worn at its edges, as pictures carried about become, but the writing at the bottom is still legible. It is in Richter's cribbed handwriting, an admonition to himself, pointed advice from one Conrad Richter to the other: "Smile, damn you, smile."

1. Conrad Richter in Albuquerque, New Mexico, *circa* 1934. Richter carried this photo inside the cover of a small notebook of quotations and personal advice. Written at the bottom is Richter's imperative to himself: "Smile, damn you, smile."

one

Pine Grove

ONE

When Conrad Richter, his mother, and two younger brothers boarded the train at Pine Grove Station in December 1900, they were departing not so much from a home—the family had lived in four different houses during Connie's ten years—as from a community, an extended family of relatives and near-relatives. Although a small town, 150 houses spaced along the six blocks of Tulpehocken and three of Mifflin Street, Pine Grove was settled, permanent; houses were known by the names of the families that built them and, more often than not, continued to live in them. By 1900 all of Tulpehocken Street was paved in red brick, a source of pride among the townspeople, as were the shade trees, maples and ashes, horse chestnuts and elms, spreading high above the streets. Behind the shaded walks, interspersed among the single and double houses on Mifflin Street and Main, as most people called Tulpehocken, were four churches, seven stores, two hotels, and several taverns. All made familiar landmarks for a young boy exploring.[1]

One of the hotels, the Mansion House, had been the home of young Connie's mother's people, the Conrads, for whom he was named, and its tap-room was the first place to look for his paternal grandfather, Mike Richter, in late afternoons after his day's work for the railroad was done. One of the stores, M. H. Boyer and Company, was his father's—or had been until John Richter had sold his share the previous summer. Until then John Richter could be found behind its walnut counters every day but Sunday, from six in the morning until his last customer departed, between nine and ten o'clock at night. Two of the churches had been the charges of Connie's maternal grandfather, the Reverend Elias Strickhauser Henry, a tall, spare man of stern countenance but lively wit. Young Connie had been timid in his presence but happy that his grandfather was so important a man. At Reverend Henry's funeral three years before, the mourners overflowed both sanctuaries of St. John's and a third service had to be conducted out-of-doors.

Both his grandfather's churches were on Main Street, several blocks apart. St. John's Lutheran Church was two doors down from the Lutheran parsonage, next to the big square Filbert house where Connie's brother Joe had been born. St. Peter's was farther down Main Street, south from Grandfather Richter's house, where Connie and his mother and brothers had lived since their house had been sold to Johnny Martin. St. Peter's was what was known as a union church, a church shared by two congregations. Two years after Elias Henry became the pastor of St. John's, the Lutheran congregation of St. Peter's asked the young Reverend Henry to become their minister as well. Pa-Pa Henry had agreed, hoping to persuade the two Lutheran congregations to join together. But that was not the way of the Pennsylvania Dutch. For forty years the twenty families of St. Peter's Lutheran congregation quietly declined invitations to worship in St. John's; they had their own reasons for remaining small and sep-arate, they said, and could not be persuaded. One of those reasons was that they did not want to give up their pretty stone church to the Reformed congregation that shared it.

North of Mill Street were the tanneries, the flour mill, the ironworks, and the rail yard. Over by the canal, below Aunt Esther Conrad's house on the corner of Mifflin and Morris Streets, was the coal yard where Ed Christ, ignoring the objections of neighbors, allowed neighborhood boys to use his shanty as a clubhouse—provided, of course, that they did not steal his coal for their stove. Connie had been born in Aunt Esther's big brick house, and there he had attended her kindergarten. When Aunt Esther became too addled to live alone, confusing him with her own brothers, his mother's sister Elizabeth—Aunt Lizzie—and her family had moved in to care for her.

Even after his family had moved from the Filbert house to their own home, a half double a few doors away from Grandfather Richter, Connie, Joe, and Fred, the youngest brother, would walk to their Aunt Esther's. There they would find his Aunt Lizzie and her husband Robert Irwin, a railroad conductor like Grandfather Richter, and their cousins Beth and Henry. Beth was named for her mother, and Henry bore his mother's maiden name, but nobody but Aunt Lizzie called her son anything but Trap. It was at Aunt Esther's that Connie and Trap laid their plans to run away to hunt buffalo in the West, hiding out with their cache of goods filched from the store. Soon after dark the runaways were pulled from their hiding place, scolded for stealing, and sent off to bed.[2]

Aunt Lizzie was lame and had trouble with the steps to the basement kitchen of the Morris Street house, but she could tell wonderful stories and play just about anything on the piano. She gave piano lessons, and as often as not when he visited, Connie would find some luckless Pine Grove youth practicing at the square piano in the parlor, and his aunt, cooking below, rapping on the pipes to call attention to missed notes and faulty timing. Although he would in later years teach himself to play after a fashion, somehow Connie escaped the piano lessons.

For most of the year, the Richter boys' life in Pine Grove was an outdoor life. Summer was best, for then there was no school and days were lazy in the summer sunshine. There was time for fishing for catfish in the lower basin of the canal, and for swimming under the railroad trestle, the best swimming hole on Swatara Creek. On warm days boys would gather by Irwin Loser's watch box, playing tag and poker for jack straws until the swallows returned to the covered bridge. That meant it was one o'clock, time for the half mile walk to the railroad trestle for an afternoon swim. Nobody took a bathing suit. For Decoration Day, called simply "the Thirtieth" in Pine Grove, each family carefully prepared its grave plot at the cemetery. Then came the parade, old Major Filbert leading the Civil War veterans in their faded blue uniforms as they marched down Main and up Cemetery Hill, there to honor the Union dead. In June churches held strawberry festivals, to which everybody was invited, and later in the summer there were church picnics, where the older boys would parade with lap blankets across their shoulders, the sign that they had charge of the family buggy and were available for young ladies desiring to see some fancy trotting along country lanes. In September school curtailed most longer excursions into the woods and fields, but there remained hours of light after the day's lessons, and Saturdays, and fall break for teachers' sessions, when they could climb Blue Mountain to look for pawpaws and persimmons, or walk the Long Trail through the hardwoods to Squire's Woods to gather chestnuts. Sundays were less appealing, indeed to young Connie Richter they were a source of dread, for inside the church while the morning sermon droned on, light seemed to dim into a depressing gloom. Forever after he would remember Sunday church services as "the menace that spoiled Friday night and Saturday."[3]

In fall 1900 Connie and his brothers were all too young to join the late-night torchlight parade to celebrate William McKinley's reelection—though Connie and Joe, when left with the hired girl, sometimes sneaked out of a window to join their friends. Nor is it likely that their mother Lottie Richter would have allowed them out to join Trap and his gang for a Halloween night of outhouse tipping and harness switching. But though they weren't the rascals that Trap was said to be—Trap was famous as the only boy ever expelled from kindergarten, and by his own Aunt Esther—there was evidently more than guilt by association. When the constable came round to report misconduct, he sometimes stopped at the Richter boys' door.

After winter frost hardened the ground and snow covered the roads, the coal sleighs, laden with anthracite for farmers' coal bins, slid silently through the back streets behind the muffled thumping of the heavy draft horses, their breath steaming. Then there was sledding on Cemetery Hill and Bird's Hill and on the Long Stretch down from Blue Mountain. When the ice froze smoothly on the upper basin of the canal, skaters slid in silent arcs across its southern end. At the northern end boys would gather to speculate about the thickness of the ice where the springs were, daring each other to be the first to venture across the places where the ice was a dangerous deep blue green. Ed Christ once ordered Josie Emerich and his ice cutters away from the area of the basin cleared of snow for ice-skating. "So it's pleasure before business," Josie sneered. "That's right," answered Ed.[4] Long since left idle by the railroads, the canal had no other function in 1900, unless it was to remind the town how directly related its prosperity was to the transporting of hard coal.

A family story has it that a Conrad was the first to discover anthracite north of Pine Grove, initiating the town's and his own family's prosperity. Be that as it may, the town grew from a crossroads village in 1830 because of the large deposits of hard coal nearby. A gap in Sharp Mountain to the north of Pine Grove, through which Swatara Creek flowed, made the town a natural junction point for the early canals and then the railroads transporting coal to Philadelphia and Baltimore. In time Pine Grove became the market town for the Pennsylvania Dutch farmers whose fields and orchards spread across the valley between Sharp and Blue Mountains and for the Irish and Eastern European miners who dug coal from the veins pitching steeply down into the hills.

The first Conrad to come to Pine Grove was Henry W. Conrad, who visited sometime after his marriage in 1810 to Elizabeth Kendall. The daughter of a Revolutionary War soldier who had crossed the Delaware with Washington, Elizabeth brought to the marriage a dowry of extensive landholdings in Schuylkill County. Those tracts may well have spurred young Henry—he was twenty-one in 1810—to think of leaving Montgomery County, where his own family was as substantial and well-connected as the Kendalls. His father Frederick Conrad, a blacksmith and farmer, had by steady industry developed his holdings to include a grist mill and a sawmill. Frederick Conrad had also found time to serve as a justice of the peace, a delegate to the state legislature for four terms, and a representative to the United States Congress for two. It was Henry who, it was said, returned from a surveying expedition bearing samples of stone coal. That might have occurred after his service as a captain in the War of 1812, or perhaps much later. After a term as a prothonotary for Schuylkill County from 1821 to 1824, Henry Conrad served as justice of the peace and deputy county surveyor, a job that would have sent him into the hills above town. But of course he could have learned his surveying, and found the stone coal, while exploring his wife's land. By 1830 he had built the Mansion House, combining an inn, store, and a tavern. Henry and Elizabeth Conrad appear not to have developed the coal lands, and the funds to build the Mansion House most likely came from Henry's inheritance; his father Frederick died in 1827.

A Jacksonian Democrat and an abolitionist, Henry Conrad was as politically active as his father had been, convincing his neighbors to establish a school in Pine Grove and serving two terms in the state legislature. There were also persistent rumors that the Mansion House served as a station on the underground railroad. One teenaged girl, Black Hettie, stayed on at the Mansion House and elsewhere in Pine Grove, serving as a nurse to some of the Conrad children. Trap would remember Black Hettie visiting his Aunt Esther in her home.

The Conrad family lived quite comfortably through the 1830s, and Squire Conrad—a title conferred upon him as a magistrate—bought a tavern in North

Pine Grove and parcels of land to add to the large tract on which the Mansion House stood, stretching from Tulpehocken Street to the Swatara. But in the years following his death in 1841, the inherited coal lands were traded away for others farther west, which proved to be unproductive, and little by little the Mansion House tract was sold off, perhaps to pay for the educations of some of his eight children. There were six girls—Catharine, Esther, Sarah Ann, Charlotte, Valeria, and Mary—and two boys—Frederick William and Victor Lafayette. Frederick and Victor both attended Gettysburg College and Seminary, traveled widely abroad, and served prominently in the Lutheran Church in Philadelphia, where they jointly edited the *Lutheran Observer*.

Esther Conrad also went away for schooling. Speaking French and German fluently, she taught languages to young ladies in Ohio before returning to teach in Pine Grove. When she returned she had built on Conrad land a house meant to last for generations, with a foundation thirty inches thick, walls of doubled brick, and windowsills hand hewn from timbers. Townspeople recognized as hers the poems signed "Hadassah" in the *Schuylkill County Herald*, but she was better known as the good Samaritan of Pine Grove, inviting any unfortunate into her home. In her last years (she died in 1908) she would sometimes escape through a window of her home to return to the Mansion House where, she thought, parents and sisters were awaiting her as they had in her childhood.

The Conrads remained the social equals of the Millers, the Stees, the Forrers, the Filberts, and the other propertied families of Pine Grove even as they slipped from equality of estate. When in 1852 the new Lutheran minister of St. John's began to call upon Sarah Ann Conrad, the third-eldest daughter, the arrangement seemed natural enough to everyone. She was only a year older than the Reverend Elias Strickhauser Henry, her birthday being September 23, 1822, and his November 30, 1823. She was pretty, socially adept, and active in St. John's Lutheran Church. And of course she was a Conrad. They were married on September 12, 1853. In time there were three children: Elizabeth Lydia, born on June 30, 1854; George Conrad, on February 22, 1856; and Charlotte Esther, on April 22, 1859. Though a minister's salary was not large and Sarah brought little from her family's reduced holdings, there was extra income from weddings and funerals, and, evidently, an occasional windfall from a horse trade. And at harvesttime each year, there was a profusion of vegetables and fruits for canning and preserving, for Elias Henry took great pride in his garden. It was a happy marriage until tragedy struck in August 1869. On a family picnic Sarah Ann slipped while picking berries, falling from a cliff to her death. Two years later Elias Henry married Elmira Seidel, a pious woman and a conscientious stepmother, hardworking and caring, but for the children never a replacement for their dear lost mother.

Elias Henry continued his ministry, traveling by buggy and by horseback to attend to the congregations of his four churches, two rural churches as well as the two in Pine Grove. Throughout all these years, the Reverend Elias Strickhauser Henry was a prominent member of the community, respected by all except the "Copperheads" whom he had angered by his abolitionist sermons. Although they never carried out their threats against him, they did, one Sunday morning, roach the mane and tail of his buggy horse. Later he would be equally vocal in denouncing the Molly Maguires, the secret organization accused of labor agitation, terrorism, and murder in the anthracite fields. Among his intimate friends he was known as a wit and a teller of tales heightened in humor by his unsmiling delivery. When he died of Bright's disease in 1897, his obituary in the *Lutheran Observer* summarized his years of service: he preached 10,086 sermons, baptized 6,408 children, confirmed 1,681 persons, married 1,240 couples, officiated at 2,489 funerals.[5] His grandson Conrad would later speculate that his years among the stolid Pennsylvania Dutch must have seemed to him an exile, but there is no evidence that he himself had such thoughts. In more than forty years service he had never once taken a vacation."The devil doesn't take a vacation," he was reputed to have said.

At Elias Henry's urging, his son George followed him into the Lutheran ministry. In 1900 he was pastor of the Lutheran Church at Shippensburg, Pennsylvania, a distance from Pine Grove. Elizabeth—Aunt Lizzie—became the family musician; the youngest child Charlotte, once she outgrew her tomboyishness, became the family scholar. Lottie took after her Aunt Esther, the family said. Like her Aunt Esther she became a schoolteacher, and for a while after the death of her fiancé, Edward Kim, it seemed that she might, like her Aunt Esther, be looking ahead to a life without a husband and children of her own.

By Pine Grove standards, the Richter family was far less august than the Conrads. When the flood of 1862 destroyed the Union Canal from Pine Grove to Jonestown, carrying away a railroad trestle and washing out sections of track, the Reading Railroad sent John Michael Richter to supervise a work gang. Brusque in speech but taciturn in demeanor, still speaking with a pronounced German accent, Mike Richter got on well enough in the predominantly German community to decide to stay. When the trestle was repaired, he became a section boss for the Tremont and Lebanon spur of the Reading Railroad, bringing his wife and family to North Pine Grove, then moving shortly thereafter to a company house on Tulpehocken, across from Canal Street. There he would live until his death in 1915.

Mike Richter had come to the United States in August 1854 from Alten-Baden, Germany, where he had been born on July 21, 1834. It has been said he came to escape conscription into the army. The son of Absalom Richter, listed in the family genealogy as a shepherd, as were Absalom's father and grandfather, Mike Richter learned English well enough to court Suzannah Michael of Reading, marrying her on February 16, 1856. Three children were born before the family moved to Pine Grove: Tillie Richter, Sarah Sophia, and on September 11, 1861, John Absalom Richter. In Pine Grove four more children were born: Mary Ann, Henry Michael, Emma Regina, and Bessie Christine.

Late in his life John Absalom Richter wrote an extended memoir of his adolescence and early manhood in Pine Grove. From this account it is known that he was a thoughtful and a pious young man, deeply affected by the deaths of his little brother Henry Michael, who died at four in 1872, and sister Bessie, who died at eleven in 1889. In his sorrow he found comfort in religion, he wrote, and by his teenage years John Richter decided that he was called to the Lutheran ministry. His father Michael had other ideas, however; when his wife Suzannah told him of his son's wish to attend college and then seminary, his response was final: "I had to work; I guess he'll have to as well."[6] Another man might have found softer words for such a hard truth, but Mike Richter did not mean to be unkind, only practical: a workingman simply could not afford to send a child to college.

During the summers of his fifteenth and sixteenth years, 1876 and 1877, John Richter worked for his father as a laborer on a section gang. At the end of the second summer John Richter saw no reason to return to school, there being no chance for him to attend college, and so his father found for him another job, that of outside man for Sherman's Store. Robust and gregarious, John Richter settled into the routines of hauling, storing, and clerking, ignoring for several years the railroad and its opportunities, which his father repeatedly offered. Eventually he became brakeman for the ballast train on which his father was conductor, and soon thereafter he agreed to become stationmaster of the Pine Grove station. His decision may have been influenced by his courting of Lottie Henry. The two had grown up knowing each other, attending the same school and church, but Lottie Henry was two years older than he and had been three years ahead of him in school. Only after the death of Ed Kim, Lottie's boyfriend and the older brother of his own best friend Eugene, did John Richter begin to take special notice of Lottie Henry. In time there was a daily correspondence between them, and though many in the town would not have thought the match a favorable one for the minister's daughter, John Richter was nonetheless of good German stock and strong in his religion. Elias Henry evidently had no objection.

After two years of letter writing, John and Lottie married on September 4, 1884. He was twenty-three and she twenty-five years old. When no children came, Dr. Seyfert gave them some exceedingly sad news. Lottie's womb was somehow turned around and she would not be able to conceive children. That sadness was then compounded by an extended separation: the railroad transferred John to the Lansdale station, north of Philadelphia, too far to travel home except on occasional weekends, and so for two more years John and Lottie wrote each other letters that crossed in the mail. Then came the news of the death of John's best friend, Eugene Kim. Eugene had been superintendent of the St. John's Sunday School, and with his loss the church fathers decided they needed John Richter back to replace him. To accomplish this, two church members offered John Richter a chance to join them in buying a store: for $1,500 he could be a quarter partner. John Richter borrowed $1,000 from his father-in-law and in 1888 returned to Pine Grove as store manager and partner in M. H. Boyer and Company and as superintendent of the St. John's Sunday School.

About a year later, Lottie had wonderful news to tell John. In spite of Dr. Seyfert's prediction she was carrying a child. After anxious months, early in the morning of October 13, 1890, Dr. Seyfert delivered to Lottie and John their first child, a boy. Smiling down at Lottie and her baby, Dr. Seyfert said, "Never was a baby more welcomed than this one."[7] Lottie named him Conrad Michael, the maiden names of his two grandmothers. A day or so later, as Conrad Michael slept beside her in his crib, Lottie had a vision of a procession of dignitaries, richly robed, coming one by one to pause before the crib and then slip away. Another family might have explained this strange occurrence as a dream, as Lottie herself reported that she believed she was experiencing until, glancing at the bureau mirror, she discovered that she could see the reflection of the visitors' backs. But for the Conrads and Henrys, who shared stories about strange happenings in the Morris Street house where Connie was born and who recognized Lottie as a sensitive, one especially aware of presences unfelt and unseen by others, Lottie's vision was a sign confirming another. Conrad Michael had been born with a caul, in German folk tradition a sign that a child was destined to live a special life.[8]

T W O

In Pine Grove parents were not inclined to be publicly affectionate toward their children. Most often they took scant notice of them except when they were in the way, and then only to shoo them. Not so John Richter. He had waited with so little hope that his son Connie seemed a gift from God, and the coming of Joe and Fred only slightly less miraculous. Joseph John Henry Richter was born on February 21, 1893, and George Frederick Richter followed on July 17, 1894. John Richter seldom passed up opportunities to show affection to all three of his children, lifting young Fred high into the air, swinging Joe about, mussing Connie's hair. Forever Connie would remember his embarrassment at his father's exuberant kisses and the sensation of a bristly wet mustache against his cheek.

Almost always Connie could find his father at the store, filling it with his songs and laughter. Outside the store was the obligatory bench for loiterers. Inside there were bins with coarse salt, flour, and corn; there were baskets and china, coal oil and nails, molasses, vinegar, cider, shellac, and paint. In the basement were kept the screws, nuts, bolts, hinges, and knives; there too was a spring that served as a cooler for perishables. Everywhere there were things to touch and smell, and usually there were customers—in and out, chatting and gossiping, asking for buttons and hoes and butter. When Connie visited, his father was almost certain to give him a dried fruit or a candy. As the oldest, Connie was first to be taken along in the store wagon for trips to the patches, small villages built by coal companies for their miners. Along the way they would sing hymns, his own soprano joining his father's bass as their three-horse team plodded up the long hills toward the meager coal towns where most of the customers seemed to owe John Richter money.

In later years Conrad Richter often recalled a favorite anecdote about his father. When the tramp Mike Whelan came to town each month to collect his soldier's pension, sometimes he would stop at Boyer and Company for a handout. John Richter was generous but also protective; in return for the handout he insisted that Mike stay away from Mrs. Richter and the boys at home. When he once caught Mike at his back door, John Richter chased him out of the yard, through the fence gate, and on down the back lane—brandishing a fence slat as he ran. That was his father to Connie Richter: easygoing and generous unless his family's welfare seemed threatened; then—and it must have been elating for the young boy to see—he changed into an avenging angel.

But it was Connie's mother who was the emotional center of his life. In photographs taken at this time, Lottie appears plain featured and overweight,

2. The Richter family, fall 1894. Joe leans on John Richter's knee, Fred rests in Lottie Richter's arms, and a carefully posed Connie Richter stands between his parents.

though in pictures taken before her wedding, she is slim and athletic, decidedly pretty with dark, deeply set eyes. To her three sons she was a careful and caring mother, strict about manners and decorum but indulgent of pranks—smiling when other mothers might have reached for a switch. When Connie talked Joe and Fred into a contest to see who could pee farthest from the back porch, they were found out mid-contest by Lottie, watching from the kitchen window. Expecting a stern countenance and quick punishment, they discovered instead a mother unable to control her laughter.[9] Lottie's hearing was slightly impaired, which meant that the boys should have been able to whisper secrets they wanted to keep. But often when they whispered she would respond with comments that surprised them, and they never could be sure if she were just a shrewd guesser or if, as others in the family said, she was gifted with an extra sense.[10]

Returning home from school or play, Conrad first looked for his mother, and when she was not there he was unhappily aware of a difference. If Sunday church services were dreaded times, Wednesday evenings were in some ways worse. Wednesday was Guild Night at church, and his parents attended every week, leaving the boys in the care of Lizzie Roden, their young maid. Long after Joe and Fred were asleep, Connie would lie awake in the dark, suffering from the "painful separation"[11] he felt when alone, longing for his mother's return. Only when he heard the sound of her footsteps did he feel better, reassured by her coming. Then almost immediately he would fall asleep, often before she came to kiss him good night.[12]

Like her sister Lizzie, Lottie Richter was a storyteller. Friends would remember and remark upon Lottie's easy smile, gracious manner, and "beautiful modulated voice,"[13] but she was nonetheless a Conrad. For all her gentle affability, there was about her a quality of reserve, an inwardness; she was friendly to all but intimate, it seemed, with none. As an adult Richter admired this quality in his mother, remarking on it in his journal as a sign of her patrician heritage. But that inner self of Lottie's must have seemed at times unreachable to a child who waited awake and alone in the dark. For that child was not altogether sure of his own bearings.

As fondly as the adult Conrad Richter would remember his Pine Grove childhood, life was not all sun-filled afternoons. Although Pine Grove was a small town, Doc Seyfert was kept busy by the ailments he was expected to treat, and his successes were often more the result of a patient's strong constitution and luck than of the medicines the doctor carried with him on his rounds. Except for the vaccine for smallpox, there were no miracle drugs in the last decade of the nineteenth century. No child escaped entirely from the childhood afflictions of measles, mumps, chicken pox, and the assortment of colds, coughs, and infections. As seasons of these illnesses arrived, and cycles of epidemics, parents worried that their children would come in contact with scarlet fever, rheumatic fever, diphtheria, or polio. They could only hope that the year's influenza strain was not especially virulent and that their children were not weakened by other illnesses when these killing and crippling diseases found them. As children grew toward adulthood, before them all lurked the specter of tuberculosis, the white plague, typically striking its victims in their late teens—and killing more people each year than heart disease and cancer combined. In Pine Grove few families went untouched by it.

Conrad and his brothers were luckier than many. Joe's childhood bout with scarlet fever left him entirely bald for life. As a teenager Fred missed two years of school with chorea, called St. Vitus' Dance because of the uncontrollable tics and spasms it inflicted on its victims. As a young child Conrad had recurrent problems with his kidneys; later he would contract rheumatic fever—and perhaps scarlet fever as well—but only his eyes seemed permanently affected, easily strained by close work.

Even when healthy young Connie was an excitable and nervous child, unable to sit long without squirming, and Sunday sermons and weekday classes were an agony of tedium, relieved only by an imagination that carried him out through the sunlit windows into the bright world outside. As he recalled his childhood, his most worrisome ailment was his acute sensitivity. It made him shy and self-conscious, a child who did not seem to fit with other children, one who would drift away from his own birthday party to sit alone on the back stairs. Late in life Richter would remember a neighbor who claimed it took young Connie an hour to walk a single block: "He would walk one step and look around, then another and look the other way, at nothing at all that she could see, and stand there as if hypnotized."[14] One day, leaving home at the usual time, he arrived at kindergarten to find no other children there. Instead of being early, as he first thought, it turned out that he was so late that all the other children had already gone home.

Was young Connie odd—so unlike other children that his behavior was remarked on by others? Late in his own life, Conrad Richter's younger brother Frederick provided a family perspective. Yes, Connie had been different from his two brothers. Not that he and Joe gave much thought to Connie's ways, or discussed them, for to his brothers Connie was just Connie, as each brother was unique, individual. Fred was youngest, the happy-go-luckiest, the one the others were charged with looking after. Joe was interested in mechanical things and seemed always to be competing with Connie, especially in athletics. He was the most like their Grandfather Richter in blunt speech. Connie was oldest, fastest, most athletic. It was Connie who was the restless sleeper—having his own bed not because he was oldest but because his tossing and turning disturbed the other two. (Once in his early childhood, his mother would later tell him, he had answered her remonstrance that he must have patience for his dinner by retorting, "I don't want patience. I want potatoes.")[15] When the three boys were invited to stay overnight at a friend's, Connie was the one who would return home before daybreak. He was the dawdler and daydreamer, the brother with the worst temper, and the one the other two would gang up on. On one occasion Joe and Fred put Connie's rock collection under his sheets. When he found the rocks in his bed, Connie threw the largest at Joe, just missing his head.

Was he a worry to his parents? Fred Richter did not remember. But there is ample evidence that religion as Lutherans practiced it in Pine Grove was troublesome to Connie Richter. As little more than an infant, he could respond to the story of Christ's birth in a manger with "Jesus can have my kibbie" [crib]; and to the Christian motifs of birth and rebirth and their promise of survival for the soul, Richter would remain congenial throughout his life. But the dark admonitions he heard from the pulpit each Sunday of the wages of sin, of damnation, of ritual sacrifice and crucifixion, these became a ghastly dream, and the Sunday services that fed it so disquieting as to be almost unendurable. With his eyes fixed on the nearest window and the sunshine outside, he rejected his grandfather's warnings to humble himself before an avenging God. Surely that was not God's divine plan for man. At some point he decided that he would never again repeat the Apostles' Creed, and he never did.

How aware Conrad's parents were of this early religious crisis is not known. As a teenager Conrad would openly disagree with his parents about religion. He and his father argued heatedly, and he avoided attending confirmation classes until he could no longer put them off without publicly embarrassing his father. But a boy as sensitive as Conrad would not have been able to tell his mother that her countenance in church, her singing of terrible songs, was part of his pain. He might confide in her that there were songs so sad that he could not bear to hear them—such as one mournful ballad in which a starving child sings, "Only three grains of corn, Mother, Only three grains of corn"[16]—but he too was a Conrad, and there were things he would not share, not even with his mother. One was his secret fear that, because he was so different from the others, he was not the child of Lottie and John Richter.[17]

The events that led to John Richter's absence from his family began three years before his departure, at the death of Pa-Pa Henry. During his long suffering with Bright's disease, nothing comforted Elias Henry as much as the presence of his son-in-law John Richter. When the pain finally ended, John found himself executor of his father-in-law's estate, and in carrying out those duties he gave long hours to the worldly remains of a man who had spent his life in the profession John Richter himself still longed to enter. At the job's conclusion, John Richter had in his possession all of Elias Henry's papers and books, and Lottie Henry had an inheritance of $3,400—not a princely sum in 1897, but more

3. Lottie Richter and her younger sons, Joe and Fred, with the family dog, Dixie. Taken by eleven-year-old Connie during the fall of 1900, this portrait would be the source for the picture John Donner describes in *The Waters of Kronos*.

than enough money to make Boyer and Company into Boyer and Richter, almost enough to buy the store outright. Certainly that was what most of his neighbors would have expected John Richter to do. Here was a first step toward raising the Richter name toward the former prominence of the Conrads. Perhaps the day would come when he could give his son a different answer from the one his father had given him when he asked to attend college. Surely John Richter thought of these things, but he thought as well, insistently, about the ministry. In the store and at church he was the same affable and outgoing man, but at home he was preoccupied, distant. His prayers at meals were interrupted by sighs and long silences, as if he were in silent conversation with an unseen presence. Finally Lottie and John told their sons that the family would be leaving Pine Grove. They were selling the store, and their father would be going to Susquehanna University in Selinsgrove, Pennsylvania, to study for the ministry. The family would join him in Selinsgrove just as soon as he found a place for them to live.

After his father departed in fall 1900, Connie borrowed a camera and took a photograph of his mother, his two brothers, and their dog Dixie in their Pine

Grove living room. The young boy would prize his photograph, preserving it carefully. That photograph would be the only framed picture the adult Conrad Richter kept on his writing desk. It would be the photograph Conrad Richter re-created in his novel *The Waters of Kronos* as the snapshot that John Donner, old and dying, carries with him when he visits his parents' graves.

> For years it had stood in a small black frame on his desk at home. Now yellow and soiled, it had started to crack. It was a picture he had taken himself with his father's old plate camera when he was ten. His younger brothers sat at a small table in the old sitting room, their mother between them smiling her warm love at the young photographer. It was a scene that never failed to bring back the old realities, the almost forgotten sideboard with claw feet, the crokinole board standing against the wall, the colored wall-hangings of his mother, the old-time shepherd dog Sandy panting on the floor, and in the background the two closed doors, one to the stairs and one to the kitchen.[18]

With this picture packed away carefully for their journey into a new life in Selinsgrove, Connie Richter, standing on the train platform in December 1900, looked back from the station to the houses and streets that had been his world. There he was John and Lottie Richter's oldest boy, a grandson of Elias Henry. He was a Conrad, who were friends of the Millers, Stees, Ferrars, Barrs, and Filberts. He was a Richter, grandson too of Mike Richter. He was the cousin of Trap and Beth, the nephew of Aunt Lizzie and Great Aunt Esther, even if she did confuse him with her brothers. Full of the adventure of the move to Selinsgrove, secure beside his mother and brothers, he would still have been uneasy about departing. In Pine Grove he knew who he was. Who would he be now that he was leaving?

A Boy's Will

O N E

John Richter was waiting at the station when Connie and his mother and brothers arrived at Selinsgrove.[1] Walking with them through the late afternoon chill he spoke animatedly about their new house, the college, and the bright prospects he saw for Lottie and the boys. The home he led them to was just at the edge of town, a double house of white clapboard with poplar trees in the front yard. Their side was the lower half, toward town, and it rented for six dollars a month. Inside they found their furniture already placed in the parlor, the sitting room, and the kitchen. There was the carom and crokinole board against the wall, and their mother's pride, the sideboard with the claw feet.[2] This was the home of a poor seminary student, and few frills could be afforded. But the small house did have three bedrooms upstairs, so Connie could sleep alone. Meals were simple but sufficient. There were breakfasts of fried potatoes and boiled or fried mush, dinners of ham or bacon and an egg, suppers of the newly popular shredded wheat biscuits with milk. On Sundays there was the weekly treat of steak, a pound and a quarter of it to divide among the family, and often a half pound of chocolate chips from Hillibish's Store or peaches in sweet thick syrup that Lottie had canned in Pine Grove.[3]

Although John Richter was thirty-nine years old, twice the age of many of the undergraduates, he had made friends easily at Susquehanna, both with his classmates and with his teachers. The house on the outskirts of town became a hub for the activities of homesick students and, in some cases, equally lonely instructors. Never happier, John Richter talked constantly of his studies. What he lacked in education he tried to compensate for with his earnest attention to lectures and books. But because he was so much older and responsible for a family, John Richter's undergraduate training was of necessity limited to a single year before seminary, and not everybody at Susquehanna thought encouraging the middle-aged man was good policy. When summer supply pastorships were offered, John Richter found that the younger, better-educated men were given the choice positions. He was assigned to small country churches.

While John Richter studied at Susquehanna University and Seminary, his sons attended the public school in Selinsgrove. Connie's first year passed without event, but during the second something went so badly wrong that at its end Connie was informed that he would not be promoted. The problem seems to have been a bullying schoolmaster, which was how Richter would tell the story in A Simple Honorable Man, the novel based on his father's life as a minister.[4] Although a good student, alert and quick-minded, the sensitive and high-strung Conrad would have been distracted by such a teacher. Whatever the source of the trouble, John Richter came quickly to his child's aid. In fall 1902, though still more than a month from his twelfth birthday, Conrad was specially admitted to Susquehanna Academy, the university's preparatory school. During their third and fourth years in Selinsgrove, father and son walked together to their morning classes, taking the short cut along the railroad tracks.

Even after enrolling in Susquehanna Academy, Connie waited impatiently each year for the beginning of summer vacation. Then he had time for reading of his own choosing, primarily popular fiction. He had been an early reader, moving from the children's books his mother read to her sons to the Frank

Nelson and the Boy Trapper books for young boys, on to *TipTop Weekly* and, when given permission to borrow whatever he wanted from a family library in Pine Grove, *Robinson Crusoe*, *The Swiss Family Robinson*, and Arthur Conan Doyle's tales of Sherlock Holmes. Free to choose at will among a room full of books, Richter developed a lifelong habit of looking for second and third books by writers who created for him the magic of lives he could enter vicariously. At Selinsgrove he read the historical romances of Robert Chambers and dime novels of Burton Standish, but by sixteen he had also read all of Shakespeare's plays.[5]

He was still happiest out-of-doors. As in Pine Grove, summers in Selinsgrove were the best times, releasing the Richter boys to play in the streets and fields around their home. Together the three boys fished in the nearby creeks and canals and paddled a canoe along the shore of the Susquehanna. Once Connie, Joe, and Fred were caught on the railroad trestle over Penn's Creek when a train whistled its approach. Because the trestle was high and long, there were perches, small platforms built out over the water, for anyone crossing the trestle to step onto, away from passing trains. When the train whistle sounded, Connie hustled Fred to a perch and then looked back to see Joe crawling in fright across the ties. Rushing back to his brother, Connie helped Joe to climb down to a pier beneath the track and then slid down himself, just as the train roared through above. It was a close call, "thoroughly scary" to the boys, and to his younger brothers Connie was a hero for his daring rescue.[6]

The family lived in Selinsgrove for four years, with only the small sums from John Richter's summer pastorships to supplement Lottie's dwindling inheritance. At times the money worries led to what Richter later remembered as "desperate penury,"[7]—breakfasts of four tablespoons of grape nuts, for example—but though the money was tight, the boys were healthy and John doing what he loved. All would remember these as good years.[8] In early summer 1904, John Richter was ordained as a Lutheran minister and called to serve the Lutheran Church in the town of Tremont, six miles north of Pine Grove. Before the family left Selinsgrove for Tremont, however, Connie was asked to make a difficult decision. He was offered a scholarship to return to the academy in the fall as a boarding student, but he would have to agree to use his schooling to prepare for the ministry. The offer seemed likely to be Connie's only chance for a college education, and his parents made clear to him that they hoped he would accept. John Richter no doubt remembered how ardently he had wished for just such a chance at fourteen, and it must have nagged at him that, in spending Lottie's inheritance for his own education, he was denying that same chance to his children. For Lottie the scholarship meant her son could continue the family's tradition of the ministry as a profession, in which her father, brother, and two uncles had all achieved some prominence.[9] But Conrad could not bring himself to accept, knowing himself to be unsuited for the ministry. He could not imagine himself confidently preaching from the pulpit. Having to speak in public always sickened him.

Even if the scholarship were not tied to study for the ministry, Connie would have dreaded the thought of separation from his family. What home would there be for him, as his parents' house had been a place for homesick students? Conrad Richter was not yet fourteen years old. He was barely five feet tall. Acutely sensitive, awkward, and diffident when with strangers, he was certain to suffer terrible longing when separated from his family. Just the thought of being so far away from his mother brought the feeling of emptiness into him. No, he could not choose Susquehanna, no matter how disappointed his parents, no matter how foolish he seemed to his relatives and friends.

And so Conrad moved to Tremont, settling with his family into another frame half-double house. Like Pine Grove, Tremont was a town created by anthracite. In 1848 a single hermit's cottage occupied the spot; a decade later there were a hundred houses and six hundred people, all brought by the Mine Hill and Schuylkill Haven Railroad, which connected the mining spur lines to the Reading Railroad. Pictures of the Tremont business district from the turn of the century show substantial brick hotels and stores along a tree-lined main street.[10] This was no mining patch, no group of small, roughly built houses next to a mine and a breaker, but Tremont was a mining town and the home of miners. Here Connie and his brothers heard the tramp of boots before dawn as miners walked to the first and second mining trains, and they watched them return in the evenings, jumping from still-moving trains to lope down from the depot to their homes below.

Connie Richter was fourteen years old his first fall at Tremont. According to an anthropometric chart he filled out at the time, on September 4 he was 5' 6" and weighed 122 pounds. Eventually he would be 5' 11", several inches above average height, a slender, athletic young man with brown hair, handsome features, and a youthful, engaging smile. In photographs from the Tremont years, he appears alert and carefree—mugging with his cousin Shorty Keeley or showing off his striped bathing suit and the family collie, Dixie. Nothing in these pictures suggests the sensitivity he and others have recorded. Richter's own recollections of his self-consciousness, and his escape into reading, occasionally surfaced in later years, as they did in a letter to Erd Brandt, an editor for the *Saturday Evening Post*. Confiding to Brandt that his early reading of the *Post* had allowed "the

4. The Richter boys mug for the camera, *circa* 1906. Connie Richter is on the left, Joe on the right, and Fred holds the leash to another Dixie.

feeling of another world and another life," he described himself as "a country town preacher's boy in a suit of donation clothes."[11]

Young Connie Richter was also acutely aware of the public appearance of his parents, a growing source of discomfort during his time at Tremont;[12] much of this discomfort focused upon his father's public presence. Even in his severe black coat and hat, John Richter did not seem to Conrad as ministerial as his grandfather had been. Though now a servant of the Lord, John Richter remained the affable extrovert he had been as a storekeeper—energetic, outgoing, enjoying the company of all people, sinners and saints alike. When John Richter spoke to strangers on the street, Conrad thought he saw puzzlement in their eyes, and perhaps the suspicion that this clergyman was trying to convert them to his own religion. At Sunday services, Conrad would squirm at his father's large gestures, his effusive prayers, his bass voice that rose in song above the combined voices of his congregation. None could doubt the minister's sincerity or his goodness of heart, but instead of being the head of the church, as Grandfather Henry indisputably had been, John Richter seemed more the humble servant, an apprentice in need of correction.

Conrad's discomfort concerning his mother was another matter. In the thinking of her eldest son, Lottie Richter deserved a better life than that of a minister's wife in Tremont. Not a large parish, even when compared to St. John's in Pine Grove, Tremont's Lutheran congregation paid its pastor only $400 a year. Family finances had to be handled carefully, and occasionally the careful watching was not enough. Nothing remained of Lottie's inheritance. In July 1906 she received a smaller sum, $616, from the estate of her Aunt Hannah Conrad. Perhaps there were yet debts from the Selinsgrove days, perhaps just normal household expenses for a family with three children; whatever the reason, that sum slipped from savings into expenditures. When it was gone his parents were driven to an ordinary enough remedy, but one Conrad would always remember and resent. His mother's sideboard with the claw feet and fluted columns, her cherished connection with the bygone days of the Conrads, had to be sold for the little extra cash it would bring. That Lottie may well have suggested the sale, perhaps even insisted upon it, was lost on her eldest son, who felt keenly the failure of his father to provide for his three sons and wife.

So too would Conrad have felt the change in Lottie's social position. In Pine Grove she had been a Conrad, the daughter of Elias S. Henry, and the wife of a citizen of substance. Now the wife of a country clergyman, she was an unpaid servant of the church. She was expected to attend upon her husband's ministry, expected to turn the other cheek at the slights and presumptions of well- or even ill-meaning parishioners and neighbors. Lottie Richter may have adjusted well enough to the changes, for hers was the way of patience. But it was not the way of her eldest son, who saw how shabbily his mother dressed and how differently she was treated. He would resent the changes deeply, and he would blame the changes on his father. However content John Absalom Richter was to be a servant of the Lord, his choice had changed the family's earthly circumstances decidedly for the worse. Selinsgrove might have been a happy preamble to the ministry and its privations, but the years in Tremont were the reality—a life of poverty for dedication and service that often was not appreciated. John Richter may have appeared not to notice, but his son did. Twenty-five years later, he would still remember indignantly "what the Church did to Father and Mother," taking his father's strength and making it "professional piety," taking his mother's "natural dignity and grace" and humbling it.[13]

Commencement for Tremont High School's graduating class of 1906 was enough of an event that the school board charged fifteen cents' admission. For this fare, the audience was treated to some undergraduate singing, two solos and three songs by a quartet, and presentations—oration, recitation, or essay—by ten of the eleven senior class members. The one member of the graduating class who did not participate was Conrad Richter, who refused to speak at the ceremony and held out against the persuasions and admonitions of his teachers, classmates, and parents, even against threats by the school board to withhold his diploma. He may well have been expected to give the valedictory address for his graduation, as members of his family recall; his report card lists grades that could have won him that distinction. But on the printed program, the valedictory address on patriotism was assigned to Joseph Murphy, Conrad's good friend. The only Richter to appear on the commencement announcement was the Reverend J. A. Richter, who delivered the invocation. Always unhappy about speaking before a group, dreading those Fridays when he would be required to speak extemporaneously before his classmates, Conrad Richter weighed the different embarrassments of speaking and not speaking at graduation and announced he could not speak. No matter how odd that made him seem, just the thought of a public recitation frightened him so badly that his stomach became upset. He would face the teasing, even the ridicule of others; he could not face the graduation audience. Even when his parents pleaded he stubbornly refused. Knowing that once his son's mind was made up, he would not be persuaded, John Richter interceded for his son. Conrad received his diploma without speaking, but only after the painful experience of sitting with his classmates as one by one they rose to speak. Would it not have been easier, less publicly humiliating, to play some small part? Conrad was, after all, an unlikely rebel, a shy boy, shrinking from any public exposure. The lesser exposure would have been to speak. But while others would have seen him as stubborn, willful, and even defiant, he saw himself as none of these. His choice was not an act of will, for there really was no choice. Sitting through the graduation orations and recitations, he must have longed to be like the others in his class. How much easier the world would be if he could put himself forward confidently as they did. But he could not speak; his nerves would not let him.

Remaining from Conrad Richter's senior year is a red leather-bound notebook inscribed in his unpracticed attempt at script: "Conrad M. Richter, Tremont High School, '06." Beneath is an index for the planned writing within, with such categories as "Jokes and Funny Sayings," "Little Incidents to Weave into a Story or Book," "Plots, Ideas, and Notes," "Novel," and "Ideas-Business." Inside this notebook, the earliest evidence of Conrad Richter's ambition to be a writer, are a few pages of jottings and many blank pages. There are seven pages of jokes, limericks, and puns ("How much did Romeo? That depends on what Juliet"). Under "Facts Worth Knowing" are the names and hometowns of the eleven members of Tremont High School's graduating class. Under "Little Incidents" are four pages of notes and anecdotes, undeveloped, and then without any comment a list of novels and novelists, popular writers whose works could be found in most lending libraries: Robert W. Chambers, George Barr McCutcheon, Ralph Connor, Harold McGrath, Owen Wister, Marion Crawford, Robert Barr, Gilbert Parker.

An avid reader and a good student, Conrad Richter must have longed for the chance to continue his studies in college. But there could be no college for the son of a poor minister—except to prepare for the ministry. And his decision on that had already been made, and irrevocably. Conrad Richter did not send his mother to talk to his father, accepting without asking the answer his father would have had to make: there was no money; he would have to work.

In his adult years, Conrad Richter repeatedly reflected on his first jobs as evidence of how inadequately his parents—especially his father—understood his nature. When Connie was thirteen or fourteen, John Richter found him a summer job as water boy for the workers building the Blackwood Breaker. Conrad's job was to carry water up the crude ladders and across the skeleton structure to the carpenters high above. He lasted the morning, forcing himself to climb with the heavy, unbalancing bucket up the ladders and across the trusses and beams. But willpower was not enough, and after lunch he went home

sick and did not return.[14] After Conrad's graduation, John Richter found his
son a job at a colliery, where Conrad picked slate, shoveled culm, and carried
machinery up into the breaker. He liked this work no better than his time at the
Blackwood Breaker. Inside a coal breaker, an outsized building several stories high,
coal was crushed at the top of the building and then sluiced through descending
levels, where slag, shale, and rock were separated from the coal and the coal
sorted by size. Such breakers were dark, hot, dirty, and thunderously loud. Coal
dust filled the air, settling onto the floors and beams on every level of the huge
wooden contraptions, and the whole structure shook and swayed as the grinders
and sorters shuttled their metal plates back and forth. It was no place for a boy
with bad nerves; after only a few weeks an exhausted Conrad went to bed with
a fever.

When he recovered, Connie took a job driving a team through the streets of
Tremont, picking up and delivering clothing for a steam laundry. Then in fall
1906 his father found him a clerk's job in East Pittsburgh, working for the West-
inghouse Manufacturing Company. Fred visited once that fall, carrying with
him on the train a chocolate cake baked by Lottie; otherwise the sixteen-year-
old boy was left entirely on his own two hundred miles from home. Many years
later Richter would remember "going from and coming back to [his] boarding
house in the darkness" and the two libraries he "haunted," the Braddock library
and the main Pittsburgh library near Schenley Park, as "oases of lifegiving greenery
and light in a gray desert land."[15] After a winter in East Pittsburgh, Conrad found
himself sick again. Unhappiness deepened into depression and finally into emotional collapse; too sick to work, he boarded a train for home.

T W O

During Conrad's few months away, John Richter had accepted a call to three
small churches in White Deer Valley south of Williamsport, Pennsylvania, and
so the home Conrad returned to was not the Tremont Lutheran parsonage but
that next to the Stone Church, Christ Lutheran, in the pastoral valley below
White Deer and Bald Eagle Mountains. Thereafter Conrad Richter would refer
to his illness in East Pittsburgh as a nervous breakdown, but the symptoms he
described—physical exhaustion, vitiated willpower, uncontrollable crying—
today seem more those of acute depression. He was genuinely sick, however,
not just unhappy; and the young man who stepped from the train at Montgomery, thin, sallow, deep-eyed, was obviously in need of a period of rest.

During the warm summer, Conrad walked the valley roads and hiked across the low mountains surrounding the small churches of his father's pastorate. Shade, Jack's, Tuscarora, Black, Stone, Nittany, Bear, and Lick Mountains: eventually he explored them all. He was especially fascinated by the "benches" on these mountains, where hunters were known to become lost, and on any sunny day he was as likely as not to set out for one of them, calling to his hunting dog Monty to go with him.[16] As Conrad's health improved, his father found for him farm jobs, outdoor jobs in the sun—haying and digging potatoes—and it was a tanned and fit young man who began work as an assistant cashier at the new bank in Montgomery the following fall. Farmers and Citizens offered an innovative service to its customers, weekly pickup and delivery of money at several stores throughout the valley, and Conrad would drive one of the spirited bay horses of Dr. Hull, the bank president, as he made his weekly rounds. On Wednesday evenings, when the bank stayed open until 9 P.M., Dr. Hull would keep his young friend company at the bank. After closing, Conrad set out on the long, lonely walk to the Stone Church through the lampless dark.[17]

While recuperating in White Deer Valley, Conrad Richter read avidly *Physical Culture Magazine* and became a devotee of Bernarr McFadden, the magazine's founder, who claimed to have built himself up from a weak and sickly child into a celebrated strong man by what he termed "kinestherapy." First in a quasi-autobiographical novel, *The Athlete's Conquest*, and then through the pages of his popular monthly magazine, McFadden advocated the virtues of fresh air, exercise, good hygiene, adequate rest, and an almost meatless diet. Exercise expanded intelligence, second sight came from fasting, and cures for disease only from natural methods following McFadden's regimen. Loose clothing was best, corsets dangerous, and physicians unnecessary. Conrad's sickness in East Pittsburgh may well have been exacerbated by a McFadden diet based upon graham crackers, but once back home with his parents he convinced his brother Joe of the potential benefits of McFadden's program, and together they undertook the regimen.[18] What attracted Richter to the McFadden program was that it promised health to those determined enough to keep to the regimen. One could make oneself stronger, more stalwart, less nervous, simply by acts of will. That first winter in White Deer Valley the two brothers slept in a bedroom with the windows wide open, and they walked together to Montgomery, Joe to high school, Conrad to the bank, convincing themselves of the virtues that were to be theirs by following McFadden's advice and eating no breakfast. Fred found he simply could not sleep in the cold or go without breakfast, and no doubt the older brothers felt their convictions confirmed when Fred came down with St. Vitus' Dance.

5.   Richter's experiments with the family camera produced this
doubled portrait of himself, *circa* 1907.

Richter remained with the bank until spring 1909, during the coldest weather
renting a room at Mrs. Piatt's boardinghouse—at a cost of a dollar more a
month than the bank paid him. On winter evenings he read whatever he could
borrow, both books and magazines. Or he would spend the few cents for admission to see a moving picture show in Montgomery, leaving the theater with a
sense of "loss, regret, and gloom" to find himself again in the "dark ordinary
streets" of the town, choosing whether to return to the "cheerless walls" of his
boardinghouse room or set out on the four-mile walk home.[19] Each week he
waited at the rail depot for the arrival of the *Saturday Evening Post*, eager for its
short stories. Sometimes the stories and books he read moved him so deeply
that, to relieve his pent-up emotion, he had to take walks in the dark.[20] When
he thought of the future, he imagined himself writing such stories. On Sunday
afternoon hikes with Fred, Connie carried along a thesaurus so that when they
stopped to rest, Fred could call out words and he name the synonyms. If Conrad
wrote stories, he did not save them, although he did write brief notes for stories
in his red leather-bound notebook. But if he was not yet writing stories, he was
more actively pursuing another dream, a personal version of the rags-to-riches
stories he found repeatedly in the popular novels he read. He wanted to make
enough money to lift himself and his family out of their poverty.

After the second winter at the bank, Conrad quit his job to establish a whole-sale lumber business, an ambitious enterprise for a man who had not yet arrived at his nineteenth birthday. Evidently his idea was to supply timbers and ties from White Deer Valley, where lumber was plentiful, to the anthracite mines above Pine Grove and Tremont, where the hills had been lumbered over. Confident of success, he hired his brother Fred to help and spent his small savings on business forms that announced "CONRAD RICHTER, LUMBER AND TIMBER." From the appear-ance of the telegram forms, order forms, and letterhead stationery, the business might have been a thriving concern: "Everything from Stick to Shingle" they announced, and "My Specialty Everything." But the enterprise never matched the success that the order forms implied. His bank account for the Farmers and Citizens Bank lists only one deposit during this period, $96.00 on April 2, 1909, suggesting that Conrad Richter brokered a single lumber deal.

When the lumber venture did not thrive, Conrad Richter attempted to extend his earnings by selling newspaper subscriptions and by writing news items as a stringer for Philadelphia newspapers. Neither enterprise brought much extra income, nor took much time from outings with his brothers—swimming, camping, and, in the fall, hunting with his hound Monty. One summer Joe and Conrad built a canoe for themselves, and in their impatience to complete it they violated the family's rule against work on the Lord's day. Grandfather Richter happened to be visiting, and he asked Connie about the noise out back. He made no com-ment when Connie explained that he was hammering down loose boards on the walkway to the outhouse, but later in the day when Conrad returned to the canoe he found awaiting him the railroad conductor's blunt judgment. Chalked boldly on the canoe's frame was, "Conrad iss a liar."[21]

If Conrad considered another job away from his parents and brothers, he did nothing about it. There were those, however, who thought the Reverend Mr. Richter ought to have found more profitable activities for his sons, then nine-teen, seventeen, and sixteen years old. By reputation at least, the three were not models of decorum. One neighbor, blacksmith Charles Hulsizer, went so far as to say: "those Richter boys are damn bad ones. I won't let my Howard associate with them."[22] When a deacon pointedly commented to John Richter that he "didn't understand why 'the reverend' kept his three boys lying around the house,"[23] John Richter preached a sermon on failure, concluding it with his resignation.

To Conrad, the failure was his. Although he knew that the real reason for the deacon's nasty comment was a church dispute that had entangled his father, the family's three years in White Deer Valley ended because the deacon recognized him as a point of vulnerability. As the oldest, he was the one who ought to have succeeded at something his parents could be proud of.

By late summer 1910, the Richter family had moved to another rented duplex house in Windber, in western Pennsylvania. This was soft coal country, rocky, hilly farming land and communities of mixed ethnic groups—mostly Eastern European miners and their families—people John Richter found as congenial as any since the patch towns around Tremont. But for a minister already middle-aged, the new charge was no advancement, and the opportunities for his sons seemed only a little better in Windber than in White Deer Valley. A church member would later write to Conrad Richter, recalling him as "the new minister's son, so grown up and sophisticated" with the "look of a dreamer in his eyes."[24] Some of those dreams were still of writing, and Richter was by then actually making his first tries at fiction. In early October he wrote to Robert W. Chambers, whose novels he had read since boyhood, asking Chambers to read what he had written. Chambers agreed, but grudgingly: "If you care to send me copies, typewritten, of one or two stories, I will take the first opportunity of reading them, and then I will find a few moments in which to write you my opinion of your chances. But believe me, my opinion is worth practically nothing; I am not a good critic."[25] Chambers's letter was the first of a collection that the young man would receive from famous people, for Connie Richter had discovered it was easier to present himself in writing than in person. On paper he could speak to anybody.

Richter never sent Chambers a story. Perhaps his first excitement about another kind of writing diverted him, for within days of Chambers's letter Richter happened upon a series of articles on newspapermen called "The Men Who Make the News."[26] The day after reading the articles, he again took the trolley from Windber to Johnstown and there, putting aside his shyness, he walked into the office of the *Johnstown Journal* and talked himself into a reporter's job. He began October 11, two days before his twentieth birthday, in the city where eleven years earlier two thousand people had been killed in the flood that demolished the town. His assignment was to cover the "undertakers, lawyers, churches (except Catholic), YMCA, Conemagh, Cambria Country, Summerset County."[27]

After young Richter submitted his first story, the crusty old city editor called him over and asked what newspapers he had worked on. When Richter answered, "Nowhere," the editor replied gruffly, "Well, you'll go farther than here."[28] Richter certainly went quickly. By the middle of the following month, he was editor of

the *Patton Daily Courier,* a small-town weekly, and in January Conrad set out to
try his luck again in Pittsburgh, this time as a reporter for the *Pittsburgh Dispatch.*
But these quick changes were less the happy result of talent discovered than the
restlessness of a young man who found the reality of working on two failing
papers—both would fold in a matter of months—less exciting than the articles
had made journalism seem. He did develop skills and habits of mind that he
would later be grateful for: "The story had to be written whether I felt like it or
not. There was no waiting for inspiration, for something that violently interested
me. In fact I had to let out things that interested me personally but which had
no place in the story as such. I had to meet a deadline. A great many stories had
to be written every day, some short, some long. I had firsthand experience with
all kinds of people. It was necessary to get information, material, and sometimes
pictures from them. A good reporter learned to tell when a man was telling the
truth."[29] And the daily necessity of gathering information, often from strangers,
forced him to overcome some of his shyness. But the assigned rounds of undertakers, lawyers, and churches neither satisfied a young man's longing for experience nor appeared to open the way to success. Soon he was longing for change.

In early December Richter sent two poems to the Literary Bureau, a Philadelphia agency that advised aspiring writers for a fee. Neither of the poems
elicited any encouragement, the bureau's staff advising him that "the short story
is what is being looked for" by magazines.[30] By early January he had sent two
stories; one they returned as unlikely to sell, the other, "The Torpid City," they
agreed to send out to editors for consideration. Soon it too would be rejected,
but Conrad Richter's real apprenticeship in fiction had begun. He had offered
two stories for sale.

A part of Richter's attraction to writing was his notion of what such a life
must be like, and his idea was a young man's, focused on success and its attendant rewards. Successful writers like Robert Chambers were well paid; they
were admired and respected in their communities as substantial citizens. They
did not live in duplex houses among the poor. At least equally attractive to
Richter was his personal response to the voices of writers who talked to him in
the pages he read. He felt keenly the power of these writers, their ability to
create, to control, to select and modify, to make a pleasing order. He must have
felt strongly and with real longing the difference between the writer's voice, the
confident self by which the writer communicates with the world, and his own
voice in daily conversations. In the works of authors he most admired there
were no false steps, no fumblings for words, no embarrassment about awkward-
ness or intimacy; the self-assured tellers of these tales seemed never to fear

failure. He responded to these personae as he wished others would see and respond to him.

Understanding that this magic was, after all, craft, that the real person behind the voice might be as timid or as uninspiring as he, Richter wondered if there were not secrets to this craft as to others, known only by initiates. If he could witness the process, if he could see intimately the daily life of a successful writer, perhaps he could teach himself what experience so far had not granted him. Once he understood the practical, the daily reality of the writing, then he would be able to test himself against that measure, to see if he himself had the inner qualities—the resourcefulness, the determination, the talent—to join these few. Although at twenty years old his record had been one of disappointments and failures, Richter believed his inability to thrive was a consequence of mistaken placement. He was simply unsuited for the jobs his father had found for him. He was neither especially strong nor especially stalwart, but he did have qualities of mind and heart that his parents apparently did not recognize. Once he rejected the scholarship to Susquehanna Academy, they seemed to have no further thoughts for his future except workaday jobs that could be done by just about anybody. Given a chance, he believed he could do more. Anyhow, he believed he deserved that chance.

With all this in mind, Richter wrote to authors whose work he had read with enthusiasm, this time asking for something more than advice. Before taking the job in Pittsburgh, he wrote to Hamlin Garland, Jack London, Ralph Paine, Thomas Nelson Page, George Barr McCutcheon, and Upton Sinclair, asking each if perhaps he did not need a private secretary, a young man with experience as a newspaper reporter and skill with a typewriter. Jack London wrote back that his wife, taking the letter by dictation, "refuses to give up her job."[31] Upton Sinclair wrote that he had a secretary, but he would consider Richter as a housekeeper.[32] George Barr McCutcheon wrote twice, once to say he might need a secretary for a trip abroad, the second to dash whatever hopes he had raised by saying the trip was off.[33] From Pittsburgh he wrote to William Dean Howells, the country's best-known writer and the editor of *Harper's Magazine*. Howells replied: "I heartily wish I could offer you a job, for your frank letter makes me wish to know you. As yet, however, I do everything for myself, and by leaving many things undone, manage." Perhaps remembering that others had been kind to him when he had similar aspirations, he added, "When you come to New York, Harpers can give you my address."[34]

Discouraging though these replies might have been, Richter kept up his hopes and continued to send stories to the Literary Bureau. In April the bureau returned "Three Little Outcasts from Paradise," rejected by ten magazines, including *Scribner's, Munsey's,* the *Saturday Evening Post,* and *Everybody's;* in May the bureau returned to him "The Secret of Health" and "The First Case," neither having found a buyer in five tries. The editors' only comment was that each story was about a thousand words too long.[35] That same month Richter expanded his search for a job, writing to famous people who lived active lives of the kind Richter found inviting. Ernest Thompson Seton, chief scout of the Boy Scouts of America, replied that he had "no vacancy at present, as I have sufficient staff to attend to all my work indoors and out."[36] Gifford Pinchot, then head of the U.S. Forest Service, wrote that he "already had two very good secretaries, and do not need another."[37] Richard Harding Davis responded more pointedly to Richter's request for his help to become a war correspondent: "Writing me for advice how to be a war correspondent is not the way to begin. . . . What I mean is that if you really wanted to be a war correspondent you would borrow the money, steal a ride on a freight train, or walk to the Rio Grande. Should you do so, I should be glad to hear from you again."[38] However much he may have longed for the excitement of the expedition into Mexico, Richter was not yet ready to strike out so boldly on his own. What he was asking, indirectly, was for sponsorship, a mentor to initiate him into a different life, the world of successful people. Having no luck with his stories or with his requests for work as a private secretary, he turned to another kind of writing. On June 13 the Vitograph Company of America wrote to offer Richter $15 to purchase the rights "as are necessary to motion picture purposes" for his screenplay "Look Before You Leap."[39] It was his first sale.

Conrad Richter worked through the summer for the *Pittsburgh Dispatch,* continuing at the job about twice as long as his first attempt at living away from his family four years earlier. Ultimately, however, the result was the same: he slipped deeper and deeper into depression, experiencing again what he would term a nervous breakdown. Years later, in an introduction to an unpublished book meant for fellow sufferers of nervous afflictions, "Nerve Energy and Its Management," Richter recounted that experience. Working nights, unable to sleep during the hot summer days, the young reporter found himself succumbing to inescapable fears, fears with no apparent causes that came to torment him so completely that any future seemed "some inconceivable damnation, . . . an eternity in hell." Unable to allay these terrors, he had no choice but to return to his parents' home, where "with rest, wholesome food, fresh air and the environment of the family fireside" he effected "a gradual, makeshift recovery."

By his twenty-first birthday on October 13, 1911, Richter was sufficiently in control of his emotions to begin thinking again about jobs, even jobs that would take him away from home. Still longing for the big break to demonstrate his worth, he thought again of becoming a private secretary. This time he decided to advertise, placing a personal notice in the *Bookman* to offer his services. While awaiting replies, Richter accepted a job as a sports reporter on the *Johnstown Leader*. Although not what he wanted, the job did allow him a place to work near the family home in Windber. He would be able to live there until December, when the family was to move to Reading, Pennsylvania, where John Richter had been called by another Lutheran church, his fourth charge in seven years. Just after his twenty-first birthday Richter received a reply to his advertisement from a Mrs. Elizabeth C. T. Miller of Cleveland, Ohio, who was looking for a general secretary who could also attend to her two boys, nine and seven years old, in the afternoons. This was not what he hoped for, and Richter delayed making any reply. A week later another letter from Mrs. Miller arrived, and then at the end of the month a letter answering Richter's request for more information. Mrs. Miller needed someone to write her business and social correspondence and to write letters in connection with her active work in charities and with her bookplate collection, which was becoming quite large. In the afternoons, her boys needed someone to "be with" them for sports and play. Could Mr. Richter come the following Sunday for an interview?[40] Mr. Richter could not, but he did finally agree to meet with her on December 3, a Sunday morning.

They met at her home on Euclid Avenue, which turned out to be a mansion; Mrs. Miller herself turned out to be the daughter and heir of Washington S. Tyler, owner of the W. S. Tyler Company, a wire manufacturing concern. Her household staff already included a butler, a cook, a maid, a chauffeur, a garage man, and a governess who looked after the schooling of the two boys. Mrs. Miller hoped to add to this staff a young man to help manage the household while she was away on vacations—which she often was—and to oversee the rough-and-tumble activities of her sons. There was no husband in the household, for Mrs. Miller was divorced. Reluctant to accept the job, Richter was at least interested enough to lie about his age, claiming to be twenty-four.

In the weeks following that meeting in Cleveland, Mrs. Miller wrote Richter repeatedly, urging him to a decision that he continued to put off. Finally, after months of delay, Richter gave up waiting for a more interesting alternative. Once his parents and brothers had moved to Reading, Richter had no reason to stay in Johnstown, and so he accepted Mrs. Miller's offer of $50 a month and room and board, and in May he moved to Cleveland. But he was not optimistic.

When he left the *Leader* he told nobody there, not even his friends among the young reporters, about his new job in Cleveland. If it turned out badly, he wanted as few people as possible to know.

THREE

By early June Richter was settled into the Miller home. In the mornings he worked with the bookplates in the second-floor library; in the afternoons he took charge of nine-year-old Tyler and seven-year-old Otto, for sports and play. It was an uncomfortable living arrangement, for he was neither guest nor servant in the household, nor was he invited to think of himself as a member of the family. Wary of gossip, Mrs. Miller did not want a man living in the house at all, but changed her mind to have him conveniently at hand at all hours. Richter dined with the family, even at dinner parties—lavish, two-butler affairs for up to two dozen guests. Unsure what was expected of him, he dreaded these events, where he would remain silent unless spoken to directly. About such matters Mrs. Miller offered no guidance at all. When she was at home, which was seldom enough, she chose to treat him with severe reserve, discouraging any questions.

Of course he was unhappy. Tyler and Otto were brats even when on their best behavior, and Richter was hard put to find a combination of cajolery and subtle coercion to keep them in line. He did try conscientiously, and the boys responded to his efforts with affection if not obedience. They would at least sit still to hear the adventures of an immigrant boy from India, Skeeks by name, about whom Conrad created stories on demand. But he was no real secretary, at least as he had imagined such a position. Mrs. Miller was simply rich and idle; there were no secrets of success to learn, no chance for sponsorship, and the only correspondence was of the household management kind. Even so, in his letters home Richter creates for himself a cherished persona, that of an upbeat, contemporary man of the world, both participator and amused observer of the goings-on around him. In them he describes "Funnyland," as he named life with the Cleveland Millers, both the city mansion with its dinner parties and trips to the theater and the farm outside the city, where Mrs. Miller took her boys for horseback riding and Independence Day fireworks. In an early letter, the young secretary describes a trip to the theater:

> Well I've gone and done it. No not married—not yet. Nor did I break
> with Mrs. M. and give her ten days. Nothing of the sort. Simply went to

a matinee at the Colonial Theater in a box party consisting of the two boys, two girls, Mrs. A.B.C.D.E.F.M. and myself. And tra, la, la. We went down in the Stearns Landaulet, with Gustave at the wheel. Gustave, accent on the last syllable please. . . .

Of course my accompaniment, in C-flat most of the time, was purely functionary, employeeical, pardon the momentary mintage, but I was there just the same. And that consarned theater proved full of people who knew Mrs. M. and the boys and girls, two young ladies from uptown. My employer kept busy bowing when the lights came on and I was busy making my blue suit and a fever sore on the audience side lip, harmonize with the plush curtains and surroundings.[41]

Here is a narrator telling tales on himself, amused by his participation in a comic world. It is of course a literary construction, an act of imagination for Richter's pleasure as well as his family's. It is the voice of Richter as he wanted to be, tried to be, but in performances that were never quite convincing to himself.

That fall Mrs. Miller offered her secretary an extraordinary adventure. She asked if he would travel to Coeur d'Alene, Idaho, to investigate for her a possible investment, a lead and silver mine. Richter readily agreed to go, asking only that he be allowed to continue the trip on to the West Coast before returning again to Cleveland. When he arrived at Wallace, Idaho, in the middle of October, his first recorded act demonstrates that his shyness would not interfere with his sleuthing: he invited the pretty secretary of a Wallace mining tycoon to a movie, an invitation she accepted. The next day he took the Missoula line north through the Bitterroot Mountains to Sildex, the company town of the Amazon-Dixie Mining Company, and there he presented himself to Wesley Everett, superintendent of the works, as a Pittsburgh reporter after a story.

Perhaps there were likelier ways to discover the true story of the Amazon-Dixie, but the reporter ruse worked well enough to get Everett's attention for several days. The Amazon-Dixie was only an exploratory tunnel, not a productive mine; following the surface vein to richer deposits required enormous capital, and Everett was looking for investors. Recognizing the unexpected visit as a promotional windfall, the burly, exuberant Everett turned his attention to giving Conrad Richter, reporter, a yarn worth writing. Richter took it all in, repeating in letters home Everett's stories, including one of fending off a grizzly with a pocketknife. Everett had the scars on his arm to prove it, Richter innocently wrote. Richter found himself thoroughly impressed, for Everett was the kind of man Richter wished he could be—self-assured, outgoing, respected by investors and miners alike. He was superbly in control, "a man's man from the toes up."[42]

Before leaving Sildex, Richter admitted to Everett his real mission: "I'd have been a hound to maintain the half-deception," he wrote his family. In the same letter he announced he had decided to invest in Amazon-Dixie himself: "Mother and Dad, you'll have to count me out of the possibility of help for a while. Having had this proposition shoved upon me by fate and found it so above par in every respect, I'm going to make good and take a block of stock. It's a gamble, I admit, everything is, but it's the biggest thing in the country and I'm going in. Only a little stock is left. . . . I have enough for the first payment. Another follows in 3 months and so on for a year or two until the vein is struck below by the tunnel in operation now. It's going to make me scrape to save but the work will do me good, I'd have spent the money in Cleveland anyhow."[43] How could he have resisted? Here was his chance, his opportunity to plunge into a risk that could change his life—and his family's life—irrevocably.

After the Coeur d'Alene adventure, Richter's duties in Cleveland were even more depressingly uneventful than before. In November Wesley Everett visited Cleveland, no doubt to pursue Mrs. Miller's interest, and Richter talked to his new friend about opportunities out West for young, willing men. Once the mine came in, Everett promised, Conrad and his brother Joe could both work for him. In less than a year underground, he claimed, they would know enough to take a superintendent's job like one of the three Everett had declined that month. The invitation seemed just right for Joe, who was interested in engineering, but Richter had different thoughts. He did not want to be a manager of men, but rather an assistant to a mining magnate—again a kind of private secretary, next to power but not exercising it, not a king but an attendant lord. In short, he was still looking for sponsorship.

There was also another reason. Although Richter wrote enthusiastically about the opportunity to his brother Joe, he still dreamed of becoming a writer; he wanted a position that gave him time to write. That fall Richter typed out on Mrs. Miller's new typewriter a story that placed a rich woman strikingly like Mrs. Miller into a predicament Richter may have found some satisfaction in—worrying that her new husband loves only her money. Richter also typed up and submitted to *St. Nicholas Magazine* two of the stories he had created for Otto and Tyler, "Skeeks" and "Skeeks in America." Both were rejected, and both would be turned down in January by the *Woman's Home Companion*.[44] But if disappointed he was not yet discouraged, and the time he spent at the typewriter was time when his mind was far away from Tyler and Otto and the imperious Mrs. Miller.

At Christmas, his first ever away from his family, Richter's various unhappi-nesses again spilled over into a letter home. Asking that they not tell anyone, not even Aunt Lizzie, Richter again confided that his was "not the kind of secre-tary job you read about in novels." A less self-conscious and private young man might have found considerable entertainment in the extravagances of Mrs. Miller's parties, and Richter himself clearly enjoyed sharing stories about the elite with his family, sending home party favors, cigars, and imported cigarettes left from these affairs. "That thing of bashfulness is gone," he wrote, but clearly his dis-comfort was not. Unsure just what was expected at these affairs, he remained a "nontalkable fixture," as unobtrusive a presence as he could make himself. And he continued to smart at Mrs. Miller's public treatment of him. Although he understood that the divorcee's curt manner was a defense against gossip, that knowledge did not make the experience any more comfortable.[45]

When not playing with the boys or attending to the household finances, Richter worked at his stories, at least fitfully. One story idea came from his trip into mining country the previous fall, about two prospectors who try to convince a blind and fatally wounded friend that they are meeting his last wish. A local-color story in the Bret Harte manner—full of quaint dialogue, evocative descrip-tions of place, and rough but warmhearted characters—"The Bravest Little Soul" drew as well upon a surprise ending in the manner of O. Henry. This time the high hopes with which he mailed the story were not dashed: on July 19 Richter received a letter from Robert Hobart Davis: "'The Bravest Little Soul,' notwith-standing it is highly improbable, is delicate and agreeable, and I should like to use it in *The Cavalier* at twenty-five dollars. If this rate is agreeable, let me know."[46] Ever more adventuresome with words when the words were delivered by mail, Richter immediately wrote to ask for more money, a two-sided argument based on the intrinsic worth of the story and how long it had taken him to write it, with an appeal thrown in about needing the money for an upcoming vacation. He was sufficiently persuasive to convince Davis to raise the rate to $35.

By summer 1913, Conrad Richter had been living away from home for more than a year. All things considered, his health had held up well. There had been a problem with eyestrain during the winter, probably from the close work with bookplates, but no hint of the trouble that ended both earlier jobs away from home. Of course conditions in Cleveland were decidedly better than they had been at those jobs. If at times homesick, he at least had the presence of the Miller boys and staff around him; he did not have to return after work to a lonely boardinghouse room. The year in Cleveland had also given him an insider's view of a group that fascinated him, the leisured rich, and the experience had taught

6.   Conrad Richter in his best suit and stiffest collar, *circa* 1912.

him, if not the secrets of making money, at least the skills necessary to provide himself with protective coloration. As he wrote home in another of the letters telling tales on himself, he was now able to cut a peach on his plate without spilling his neighbor's wine. But he was still ill at ease. Acutely aware of the qualities society approved of in its young men, he could create a persuasive imitation. It was easiest in letters, where only words could betray him as an impostor, but given time to prepare himself he could create a convincing portrayal of Conrad Richter, urbane secretary to a wealthy Cleveland family. In a photograph taken of him standing with his foot on the running board of one of Mrs. Miller's cars, he seems comfortably in place, a handsome young man smilingly at ease. In a formal portrait at about the same time, his stiff demeanor in his high collar and tightly buttoned suit, his carefully slicked down hair, seems no less genuine than that of all the other swells who posed just as stiffly in their high collars that year. But beneath the public composure, the acutely self-conscious Connie Richter

7.   Richter in his bathing suit at Rye Beach, New Hampshire, August 1913.

still squirmed at the thought of exposure to the coolly critical eyes of those whose savoir faire came from privileged life, not from books. Whatever he was to others, to himself he was still the country parson's son in masquerade.

That August Mrs. Miller chose Rye Beach, New Hampshire, for her summer outing with the boys, taking Richter along for the six-week vacation. The entourage went by train to Boston, then by one of the family cars—shipped ahead to await them—on to the small family resort. Among the families vacationing at Rye Beach, Richter met Johanna Kenngott, an au pair from the Black Forest. She smiled at him when he told her that his grandfather had been a shepherd in the Black Forest, tempting Richter to try out his Pennsylvania Dutch. When he did so she blushed, explaining that he must not call her "du," lest people think they were engaged.[47] But she laughed easily, lessening the sting of his mistake. And besides, she was quite pretty.

As the summer days passed, Connie Richter and Hanna Kenngott sat together in the sunshine, talking as the children romped along the pebble beach. They made an attractive couple, he tall, slender, gangly and strong shouldered in his tank top and bathing shorts—a handsome young man who did not look the twenty-five he claimed to be—and she blonde and fair, outgoing and pretty. In the evenings, after the children were asleep, they would meet with the other young people gathering around campfires. Two things especially attracted Richter to Hanna. She was always happy it seemed, and her happiness was infectious. Once they were good friends, Richter discovered that her smiles and laughter were a bright facade, for her employers treated her badly. Then he confided in her that he too was unhappy, that his job was not what he had hoped it would be. On her last evening at Rye Beach Hanna walked with her girlfriends to the community campground, there meeting Conrad to say good-bye. He promised to write, and so too did she. Her letters suggest that there were other promises as well.

Back in Cleveland, the summer outing over, the months stretched before Richter in an attenuated and depressingly unbroken pattern. Even thoughts of Hanna were unconsoling, for she was far away in the Black Forest and the letters she promised had not yet arrived. Richter told himself that he would work on his short stories whenever he could: if he could sell his stories he could escape from Cleveland and the Miller household. He had by then a copy of the *Cavalier* for September 6, 1913, with his first published story. As would happen often enough to other stories, the editors had chosen for it a different title, "How Tuck Went Home." When he completed stories that fall, he sent them out directly to magazines. In October the *Cavalier* returned "The Sister of Rudd," with the comment that though he wrote "with a certain distinction," Richter "ought to pay more attention to plot." *Adventure* rejected "James Stacey" but did invite him to "come again." The *Smart Set* liked "Nell Hogan, Shoplifter" well enough, but it came too soon after a similar story for them to use it.[48] Although he had been advised by the editor of the *Cavalier* that stories of selfless sacrifice, as he had created in "The Sister of Rudd," were too improbable to succeed, stories of altruism continued to work in the young writer's imagination. "The Bravest Little Soul" was also an improbable story about friends trying to help one another, but it had sold, perhaps because the exotic place and peculiarities of the people kept it from the criticism that contemporary, cosmopolitan people just did not behave that way. Richter tried again, this time setting his story in the hard country of his father's western Pennsylvania ministry. Instead of a college student taking the blame for his friend's errors, as in "Rudd," he created a country deacon, cruelly unbending in his pious rectitude, who asks for and receives the weight of a childhood friend's bundle of unrepented sins.

Richter called his new story "Brothers of No Kin," and he chose for this fable of sin and retribution a narrator who is very much of the present—glib, cosmopolitan, determined to connect himself with his audience: "Ebenezer Straint, deacon, was not a man like you or I. In either your town or in mine, a hard-headed, shallow-minded religious crank he would have been, a church fool and stiff pedestrian in the strait and narrow path. Youth would have laughed and cynic would have sneered. . . . Even a doubtful Christian as you or I would have called him an obstinate, bigoted, old illiberal, and shaken our heads sadly over his good in this world of yours and mine."[49] This relic of nineteenth-century absolutist religion is not Richter's father nor his grandfather, but he is surely the worst of Lutheranism as Richter had experienced it in his childhood and adolescence. For Ebenezer Straint, faith is ever an oppressive thing, a burden taking all joy from life, unbearable except in the knowledge of its alternative, eternal damnation to those too foolish to heed the coming retribution of the Lord. But if such faith is an anachronism, Richter's modern narrator understands that the choice it leads to is stunningly human, heroic in its self-denial and mythic in its repetition of the ritual sacrifice of one life for another. How can the deacon choose damnation for himself and salvation for Jeremiah Ritter, his only friend? In their oppositions they have each lived their lives as ultimately as humanly possible, one denying all pleasure, the other refusing any self-denial. By the deacon's religion, he deserves to be saved, his friend damned. But impervious to all other earthly temptations, the deacon is trapped by his love. He prays to take upon himself the sins of this friend, and his prayer is answered. A life's guilt lifts from his dying friend's soul and drops oppressively on his own.

Richter wrote "Brothers of No Kin" in October 1913. That October in Cleveland, as fall settled toward the gray afternoons of November, Richter waited for a letter from Johanna Kenngott that did not arrive. Alone and unhappy, restless in his life of menial chores, he felt his unhappiness slipping into despondency, and he waited with growing dread for his mind once again to slip from his control. He typed his story in the second-floor study of 3738 Euclid Avenue, the mansion of a woman who frivolously abandoned her children to an untried, an unknown young man so that she was free to chase whatever pleasures caught her fancy. He worked remembering the painful church services of his childhood, the arguments with his father about the articles of faith, his apostasy in the eyes of his parents. Balanced between two worlds he repudiated, the cruel admonitions of the church and the hedonistic escapes of the secular rich, Richter wrote his story about one group for the other; and he himself was mediator and interpreter.

Richter's narrator is a version of himself, of Conrad Richter as he wanted others to see him—very much one of them, understanding their values, seeing man's faith in science and human discovery as a comfortable improvement on the lives of the likes of the deacon, and even on the life of his own father. But his direct address to his readers carries as well the contrasts Richter saw and felt himself, especially in Cleveland among the excesses of the leisured rich, between modern relativism and the bedrock of religious fundamentalism. His was a story less about religion than about love, but that love came only out of deeply held conviction; indeed, without the conviction, could there be such love? Could Jeremiah Ritter have made the same sacrifice for Ebenezer Straint? Richter's narrator understands and accepts his place among the moderns, but his feelings of brotherhood are at least ambivalent. It is cool wonder but wonder nonetheless in his voice as he describes Ebenezer Straint's departure from his home: "It was a steep and sandy Allegheny road, a stony, endless road, that has never been traveled by you or me."[50]

Without doubt "Brothers of No Kin" was the best story Richter had written, and remembering William Dean Howells's letter two years before, he sent it to *Harper's Magazine*. Quickly came a reply, not from William Dean Howells but from "Editor, Harper's Magazine": although they had read his story "with sincere interest" and found it "original and striking to such a degree" that they welcomed another submission, the story was "not precisely" what they wanted for their magazine.[51] Four months later, in mid-February, the *Forum* accepted "Brothers of No Kin." But by then Richter's mind was elsewhere. The emotional disorder that had afflicted him twice before had returned in full force, and Richter again found himself the victim of unnameable fears and insomnia.

It happened, evidently, in November. Perhaps about the time—shortly after completing "Brothers of No Kin"—that Richter began a story titled "The Old Debt." Whether then or later, the story is a piece of wishful thinking about the job in Cleveland and his relationship with his mother, and it has bearing on his depression during fall 1913. In "The Old Debt" a young man, after several years working as a private secretary to a wealthy family, returns home in minor triumph. Where before he has been unable to hold any job, a burden and a worry to his minister father and especially to his mother, now he presents himself an alert, confident, sophisticated man of experience and presence. Turning aside all questions, he carries his mother out of her modest parsonage home into a posh New York hotel, hires a limousine to take her about, and insists that she spend largely on herself as she has never been able to do. The spree concluded, the secretary returns his mother to her home and sets out for the West, revealing for the first time that he has been fired from his job. As he departs, he borrows $100 from his father, having spent every penny he had saved but prepared confidently to begin again.[52]

Part of the wishful thinking for Richter was of course the daydream of lavishly rewarding his mother, compensation for the failures of both the father and the son. If during this time, as he later told his daughter, he was writing stories while waiting to be fired because of his nervous condition, then he wrote knowing another of his failures would soon be visited upon his mother. The story was his version of how he wanted to go home, how he wanted his family to see that his time among the rich had changed him, made him knowledgeable of their ways, gave him information that was empowering. But in the story the young secretary's success is finally an illusion, just as Richter knew his own to be. After completing "Brothers of No Kin" Richter asked for and received time off to visit his parents in Reading, a visit that may well have started his thinking about "The Old Debt"; but soon Mrs. Miller was writing to ask if he could be back in time for Otto's birthday party.[53] That was the reality of his job, behind the illusion he preferred others to see.

In an act of will Conrad returned to Cleveland, putting aside his longing for the home of his parents to supervise a boy's birthday party. But his will was less and less able to hold together the public presence he relied upon in Cleveland. Long suppressed feelings came frighteningly to the surface of his mind, not only at night, which was bad enough and draining, but at other times, too, times when he guardedly presented only a public posture. Richter sought out a young Cleveland neurologist, hoping that this new field of medicine would offer him an explanation of his condition and a cure. During the hour examination, Richter told the neurologist about his physical maladies, the coppery taste on his tongue, the ache in his chest, the insomnia, the anxiety, the despair. He did not reveal to the doctor the fears assailing him. These were, Richter would later write, "too monstrous, shocking, unseating to reason."[54] At the end of the examination, the young neurologist pronounced him physically fit, perfectly well—a conclusion Richter immediately rejected. "Something can't be nothing," he said to himself; "It can't be just a word like neuresthenia."[55]

Knowing he had held back information, Richter turned desperately to the only vehicle by which he could admit the specifics of his frightening urgings. He decided to write to authorities on brain disorders whose names he discovered in the Cleveland library. As he had written to writers when trying to find a job, he wrote to Jacques Loeb, M.D., of the Rockefeller Institute for Medical Research in New York and author of *Comparative Physiology of the Brain and Comparative*

Physiology; to Richard C. Cabot, M.D., in Boston, a specialist in nervous disorders; and a Dr. Dubois, in Berne, Switzerland, whose *Influence of the Mind upon the Body* had been translated into English. It is likely he wrote to others as well. The replies from these three were kind, extensive, and thoughtful, but finally they gave Richter no more hope than did the Cleveland neurologist. His case was "merely a nervous one,"[56] probably hereditary, and their best advice was to avoid stressful jobs, give up studying foreign languages for a time, and exercise outdoors daily. Their replies do disclose what Richter had not revealed to the doctor in Cleveland. To them he admitted, as Jacques Loeb put it, "the irresistible desire to commit blasphemy." About these libidinal impulses forcing themselves into the tightly controlled public presence of Richter, Dr. Dubois wrote, "Ideas without acts have not importance."[57] Jacques Loeb wrote: "Your whole worry about your condition is due to the fact that you think your [illness] is something to be ashamed of, which is not the case. Even if you should yield to it, and should swear sometime, there would be no wrong in it. The main thing is that you get rid of your fear that you might say something that is not proper." Just how Richter was to rid himself of this fear, Loeb did not say.

Never had Richter felt more alone in the world. Separated from his family and missing them intensely, despondent that no letter had arrived from Hanna, forced by his job to maintain a pose in an uncomfortable public situation while his mind tricked him with unexpected and unexplainable urges to say shocking things, he wrote to Richard Cabot a second time, posing a desperate cure. With both relief and despair he read Cabot's reply: "No brain surgeon could take away your memory and leave your life intact."[58]

Richter returned to his parents' Reading home for the Christmas holidays; either just before or just after that visit he received a long-awaited letter from Johanna Kenngott. But neither her letter nor the news that the *Forum* had accepted "Brothers of No Kin" gave him relief from his depression. In his letter to Hanna telling her he had been ill, he wrote that it was best that they be just friends,[59] and he began to prepare for the inevitable dismissal from his job. Finally one morning he was unable to pull himself from his bed, unable to control his crying. When the paralyzing depression did not abate, he knew he could not stay in Cleveland. There was no place for him to go but back to the parsonage in Reading, once again a failure, once again a burden and a worry to his mother.[60]

Early Marriage

O N E

Back in his parents' home in Reading, rest and the comforting presence of his family eased the intensity of Richter's depression, and he pulled himself together to work.[1] By the end of February 1914, he had collected seven letters of recommendation, including testimonials from Wesley Everett of the Amazon-Dixon Mining Company, from H. D. Hoover of the Carthage College of Character Culture, from Charles T. Aikens, president of Susquehanna University, and from H. H. Hower, advertising manager of the F. B. Stearns Company, makers of the Stearns automobile, who noted Richter to be "greatly interested in the automobile trade."[2] Missing is any word from Mrs. E. C. T. Miller herself. It is not clear how energetically Richter presented these letters to potential employers. He may have traveled as far as Buffalo, New York, in his searches, carrying a personal introduction from Everett to city hall, naming Richter "a hell of a good fellow."[3] But given his collapse in Cleveland it is unlikely that he would have pressed for a job taking him far away from his parents and brothers, both of whom still lived at home. It is quite clear that he quickly set himself an ambitious writing routine, turning out stories over the next months in numbers he would never again match. Working in his father's study, a second-floor bedroom in the parsonage at 813 North Eleventh Street, he typed away at his stories, drafting and redrafting at a pace that did not suggest a cautious recuperation but rather a frantic drive to succeed.

A great deal was at stake for Richter: the stories were his way to set aside a record of repeated false starts and early quittings. Fearing that his talents did not match his ambitions, his sense of himself hung upon each story. The best he posted immediately to *Harper's*, *Munsey's*, or *Hearst's*, and when they were returned— as they all were—he sent them to the second echelon of magazines, to *People's*, *Everybody's*, or *Adventure*, where publication was less prestigious and less remunerative. Some he sent to the *Editor*, a magazine offering a service like the Literary Bureau, critical help with stories for a fee. On February 28 *Munsey's* returned "A Sample of God's Repair Shop" with a brief opinion and some encouragement. The advice is typical: "I think this story is promising in its characterizations; you made me interested at once in Martin, the description of the children; and their dialogue I think is excellent. But why on earth did you kill it altogether by having the man go and get drunk? You lowered him about ten miles when you did that. You write too well to fall back upon such a cheap-and-easy device for getting him back into his own house. . . . I shall be very glad to see some more stories of yours. I think your work has materially improved. But remember, we have to have strong plots and quick action. We cannot use character studies."[4] Repeatedly Richter heard the same message: editors all wanted strong plots, which Richter's stories did not sufficiently offer; and they wanted stories that were positive influences—tasteful, even didactic tales for modern readers. They would not buy character studies, nor were they interested in the ironic or satiric. Having no strong sense of a subject himself, Richter attempted to follow their collective advice, trying to be more plotty, more uplifting, more contemporary.

That spring two voices became distinct among the letters about Richter's stories. The first was that of an A. L. Kimball, who wrote critiques of stories for the *Editor*. Early in March A. L. Kimball wrote to Richter: "Your work is unusually good. You have original ideas and the ability to work them convincingly. We feel certain that short story success will come to you."[5] Although Kimball's simple declarative sentences have a formulaic ring to them, unlikely to convince a writer as full of self-doubt as Richter, the five pages of advice about two stories, "The Phantom Special in Yellow" and "Marked Down," did provide concrete suggestions for revision and encouragement that, if Richter stayed steadily at his work, he would soon be selling stories. For a writer struggling with his own fears of inadequacy, A. L. Kimball's letters, as much pep talks as practical criticism, would become a needed prop as the months passed without a single story selling. As their writer-critic relationship developed, A. L. Kimball discovered herself as not Mr. but Mrs., and that helped Richter to confide in her. Later she would send Richter her home address, for use when he was especially despondent, adding that she was not so very much older than the aspiring writer.

The second voice came through letters of rejection from *Hearst's Magazine*. Signed only with the initials I.M.P., these letters were sometimes longer and more detailed, always sharper, wittier, and—once I.M.P. had corrected Richter's mistaken assumptions about her position and sex ("P.S. 'Reader' is the word. Thanks for the flattery. Also the word 'he' should be amended to read—otherwise"),[6] more playful and flirtatious. But for all her playfulness, I.M.P. in her criticisms cut sharply to the center of each story, assessing and suggesting, and she too encouraged Richter even as she teased him. When Richter in one of his cover letters for a submission, on stationery he had collected from trains and hotels during his trip west, politely protested her idiosyncratic editorial style, I.M.P. soon replied:

> Dear Mr. Richter,
>   Never mind—even if you don't enjoy it, I do. Not that it seems to help you any; I've got to return these just the same. Fact is, absolutely nothing is being bought in this office just at present. We are endeavoring to exist in status quo; to live on our fat, like a bear in winter, for reasons of editorial (not financial) policy. Of course, the drought may break at any moment—who am I, to read the will of Allah? . . . For a small commission, I will gladly steal, purloin or abstract such gilt-edged stationery from such glittering caravanseries as you may designate— supposing your present supply runs out. Could anything be fairer than that? The hotels are so convenient, here.[7]

Whatever Richter might have made of I.M.P.'s remark about convenient hotels, he was encouraged enough by the personal attention to send another story by return mail. Quickly came I.M.P.'s assessment: "I don't like this story so well. I could tell you why, but must I? I don't think it's good. You seem to have just gone out of your way to make trouble for your harmless characters, and that's not artistic."[8] What was he to do with such a reply? First editors complained that his stories were too much character sketches, and when he created more difficulties for his characters, they told him the difficulties were contrived. In discouraged puzzlement he wrote to Mrs. Kimball, explaining his youth, his concentrated hard work, and his disappointment in getting no further on with his craft. On April 11, A. L. Kimball replied with motherly advice: "We are glad to have your letter and have noted carefully the confidences given. We thought you an older man, but your youth stands strongly in your favor. You have much zest to impart to your work."[9] Within two weeks, I.M.P. was to offer her own response to Richter's pleas for advice: "I have read the enclosed story, and I think it's rather good as a bit of genre drawing. In brief I like it. But yes, you are not simpatico; your critics were right. Now that wouldn't matter so much anywhere else than in America. But the Americans like sentiment; they would rather an author were even maudlin than otherwise. And you don't feel for the people you write about. That doesn't disturb me; I like the brutal facts; but I see where others would fall foul of your work."[10] In the same mail came another, briefer letter from I.M.P., rejecting another story but offering Richter her greatest encouragement: "Never mind the trouble. I'm computing the odds on whether I can get a story of yours accepted here yet!"[11]

When Richter tried Robert Hobart Davis again at the *Cavalier*, sending him a story based upon his own experience as a private secretary in Cleveland, Hobart's reply was doubly hurtful: "'Mrs. Wharton's Secretary' is a very uninteresting young man and I do not think he is worth the space you have given him. . . . Try again and make an effort to get somewhere."[12] About the same time Richter wrote I.M.P., employing with the aptly acronymed reader a different strategy. Thanking her for her efforts to place one of his stories, he asked if he might not show his appreciation by taking her to dinner. No doubt his motives were mixed, hoping to sell one of his stories and curious to meet the vexaciously witty woman. I.M.P. put Richter off, writing as always amusingly and bluntly to the point: "Let me warn you that editorial integrity is proof against even a dinner at Childs'—if you were thinking of it as an investment! . . . If the worst comes to the worst, you can bring me an 'all-day sucker,' and we'll let the dinner thing go."[13]

By late July the folder of rejection letters had become thick. I.M.P. had not succeeded in placing one of his stories at *Hearst's*, and A. L. Kimball's counsel had not led to a single sale. Although editors praised his craft, they found his plots too slight, his stories, as I.M.P. had said, too short on the milk of human kindness. Were there yet techniques of craft he needed to master? Or were the failures simply the unchangeable outcome of too thin a talent? Richter had done all he could think to do to meet editors' expectations, including reading all the stories they published in their magazines. But something was always wrong. It seemed to make no difference whether he trusted his own intuition or slavishly followed advice. Neither way succeeded, and what good did it do to talk of intention or achievement when no editors would accept his work? To be read, he had first to sell, and how could he do that? He could not stay at home with his parents forever, and his savings from Cleveland were running out. Nonetheless he persevered, working through the warm weeks of July. Some evenings he would join Joe for walks about Reading, and occasionally he would go with his brothers to see the latest films. When Joe and Fred went off for a week's visit to Pine Grove, Richter stayed dutifully at his typewriter, worrying out new stories and trying again to write scenarios for the motion pictures, scripts for one- and two-reelers for film companies gobbling up treatments for their new entertainment. To make himself look older, he grew a mustache. When his eyes gave him trouble, he went to a doctor for prescription glasses—choosing pince-nez frames which made him look almost professorial. With those he returned to his room and his work, often typing far into the night. At the end of July, *Women's Stories*, a cheap-paper monthly, wrote to offer $25 for "The Old Debt," Richter's story about a young man's gift to his mother. It was his first sale since "Brothers of No Kin," for which he had still not been paid. In between these sales, thirty stories had been rejected.

On their return from Pine Grove, Joe and Fred told Connie about the group of young people they met there. Richter was especially interested in their descriptions of the young women—Adah Schucker, Pauline Sutton, and the leader of the group, a small and pretty young woman known by the name of Harvey. Harvena Achenbach was only four years old when the Richter family left Pine Grove for Selinsgrove, and Conrad did not remember her. Listening to his brothers' reports, Conrad was sufficiently enticed to be talked into taking a brief vacation from writing, and he agreed to join them for a second visit in early August. Although Trap Irwin was gone from Pine Grove, working for a railroad in the West, cousin Beth lived there with her husband and child, and Aunt Lizzie still lived in Aunt Esther's house on the corner of Morris and Mifflin Streets. There the three boys would be welcome. Conrad, Joe, and Fred arrived in Pine Grove on Saturday, August 8, and by the next day—or so he would always say—Conrad's heart had settled forever upon the small, dark-haired woman of eighteen who wanted to be called Harvey.

When Joe and Fred introduced Connie to the Pine Grove gang, Adah and Pauline smiled and shook hands with the oldest Richter boy. Harvena Achenbach did not offer her hand, and she looked at Conrad in a way that discomfited him. She was pretty, he thought, attractively trim in the style of the time, with blue gray, slanting eyes and doll-like pink cheeks. Did she see through the mask that he used to cover his habitual shyness and social uncertainty? In his travels Richter had learned a thing or two about talking to young ladies, and he knew the tactical advantage of direct questions. "What are you thinking of?" he asked her. Whatever answer he expected, her reply was characteristic of her surprising candor. "Of you," she said, and her answer stopped his heart.[14]

Harvena Maria Achenbach was no shrinking violet. But for her exceptional composure, making her appear disconcertingly at ease, she might have seemed even devil-may-care. Pert and fun-loving, she joined in whatever sport or play was at hand, tennis with the gang or wrestling with her younger brothers. Even at eighteen she was still something of a tomboy, as Conrad's mother had been; and if he remembered the pictures of his mother from before her marriage, he would have seen that, though smaller than his mother, Harvena Achenbach looked remarkably like Lottie Henry at eighteen. As the first days passed, Conrad found he liked everything about this young girl except her inattention to him. He liked her fearlessness, her willingness to say or do anything she chose, ignoring what others might think. So often discouraged himself, so self-conscious of his own actions and of how others saw him, he watched her with fascination. He liked her rueful way of talking, as if telling stories on herself, and he liked the lilt to her voice, so different from the Pennsylvania Dutch cadences of her family and friends. Like Hanna Kenngott, she seemed irrepressibly happy, and he listened for her laughter and for her voice among the other voices singing. Even when she was quiet, Conrad felt her steady self-assurance. Others could interest her, but not persuade her or turn her. Without thinking, she knew what she thought. Perhaps best of all, most delightful to a young man who often felt stiff and uncomfortable when with others, she had the knack of making him easy.

Trying not to seem obvious in his intentions, Conrad looked for ways to be near her as the Richter brothers joined the Pine Grove gang for picnics and corn roasts, tennis games and swimming. At the end of each evening, they would all walk arm in arm up Main Street, singing temperance songs:

We're coming, we're coming, our little band,
On the right side of temperance, we've taken our stand,
We don't use tobacco for really we think
Them that uses it is liable to drink.[15]

When he could arrange it, Connie's arm would be linked with Harvey's for the evening march. One afternoon on the walk up Bird's Hill to a corn roast, she let him button her sweater, but then she slipped away to join her girlfriends, leaving Richter to walk alone.

One matter disturbed Richter from the beginning. Although no one seemed more vital and alive than Harvena Achenbach, Conrad knew that her family was afflicted with tuberculosis. Her mother had died of it when Harvey was twelve; an aunt and an uncle had also died of it, and only weeks before, the Achenbach family had buried her older sister Alma, dead at nineteen. By the thinking of the day, the entire family was afflicted with the disease; Harvena Achenbach was marked as a victim and almost inevitably would succumb, probably in her early twenties. Having suffered such losses and knowing her own danger, how could she seem so untouched by these things? Here was a lovely young woman bearing far more than he, and yet she seemed unconcerned.

Richter also knew that he was not alone in his attention to her. After the death of her mother, Harvey had been befriended by the Strickler family in Lebanon, Pennsylvania, a family whose zest for life matched her own. Often she would visit them in Lebanon, a short train ride from Pine Grove. Among the young people of Pine Grove it was understood that Paul, the Strickler son who squired her about when they were together, was her young man and that if Harvena ever married, it would be Paul. But Harvey was not one to let others make choices for her. By the fifth day of Conrad's stay in Pine Grove, she was overtly encouraging his attentions. After a wedding in Suedberg, which Richter attended to hear Harvey sing "I Love You Truly," Harvey allowed him to hold her hand as they walked along the railroad tracks to the station. Elated, Richter "dared the crowd" by whistling "Here Comes the Bride" as the two led the evening march up Main Street.[16] The next morning he and Joe waited for her on the steps of the armory, where she had promised to join them if she could get away from chores at home. When she did not arrive they went swimming. Later in the day, walking a back street to Aunt Lizzie's, Richter saw her in her yard, playing ball with her younger brothers Lyman and Stanley. Seeing her unexpectedly after missing her all day, he was quite sure he loved her. Late the next afternoon he told her so. Sitting with him at the foot of Bird's Hill, looking up at him "half laughing, half ashamed,"[17] she admitted she loved him too and had from the first moment she saw him.

By Tuesday morning, August 18, when the brothers boarded a train for home, Conrad and Harvena had already established the pattern of their courtship. Connie would be ardently, single-mindedly intent on his "girlie-mine"; Harvey would be coy, reticent, needing to be persuaded. For all her exuberance, her bright cheer, there was about her, as there was about his mother, an inwardness, a central self composed and separate from others. That to Conrad seemed untouchable, and though he was older and, he thought, wiser about the world outside Pine Grove, and one of his delights in his relationship with Harvey was in instructing the ingenue, what he wanted most was to touch that inner being. He worried that, though she was happy to be with him, she turned from him to others with what appeared to be equal pleasure. To such single-minded commitment as his, anything less than rapt attention seemed uncertainty, and he could not keep from feeling that her love was not as wholehearted as his. He was the beseeching suitor, she the hesitant and resisting one. It is impossible to know just how resistant Harvena Achenbach was. She could hardly be called inattentive or uncaring when before his departure she accepted Conrad Richter's proposal of marriage, agreeing to marry just as soon as his stories began to sell. But her feelings for him might be, he would write worriedly, "only your '14 love"— a fleeting romance that would not outlast 1914.[18] Afraid to rely upon the happiness that marriage to Harvena promised, he brought his uncertainties into each of his daily letters to her.

As soon as he arrived home in Reading, Richter sent Harvey a postcard, using the names he and Joe kiddingly had called each other since boyhood: "Uriah and Phaeneus know your life will be so sweet as to walk through life in your stocking feet." In a similar spirit he would send her a photograph of the two brothers at the piano singing "That Old Gang of Mine," with an inscription signed "Caruso and Paderewski." But such lightheartedness was infrequent. In the late afternoon of the day they parted, Richter began his first letter. He continued it the next day, hoping to mail it after the arrival of a letter from Harvey. When none arrived, he posted his own with pleas for her to keep her promise to write often. If she made that promise, she was not to keep it, and as the weeks passed Richter wrote Harvey daily, dwelling upon his loneliness and his disappointment at her infrequent replies.

When a letter from Harvena did arrive, Richter answered immediately, telling her that her letters raised his spirits and renewed his hope, which often desperately needed renewing. It would be a refrain running through all his letters to

Harvey that fall and winter. Now that he was betrothed to Harvey, there was the future to think about, bringing on spasms of anxiety and self-doubt. What if his stories did not sell? Soon after their parting, he advised her not to call the ring he had sent an engagement ring. It was better to keep their plans to themselves, he wrote, for "if nothing turns up for me, I am helpless to marry you."[19] Richter had as well other reasons for thinking it best to keep their relationship secret. Harvey was, after all, more than five years younger than he. Attracted to her youth and inexperience, Richter enjoyed the complex roles of lover as well as "pal, comrade, big brother";[20] but he remembered the times when she was less than gratifyingly attentive to his explanations and counsel. Would she tire of him? Had she already begun to do so? At times Richter found himself imagining the worst. Then he would implore her to write in letters evidencing some of his least attractive qualities, his self-absorption, his insecurity, his penchant for secretiveness, his pessimism about the future, and his dread of public ridicule. Evidence of his wobbly emotional balance showed most dramatically in letters after the mail carrier passed without stopping at the Richter house on North Eleventh Street. Then Richter could not keep himself from querulousness, as he himself would later see clearly enough to relegate two of these letters to his "Bad Letters File," a collection kept to remind himself how not to write to anyone.

Richter also worried about Harvena's health. For all her vitality, she was thin, not particularly strong, and susceptible to coughs. As the oldest daughter at home—her sister May was away at nursing school—she kept house for her father and her younger brothers Lyman, Arthur, and Stanley and her sister Grace. She cooked, she cleaned, she did the family wash. Richter worried that she was not able to bear such a burden, and repeatedly in letters he urged her to take better care of herself. If she let herself become weakened, she would be unable to ward off tuberculosis. Clearly he had this in mind when he urged her to write more often, except if she needed to rest. And he may well have been thinking of her precarious health when he wrote on August 24 that "we'd better not have children—for their sakes—so that they might not know sorrow some day."[21]

When Richter next visited Pine Grove, Harvey admitted to misgivings that were understandable enough, given that Conrad was regularly telling her how she was disappointing him. As always fearlessly forthright, she told him that she was different from him and that she would not try to be something other than what she was. Richter answered that he did not want her to be like him; rather, he insisted that her difference was good for him, helped him.[22] At the end of his visit, Harvey was unable to say that she was certain of her feelings, adding anxiety to his depression when he returned to Reading. In his letters Richter urged her to find some way to test her feelings and to write quickly to tell him the outcome. Later he would write in an agony of jealousy, hearing that she had visited the Stricklers—and therefore seen Paul Strickler—without telling him. But however mixed Harvena Achenbach's feelings, she was true to her commitment as she understood it. Although the difference in personalities led to growing tension that could escape only in outbursts of anger and blame, the differences also energized their relationship, such as it was—he wholeheartedly committed, she returning his love but simply incapable of matching or even appreciating such attention as he focused upon her. Whatever proofs Harvey found to reassure herself, in October she visited Reading to meet John and Lottie Richter. During that visit Conrad and Harvey announced that they planned to marry just as soon as Connie could support them both.

When Harvey returned to Pine Grove, Conrad reported that his mother was pleased with her prospective daughter-in-law. John Richter offered no comment, but Conrad was sure he liked her because "no one could help doing that."[23] Shortly thereafter, Connie's grandfather Mike Richter offered his own brusque assessment: "Connie has a nice girl. She isn't very big, but she's all right."[24]

T W O

Several years later Mrs. Kimball from the *Editor* wrote that during this fall Richter was sending her wild letters on scraps of paper, full of his hopes to marry and move to California. These plans would fill Richter's happier letters to Harvena, air castles of future felicity. Just as soon as his stories began to sell, he wrote, he would come to carry her away from Pine Grove, to "start up alone, by ourselves" to prepare for "they who are to come"[25]—the two children, whom, despite Conrad's earlier worry, they had decided to have. One would be a girl, named Harvena for her mother, and they would call her Vene. The boy, named for his father, they would call Junior. When Richter wrote of these children, he wrote as if they were already living with their mother, waiting for their father to return home.

This daydreaming was almost solely Conrad's. If Harvena was content to listen to fanciful stories about the future, she resisted at the first signs that these escapist fantasies might turn into realities. To his insistence that for her health they must at least be ready to go to California, she answered an adamant "no." Her future included Pine Grove, her family, and her friends, and she must have felt that Richter's plans to go away together, delightfully childlike in their combined specificity and indefiniteness, were not the bedrock on which marriages could successfully be built. Though only eighteen, it was Harvena who better understood the practical circumstances of adult life. But if Harvena was the realist, she was not the pessimist; Richter typically was the one looking ahead and seeing the specter of unhappy times. In a November letter he wrote, "You and I dearest must always stick together no matter what. But perhaps there are fires to go through."[26] The odd turn of thought at *but* suggests that the reason for sticking together is not to put out the fires but rather that the fires threaten whether they are together or not. Perhaps here Richter has jumped associationally to his fears about Harvena's health, but more likely this thought is an example of his lack of confidence in life itself and of his own secret worry that he was not quite up to what lay before them.

Whatever Richter's fictions of future life, the practical matters of the moment made them seem far distant. First of all, until her sister May returned from nursing school, Harvey was needed in Pine Grove to keep house for her family. May planned to return home, but her plans, at least as Harvey reported them to Richter, were exasperatingly indefinite. As great an obstacle was the couple's lack of any source of regular income. In August Richter received from the Vitograph Company of America an offer of $25 for his movie scenario "The Passing of Tombstone Mike."[27] Twice that fall he would sell scenarios, for a total of $75,[28] and one story sold, "The Tangle of Lace" to *Women's Stories* for $25.[29] By Conrad's desperate lover's figuring, he and Harvey needed at least $35 a month to live—a more realistic estimate would have been at least twice that—and there could be no certainty that even these small sales would continue with sufficient regularity to pay the landlord and grocer. Richter still had his 8,000 shares of Amazon-Dixie Mining stock, but the chances of the stock ever paying dividends grew fainter with each passing month. Reluctantly he wrote to Harvey, accepting her practical advice: "But dearest, I believe you are right. Writing is not the thing for you and me."[30] He was not yet ready to give up his writing, but if they were to marry soon he would have to find some other way to earn a living.

Richter's thoughts turned again to avenues he had traveled in the past, finding something available locally that he could market outside the area. Pretzels were known elsewhere in 1914, but in Reading, Pennsylvania, pretzels were a dietary staple—by common agreement delicious, nutritious, and cheap. Richter guessed that the person who successfully marketed Reading pretzels outside central Pennsylvania could make handsome profits as a wholesaler. The problem was simply one of effective marketing. Using the last of his savings from Cleveland, Richter prepared his campaign. As he had with his lumber business at White

Deer Valley, he began by creating an appropriate image for success, letter-head paper and business cards, with dark brown ink on golden yellow paper, announcing the opportunity to buy pretzels from "The Richters, Makers of Cris-pretzels—Conrad Richter, President." The promotional campaign was persuasive enough to prompt John Wanamaker, owner of the New York and Philadelphia department stores, to reply personally that he would order a product so effectively presented if his stores had grocery departments. Stores in other cities did agree to try the Reading pretzel, but orders—and, more important, reorders—were slow in coming. Although in time the venture would make a modest profit, in fall 1914 young entrepreneur Richter had no money on which to live.

To solve that problem, Richter began looking for a job, filling out an appli-cation for the National Organization of Employment Specialists, a New York firm with offices in Philadelphia, Pittsburgh, St. Louis, and Chicago. Again he lied about his age, listing himself as twenty-eight and his year of birth as 1886. He was 5'11" tall, 165 pounds in weight; his health he listed as good, with no physical defects. In the blank beside marital status he typed "soon" and by church affiliation, "Lutheran, but liberal." He acknowledged that he had not attended a college but added that he had "been constantly at the grind of higher education by self," and he knew "a smattering of German and Italian." With some adjust-ments so that the years and months of employment would not invite unwanted questions, Richter listed his various employers from the Farmers and Citizens National Bank to Mrs. E. C. T. Miller, noting that from April 1908 to July 1910 "I was out for myself in the wholesale lumber business" and that he left the Cleveland job in February 1914, "to be nearer my fiancée and people." Since February he had been employed as "manager" by the Richters, Reading whole-salers. What Richter had in mind was another job as a private secretary, some-thing that would allow him the money to marry and the time to continue writing. Failing that, he was interested in being an investigator, a salesman, an editor, a reporter, a correspondent, a clerk, a cashier; but he was open to any alternative, he wrote: "To your competent judgment I leave the problem of placing me to the best advantage for myself and my employer. . . . As to location, I am prej-udiced against no particular section. However, for the sake of my wife-to-be, I should prefer a locality with good air, not too damp and cold." But his solicitude for Harvey's health had its limits: "Disregard this rule, however, if necessary."

In December Richter promised Harvey that he would continue his writing only until the end of the year. If by then there were no sales, he would give up stories and put all his time to marketing pretzels and finding a job. Richter did not give up easily. On Sunday, December 13, he wrote a first draft of a new story. The next day he worked on a movie scenario, and on Tuesday he wrote another. On Wednesday, December 16, he spent his morning finishing up a third scenario, his afternoon typing the final version of the story, and his evening packing crates of pretzels.[31] During this time Richter first began to fashion a story based upon the experience of his friend from Rye Beach, Hanna Kenngott. That fall Richter had received from Hanna an answer to a letter he had written to her months earlier, before he met Harvena. She was back again in the United States, in Brewster, Massachusetts, and terribly unhappy. Although the family for whom she worked was pleasant and kind to her, she was caught in the United States when the hostilities in Europe turned into war, and she found herself unable to return home to be with her family. From Hanna's moving explanation of her predicament, Richter created a story of a young woman from the Black Forest whose irrepressible laughter masks her anguish at the loss of her parents and brother, all victims of the war, and her deep longing for home.

As with most of his stories, Richter's primary difficulty in "The Laughter of Leen" was in working out a suitable plot. For him, the idea was already full of that something Mrs. Kimball had called "purpose," and that something to Richter was the combination of the pathos of the young girl's situation and the indomitable spirit with which she refused to succumb to her suffering. For inspiration he had not only his own memories of Hanna at Rye Beach, where her smiles and laughter covered her mistreatment by her employers, but also the unfailingly bright spirits of Harvey in spite of her family's difficulties and her own affliction. The problem was to create a vehicle to allow that force of character to show itself to readers, and to do so Richter chose to create a conflict between a coldly imperious mother of an undisciplined child and a new governess named Leen. Looking on as the two wills and personalities clash is a brother of the child's mother, a moody young man who is despondent because his business plans have not yet been realized. The mother is a characterization of Mrs. Miller of Cleveland, and the brother, evidently, a fictional version of Richter himself. The focal point of the tale is Leen's laughter, which disturbs the household decorum. Asked to restrain herself, Leen refuses, and when pressed by the brother to explain her intransigence, she admits the sorrow she is holding within. If she cannot laugh, she says, she will surely die of heartbreak. At this disclosure, the brother is so struck by her courage that he takes the lesson himself. Her laughter becomes a tonic and her spirit an inspiration.

In summary, the story seems ordinary enough, undistinguished from the other forty-six separate submissions, stories, scenarios, and poems of 1914. But for Richter it was the only story of this year's apprenticeship that approached

"Brothers of No Kin" in its accomplishment. Reading his story years later, Richter recognized in it the ineffable something that gave his best stories magic, raising it above others that would sell to better magazines, for much more money. His intuition told him that the quality of experience captured, the emotion evoked, separated "The Laughter of Leen" and "Brothers of No Kin" from his other early stories. Only these two were fundamental; by comparison the others were trivial and formulaic. Just what made this magic, Richter could not himself specify. But in later years, when he insisted that his wife and daughter (even as a child) listen to drafts of his stories, he would ask them if a character seemed real or an action believable; but what he really wanted to confirm was that the story moved them. He would note their comments in his journal and notebooks, but what he noted most carefully were their exclamations of pleasure or displeasure and his own sense of how strongly the story made them feel. But he only got to the point of trusting his two listeners much later. At the end of 1914, he was still relying on the judgment of magazine editors and on his reading of the stories in their magazines.

When by late January neither the stories nor the sale of pretzels brought the income to marry Harvena, Richter kept his promise to his fiancée to put his writing aside and look for a job. For a time he considered an offer of a New York settlement house, room and board in return for teaching evening and Sunday classes, giving him time during the day to sell the Richter Crispretzels to New York stores. But what finally brought him a job was another letter addressed to people he did not know. This one he sent to businessmen in Reading, announcing himself eager to put his talents to work for a good company. Promising that he could "handle almost anything from a typewriter and adding machine to people and automobiles," Richter summarized his work experience—"clerk, salesman, managing secretary, banker, and newspaper reporter and editor"—and added that he had "a number of interesting credentials."[32]

One of the people who received this letter was Harry Hayden, general manager of the A. Wilhelm Company and president of the Reading Chamber of Commerce. Financially involved in the New York publishing firm of Hinds, Noble, and Eldredge, Hayden had recently suggested to his brother-in-law, Tom Hinds, that the mail order division be moved to Reading, where its overhead would be lower. Richter seemed to Hayden to be a likely manager for the division. He was young and energetic, and he was willing to work for a small salary.

Richter was elated by the possibility. With his marriage seeming more immediate than before, Richter made the obligatory call on Gregory Achenbach to ask permission to marry his daughter. Richter met his future father-in-law in the

8. Conrad Richter at home in Reading, Pennsylvania, 1914. His close work reading and writing stories led to the pince-nez glasses, tucked into his jacket pocket.

Achenbach family study, Gregory Achenbach sitting at the desk where he performed his duties as a justice of the peace. In a manner that well may have reminded Richter of his grandfather Mike Richter, Achenbach told Conrad plainly what he knew to be a painful truth. His family was infected with TB. It had killed his wife and his daughter Alma, and though he could not yet see it in Harvena, surely it would show itself soon. Although Richter could not have expected such a statement, he knew without thinking his response. "Then she needs someone to take care of her,"[33] he replied.

Gregory Achenbach did not attend the wedding, which was secret and probably unplanned. Gregory Achenbach did not even know in advance that the wedding was to occur. Just before midnight on March 23, Lottie, John, Joe, and Fred gathered in the parlor of St. Peter's Lutheran parsonage for the marriage of Conrad and Harvena. The ceremony was completed just after midnight, making the official date of marriage March 24. The unusual hour was at Conrad's insistence; he wanted the marriage to be at midnight so that each year he and Harvena would have two anniversary dates to celebrate.

THREE

After only four days together as man and wife, Harvena said good-bye to her husband at the Reading Railroad Station. Still needed in Pine Grove, where her family awaited her, she returned to break the news to Gregory Achenbach. "Tell me what your father said," Richter wrote to his bride, anxious about his reaction. But he urged her to keep the marriage a secret from everybody else. Far better to wait until they could announce his new job as manager of a division of Hinds, Noble, and Eldredge. Then there would be less gossip about their rash behavior. He reminded Harvey that "it won't be a secret at all if more than two or three know it," and when she wrote that she had confided in Pauline Sutton, Richter replied that he was glad that she now had someone to talk to, but he hoped she would not tell others, not even her older sister May. He encouraged her to be just as secretive with his own relatives: "I believe Beth would think more of us if we didn't tell her all our affairs—she knows enough already. So if you haven't told her yet—do not tell either her or Aunt Lizzie."[34] But such secrets never survive long in a large family or a small town, and in less than a month the couple gave up their attempt and sent announcements of their wedding to relatives and friends. By then the job with Hinds, Noble, and Eldredge had developed into what was almost a sure thing. But it was still not final.

As the first letters of congratulation came in, Richter went off to the publishers' New York office, there to prepare cost estimates for moving the mail order division to Pennsylvania. His letters to Harvey were full of news about the New York office, about bungalows he saw advertised for under $1,000 and about the Union Hotel, where he stayed for one dollar a night. On April 23 a telegram arrived for Richter at Hinds, Noble, and Eldredge. It was from his father: "Call up Mitchell Kennerly New York Telegram received for photograph Don't understand." Richter immediately recognized the name, for Kennerly was the editor of the *Forum*, the magazine that still owed him for the short story "Brothers of No Kin," published well over a year before. Just that month he had asked the staff of the *Editor* to intervene on his behalf. Knowing they had sent a strongly worded letter, Richter hoped Kennerly was finally going to pay him something for his story. But what Kennerly wanted was for Richter to send a photograph of himself to the *Boston Evening Transcript*. In the first year of what would become an annual event sponsored by the *Transcript*, "Brothers of No Kin" had been chosen by Edwin O'Brien as the best short story of 1914. Richter was elated, but that elation was quickly undercut. On April 27 Kennerly finally sent Richter his money: for the best story of 1914, Richter received a curt note of apology for the delay and a check for $25.

At the end of April 1915, the board of directors of Hinds, Noble, and Eldredge voted to proceed with plans to transfer the mail order division to Pennsylvania. When Richter again returned to New York to prepare for the transition, Harvey managed to get away from home and go with him—their week in New York to be their honeymoon. After a night at the Union Hotel, they moved to a room on Eighteenth Street across from the Hughes Chocolate Factory. Each evening Harvena would wait for Richter to return from work, and they would then walk together about the city, discovering small restaurants with modest fare.

On their return from New York, Harvena stopped in Reading long enough for the couple to look for a place to live. Lottie Richter invited the young couple to stay in the parsonage, but Conrad and Harvena wanted a place of their own. Although they could afford only a single room, the room they found had a fireplace to keep the room cozy in winter, and Mrs. Eddye, the landlady, seemed pleasant and helpful. Conrad's typing stand would be their dining table, and the broad ledge at the foot of the bed their sideboard. When one of Harvey's family or friends came to visit, Mrs. Eddye agreed they could rent a spare bedroom for the night.[35] Far more often as the weeks passed Richter spent his nights alone in the one-room apartment on North Front Street. When May finally returned to Pine Grove, she arrived sick and had to be hospitalized briefly. While she recuperated, Harvena was needed in Pine Grove. Even after May recovered sufficiently to take over the household chores, Harvey regularly returned to Pine Grove for visits. Having few friends in Reading, her days in their single room passed slowly. Then, too, the gathering summer heat in Reading left her weak and breathless; she breathed more easily in Pine Grove.

By the end of May the papers had been prepared and filed to incorporate the Handy Book Company in Pennsylvania, with Richter named as president. Later he would claim this to be a joke of the Hinds brothers, Tom and Roger, who with Harry Hayden were the owners of the new corporation. In reality he was manager of the office at 1 Reed Street, and until the incorporation was complete he was the only employee.[36] Soon thereafter he hired his brother Fred, conferring on him an equally inflated title of secretary-treasurer. Together they set up the business, which consisted primarily of mailing out advertisements and filling orders as they arrived at the Reed Street office. Especially in the early months, their primary occupation was stuffing envelopes with circulars and boxes with books.

During the early months of their marriage, Richter worried about money. Although his salary of $25 a week covered their immediate expenses, it allowed little for luxuries and nothing for savings. Richter wanted a car and a house for himself and Harvey, and he wanted enough money in the bank so that, if Harvey should begin to show the telltale signs of tuberculosis, he could take her immediately to California or any other place where the air was dry and cool. Unable to ask for more salary until he demonstrated that the firm could afford it, he decided the most likely way to increase his income was to try harder to crack the short story market. In May, Richter wrote to Mrs. Kimball, suggesting a campaign to sell his stories in the wake of the "Brothers of No Kin" success.[37] He also wrote to the *Transcript* to wonder if, since they were so taken with his story, they might not be interested in purchasing others. They were not. But others were interested, including Bruce Barton, who wrote to ask for submissions for *Associated Sunday Magazines* and *Every Week*. Even Mitchell Kennerly brazenly wrote to say that the *Forum* would like to read more of his stories. Then Paul R. Reynolds, a highly regarded New York literary agent, wrote to offer his services. When Richter accepted, Reynolds quickly sold the second serial rights to "Brothers of No Kin" to *Illustrated Sunday Magazine* for $50—double the price of the original sale. Later Reynolds sold a second story, "The Wall of the House of Ryland," to *Illustrated Sunday Magazine*, again for $50; but he declined to submit "The Laughter of Leen" to editors, returning it with a note saying he found it "almost impossible to sell anything that has any connection with the war."[38]

After Reynolds turned the story down, Richter wrote to another of the agencies that had asked for his work, the Paget Literary Agency, choosing the brother and sister team of Cora and Harold Paget because they handled movie scenarios as well as stories. To them he sent "The Laughter of Leen" and "The Forbidden Root," a new story; several children's stories; and "Brothers of No Kin" for movie consideration. None of these seemed to the Pagets to be especially promising, but they agreed to send out "Leen" as having "a chance, though . . . not perhaps a very good one."[39] Like Reynolds, they saw little market for stories dealing with the European war. Disappointed that the attention "Brothers of No Kin" had received had not led to other sales, Richter found himself less and less inclined to turn to his typewriter in the evenings. When Harvey was in Reading that summer and fall, they would walk the city streets in the early twilight. When Harvey was away, often Richter escaped from the close heat and loneliness of their room to spend his evening in the pleasantly lit public library, reading magazine stories, or in the cool dark of a movie theater.

On a weekend visit to Pine Grove Conrad and Harvey met Mulford Foster. Having heard stories about a man who was not "afraid to tell people right out that he likes snakes,"[40] they took a train to the whistle stop of Cold Spring where they discovered Foster and his wife Fridel. Only a few years older than Richter, Foster was about as different from him in personality as the deacon from his friend in "Brothers of No Kin." Where Richter was reserved with all except his closest friends, Foster was mercurial, talkative, easily familiar, and always laughing. Like Richter, Foster had dabbled in all sorts of work, including newspapers and motion pictures. When Richter visited his farm in Stony Creek Valley, Foster was attempting to make for himself a career as a naturalist, herpetologist, and lecturer on animal life. His most recent project was to develop a nature camp at his farm, and green lumber to build the cabins was stacked for seasoning beside the farmhouse.

Richter saw Foster's talent for talking about wildlife as he had White Deer Valley's lumber and Reading's pretzels, an opportunity waiting for the right promoter. By December Richter had developed a scheme to serve as Foster's agent and business manager, wondering in letters to Harvey if the initial outlay in printing costs was not well worth the potential profit, which might include a chance to live in Stony Creek Valley—as beautiful and untouched as any place Richter had visited since White Deer Valley. Before the end of December he had written and sent to Foster sample fliers, circulars, and letters for promoting a lecture tour, and soon Foster and his wife Fridel were encouraging the Richters to build a cottage in the valley, on their land. It would be, Richter thought, an almost ideal place for Harvey to rest—a high cool mountain valley. There Harvena would be close to Pine Grove and able to visit her friends but otherwise separated from the people and activities that always tempted her to overtire herself. To his surprise, Harvena agreed.

For Richter, the prospect turned on what he was able to get out of his typewriter. In January the Pagets reported that after five rejections they had finally sold "The Laughter of Leen" to *Outlook* for $100. That was a start. By the end of January he had sent several new stories and movie scenarios to the Pagets. About the stories Cora Paget was at least mildly encouraging—except for one story, "Bobby Shafto," that she returned almost immediately with discouraging suggestions for wholesale revision. Richter angrily wrote by return mail to disagree, but then put his disappointment aside and began to revise. Overnight he rewrote the story and returned it, and Cora Paget replied almost as quickly that Richter had "done splendidly with it," that she was now "thoroughly enthusiastic"[41] and so too was her brother. If anything, Harold Paget's enthusiasm was even more pronounced. Writing the following day "to butt in on general principles," he urged Richter to put aside movie scenarios and to stick to stories: "a man who has your unusual talent for making good literature in the field of fiction, has no right to give his energy or time (surely I am right?) to such things as movies are made of—at least at present." It was "only a matter of a year or two," he wrote, before Richter would be making $5,000 to $10,000 a year from the magazine market alone.[42]

On his next trip to New York Richter told Tom and Roger Hinds about Harold Paget's rosy picture of his future writing stories. He added that the publisher Dodd, Mead had written to him about publishing a novel, and he had even been asked for permission to publish "The Laughter of Leen" in Braille. Roger and Tom Hinds would have listened to Richter thoughtfully. After less than a year in Pennsylvania, the Handy Book Company was already showing a profit, but they were reluctant to bet on Handy's continued improvement by giving Richter a larger salary. Instead they suggested an alternative: a continued salary of $1,300 a year, plus 40 percent of all profits beyond the first $2,500 a year, in cash or in stock. Although it took till the following December to complete the contract, their offer of a chance to share in the company's profits was sufficiently a bird in the hand to be chosen over the covey Harold Paget thought he saw hiding in the bush. For the time being, story writing would remain an avocation. While Handy Book Company continued to prosper, the

Pagets' efforts to sell Richter's stories did not. Not even "Bobby Shafto" found a buyer, and not until October would there be another sale. Then the *Ladies' Home Journal* bought "The Girl That 'Got' Colly" for $250—over two months' salary from Handy and a tidy enough sum for an avocation, but it did not match his anticipated share of that year's Handy profits. It would not pay for a home at Cold Spring.

Richter's decision to stay with Handy—if he ever seriously considered quitting—was made after a new proposal from Mulford Foster. On February 21 Foster wrote to advise Richter against trying to build that year, when neither couple had the cash to do what they wanted. Instead, he and Fridel thought Harvey should come to stay with them when the weather got warm, with Richter to come on weekends. The proposal suited both Conrad and Harvena, giving them a chance to try out the living arrangement. But though plans were made several times, and Foster wrote repeatedly that he and Fridel expected Harvey the next week, or the one after that, the months passed and the Richters did not arrive. Finally in August, when the summer heat and humidity in Reading were at their worst, Richter took his wife to Cold Spring Farm to stay until Labor Day. They did not tell the Fosters what had prompted them, finally, to accept the invitation. It was Harvey's health, but with an added concern. Harvey was just slightly more than two months pregnant.

While Harvey was at Cold Spring Farm with the Fosters, Richter turned his evenings to a different writing project. For several years he had been in sporadic correspondence with John Martin, whose *John Martin's Book* for children had published a serial story of Richter's, "Seventy Secret Passageways." Martin liked Richter's stories for children and had written several times with new propositions, but Martin paid so little—$5 a chapter—that Richter repeatedly had declined. Now Richter decided to try his own children's magazine, to be published by Handy and marketed with a gimmick that Richter was sure would attract young readers. For a dollar subscription, a child would receive an issue every other month, each with a special cover printing the child's name and announcing the magazine as his or hers exclusively. Thus to his brother Joe's first child, Richter sent a first issue with a cover announcing "Joey Richter's Magazine."

The first *Junior Book Magazine* was published in fall 1916; by summer 1917, Richter had mailed four more issues. Under an array of pseudonyms Richter wrote all the stories and poems in each. Some of these names were the products of his fancy—Tucker Blue, Robert Clearing, Polly Heather. Others were the names of relatives and friends—Elizabeth H. Irwin (Aunt Lizzie), Addison M.

Rothrock (the family doctor), Richard Kendall (a great-great grandfather who had crossed the Delaware with Washington). Under his own name Richter published only his Skeeks stories, first created to entertain the unruly Miller boys in Cleveland. Like other Richter promotions, the idea for this magazine was good enough to succeed if he had found the capital and time to develop it; the stories and poems themselves were at least as entertaining as what children found in magazines like *John Martin's Book*. But like the Crispretzel venture, the early subscriptions did not match what must have been, as a second job, an enormous effort expended to write, edit, and publish each issue. When the war brought on paper shortages in 1917, *Junior Book Magazine* became one of many marginal publishing ventures that had to be abandoned. Richter's disappointment may well have been lessened by his release from all the extra work, especially at a time when his thoughts would have been elsewhere.

On the morning of March 13, 1917, an excited but tired Conrad Richter awoke his father-in-law to tell him he was a grandfather. After a night's labor unusual only in that throughout it she had not once cried out in pain, Harvena had given birth to a healthy baby girl, already named Harvena II. According to a family story, Gregory Achenbach was astonished by the news. Harvey had carried the baby so low and had so successfully disguised her condition with loose clothing that only Lottie Richter had known for sure about Harvey's condition, and she only because her daughter-in-law had told her.[43]

In the hospital, Harvey had an unusual experience. In an eerie correspondence to Lottie Richter's visitation by dignitaries after the birth of Conrad, Harvey awoke to see her mother come into the room, softly lift back the blankets and smile down upon her first grandchild, then depart as she had come, through the unopened door.[44] As with the procession of dignitaries who came to see the sleeping baby Conrad, the least provocative explanation was that the experience was a dream, perhaps brought on by Harvena's having heard from Richter or his mother the story of Lottie Richter and the procession of dignitaries. But to Harvena this experience was no dream, and the memory would remain vividly with her throughout her life. Ultimately it became the foundation of her conviction in life after death, or, as Richter would later prefer to call it, the survival of the soul.

When the time came to bring his wife and child home from the hospital, Richter arrived in a chauffeur-driven limousine to carry the mother and infant daughter to a new home, a white duplex with a large lawn in the Reading suburb of Mount Penn. In the days after Vene's birth, Richter had rented the house and scurried about gathering furnishings, without telling his wife how he was spending his time away from the hospital. Although Harvey had promised to remain in bed for a month after Vene's birth, such promises were easier in the making than in the keeping, especially for a patient as impatient with restrictions as Harvey turned out to be. At the end of the month, it seemed to Richter that Harvey was still not fully recovered. He continued to worry through spring and into summer, for his wife did not appear to have regained her strength. What little weight she had gained during her pregnancy she had lost in the weeks thereafter. Her cheeks were thin. She had almost no appetite. She tired easily and was easily chilled. The little cough that sometimes followed her laughter now seemed habitual. These, Richter knew, were telltale signs that tuberculosis was insidiously active in her lungs. When August came Richter again took his wife to Cold Spring Farm. He visited on weekends, whiling away the brief hours playing with his daughter and talking to Foster about the lecture series and plans to bottle and market Cold Spring water. A cottage at Cold Spring was still Richter's aim, and it seemed ever more important when a polio epidemic broke out in 1917; New York City had an alarming number of cases, and one case was reported in Reading. Richter wanted to keep his daughter as far from infection as he possibly could.

In May of that year Richter had taken time from a business trip to Hinds, Noble, and Eldredge to visit the Pagets, hoping they had sold a railroad story he had sent them, "Swanson's Home Sweet Home." Impatient with the Pagets' lack of success, Richter spent another afternoon in New York trying to find another agent, but later that month the Pagets wrote that *Everybody's Magazine* had offered $250 for the railroad story. Cora Paget used this good news as an opportunity to pass on less pleasant information to a client who was especially thin-skinned about criticism. At Richter's insistence she had pressed editors about just where Richter's stories were deficient. The answer from the staff at *Every Week* had been that he was characteristically "inclined to be long-winded and too indirect in treatment."[45] Paget herself added that she thought Richter was trying too hard to write for the *Saturday Evening Post*. Certainly the *Post* was a goal Richter aspired to. Putting away *Junior Book Magazine*, he turned his attention to writing stories that were crisply to the point.

Even before Harvey and Vene returned to Reading after Labor Day, the first of the new stories found a buyer. In August *Every Week* bought "Nothing Else Matters" for $300. Then in September the *Saturday Evening Post* accepted a story, paying $350 for "The Sure Thing," and a month later *Every Week* bought its second story for $300, "The Pippin of Pike County." With that sale the Pagets wrote that they were out of new material to circulate, and they urged Richter to send them something soon. Was this, finally, the break Richter had longed for? He must have thought so, and he devoted his evenings to writing more stories. By December he had sent the Pagets three stories and an article about Foster and his farm, "The King of Cold Spring." The house at Cold Spring and the Model T to travel in now seemed a sure thing if his luck continued. But how should he continue? Should he quit Handy and write stories full time? This time he was strongly tempted, and Harvey, ever the more daring of the two, urged him to do so. But he delayed and delayed, telling himself he needed better information. He wrote to Cora Paget to ask her advice, and she answered with some obvious addition: if he wrote two stories a month and sold two-thirds of these stories for $250, the gross sales would be $4,000 and his net profit after commission $3,600.[46] But interspersed among the Pagets' letters of encouragement were cautionary comments about the new group of stories, then the suggestion that Richter come to New York to talk to them about his writing, and then reports of rejections from editors. Although several stories had sold, the evidence was substantial that his best stories were still only marginally salable. He simply could not yet count on selling a story as he wrote it. What if he moved his family to Cold Spring and no more stories sold? Once again Richter decided to keep his job at Handy Book Company until his stories were selling more regularly.

FOUR

Looking back a decade later, Richter was satisfied that choosing to continue at the Handy Book Company had been his only reasonable choice. A world war was in progress, and the United States had finally been forced into it. Twenty-seven years old and the sole support of a wife and child, he was unlikely to be drafted. But he did have a family to take care of, and the war effort could at any time bring more drastic shortages and sacrifices than just paper. Who could predict the many ways his family might be affected? His only choice was the safe one of remaining with Handy. Over the next five years as he continued to manage the book company, he would write in his spare time, a steady if modest output of stories, and from these stories came occasional publications. But as he completed a story, working at night and on Saturdays and Sundays, Richter was never sure that he or an agent would be able to place it. Every story was a gamble, and the point of the gamble was to make money for his family. He was less interested in the stories themselves than in selling them. As he wrote Harvena, after "we have a little pile and a Ford" there would be time enough to think about art and immortality. But until then, he announced, "I'd rather ten hundred times make my family happy now than have somebody two hundred years from now say, 'Didn't he write a nice story.'"[47]

That the stores were seen as a source of income may have been a key factor in their marginality, for the stories were written by a storyteller with no compelling stories to tell. Even when the stories had titles like "Suicide!" what the readers found in them were comfortable conflicts and easy resolutions. In "The Sure Thing" a conservative young man, tired of disparaging contrasts to flashier types, defeats a confidence man's sale of speculative stock by himself promoting a silver and lead mine. When the mine goes bust, he discloses that he never actually bought the stock, but put the money all in a safe but unexciting bank account at 3 percent—winning for himself a better job and permission to marry his sweetheart. This story, sold to the *Saturday Evening Post*, was Richter's only sale to that magazine for many more years. In "Forest Mould" a father concocts an elaborate fraud to shock his dilettantish son into discovering the work ethic. This sold to *American Magazine*. In "The Girl That 'Got' Colly" a well-meaning friend tries to cure his buddy of lovesickness for a movie star. The *Ladies' Home Journal* purchased this story. These stories were ordinary enough fare for the popular press, an adequate accomplishment for a writer who had not written "Brothers of No Kin." They were written to match the stories Richter read in magazines, following the advice of agents, editors, and counselors like Mrs. Kimball. They are stories with a message—a practical, positive moral such as those editors repeatedly said they wanted. In them people learn from experience to be better people, more understanding of others, and more satisfied with simple pleasures. What made "Brothers of No Kin" different from these stories was that in it Richter discovered his own emotional response to the special circumstance of a man facing an inevitability and behaving as he did because he simply had no other way to behave. This is of course a quality of tragedy, and when Richter would ultimately find his vision, it would be far closer to those of his dour contemporaries Faulkner, Fitzgerald, and Hemingway than most readers would discover. Like theirs, his world is tragic in the modern vein usually associated with literary naturalism, but where his more celebrated contemporaries found little more than an admirable endurance in their characters' lives, Richter in his most moving stories created characters whose personal commitments allow them to rise above simple endurance—as does the deacon in "Brothers of No Kin"—though they themselves would not see their choices and actions as anything other than ordinary.

One other early story hints at a vision of life Richter was as yet unable to share. That story is "The Laughter of Leen," in which a young woman holds herself from collapse by an internal resolve, enduring her sorrow by releasing it into laughter. In these two stories Richter revealed something of his own accommodations with a world he found terrifyingly unpredictable, touched a deeper layer of his own beliefs. Both are imagined stories rather than plotted stories, stories that begin with some piece of Richter's life—his conflict with Protestant fundamentalism, his memory of Hanna Kenngott's happy laughter when he received her sad letter—and then develop out of his sympathy and understanding for people in such a situation. In contrast the other stories of these years are illustrations of a writer increasingly in control of his craft, devising stories that have a basic message: country ways are better than city ways, simple lives more deeply satisfying than those that are complicated by modern aspirations and values. They share this message with "Brothers of No Kin" and "The Laughter of Leen," but these other stories are not stories that matter. When in the late 1930s his daughter Vene was trying to learn the craft of fiction, Richter posed for her a simple explanation for plotting: think of a story as a version of the tale of Joseph and the coat of many colors. The writer puts his Joseph in a hole and sees how he gets out.[48] In Richter's stories of the late teens, the holes are deep enough, but the shovel marks of the author are all around—and as I.M.P. had once remonstrated, "that's not artistic." Nor do characters discover their own ways out of the holes but rather find escapes prepared by the author. Just as damagingly, what these characters risk is not really all but a substitute, an ersatz all—a writer's concoction for purposes of a suitable and comfortable moral. However ingenious and complex, none of these plots is finally satisfying as plot.

But though these are mediocre stories, the story of their writing cannot be so easily dismissed. The real impulse behind their writing, for Richter, was to provide for and protect his family. Writing was a hedge against the future, insurance against whatever fires lay ahead, tomorrow or the day after that, fires that would endanger Harvey and Vene, fires that would test his courage and his will. Richter's fears were not simply phobias. Behind them there were his own illnesses, inexplicable depressions, and emotional collapses; there were Harvey's lung condition and her sister Alma's early death. And there were Vene's illnesses. In 1918 Vene came down with the influenza then spreading across the country, lying virtually lifeless for two days before her fever finally broke. Two years later, she suffered through scarlet fever, necessitating that their house be quarantined. When Dr. Rothrock came he wore a hooded robe almost as frightening to her parents as to Vene. During these illnesses, Richter and Harvey could not keep from their minds other illnesses that did not have happy endings.

At the time of Harvey's pregnancy, Richter's cousin Beth suffered a devastating loss. In 1916 her only child George was eight years old. An exuberantly imaginative and happy child, Kaptain Kiddo, as he was called, was a welcome visitor in the home of his Aunt Lottie and Uncle Jack. Cousin Connie was a special friend. Kiddo typed funny letters on Connie's typewriter, and he made up funny telegrams. Connie wrote telegrams back to him. Then one day Richter's mother answered the telephone and—for only the second time in his life—Richter heard her cry out in anguish. Kaptain Kiddo was dead, taken by diphtheria.

After Kiddo's death, how could he and Harvey admit to Beth what must have seemed a wounding happiness, the coming of their child so soon after she had lost hers? And so Harvey's pregnancy remained their private joy and their secret worry. After Vene was born, their early euphoria slipped into anxiety as she suffered one illness after another. Together they kept a social face on their worries, but the front was only for others. Comparing Vene's sniffles and coughing to her cousin Joe's most recent illness, Richter admitted candidly to his mother that "Joey's cough was much worse . . . but we mind things like that more than others."[49] They probably did. Certainly they believed they did. And their careful watching over their only child intensified when Harvey's failure to recover from childbirth led inevitably to the conclusion that for them there should be no more children. There would not be a Junior, for the risk to Harvey was too great.

Richter's way of dealing with sorrows and worries was to press himself to work harder. Against all the possible events he could not do anything about, he would insulate himself with what he could do. He worked and planned for the money to buy their own home, their own car; uncertain of his own abilities, he tried to work longer and harder than others, to be more dedicated to his goals. When he was not working at Handy or writing stories, he was reading to improve himself, bringing home piles of books from the public library. Especially for a man whose nerves could not take any great strain, all this was more admirable in the idea than the reality. Such single-minded attention to work would exasperate any mate; it irked Harvey especially, for she did not agree that their situation called for such measures. She did not see the point of Richter's obsessive working, and she certainly did not agree that she should be more directed herself. Always more social than her husband, for relief she would take Vene to Lebanon, where the Stricklers insulated themselves with laughter, and to Pine Grove, where her family and friends led ordinary lives and took time for ordinary pleasures.

Jobless and broke in Reading before their marriage, Richter had resorted to a lover's stratagem for Harvey's birthday on January 12. Writing of himself in the third person, he promised devotion in place of the gift he wanted to give but could not afford to buy for her, a traveling bag for their honeymoon: "He gives to his sweetheart the promise to be always good and kind. His sweetheart knows that he is always so when his nerves are right—but now he will be the same, no matter his nerves. With God's help and his sweetheart's and his own, he will master his nerves—he is master now, for her sake, Harvey's."[50] But he was not master of his nerves, and so this was a promise he could not keep. One evening when Richter arrived home Harvena was not at the door to greet him as he expected. His irritation at not being met exploded into anger when Harvey explained that she had been in the attic and did not see why she should have come down to wait for him. When the fight ended, she remained steadfast—stubborn, Richter said—that she was in the right; for his part, Richter was sure that this seemingly minor incident really symbolized a fundamental failing in his wife. For years, even decades afterwards, when trouble arose Richter would remember and speak bitterly about her not meeting him at the door. For her part, Harvena would remember this fight and others when she advised Vene about relationships with men. Marriage, she told her daughter, was always a battleground; she also told Vene that, if she had not been sick with a baby to care for during those years in Reading, she would have left her husband and returned to Pine Grove.[51]

In the end of April 1918 Harvey and Vene moved to Cold Spring Farm for the spring and summer and perhaps for the year. To reduce the cost of keeping two households, Richter gave up the house in Pennside and moved into a rented room on Clymer Street. For the time being, he would be with his family only on weekends. Perhaps Harvey's health led her to agree to this arrangement; perhaps she thought of the move as relief from her daily life with a difficult husband. Richter's letters to his wife make clear his thinking: in moving his family and furniture to Cold Spring he was resurrecting yet again his plans to support his family with his writing. In January 1918 the Pagets had sold "The Go Getter" for $350; that same month "Nothing Else Matters" appeared in *Every Week*. In March, Richter read his story "The Pippin of Pike County" in *Every Week*, and the next month "The Go Getter" in *Country Gentleman*. These spurred his hopes that selling stories to magazines would finally pay for the life he wanted. Until then they would rent Foster's house at Cold Spring, and there he would keep a more relaxed schedule, relieving himself and Harvey of the tension of so much work. The present arrangement, working for Handy during the week and seeing his wife and child only on weekends, was a shift until some story sales made it possible to quit Handy. "This week-end business is all right," he wrote to Harvey, "but I'm looking forward to the time when I can see you and Baby every day. A little farm somewhere within running distance of a good movie and we'll be happy. Work for me every morning and then recreation in the afternoon and reading and studying in the evening."[52] But in the meantime he promised himself that he would write at least a thousand words each day he was at Cold Spring, and he urged Harvey to help him keep his commitment.

Early that year he had interested *Everybody's Magazine* in a series of business stories, mysteries that would be solved by the application of business principles. Although *Everybody's* had already rejected the first, its editor wrote that they were still interested in the series. Disappointed by the rejection, he nonetheless wrote Harvey that he was "getting my nerve back again" for the series would "mean such a big thing" that "we must bend every nerve to it."[53] To Richter that "we" meant more than polite inclusion. He wanted his wife's active participation in his writing; he wanted her to care about his stories, to read them in drafts, to encourage him to keep working. Later that summer he would write to Harvey about Kathleen Norris, who had said in an interview that she probably would not have succeeded without the help of her husband, who mailed her stories out and intercepted the returns so that she would not see them and be discouraged. "Oh, Darling, I want you to want to do things—to help me," Richter wrote, adding "And—think, sweetheart—Kathleen Norris says that now she has . . . more money than she could possibly spend."[54]

That spring Richter's parents moved to a new pastorate, in Milton, Pennsylvania. Fred had been drafted into the army when the United States joined the allies in the World War, and Joe's job with the electric company often kept him away from home. Alone in Reading, about once every two weeks Richter would spend an evening at his brother Joe's home; another he would go to pass an hour with Merritt Beuchler, husband of his Aunt Emma, in his railroad dispatch office. Many nights he whiled away an hour or two in the public library, and often, he admitted in his letters, he spent the eleven cents to see a movie—William S. Hart in *The Square Deal Man*, Kitty Gordon in *Tinsel*, Theda Bara in *Cleopatra*, and Billie Burke in *Let's Get a Divorce*.[55] His favorite was Mary Pickford, he wrote to Harvey, because she reminded him of his wife.[56]

Away from his wife and daughter, Richter worried about his relationship with Harvey. It upset him that they often fought during the little time they had

together. To the extent that their arguments were his fault, he was determined
to change. But he believed the fights were not altogether his fault, and he was
equally determined to convince Harvey to work to improve herself. What to
Richter seemed most in need of correction in his wife may have seemed to others
the strengths of her character: her sureness of self, knowing her own mind and
being unafraid to speak it. But to Richter these traits were the worst of the Pennsylvania Dutch heritage—stubbornness, insensitivity, and a prideful refusal ever
to admit, even to herself, that she was wrong. To persuade her, he tried every
ploy he could think of. While she was at Cold Spring Farm he wrote to her,
"You've got to get right so you can start getting me right."[57] In another letter he
wrote, "Darling, sweetheart, everything is coming fine—just one thing now and
you can do it—because when conditions are right you are simply ideal. . . . I'll
keep gently reminding you till you have yourself under control."[58] Three days
later he wrote: "Sweetheart when I see these movies I always think that I have
right at home a movie queen who can beat any of 'em after she's right and who
can beat all except Mary Pickford and maybe one or two more already. Naturally she's sweeter and prettier and gentler than any of them, but she hasn't quite
control of herself to show it always."[59] By control Richter apparently meant the
ability to overcome impulse by careful imposition of personal will. This was his
own attempt, more notable in the effort than in the success; but to Harvey, the
idea itself was uncongenial, and she resisted his attempts to impose his personality upon hers.

In midsummer a problem at Cold Spring caused them to put aside the issue
of Harvey's character. Fridel Foster turned out to be a gossip, and Harvey discovered that she was carrying tales about her. The two had words about it. One
night someone began dynamiting fish in the creek, frightening Harvey so
thoroughly that she stayed up all night with a gun in her lap, protecting Vene.
Then Fridel gave Harvey a squab to eat that Harvey believed to be spoiled, and
she decided Fridel had done so maliciously.[60] After that, there was no chance for
the arrangement to last. Early in July Richter drafted a letter to Foster to say that
it was impossible for Harvey and Vene to remain at Cold Spring, where they
were victimized by someone who was "double tongued, double faced, and double
charactered."[61] After a conversation with his lawyer, Richter sent Foster a milder
version, regretting that they would be leaving Cold Spring because they had
been "unpleasantly surprised and disappointed in Mrs. Foster" and concluding
with a pointed request: "Kindly do not repeat untruths about us. This we absolutely insist upon."[62] In the same mail he sent a letter to Harvena urging her to
say nothing to Foster or his wife except that he would speak for them when he

came. He warned Harvey not to let Vene play out of her sight and to watch care-fully her milk, for Fridel might tamper with it. He also reminded her where he kept his revolver, in case of any threat.

At the end of the month Richter moved his wife and child to the Pine Grove Hotel, where Harvey asked to stay until the summer heat abated. At the Pine Grove Hotel she was free from housekeeping, and she could take her meals at Mrs. Yocum's boardinghouse. Then, too, her friends in Pine Grove helped the time pass quickly, and with care and rest perhaps there she could grow stronger as they had hoped she would at Cold Spring. Back in Reading, Richter wrote to say he agreed with her decision, guessing that they would both be happier—Harvey because in Pine Grove she had her friends and leisure, he because his Harvey would be growing healthier. But alone in Reading, Richter found him-self without any way around Harvey's choice: she preferred a hotel in Pine Grove to a room in Reading with her husband. Was this the end of their marriage?

Compounding this private fear was Richter's concern about being the subject of gossip. Even before Harvey and Vene were safely out of Cold Spring, Richter was already worrying about what people would say: "Sweetheart—I wish you could let the girls know that I am wanting you to go to the hotel—it may sound selfish—but I am so sensitive—I wouldn't feel comfortable in Pine Grove if I thought people thought it was you who had elected the hotel life to home life—as though home with me wasn't enough."[63] When he telephoned the Pine Grove Hotel at 8:30 on a muggy August night, Harvey was out with her friends, which did not lift his spirits any. But he kept his temper in check and chose with care what he wrote in his daily letters. Resorting to the rhetorical ploy of making a point by saying he did not need to, Richter wrote that he knew he did not have to worry that she would neglect Vene to be with her friends.[64] He wrote as well that he was looking for another house to rent, so that when the weather cooled she would have a comfortable home to return to.

Richter spent the early fall living alone in a room on Clymer Street; his twenty-eighth birthday he spent hospitalized, recuperating from the virulent influenza of 1918, which would eventually infect both Harvey and Vene.[65] It was not until late October that Harvey and Vene rejoined Richter in Reading. As winter came and passed and another summer with its heat returned to Reading, Richter restlessly kept at the dull but secure Handy Book Company, hoping for a string of story sales that would permit his escape. There were flurries of sales. In summer and fall 1919 Richter sold three stories, "Cabbages and Shoes" to *Everybody's Magazine*, "Forest Mould" and "Suicide!" (published as "The Man Who Hid Himself") to the *American Magazine*. Having broken with the Pagets, Richter kept the combined $750 these stories earned him. With this money and a $1,000 second mortgage for a down payment, he bought a house on the north side of Twenty-fifth Street in Mount Penn for $5,200. With the money from his 1920 sales, "Smokehouse" to *Country Gentleman,* "The Wings of a Swallow" and "Tempered Copper" to *People's Favorite Magazine,* and "You're Too Contwisted Satisfied, Jim Ted" to the *American Magazine,*[66] Richter bought the car he had long waited for, a used Model T Ford. Little by little he was working toward material security for his family. Handy Book Company provided them with their daily needs, and his stories, when they sold, provided opportunities to get ahead. Although there continued to be times when Richter found himself thinking about a different life, a writer's life, the possibility seemed to have slipped away. Unexpected circumstances like the falling out with the Fosters had kept him from it; so too had his own unwillingness to make the kind of decision his father had, gambling the welfare of his family to pursue his own dream.

Richter's thirtieth birthday passed and he began a new decade of life. Like many others with unmet aspirations, Richter at thirty was resigned to, if not wholly content with, his life. Through the second decade of the twentieth century, through emotional breakdowns and job changes, through marriage to Harvey and the birth of Vene, through the Great War and his wife's precarious health, through all these he had held on to his hopes to make a name and a fortune for himself with his stories. Although that possibility seemed to have passed, he still yearned for something more than his life had given him. He still kept his 8,000 shares of Amazon-Dixie Mining stock. And after he put his daughter Vene to bed with a story about Skeeks, he still turned to his writing desk to work on another short story to offer to the magazines.

Pine Tree Farm

O N E

Pulmonary tuberculosis is an insidious disease. In the early stages of the disease, victims are often unaware they are afflicted, and even in moderately advanced stages there may be few signs that the disease is active. Perhaps the victim catches cold more readily than others or has difficulty throwing off a light cough or hoarseness that lingers after a cold. There may be shortness of breath, a loss of weight, a sense of fatigue at slight exertion. Flushed cheeks may be the telltale sign of a slight fever each afternoon. But these symptoms are so imperceptible that there seems little cause for alarm until the lungs are deeply infiltrated by the tubercle bacilli. Only then does bloody sputum signal the onset of the advanced stages of the disease, the stage known throughout the nineteenth and early twentieth centuries as "consumption," when pockets of infection break through into the bronchial passages, causing hemorrhages of bright red blood.

There is no record to establish just when Harvena Richter began coughing blood, or when she finally admitted her condition to her husband. Richter believed that the onset of his wife's advanced tuberculosis resulted from Harvey's overextending herself selling books for Handy, or perhaps the first hemorrhages followed her bout with the flu in 1918, as some of her family would remember.[1] Whenever it began, Harvena hid her illness as long as she could. Decades later Richter told his daughter that when he asked his wife why she had kept her condition from him, her answer had been typical of her exasperating way of looking at things: "I don't like to tell every little thing,"[2] she said, as if she had been keeping to herself some minor household mishap. Another explanation would have occurred immediately to Richter; her secrecy was another instance of Harvey resisting his attempts to take her to a more healthful climate.

However alarming the news was to Richter, Harvey's condition must have seemed the arrival of an inevitability. Having studied thoroughly all available information on tuberculosis, Richter had seen signs that her incipient tuberculosis, as her doctors called her condition in the early years of their marriage, was not incipient at all. He had watched her appetite decline and her slight body become even more birdlike. He had listened to the cough with which her laughter would habitually end. He had seen how easily she tired from slight exertion. Richter understood as well that there was no cure for Harvena's tuberculosis. The best that could be hoped for was that the disease could be arrested. At this time, there was a widely accepted and practiced means of treating the disease, and the regimen that was the heart of the treatment was available to any who wished to know, as Richter certainly did, in magazine and journal articles, in pamphlets distributed by the Public Health Service,[3] and in a magazine devoted entirely to the "cure," the *Journal of the Outdoor Life*. This treatment was first successfully practiced in the United States by Dr. Edward Livingstone Trudeau, who almost by accident succeeded in arresting his own advanced case. Believing himself in the final stages of the disease, he had gone to a favorite cottage in the Adirondack Mountains above Saranac, New York, to await death, and there he discovered that the brisk air and long days of rest were therapeutic. Trudeau's sanitarium at Saranac Lake led to that community's reputation for its salutary climate, and by the early twentieth century "health seekers" had turned the small community into a town of private sanitariums and "cure cottages." Many died there, but many others, after extended stays, were able to return to their homes to live almost normal lives.[4]

The key to the Trudeau treatment was a miserly hoarding of all energy by restricting the patient to virtually absolute rest. Such prolonged inactivity was of course easiest when the patient felt sick, but total rest was most critical when energy and lighter spirits began to return. According to Trudeau, this was the most dangerous period, for the body desperately needed every bit of its stored energy to fight the disease exactly when patients, feeling improved, were eager to waste their improvement on walks and visits with relatives. Second in importance was a regular diet of wholesome foods, a difficulty in that the disease typically depressed the patient's appetite. The Trudeau method insisted that patients force themselves to eat small meals many times daily. The third order of the regimen was to spend as much time as possible outdoors in fresh air, preferably cool mountain air. For this, sanitariums and cure cottages provided private sleeping porches, enclosed verandas with windows that could be opened for maximum ventilation. On these porches patients would spend most of their days and nights, protected from the elements as they whiled away months of unbroken rest.

About one subject experts disagreed. Trudeau believed that relatively high altitudes were best for patients, thin air being easier to breathe. But because winters in higher altitudes were too severe for many, others held that California offered a better climate, especially the southern part of the state near the ocean, where the annual temperature variation was not great and the air was characteristically dry and cool. Other places thought to be therapeutic were Denver, Colorado, along the edge of the Rockies; communities in North Carolina along the Blue Ridge; and a number of places in the high desert of the Southwest. Of these, Albuquerque, New Mexico, was the most popular, a mile high like Denver but warmer and drier year-round. This debate about the most healthful climate, well known to Conrad and Harvena Richter, was the source of an ongoing argument between them. As Richter wrote to Jim Manning, his best friend from Tremont High School and himself a victim of TB, he had been trying to get Harvey to go to California ever since their marriage.[5] At least, he tried to persuade his wife, they should leave Pennsylvania for a year in a better climate, to allow her to regain her strength. But Harvey had repeatedly refused, and on her side she had the pronouncements of public health officials in such states as Pennsylvania and New York, who argued that climate was less important than the quality of care, as sanitariums in northern Europe demonstrated with records of success virtually indistinguishable from those located in more temperate climates.

At least as often Richter and his wife argued about Harvena's refusal to keep
to a regimen of unbroken rest. When she was sick, she would follow the doctor's
orders and live the restricted life of a semi-invalid. But just as soon as she felt her
vitality returning, no cajolery or admonition could keep her off her feet. Invariably she would overextend herself and suffer a relapse. As Richter saw it, her
joie de vivre threatened to kill her, for she was incapable of disciplining herself.
Suggestions such as his mother's, that Harvey bob her thick braids of hair and
thereby save a bit of energy, were simply of no help, however well meaning.
The combination of Pennsylvania's hot humid summers, damp cold winters, and
Harvey's irrepressible spirit meant, Richter knew, that he was losing her.

Richter attacked the problem with his usual thoroughness, searching out
doctors with reputations for success in treating tuberculosis, interviewing public
health officials, and writing letters to experts asking their advice. In time Richter
decided that his only choice was to bring the mountain to Mohammed. If
Harvey would not leave her friends in Pennsylvania, then he must find a country
place for her to practice the Trudeau regimen. With this in mind, he began
looking for a hillside farm among the low mountain ridges running across the
middle of Pennsylvania—a farm close enough to Pine Grove so that Harvey
could visit her family and friends, but not so close that she would be continually
tempted to overtax herself. This must have been one reason why in spring 1922
he suggested to Harry Hayden and the Hinds brothers that Harrisburg, Pennsylvania, was a better location than Reading for the Handy Book Company. If
he could move Handy to Harrisburg, he might have better luck finding a place
in the mountains north of Harrisburg, an easy train ride from Lebanon, where
the Stricklers still lived, and from Pine Grove.

On a summer day in 1922 Richter drove his skittering Model T Ford up the
rutted red shale road of Clark's Valley and found the place he was looking for,
Pine Tree Farm. The farm's 186 acres stretched irregularly across the north face
of Short Mountain, almost to the top, with the house and barn on a shoulder of
land about halfway up the slope. Only the land across the shoulder was suitable
for farming, and those fields were overgrown with weeds and scrub maples and
locust saplings that would take weeks to grub out. The rest of the land was woodland and the remains of woodland, the stumps left after the larger trees had been
lumbered out. The farmhouse itself, enlarged from a log cabin—the first in the
valley, Richter discovered—was a solid enough structure but in need of sub-
stantially more work than just scrubbing, painting, and wallpapering. There was
no running water in the kitchen and no bathroom indoors; there was neither

9.   Richter poses with Harvey and Vene at their home in
Pennside, a suburb of Reading, *circa* 1921.

electricity nor gas for lighting. The barn was a skeleton, and both barn and farmhouse needed new roofs.

Despite the months of work that would have to be done, Richter knew
immediately that the farm was exactly what he wanted. Its woods and fields were
just as he had imagined his own farm, and Clark's Valley was even more beautiful
than White Deer Valley and Cold Spring. It was, as Richter would say repeatedly, "the prettiest backwoods valley we had ever seen."[6] He was determined to
have it, and if he had second thoughts, the illnesses Harvey and Vene suffered
the next winter ended them. Five-year-old Vene came down with German measles,
diphtheria, and then whooping cough all in one month, and Harvey, once again
overextending herself, ended up bedridden, coughing blood.[7] On February 22,
1923, Conrad and Harvena signed the settlement papers in Harrisburg. Shortly

thereafter he moved the Handy Book Company to Harrisburg, taking a room at the Engineers' Club during the week so that he could supervise the workmen transforming the run-down house and overgrown fields. On afternoons when he could escape from the office, he drove north from Harrisburg along the Susquehanna River, past the village of Dauphin to Clark's Creek and the road that wound along its edge up into the valley. From his office to Pine Tree Farm was twelve miles.

On weekends Richter returned to Reading, reporting on the week's activities. During the week he wrote to Harvey almost daily, mixing his worries about the high cost of every improvement with descriptions of wildflowers, anecdotes about the local workmen and lunches of wild berries picked from the fields, and the summary of a conversation with a Harrisburg man who had said without prompting, "If I had the con, I'd go up to Clark's Valley and get well."[8] To supply running water to the house, Richter had a springhouse built high above the farm and a pipe laid down through the woods and fields. He had a bathroom installed in the house and added a new front porch and, over the kitchen porch, a second-story sleeping porch for Harvey. Electricity was not yet available in the valley, but a telephone service line had been strung along the road beside Clark's Creek. Not wanting Harvey to be alone without a telephone while he was at work, Richter paid the high cost to bring a telephone line from the valley to the farmhouse. When all the work was completed, including fresh coats of white paint and new red roofs for the house and barn, the improvements cost more than the $4,500 Richter had paid for the farm. But the price did not matter. Richter had what he wanted.

If life at Pine Tree Farm did not turn out to be quite as Richter had dreamed of country life—writing in the morning, recreation in the afternoon, reading and study at night—it was closer than he had ever come. By the second summer's slow period at Handy he was driving to the office only on Mondays, Wednesdays, and Fridays. The other days of the week were like the summers of his childhood, a life outdoors, exploring the farm with Harvey and Vene, carrying guidebooks to identify flowers, birds, and trees. When Harvey rested each afternoon, he took his daughter to the creek to fish and swim or high up onto the mountain in search of mosses, which became her special subject for nature study.

Vene was six years old the summer the family moved to Pine Tree Farm. Although she walked and talked late, she had taught herself to read at three, and by eight she would be reading Thoreau with her father. A happy child with blonde curls in ringlets around her face, she seems in family photographs a picture of health. But remembering her bouts with three contagious diseases their last winter in Reading, when she had attended a private nursery school, Richter and Harvey decided they would not risk sending her to the one-room schoolhouse a mile from the farm. Instead they kept her at home, where Harvey taught her the Calvert Course, a school program for shut-ins. This would be supplemented by nature study with her father and, when a piano found its way into the farmhouse, by music lessons. When the day's schoolwork was completed, Vene could play outside with Brimsey, their Newfoundland dog, and later with Beowulf, the pick of Brimsey's third litter, a "hippopotamus of a dog" weighing forty-five pounds at only sixteen weeks of age and at full growth well over a hundred.[9] Richter also undertook to teach his daughter sports, as he had the Miller boys many years before in Cleveland. But however comfortable Vene was in the out-of-doors, she was not athletic and Richter was not a patient coach. Among her recollections from those years would be memories of her father's exasperated loss of temper when she simply could not learn a proper scissors kick for the high jump.

Evenings inside the farmhouse were cozily comfortable, even when winter winds blew across the mountain and the house creaked and shivered. A happy memory forever after was Richter's recollection of reading by Aladdin lantern at the dining room table while Vene practiced the piano and Harvey finished up the supper dishes. The hard coal furnace in the cellar kept them warm throughout the cold spells, though tending it was Richter's least favorite chore. The cellar was dark, dank, and musty, giving Richter unpleasant sensations. Usually he would ask Vene to go with him when he stoked the furnace, but she was long asleep when he tended the fire for the last time each night. Alone in the cellar, he said, he felt presences there, reminding him that valley residents believed their house to be "the most haunted in the valley."[10] One night Vene saw something grayish floating through a hallway; on another a neighbor from the far ridge reported seeing a light passing from room to room, long after Richter and his family were asleep; and on another Richter and Vene followed two bobbing yellow lights, will-o'-the-wisps, which seemed to float into the wind before coming together in a flash and disappearing at the spot where only a foundation remained from an early cabin.[11] When Harvey and Vene visited overnight away from the farm, Richter usually chose to stay in Harrisburg at the Engineers' Club. At home by himself, the farmhouse at night was just too lonely.

Almost from the day they arrived at Pine Tree Farm, Conrad and Harvey were drawn into the community of their valley neighbors. Although there were telephones in houses closer to the road, people tramped the long lane to introduce themselves and ask to use the phone, staying afterward to visit—the valley standard for neighborliness. A valley girl became their first maid that summer. When she stayed home one day to have a baby, the sister she sent to replace her continued on as maid until the day she stayed home for the same reason. Richter hired other neighbors to help clear the fields of scrub growth and to plant seedlings of pine, hemlock, elm, Lombardy poplar, and Norway spruce on the slopes below the farmhouse. Later he hired others to work at the sawmill he set up to harvest some of the timber above the farmhouse, primarily the chestnuts then dying of blight. The sawmill, an exasperation from the beginning because Richter's notion of a day's work was different from the hired help's, was finally sold, leaving him, Richter wrote, with little to show for it but anecdotes.[12] But even that was not such a bad bargain for an outsider who actively courted the valley people, especially the local characters. Driving along the creek, he would stop to pick up walkers, hoping that they would repay his kindness with conversation about local happenings. When they did, he often recorded these in a journal he began in spring 1925.

Originally meant to be a diary of his explorations of the flora and fauna of Clark's Valley, the journal soon became a record of his thoughts about daily happenings, and often these thoughts were about his neighbors. Several valley residents eventually took a prominent place in the journals. One was Petey Meyers, owner of the local general store. Another was John Minsker, who was supposed to farm Richter's fields. A scion of the first family to settle the valley, Minsker was more woodsman than farmer, neglecting his fields to hunt or trap or just loaf and talk. As dark settled on summer evenings, Richter would sit with Minsker on the porch steps, trading stories as the night's first owls called across from Peters' to Short Mountain. When Richter came to write about pioneers westering into the virgin forests of Ohio, John Minsker would become his model for Worth Luckett.

Although a successful businessman approaching middle age, Richter had not yet outgrown his adolescent self-consciousness in public. This acute sensitivity was enough of a factor that in his tenth anniversary letter to Harvena he wrote: "I want to take you to the theater again and go to lunch with you. If I only weren't so accursedly shy."[13] But Richter's habitual shyness and self-consciousness disappeared once he made the turn onto the Clark's Valley road. In Petey Meyers's store he felt enough at home to sit with the local men gathered around the stove, enjoying their country outlook and mannerisms. But he would never stay for long, excusing himself by saying that he had to get back to Harvey and Vene. One night Petey Meyers asked him, "What will they do when you die, if you keep overprotecting them?"[14]

If the residents of Clark's Valley found Richter's ways different from theirs, they evidently liked and even appreciated him. At his neighbors' urging he accepted an appointment as a township supervisor, and he repaid their confidence by talking the other supervisors into paving the road through the valley, then taking on the exasperating job of supervising the workers—many of whom had worked at Richter's sawmill. But if Richter took pleasure in the idea of himself as a country squire, he gleaned at least as much satisfaction from being thought of as just a neighbor, like any other in the valley. When he gave Petey Meyers a copy of his newly published *Brothers of No Kin*, his first collection of stories, he noted with pleasure Meyers's comment the next time he visited the store: "'I sat down still and read that book you gave me. I like a story just about as long as them. These here stories that run through a whole book are too long for me.' Just that. Nothing more. Whether he noticed that the stories were by me, he did not say. If he did, he took it as a matter of course. Alec Stricker saws lumber. Bill Fleager shoes horses. Will Minsker raises apples. Houckey keeps bees. And I write books. One is no more strange than the other."[15]

TWO

If Richter's primary reason for buying Pine Tree Farm was Harvey's worsening health, it was not the only one. There was of course his own longing for a back-country farm, a favorite daydream throughout his adult years, and there were his worries about his own health and about Vene's health as well. Then, too, Pine Tree Farm offered a haven for his mother, Lottie Richter, who after a life of worrying about imagined diseases found herself with a heart weakening demonstrably as she approached her sixty-fifth birthday.[16] In warm weather Lottie Richter visited the farm for as long as a month at a time, freeing her from the chores at the parsonage of John Richter's latest charge, St. Matthew's Lutheran Church in Allentown, Pennsylvania. In addition, there was Richter's restlessness at the Handy Book Company. Through his first years at Handy, Richter had thought of it as a way station, a step toward better things. But other opportunities had not come, and Richter's attempts to market his talents as a sales writer had led only occasionally to contracts to develop promotional campaigns for such products as office paper supplies. Even an ingenious booklet, "Seven Sales-Writing Principles," a private publication intended primarily to bring him more consulting business, had only a modest success. Its ideas for sales and marketing, now commonplaces of modern advertising, were evidently too radical for businessmen in

1921. At any rate the booklet did not bring him the writing and consulting contracts he hoped for.

Richter's only public statement about his work at Handy is buried at the end of "Seven Sales-Writing Principles" in the form of a testimonial from Robert Clearing—a favorite Richter pseudonym. There Robert Clearing writes as vice president of the Handy Book Company: "I have always said that Conrad Richter built this business. His uncanny business analysis, his absolute knowledge of the principles of successful business, gave us selling plans and letters that went out and brought back the business when personal solicitation had failed. He did not do this once, but repeatedly, and he is still doing it."[17] Although this is obviously the prose of sales promotion, an example of Richter's ability to engage in puffery while sounding the tones of the practical businessman, there were in fact accomplishments at Handy about which Richter could have spoken with pride, including his ability to write successful sales copy. He had indeed turned Handy into the only division of Hinds, Noble, and Eldredge that turned a profit in the years of recession and inflation following World War I. But public pride in Handy's success gave way in private to his underlying dissatisfaction. Handy's books— "Helpful books for the student, teacher, and preacher"—were to his mind marginal publications, sold primarily because of his advertising copy, and to people who, Richter suspected, found them of little real practical value.[18] When he subjected himself to his own careful scrutiny, he was never happy with what he believed he had achieved at Handy. Although Handy provided a comfortable living and gave him time to do other things, it no longer offered any challenges. And with each passing year his opportunities to grow beyond it seemed narrower and narrower. Nor was he any better satisfied with his other writing, his short stories. "There's been a lot of ink spilled about my promise," he wrote in 1922 to Willard Hawkins, a story consultant. But since "Brothers of No Kin," he admitted, he had accomplished nothing to meet that promise.[19]

Richter's worries about his wife's health and his own, his dissatisfaction with Handy and with his writing—these kept Richter looking for ways to improve his life and that of his family. In his restless yearning for something better, he continued his longtime practice of omnivorous reading, carrying home armloads of books from both libraries in Harrisburg. These he read impatiently, skipping passages, pages, chapters; but he did not put down any book until he was sure he had mastered what it had to offer. Much of his reading was related to science and medicine. At the beginning of his relationship with Harvey he had read everything available on tuberculosis, as even earlier he had emptied the public libraries of whatever he could find to help him pursue his own study of nervous conditions and a wide range of subjects he believed associated with his problem—physics, chemistry, electricity, psychology, and psychoanalysis. Trying to keep up with the early twentieth-century explosion of writing about science and scientific theory, he read first articles in popular magazines and then the books and professional articles on which they were based. He read Freud on psychoanalysis and rejected his theory of infantile sexuality. He read John B. Watson on behaviorism and dismissed him as well. He investigated Coeism, a popular movement of the early twenties that argued the power of positive thinking to change oneself: by autosuggestion one could make oneself what one wanted to be. Such a theory was congenial to Richter's longtime belief (dating back at least to his fascination with the theories of Bernarr McFadden) that a mind properly focused could overcome a body's weaknesses, and it might well have been at his encouraging that Harvey became briefly a devotee of this fad, now remembered primarily in its motto, "Every day in every way I am growing better and better." Richter investigated as well Christian Science, the teachings of Mary Baker Eddy which carried Coeism one step further, arguing not that one can become what one believes but that one already is what one truly believes, and the world is too. He was at least sufficiently approving of Eddy's ideas to recommend Christian Science to John Minsker when local doctors were unable to relieve his eye troubles.[20]

Beyond his personal search for the causes and cures of nervous afflictions, Richter's interest in the scientific, philosophical, and psychological movements of the day was complexly motivated. Part was simple curiosity, a longing to know, and part was an effort to make up for his own limited education, about which he remained acutely sensitive. With his mixed feelings about experts, both his attraction to the mystique of specialized knowledge and his distrust of the pronouncements of authority (reaching back to the Sunday services of his childhood), he needed to discover for himself, to assess to his own satisfaction, to prove or disprove what others—experts—pronounced with such conviction. And there was as well a real need to prove to himself that his mind and character were strong enough to participate in the best thinking of the day. Like his father before him, reading Elias S. Henry's personal papers from behind the counter of his general store, Richter saw in the books he brought home a life of larger possibility, a life he longed to test himself against.

By the early twenties Richter was writing knowledgeably about the theories of Herbert Spencer, John Fiske, and other proponents of evolutionary naturalism, who argued that natural selection was the primary cause for change in a world ordered only by natural law. Richter was convinced by their description of evolution, and he accepted that the organizing principles for evolution were mechanical laws; but he rejected any macrocosmic formulation that did not begin with a divine being. "I am not afraid to trust God," he wrote to Stewart Edward White, separating himself from "the materialist or mechanist."[21] Given this belief, it is not surprising that Richter would be fascinated by psychic research. By 1924 when he joined the American Society for Psychic Research, he was already writing letters to magazines denouncing what he saw as smug dismissals of serious psychic investigations (though his discomfort with how these letters might be received led him to sign them "Robert Clearing"). This interest in and championing of research into the paranormal may well be a key to another impulse underlying Richter's restless inquiry into ideas, for it suggests that a primary reason for Richter's unsettled state was his uneasiness about the still unfathomable nature of the world around him. Approaching midlife, Richter was no more sure of what lay ahead than he had been as a young man when he wrote to his sweetheart "perhaps there are fires to go through," and he remained just as unhappy about those worrisome possibilities and just as distrustful of his ability to face them. To know himself and to be comfortable in his relationship to the world outside himself, he had to know first the nature of that outside world—and this continued to elude him.

Having rejected the religion of his father and grandfather, the religion that gave both men a secure self-definition through their belief in an absolute connection with a larger entity, he had found no alternative to provide himself with an equally satisfactory explanation of his place in the order of things. God to Conrad Richter was less an intimate presence than an idea of universal meaning and order, an idea that, unfortunately for him, offered no satisfactory feeling of sponsorship. Those Richter most admired in the world, men like his Grandfather Henry and Wesley Everett of the Amazon-Dixie Mining Company, were men who were sure of themselves, secure in their places. They had an innate confidence Richter knew he lacked. Even his father, John Richter, with whom Richter continued to quarrel about religion, was impervious to what his son saw as the faith-demolishing discoveries of modern science. While Richter could not accept the myths of his father's religion, he could feel within himself the cost of rejecting them—the loss of the sense of personal well-being such belief brought to others. In its place Richter had only what he could discover about the beauty and order of the universe, and psychic research gave hope of providing at some point the empirical verification demanded by modern thinking to prove the two things Richter most wanted to be sure of: that life was meaningful, and that the soul survived after the death of the body.

Such verification was enormously important to Conrad Richter. Without it he remained alone with his deepest fear, that he was unsponsored and unguided in a universe that was indifferent to him—that his individual mind was only an accident of natural law, lost among what Bertrand Russell would call "secular hurryings through space." In this context, his brave "I am not afraid to trust God" could perhaps more accurately be restated, "I am afraid not to trust God." As a modern man Richter placed his faith in science, but in science as a corrective: having exposed the myths upon which Western religions were based, science had the responsibility to go beyond that work to corroborate the rightness of man's age-old intuitive reliance on something larger than himself. Richter read Bertrand Russell, the atheist philosopher, with earnest care and discomfort, and though he rejected Russell's arguments, he considered them important enough to take his family to Washington, D.C., a day's train ride from Harrisburg, so that he could hear Russell speak in person. After the talk, Richter made notes for himself about what Russell had said, testing these against his own experiences and rejecting Russell even as he admired the cockiness of the single small man with his "squeaky voice" and "dry, spasmodic chuckles" pronouncing "revolutionary things."[22] But to refute Russell completely, Richter needed the proofs of modern science. Those proofs, he believed, would have to come from psychic research.

Throughout his life Richter called himself a student of psychic research, meaning by this that he was an interested observer but not an active participant. He was to engage himself, rather, at first fitfully and then later with dedication, in a different aspect of the search for the era's version of the philosopher's stone. Gathering everything he could from his reading, he began in the early twenties what he was soon calling his "serious writing," and by 1923 he was to write a friend that he had completed a manuscript putting forward his own theory of the psychology and neuropsychology of nervous afflictions that attempted much more, as is suggested by his working title, "The Keys of Life."[23] Although this manuscript has not survived, it was the basis for Richter's letter to the John D. Rockefeller Foundation, asking for financial support: "Some years ago I stumbled on something as Edison stumbled on his phone. I have been working ends of days and hours of nights in analyzing the psychic elements of life and man as the pioneering chemist analyzed those of matter. My hope was that if we could find the fundamental elements which mechanically control life, we could carry on consciously the work of understanding evolution which the forces of nature have done unconsciously."[24] What Richter believed he had discovered was the root cause of his own nervous condition, and he was not put off when, as he must have expected, the Rockefeller Institute declined to support his research. In response to doctors who found in him no signs of physiological disorder— leading to the unacceptable inference that the fault was his own inherent weakness—Richter constructed a psychology based on several assumptions that were if not unique, certainly unusual and without standing in medicine. The key idea of this mechanistic theory was that "vibration," the energy flowing between particles of matter, was the source of all human action and thought. Although his description of vibration in cells was to be understod as metaphoric, the cells not being biological cells but rather individual life units, Richter's elaboration of this idea led him finally to attempt detailed explanations of biological and chemical actions.

Richter called the book he was to write about this theory *Human Vibration: The Mechanics of Life and Mind*,[25] and he wrote it deliberately for a general audience— both to find a wide readership and to disseminate what he thought to be helpful knowledge to others who suffered from acute sensitivity and nervousness. In this theory, opposition to the free replenishment of energy in cell groups is the "plan of life," because "without limited energy, desire and evolution could not take place."[26] In Richter's theory evolution is nothing more than the mechanical process of "raising an individual's general vibration scale," which occurs when a high cell group, to meet an extraordinary need for energy, raises lower cell groups to its level to use the added energy flow.[27]

If this "commanded vibration" creates more than full energy flow in the associated cell groups, the result is "inharmony," a painful energy hunger. Although prolonged energy hunger can cause nervous breakdowns, in more moderate instances the inharmony brings about a new level of full energy flow, which can be tapped again when needed by a second process for raising the vibration rate, which Richter calls "applied energy." Because in higher evolution the battles requiring new energy rates are mental rather than physical (having to do, for example, with one's emotions at the death of a loved one, rather than with a physical struggle for survival), the higher level means an evolution of consciousness: "where before we were indifferent, now we are said to understand."[28]

Full energy flow (harmony) "motivates all behavior"; all organisms "desire" naturally to get from inharmony to harmony. Therefore happiness is not merely having energy, but having it in rates that do not bankrupt the supply. People do not desire evolution, but rather the opposite, harmony; but selfish mechanical desires to satisfy energy hunger result in sympathy for others, "the mark of evolutionary progress," for witnessing in others what one has experienced oneself excites associationally the former vibration rates.[29] Similarly, education occurs when one person succeeds in exciting cell groups in another who is sufficiently evolved to respond with correspondent vibrations. Modern evolution, then, rests on human consciousness: the more evolved a person, the more readily he or she will respond to the plight of others. In this description of things, Richter acknowledges and accepts John Fiske's definition of evil: "simply the characteristics of the lower state of being looked at from the higher state."[30]

Of the higher states of evolution, Richter distinguishes two qualities. The first is intellect, the ability to associate—that is, to raise one's vibration levels in response to something outside oneself. High intelligence means "association considerably above the average in quantity on a given subject or subjects and about the human average or less in vibration rate."[31] The second is understanding, in which association "may be below the average in quantity but considerably above the average human vibration rate." People of high understanding "feel rather than reason,"[32] and in doing so they expend far more energy than others with lower vibration rates and are therefore likely to suffer from nervous afflictions.

At the heart of Richter's theory is his optimistic assumption that scientific analysis will ultimately be able to explain even such "vague phenomena as consciousness, happiness, and the soul"[33] as recordable and measurable manifestations of mechanical laws of energy and matter. As Richter put it in *Human Vibration*, "The only fact or truth we know is mechanical."[34] For humans, this means that "we can do what we wish. But in what we wish there is no choice. It is fixed by evolution and to a lesser degree by our environment."[35] It also means that "even God is bound by mechanical law."[36] In at least the first of these assertions Richter is not far from Herbert Spencer and the mechanists. He is fundamentally opposed to them, however, in his reliance upon the transcendental. Richter's theory rests on the assumption that evolution is purposeful, and that its purpose is the development of individual consciousness ever closer to an ultimate knowledge of God. To attain such knowledge, the imperfect human vessel for understanding must grow in capacity; and that growth comes primarily when one undergoes experiences of hardship and pain.

In his early rejection of the Lutheran conception of God as an avenger, Richter found himself up against the question: if there is a God and He is a loving God, then why is there such random suffering and death? How do all the dark, painful, yet utterly ordinary conditions of each person's life evince a benevolent God? In Richter's theory, cell deprivation—the depletion of electrical energy (especially through stress caused by pain)—is the engine of progress. Only through energy starvation do cells and thus organisms grow stronger, and the strength that accrues is not only energy for work but for understanding. Thus adversity, which brings with it demands for strong energy flow, is the opportunity to grow. And since growth, the attainment of higher levels of understanding, is the purpose of life on earth, adversity is necessary and ease is, however longed for and enjoyed in the moment, ultimately wasteful and self-defeating. That is to say, normal estimates of success and failure, good and ill luck, are false indicators: striving is the only source of benefit. Ultimately a loving God offers all humans the opportunity of highest attainment, through personal choice and action. And He gives all people, as a part of mechanical law, the power needed to achieve this level, the will to act, and the desire to act rightly. One has only to take advantage of adversity.

Here for Richter was the great difference between his conception of human psychology and that of others. Freud explained aberrant behavior as idiosyncratic and sex-related; Watson explained all behavior as environmentally conditioned. Both theories to Richter were demeaning of humankind, reducing thought to stimulus-response. Equally demeaning were the theories of the evolutionary naturalists, for they denied a purpose to evolution by denying God. In contrast, Richter's theory, while resting on a mechanistic understanding of behavior, ultimately confirmed human experience as meaningful, even sacred, and answered what to him was the riddle of the universe. All he needed was for psychic research to verify empirically that the spirit survived the death of the body.

THREE

After the Rockefeller rejection, Richter continued working in his spare time on the book explaining his theory, but by the end of the first year he had written only the opening chapters. Other matters distracted him, including his mother's failing health. For Lottie Richter the early months of 1924 were a mixture of good days followed by lengthening bad spells, though she remained in good spirits, enjoying her visits to Pine Tree Farm and occasional outings with family members. One reason Richter bought an almost new Dodge touring car, larger and more comfortable than his well-worn Model T, was to take his mother on these outings. Soon after buying the Dodge, Richter bundled Harvey and Vene into it and drove to Syracuse, New York, where John and Lottie Richter were visiting Fred and his wife Emily. (On his release from the service Fred had followed his girlfriend, Emily Derr, to Syracuse, New York. There he found employment with the company for which he would work until retirement, the Onondaga

Pottery Company, winning the job with his oldest brother's active assistance: Conrad wrote the initial letter of inquiry Fred sent to Syracuse businesses, and he wrote a letter of recommendation so convincing that Fred's boss would comment on it at Fred's retirement.)[37]

From Syracuse, Richter took his parents on a swing north to Niagara Falls, camping out several nights along the way. Throughout the trip Lottie was in high spirits and in remarkably good health, prompting Richter, once back at the farm, to urge his parents to spend half of their savings of $1,000 to buy a new Model T. Richter's letter pressed his reluctant father, reminding him that even his mother agreed that her spirits were bound to be raised if she could look forward to a ride each day away from St. Matthew's parsonage. Besides, Richter pointedly reminded his father, she had helped save the money, and it had been her inheritance that paid for his college and seminary. Surely her happiness and health were worth $500, and Richter urged his parents to spend half their retirement savings and just "forget about it." Their three sons, all successful, would be able to take care of them if need be. With his letter he sent a check for $81.52 to cover the remainder of the purchase price of a new Ford coupe, $581.52.[38]

But John Richter delayed, and his procrastination added another item to Richter's list of his father's failures of his mother. On October 8, 1924, Charlotte Richter's heart gave out. As with many such deaths, after months of worrying there had been no warning at all. The funeral was on October 13, Richter's thirty-fourth birthday, a clear fall day full of the warm sunlight of Indian summer. Richter would remember it as "ghastly bright and fair."[39]

Nobody took the death harder than Conrad Richter, though to those outside the family there were few signs of what Richter was holding within him. In addition to blaming his father, he blamed himself for refusing his mother's final request to him. When he had last visited Allentown, Lottie Richter had asked to return to Pine Tree Farm. But a new doctor insisted that she remain available for daily treatment, and so Richter deferred to his father's protests and did not take her home with him. At the time it seemed, of course, the prudent decision, following the advice of a doctor recently trained in the latest medical procedures.[40] But with her death, Richter's feelings of loss were compounded by a devastating remorse for having failed her. In the irrationality of sorrow, his denial of his mother seemed to confirm his mother's judgment of him. As she had more than once said to him as a young man, he and his stories both "lacked the human touch."[41]

The day after his mother's death, Richter wrote to *Woman's Home Companion*, asking them to delay publication of "Mother Cuts Loose" and to publish it under the pseudonym Robert Clearing because "much of the story was written from life."[42] He then tracked down a distant relative in California to buy the cemetery plots next to his mother's. When the Hinds brothers and Harry Hayden told him in November that they were planning to sell Handy, he arranged to borrow $23,000 from a Harrisburg bank and bought the business himself. But even the excitement of taking over ownership of Handy did not lift his sorrow. Each morning he awoke to experience again the pain of her death—a time he would remember as the "zero hour," when everything was "heavy, hopeless beyond words."[43] For a brief while he called his Aunt Lizzie "Ma," evidently at her suggestion, but he gave that up long before his cousin Beth died on May 13, 1925, days after giving birth to her second child. At her funeral Richter could not keep himself from speaking crossly to the minister when he stepped on Lottie Richter's grave. Then Aunt Lizzie died on January 26, 1926. Within fifteen months he had lost three of the most important people in his life, both his real and his surrogate mother and his favorite cousin. And to these were soon added the loss of his Aunt Emma, his father's sister, and his best friend from high school, Jim Manning, who finally succumbed to tuberculosis. There had been other losses in Richter's life, but never so many, so close together—and of course no loss could equal the devastating loss of his mother.

Within a month of Lottie Richter's death, Richter drove to Philadelphia for what would be the first of a series of visits to psychic mediums, attempting to establish contact with his mother. His search began, once again, in the library, where he found descriptions of communication with spirits in an afterlife. He read the accounts of Arthur Conan Doyle, the most celebrated writer on the subject, and he read a number of testimonies written by people who claimed only that their unverifiable narratives were as factual as they could make them. Some he found more believable than others. Richter read Albert S. Crockett's *Revelations of Louise* "incredulously" until he chanced upon the testimonies of several prominent people at the end of the book, after which he reread "with new respect" Crockett's account of his communications with his dead daughter by means of a Ouija Board, table levitation, and finally through the medium of a half sister of the dead daughter, who was unknown to Crockett until he was informed of her existence by the communicating spirit. Then Richter wrote to Crockett, a former newspaper reporter for the *New York Times*, to ask his help in finding mediums. In a second letter Richter urged Crockett to join the American Psychical Society, where his testimonies would be valued, and recommended Anna Hude's *Evidence for Communication*—especially "a most convincing account" of a deceased father's communication with his son. "And yet," Richter wrote, "I doubt every day. I think we all do when the energy is low."[44]

Of the works Richter read during this period, Pierre-Emile Cornillier's *The Survival of the Soul and Its Evolution After Death* had the most marked and lasting influence.[45] Published in English in 1921, *The Survival of the Soul* is a narrative account of the French artist's extraordinary experiences with a young medium just before World War I. Through this medium, spirits from the astral world convey to Cornillier their desire to help Cornillier understand the relation between earthly life and the astral and to gain proof of the survival of the soul. The book is Cornillier's record of many sessions over several years in which he received messages from a spirit named Vettellini and others, including his own father, who explain that they are all souls in process of evolution, as are all humans, and that each goes through a series of incarnations as part of that evolution. After the death of the body, the spirit returns each time to the astral, to a level determined by the degree of evolutionary advancement in the last incarnation. Because higher spirits in the astral are unable to communicate with living people, they occasionally employ lower spirits as intermediaries, though this often results in imperfect communication. In Cornillier's special case, his fortuitous acquaintance with an exceptionally receptive medium allowed these spirits to employ him as a scribe for a book to reveal the mysteries of death and birth and of the life beyond. Unfortunately, the illness of the medium and the outbreak of World War I ended the communication before unimpeachable proofs could be obtained.

To Richter, Cornillier was extraordinarily persuasive in the detail he was able to offer and the complexity of his explanations of relationships. Perhaps equally convincing to Richter, Cornillier's account seemed to verify much of his own thinking about the meaning of life: that terrestrial life is an ordeal for evolutionary advancement and therefore meaningful; that spirit protectors could influence individual lives; that by intense concentration living beings could improve themselves (as a spirit explains to Cornillier) "[to] correct a certain feebleness of will, for example; [or to] mitigate nervous troubles or physical ills";[46] and that the soul does indeed survive the death of the body. All these gave Richter renewed hope; so too did this seeming verification that it was possible to speak again with his mother.

While reading about psychic research and visiting mediums Richter began in earnest to write the study he eventually published as *Human Vibration*. His original goal—to find a general theory to explain the particulars of his own nervous nature—remained the book's central purpose. It would be Richter's public defense of his theory of the evolution of consciousness, drawing upon the mechanists' belief that natural laws explain human actions and upon his own belief that these laws are intimately tied to a supreme being toward whom life reaches. But underlying this argument is another, without which Richter's theory loses its meaning, and that is that there is life after death, the survival of the soul. As Lottie Richter's death spurred his search for proof of an afterlife, it served as well as a catalyst for the concentrated and prolonged effort to write his first book-length work. Not very far beneath the surface of *Human Vibration* is the dread that filled a young boy on guild night, when he lay in the dark waiting for his mother to return home.

Unable to find a publisher for *Human Vibration*, Richter paid to have a thousand copies printed and bound for distribution through the Good Books Corporation, as he renamed the Handy Book Company when he bought it from Harry Hayden and the Hinds brothers. Late in 1925 he sent out more than a hundred copies to newspapers, magazines, and journals and to a long list of people he thought could be influential in the book's reception—noted writers, scientists, doctors of medicine, and even university presidents. Given his topic and his own anonymity to this ambitious list of recipients, Richter had to be pleased by the letters he received in reply. Joseph Collins, a New York neurologist widely known for his newspaper column "The Doctor Speaks," began an encouraging correspondence and wrote a laudatory review for the *Bookman*. Novelist Stewart Edward White wrote to offer comments and congratulations, as did Professor William Lyon Phelps of Harvard, Professor David Starr Jordan of Stanford, Thomas Masson, Luther Burbank, and a host of others. Nonprofessionals were for the most part more sympathetic and accepting than scientists, especially those working in related fields. But even such respondents as Stanley DeBrath and Hans Dreisch, respected researchers in telecommunication, and A. S. Holmes, of the Psychological Laboratory of the University of Pennsylvania, encouraged Richter in lengthy correspondences, paying him the compliment of taking issue with his theory in substantive ways.

Sales through Good Books were modest but strong enough for Richter to convince Dodd, Mead and Company to take over sales and distribution of *Human Vibration*, tipping in its own title page and designing a new dust jacket with admiring quotations from Luther Burbank, William Lyon Phelps, Joseph Collins, and Steward Edward White. Soon Richter was thinking of an expanded edition of *Human Vibration*, one taking into consideration the responses he had received.

Later he decided that he needed a wholly new presentation, in a new format, to convince influential scientists that his theories deserved more than polite encouragement. The problem with *Human Vibration*, Richter decided, was its tone and manner of presentation, which he had chosen deliberately to help him reach general readers. This manner of presentation had the unfortunate effect of inviting the skepticism of scientists, who were all too willing to dismiss him as a materialist because of his explanations of thought and action as mechanical, or who were disinclined to read him attentively because, he discovered, in scientific circles the word "vibration" had about it "a charlatan air."[47] To counteract these responses, he began a second book with the weighty title of *Principles in Bio-Physics*, in which he would attempt a more formal and rigorously scientific working out of his explanations. This second book would occupy much of his time for the next year.

FOUR

After publication of *Human Vibration*, Richter speculated that his new life at Pine Tree Farm had been a catalyst for its writing: free from the distractions of town life, he was encouraged to think deeply. Country life was the spur to another kind of writing Richter first undertook in spring 1925, descriptive writing about the natural world of Clark's Valley. After days outdoors, Richter often spent his evenings reading books by and about others who shared his love of nature. While he was still regularly reading fiction—noting in his journal such works as Joseph Conrad's *Tono Bungay*, Sherwood Anderson's *Death in the Woods*, Thornton Wilder's *The Bridge of San Luis Rey*, and Willa Cather's *The Professor's House*—and still reading widely to pursue his psychological writing, he was happiest reading the evocations of the natural world he found in the writings of naturalists John Muir, John Burroughs, Luther Burbank, and John James Audubon. He found much of the same enjoyment in novels and memoirs that transported him imaginatively into childhoods that reminded him of his own: James M. Barrie's *A Window in Thrums*, W. H. Hudson's *Far Away and Long Ago*, and Sergei Aksakoff's *Years of My Childhood*. In his journal he would note correspondences, recalling his childhood sicknesses, his difference from other children, his love for the out-of-doors, and his mother's special affection for her odd young child.

For some time Richter had been drawn to the biographies and "life and letters" of the writers he was reading, and he was especially interested in published journals, reading those of Ralph Waldo Emerson, Henry David Thoreau, John

Burroughs, and others. Eventually he attempted his own journal. After a false start in 1923—nine entries in three months, all about the weather, in February 1925, Richter tried again, and this time he found his voice. He would continue to write daily in this journal, one loose-leaf notebook each year, for the next forty-three years. It is almost from the beginning a curiously double-perspectived document, both a personal diary—at times intensely private—as well as writing that has in mind an audience. He thought of it as a record of a writer's life even as early as 1925, when he would have hesitated to use the term to describe himself, and while one seldom senses that Richter is consciously talking to readers, he habitually wrote so that a mind other than his own could understand. There are few private codes or symbols, though there are some, few ellipses or other evidences of mental shorthand. He made no effort, however, to improve his cramped, difficult, at times illegible handwriting.

This journal was a trying-out place for Conrad Richter's thoughts about nature, and as such it demonstrates that he did not naturally have the knack for descriptive writing. As he himself recognized years later, his entries were too derivative of what he was reading in other journals. But if his nature writing did not match the evocations of nature he so enjoyed reading in others' journals, the journal entries show that his reading of these writers was opening to him new possibilities, changing not only his writing but his conception of what was expressible in writing, even in his short stories.

When Richter bought Pine Tree Farm, he counted on the sale of stories to help pay for it. Even earlier, before he found the farm, he had written to a new agent, Curtis Brown, that he was taking his friend Carl Clausen's advice that in choosing stories to write he "lay off art and try a bacon bringer."[48] A writer of detective stories, Clausen's letters to Richter were decidedly cynical about a writer's chances to fare well with editors and publishers. As Clausen saw it, there was no art possible in a story market ruined by the likes of the *Saturday Evening Post*, *Redbook*, and *Cosmopolitan*, where editors bought stories as they might buy bread, only when they were hungry.[49] Whether or not Richter was influenced by this view, his comment about a bacon bringer may well have been a response to the depressed story market, which had brought him in 1921 just two sales, for a total of only $140, and would bring him in 1922 a single sale, "Over the Hill to the Rich House" to *Outlook* for $75. Under these conditions, counting on story sales to help pay for Pine Tree Farm was at least a feat of unusual optimism for Richter, optimism verified when, even before Richter and his family moved into the remodeled farmhouse, *American Magazine* purchased "Rich Relations" and "Hemingway's Baby" (published as "Teddy Saves the Day"), each for $350.

Richter submitted both of these to the editors, having long since lost patience with Curtis Brown's lack of success with the several stories he had sent to him.

Neither of these stories were included in *Brothers of No Kin*, the collection Richter gathered that summer for publication in early January 1924 by Hinds, Hayden, and Eldredge (renamed to reflect Harry Hayden's growing financial interest in the concern), though this omission does not necessarily suggest Richter's lesser regard for these stories, at least as bringers of bacon. All his stories were intended, he wrote modestly to Bill Breck of Brandt and Kirkpatrick, who became his agent in 1924, "only to furnish a little entertainment, and perhaps a stray ray or two of human warmth."[50] Although he remained intensely sensitive to each rejection (asking Breck not to write to him about stories that had been returned by editors, for such news always incapacitated him for an hour),[51] the stories he was writing were far from the center of his life. He wrote them for money, just as he prepared *Brothers of No Kin* to provide some needed extra income for Pine Tree Farm. Having so little invested in these stories, he was quite willing to accept Bill Breck's advice that he concentrate on stories about "good, solid, middle-class, down country people."[52] He even wrote to Merle Crowell, editor of the *American*, asking if Crowell would explain in advance what kind of stories he was looking for, so that he might try to accommodate.[53] Richter wrote this letter in 1924, when he was perhaps especially eager to glean more income from his pen, and he sent it to the only editor who had bought his stories the preceding year. But while Richter was apparently following Clausen's advice to write stories to meet the expectations of editors, he was to find it increasingly difficult to do so.

Richter continued to write stories, typically about six a year, and he continued to have modest success in placing them. In 1924 "Mother Cuts Loose," after twenty-five rejections and several substantial rewritings, sold for $400 to *Woman's Home Companion*. That same year "Father Had No Tact" sold to *Elks Magazine* for $200; and later *American Magazine* took "Derickson's Gagoo" for $400. In 1925, a year when Richter's writing time was taken up primarily with *Human Vibration*, Richter managed two sales to *American*, "The Man Who Retired" and "The Exaggerator." Each of these brought in $450. Remarkably, he was able to write these stories despite the less-than-enthusiastic reviews of *Brothers of No Kin*, which trickled in during 1924. The most perceptive and most crushing review was by Isabel M. Paterson in the *New York Tribune*, in which the former story editor for Hearst's contrasted the story "Brothers of No Kin"—"a powerful and original bit of fiction, though a trifle bare"—with the other "dozen stereotyped and unmistakably imitative offerings." It was perhaps the more devastating because his old pen pal I.M.P. was obviously taking pains to be kind as well as honest, praising Richter's talent though admonishing that it was "a gift never meant for the *Saturday Evening Post.*" To Paterson, Richter's collection was a kind of fable for young writers, in which "the good fairies who presented Mr. Richter with a fine talent wrapped it in so many napkins that he became weary trying to unfold it and fell back upon the supposedly easiest way." But "writing down is an impossible feat," Paterson warns. "Mr. Richter's one good story is considerably above the popular level; the others are equally far beneath it."[54]

Years later Richter had learned that he could not read any critical commentary of his own work, suffering too much whether the reviews were good or bad. About the reviews of *Brothers of No Kin* he wrote nothing in his journal, nor did he comment to his agent—unless, of course, one reads his deprecating remarks to Bill Breck about his stories as an indirect defense. But he was certainly aware of them and especially stung by what he thought to be Isabel Paterson's mean-spirited review. When he sent out review copies of *Human Vibration*, the only New York newspaper he excluded was the *New York Tribune.*

In spring 1925 Richter converted the summer kitchen, attached to the west side of the house, into a study for himself. With new hardwood floors and a new stone fireplace it was an attractive room and comfortably furnished. Here, Richter thought, he would be able to write his stories with greater concentration and perhaps better result. He would have preferred to abandon writing stories altogether, though realistically, he reminded himself in his journal, he needed them as he needed Handy Book Company, to provide the income for his other interests—and he warned himself in his journal that, when in the comfort of his new study, he ought not to feel superior to *American Magazine*, which was the primary source of his writing income.[55] A little over a month later, worrying in his journal over his life choices, he would list "publishing and fiction for livelihood, 'Psychology' and nature writing for pleasure."[56] Even comfortably settled in Clark's Valley, Richter's felt need for a secure livelihood was quite real, and there remained in him still a deep-seated need to be successful in other people's terms. On a visit to Pine Grove he talked to his brother-in-law Art Achenbach about together buying the local newspaper, the *Pine Grove Herald,* and "making a real paper and profitmaker out of it"[57]—an impulse recalling the lumber business in White Deer Valley, the pretzel wholesaling in Reading, and even the sawmill venture at Pine Tree Farm. After another trip he noted in his journal that a butcher he had met, about his own age, already owned three farms and had bought a house for his father, all from his earnings. The implied criticism is apparent enough: Richter thought he should have been able to do as much, or at least more than he had done.[58] This sense of restless ambition was a trait Richter believed he inherited from his father, as he speculated after coming across a copy of "Shine for a Dime," a Christmas cantata written in 1888 and copyrighted by John A. Richter and H. S. Saul. Guessing that his father "engineered and dreamed out" the cantata, Richter would write in his journal: "The part of me that wants to accomplish more in the future than in the past—that I get from my Father. . . . I can see my Mother doubtful at first as to the venture, yet silently doing her share and in the end perhaps contributing as much as Dad. Most of what understanding I have, I get from her."[59] Did he mean, here, "understanding" as he had defined it in *Human Vibration*—sympathetic feeling for others, as opposed to "intellect"? Probably so. This combination of "understanding" and "wanting to do more in the future" remained key factors in the psychological makeup of Conrad Richter, as they were factors in the reading Richter was doing and the writing he hoped to do, even though the summer kitchen turned out to be a room he could not work in—too quiet and too far from the life of his family—and though 1926 and 1927 turned out to be dry years for stories, with only one finding a buyer. Late in 1927 when Bill Breck wrote to offer some advice on revising one of these stories, Richter declined to consider the changes. Acceding to Breck that his suggestions might lead to a story with "more pep and more of a surprise climax," Richter also wrote that the revised story would have as well "more hocum," and concluded: "hocum . . . simply won't come out of my typewriter anymore. If it means my stories don't sell, they don't sell, and I'll have to forget them."[60] Of course the story Breck had suggested Richter rewrite may have had something to do with Richter's intransigence. Although the story has not survived, its title suggests that it was drawn upon personal experience, one still painful to him. The story was entitled "Mother Buys a Car."

New Mexico

ONE

In fall 1926 Harvena Richter suffered a deep coughing spell
that ended in a hemorrhage. It was, Richter thought, her first
hemorrhage in nearly four years, but later Harvey admitted
there had been others that she had kept from him. Because
they were traveling by car when the hemorrhage occurred,
she could not hide the bright red blood that soaked first
through her handkerchief and then his. Nor could either of
them avoid the unhappy truth: Harvey had not gotten better
at Pine Tree Farm; her tuberculosis was still dangerously
active.

In Conrad Richter's life no single circumstance was more consequential than Harvena Richter's failing health. Had she improved at Pine Tree Farm as they hoped, Richter's career as a writer would have been unrecognizably different from what it became. However restless and dissatisfied he was with his occupation as the owner of a small publishing house, he would not have given it up except under a circumstance such as this—Harvey's desperate illness. Whatever his dreams of making a living as a writer or of helping others with nervous afflictions, he would not have sold the Good Books Corporation without a surer financial future than either promised. And even if he had somehow gotten out from under the workaday duties of the Good Books Corporation, his sense of his life and his hopes for the future were decidedly different in Clark's Valley and Harrisburg, Pennsylvania, from what they would be in the high desert of the Southwest—and from the writing that would come from his life there.

During a slow period at Good Books, Richter recorded in his journal a lament he had shared with Harvey: "A new issue of *Publisher's Weekly* filled with countless (almost) books and several new publishers, fills me with the realization that I am trying to make a living in an already highly congested field. God knows there are many books already without my adding to the numbers. God also knows that I care little about the educational and orthodox religious books I publish. . . . I have long wanted to make a change—to step into a place where I could be helpful—but I have never had the courage."[1] Settled into his routines, wary of disasters he could not anticipate, Richter knew that only an impending catastrophe could extricate him. One such catastrophe—though an unlikely one—would be the failure of his business; by far the greater danger was Harvey's illness. Throughout the Pine Tree Farm years she continued the sequence of partial recoveries and incrementally more severe setbacks that had characterized their years together. One of these was alarming enough to prompt from Richter's Aunt Lizzie, before her death, some of her toughest language: "Don't let Vene be raised by a stepmother," she wrote to Harvey.[2] But it would take much more than blunt talk to break the pattern that led imperceptibly but inevitably downward.

The evening of Harvey's hemorrhage Richter explained to Vene that "something serious" had happened to her mother, so serious that she would have to give up teaching her daughter. Later that night Richter noted in his journal, "If sending Vene to school does not bring a steady gain in [Harvey's] weight and health, then something else must be attempted at once."[3] Within a week he proposed renting a house in Harrisburg for the winter, arguing with Harvey, who did not want to go, that the change would mean better care for her and a better school for Vene.[4] The family did not move to Harrisburg that winter, and

10. Pine Tree Farm in Clark's Valley, Pennsylvania, *circa* 1927. Here Richter hoped Harvey would recover from tuberculosis; her failure to do so led to the farm's sale and the family's departure in 1928.

Vene did not attend the local school until the following fall. Nor did any other unnamed changes come about. One reason Richter delayed was that Harvey continued to resist any changes, speaking of her health so lightly and matter-of-factly that it was hard to believe that the issue was, after all, her own life. Another reason was that, though she got no better, Harvey did not appear to get any worse. In January her doctor reported that her case was no further advanced than it had been several years earlier—relieving Harvey more than Conrad, whose opinion of the medical profession had never been high.[5] That month he wrote to *The Journal of the Outdoor Life* to ask for an opinion of the climate and care facilities for health seekers in Asheville, North Carolina. Richter also began a new group of short stories, preparing to support his family entirely by his writing, should that become necessary. And he began to talk about selling the Good Books Corporation and Pine Tree Farm.

During spring and summer 1927 Richter spent as much time as he could out-of-doors, filling his journal with the record of his nature trips with the Harrisburg Natural History Association. Harvey remained in bed almost all of each day, but in other ways their lives seemed little different from earlier years at Pine Tree Farm. Weekdays Richter drove to Harrisburg to oversee Good Books, while Harvey continued with Vene's schooling. From the beginning this had been a formally set-out part of the day, during which Vene pretended to be attending a real school with a real schoolteacher other than her mother, even giving her teacher a name, Mrs. Barnes. After Harvey's hemorrhage the school-room was Harvey's bedroom, and Mrs. Barnes remained in bed.

That spring Richter's neighbors asked him to serve as township supervisor, and for the rest of the year he felt obliged to keep track of the workers paving the road. Evenings he spent reading and writing, or avoiding this work (and later feeling guilty about it) listening to his radio. After the evening's work was done, he turned to the journals, letters, and biographies of other men who shared his love for the natural world. In March he mentioned in his journal that he was reading Emerson's journals, in April the *Life and Letters of John Muir*. In May he discovered *Years of My Childhood*, Sergei Aksakoff's remembrance of his child-hood in Russia, leading Richter back again to *Far Away and Long Ago*, W. H. Hudson's story of his own childhood on the pampas of Argentina. Both these extraordinarily vivid accounts recalled to Richter memories of his own child-hood, which, in the years immediately after his mother's death, he began to think of as the happiest part of his life. Hudson and Aksakoff, he decided, were "his" writers, as was Willa Cather, who achieved in fiction the intimate evoca-tions of the natural world Richter admired in Hudson's and Aksakoff's auto-biographies. In October he would write to himself that "a few books but the best, Hudson, Burroughs, the Bible, Shakespeare, Wordsworth, and a few more, mean more than all the magazines and novels one reads with such avidity. What I have lacked has been cultural background of knowledge and reading. I am ripening slowly . . . at the age of thirty-six."[6]

Spurred by his reading, Richter attempted his first nature article, "Not in the Nature Books." This was rejected by the *Atlantic*, but with kind words, and so he rewrote and resubmitted it, only to have it rejected again. Disappointed, he delayed writing another; but he remained convinced that his special group of writers was teaching him a different and better kind of writing, a personal expres-sion that openly acknowledged private emotions. Growing within him was the realization that what he admired most about these writers was not their ability to evoke their own sense of wonder at the natural world, but that they were able to do so without embarrassed self-consciousness. The secret to the evocation was in the candor: "when one has these feelings within him, he should quietly and simply put them down with what moving beauty he can, and not hide them from [the] Anglo-Saxon gaze as something to be ashamed to present."[7] For Richter this discovery would be perhaps his most important writing lesson, the one he worked longest to master.

In November Richter threw out virtually all his old notes for short stories, dismissing them as "a dead level of high school mediocrity"—as he then could see from his new perspective: "This much the farm and Burroughs and Hudson have done for me, made me a different mind than before."[8] If only he had been taught to read such books at an early age; then he might have "come sooner out of stock hackwork, making over and over what others had made, and into explaining and expressing new combinations as I saw them."[9] An attempt at just such a new expression was "Melody in a Minor Key," a story he completed in early September. Sending his new story to Bill Breck, he announced its difference: it was, he wrote, "a labor of love with me and not money" and a story "which many might not understand."[10]

In spite of Richter's enthusiasm for this new way of seeing, story writing remained a secondary occupation. He continued to believe that his important work was his other writing, his theory of "bio-physics" (soon he would be calling it "psycho-bio-physics"), despite rebuffs that might have discouraged a less ardent commitment. A year earlier, thinking about his future, he had divided his primary activities into two categories: for profit, he wrote stories and published books; for recreation, he studied nature and pursued his nerve theories. By summer 1927, worrying about Harvey, he summarized somewhat differently: "The three chief interests, purposes, that I cannot discard, my bio-physics, Harvey's health, and the earning of money to support the success of the first two."[11] This recommitment to Harvey's health and to his energy theories came just months after both Joseph Collins and Harvey had told him they found his *Principles in Bio-Physics* unreadable, prompting another version of his old complaint against Harvey, that she was not sufficiently attentive to him:

> Tonight I received back the first of the three sets of proof of [*Principles in Bio-Physics*]. Dr. Collins can make neither head nor tail of it. I do his mind the honor to think he was tired. I asked my wife to translate some of his pencilled comments in the margins of the first galley—as far as he went—and she agrees with him that it is incomprehensible. She gives me but cold disinterest when I try to arouse a little encouragement. I see that what I do in the future like what little I have done in the past I must

do on my own faith and conviction. Once I am successful and others send
me thanks or commendation, then she is convinced, even enthusiastic. I
am appointed a township supervisor and she is enthusiastic about that.[12]

Richter promised himself not to be deterred. Finding no publisher for *Principles in Bio-Physics*, he published it at Good Books. As with *Human Vibration*, he
sent review copies to a wide and disparate group of professionals and scientists,
and to the various journals and newspapers he hoped would review his book.
But others evidently found his formulas as indecipherable as did Dr. Collins and
Harvey, and very little comment came back to him. When his subscription copy
of *Science Newsletter* arrived and he discovered that his book was not reviewed or
even listed in "Books Received," Richter vented his anger and exasperation in his
journal, then admonished himself to keep control of his emotions. "I dare not
grow bitter," he wrote.[13] Almost immediately he started to work on another book
about his theory, one Joseph Collins urged him to write. It was to be a book of
practical advice to fellow sufferers from nervous afflictions. The basic ideas did
not change in "Nerve Energy and Its Management"; indeed, the underlying
principles and primary arguments for his theories would not change substan-
tially over the remaining years of his life. Only his purpose and intended
audience changed for "Nerve Energy." Like his father ministering to the families
of mine workers in coal patches, he was taking his message to those who needed
him. By late December 1927 he had a manuscript ready to send to Collins.

After Vene began the new school year at the one-room school in Clark's Valley,
Harvey finally began to recover her strength; but an ill-advised vacation trip to
Washington, D.C., brought her back to Pine Tree Farm weak and coughing.
Soon thereafter a worried Richter arranged for the state director of tuberculosis
sanitariums to examine Harvey. His diagnosis was the bluntest they had ever
received: her tuberculosis was so far advanced that it would not be arrested in
Pennsylvania. He recommended at least a year in Asheville, North Carolina,
which was closer to home than the alternatives in the West and Southwest and
a better choice than Saranac Lake in the Adirondacks, where the winters were
often severe. To Richter's surprise, Harvey agreed to go.
    In January Harvey's sister May came to stay at Pine Tree Farm while Richter
made trips to New York to talk to Joseph Collins about "Nerve Energy" and to
Asheville, North Carolina. In New York, Collins approved of Richter's manuscript and promised to help him find a trade publisher, but that was the only good
news he received. His agent Bill Breck told him that in the story market there

was "a decided change in the tone of successful stories—a young rather than an old note." Even the *Farm Journal*, Breck advised, wanted only stories of city life.[14] All over New York Richter witnessed signs of what he called "a flapper air, a country club air": "The city seems pleasure mad—a light air of inconsequence, a respect only for power, style, and money, and a disregard for such things as motivated John Burroughs, John Muir, and W. H. Hudson."[15] This was hardly the best time to offer "Melody in a Minor Key," and, as he guessed, it was returned to him shortly, rejected by seven magazines.

His second trip was more disappointing than the first. The weather was not only cold when he arrived in Asheville, it was a raw cold, "like a butcher's ice-box."[16] The town, to his eye, was slovenly and not at all prosperous, and the countryside, all low hills and scrub pines, had none of the natural beauty he needed to be happy. Nor did he care for the Southerners he talked to: "They have ease and poise, but they lack something," he noted in his journal, their minds seeming to take "familiar, charted and worn routes."[17] Richter's disappointment was so intense that it was physically painful. On his trip home he experienced a pain in his abdomen that grew to such intensity that in Richmond he left his hotel and spent the night in a hospital waiting room with a hot water bag placed on his stomach. He refused all other treatment. Once in Harrisburg Richter went immediately into Dr. Hartman's private hospital, where he reluctantly agreed to an emergency appendectomy. His opinion of doctors was not raised any when he awoke to discover that the surgeon had removed a healthy appendix, had even carried the pinkish bit of intestine out to show Harvey and Vene. The doctor's diagnosis: unusually acute gastritis.

When Richter returned to Pine Tree Farm after two weeks in a hospital bed, the issues of the farm, the business, and their residence for the near future were all decided upon. Harvey had taken a critical turn for the worse: as quickly as Richter could sell his business and farm, he would take her to Saranac Lake and then before winter to the Southwest. By the end of March Richter had sold his business to two of his competitors, the J. W. Wilcox and Follett Company of Chicago and the Evangelical Press, a Harrisburg wholesaler of religious books and supplies. When the notes were all cleared he had about $10,000 from the sales, a net profit of more than $3,000 a year for his brief ownership, in addition to the salary and dividends the business had paid him. The farm proved more difficult to sell, its $10,000 price placing it far above the means of the most likely buyers, his Clark's Valley neighbors. When spring passed without a substantial offer, Richter grew impatient and accepted a low bid from Donald McCormick, his banker, who took on the farm as an investment.

Within two weeks of the sale to McCormick, Richter and Harvey had sold, stored, and given away their furniture and household effects; found a home for Beowulf; and said their good-byes, some of them tearful, to their neighbors in Clark's Valley. They departed on a warm morning in early July, with Vene joining her father on the front seat of the family Dodge and Harvey reclining on the rear. They stopped first in Pine Grove, then drove on to Reading to his brother Joe's home. From there they continued on to Syracuse and the home of Fred and Emily Richter, where, on July 13, Richter invested some of his available cash in the business where Fred worked, the Onondaga Pottery Company, and in other stocks and bonds. All told, Richter had accumulated $18,000 in cash and negotiable mortgage and loan documents, enough, he believed, to support his family for five years. But of course he preferred to live as much as possible on interest and keep his principal intact, and so even at the beginning he was looking for bonds with a high yield and stocks with good potential for appreciation.

In his first journal entry from Saranac Lake, July 17, Richter remarked simply that he was "too tired, too worried over Harvena's cough to enjoy it here yet," but his description of the cabin they found—yellow pine sides, spruce rooms within, with knots everywhere—was approving. Richter had at first hoped that the family might stay together in a cabin, Harvey resting each day while father and daughter explored the countryside. But by July 21 he had visited four sanitariums, finally deciding on one on Franklin Avenue. On August 5 Richter and Vene moved to an apartment close to the sanitarium. It was small and bright, with modern furniture and a sugar maple outside the window, all of which were in its favor, and there Richter hoped to be able to write again. But he found he could not write anything to satisfy him, not even stories that, so often in the past, he had been able to turn out in two or three days of concentrated work. There were many distractions, including the woman overhead who was difficult and noisy, a banger of windows. When Vene reported she was also a wearer of lipstick, Richter smoldered, "I hope it poisons her."[18] In fact the whole artificiality of Saranac Lake upset him; it was a town with no reason for being but to provide care for tuberculars. He was even provoked by the sight of the many young people, recovered enough to be ambulatory, lounging about town in their stylish clothing. To his eye and ear they affected the mannerisms of the country club set, pretending to social stations, he imagined, that their hardworking parents were paying for. How much better to be sick among one's own people, like the ordinary folk of a Clark's Valley, who naturally sympathized. How different they were from the predatory residents of a town whose only source of livelihood was the sick and the dying.[19] Daily he visited with Harvena, keeping track of her afternoon fevers and listlessly lounging on her sleeping porch. In the presence of Harvey and Vene he kept on his bravest face, but he hated the forced idleness of Saranac Lake, he hated being separated from Harvey, and he was increasingly worried by her lack of progress. Almost a month exactly after Harvena entered the sanitarium, Richter insisted that she be examined by Dr. Price Woods, the doctor he decided was the area's most accomplished specialist.

Writing to his banker the day after that examination, Richter summarized Harvey's condition as bravely as he could: "An examination last night by perhaps the best specialist here was not encouraging, but we are trying to whistle and keep our courage up."[20] In truth the news from the examining specialist was worse than any Richter could have anticipated: instead of one tuber in one lung, as the Harrisburg doctors had all agreed, the specialist's fluoroscope showed one lung too riddled to be any longer functional and the other already infiltrated by visible tubers. Woods advised Richter to take his wife immediately to the Southwest. Only in the dry climate of the high desert was there any chance for a case as advanced as hers; and even there, he warned, Richter must understand that the Trudeau method would just hold in abeyance for a while longer what was inevitably a fatal case.

As bad as this news was, after a month of inaction and worry it was at least some relief to have a definite purpose and a destination. The night before departing, having sold his Dodge for $100 and bought three railroad tickets to Albuquerque, New Mexico, Richter wrote the final journal entry of his five weeks in Saranac Lake:

> For weeks I have done little or nothing—and I have not even health to show for it. I have driven the old car about the streets and hills, I have read the morning Saranac paper, the *New York Times* which came later, the evening local *Enterprise*; I have studied the stock market and the financial reviews and reports; I have calculated interest return and mental profit; I have wished it were cooler, less sultry, would clear off; I have sat on one of the beds on Harvey's sleeping porch or lay down on the apartment couch; I have done other useless things but mostly the above. Now we go tomorrow to New Mexico. I pray we may have a little home, a little work, and a little rest.[21]

Here as elsewhere the journal records Richter's inability to reconcile himself to a leisure life, his impatience with himself and with almost everything around him. There is a single exception. There is not a cross word about Vene, no word of even minor complaint or criticism. It is in just this, in what he does not say, that one senses how tightly he was holding on to her.

Two other events occurred at Saranac Lake that Richter would remember vividly. The first came about during the night of August 20, a kind of epiphanic bringing back of his childhood. Unable to sleep he heard the footsteps of someone outside, coming to the apartment house. Those sounds aroused in him the memory of Wednesday nights in Pine Grove, and he was once again a child, feeling the relief that came only on hearing the footsteps of his mother returning home from Guild Night. Soon she would be climbing the steps to tuck him in.[22] The second was decidedly more eerie. Startled out of sleep the very next night, Richter had the unpleasant sense of another presence in the room. Telling himself that it was not necessarily evil, he "let [himself] fall into a sleep or trance despite the repugnance." Moments later he felt "suddenly rigid, as if bound . . . by some powerful psychic chords." Unable to speak or move, he felt as he had at Dr. Hartman's hospital, when physically but not yet mentally under ether. Then from the window came a bar of bluish white light, burning into his left breast and on to his right. For a brief while he was apparently unconscious, waking to find himself weak and trembling. The next morning he remembered the experience clearly but no longer felt any dread or fear; in the daylight the coming of the blue light seemed no more frightening than if he had been in a hospital under a healing lamp. What could he make of this? He had only one thought: "I recall the stories of light the higher spirits in *The Survival of the Soul* directed, and sometimes I wonder if it were possible that I witnessed one of them."[23]

T W O

To the loafers at the Albuquerque train station of the Santa Fe Railroad, there was nothing unusual about the family that stepped from the train. A father, an obviously sick mother, and a young daughter: families just like this arrived each day to huddle hesitantly in the harsh white sunlight before making their way to a hotel or boardinghouse. These were simply "health seekers," as the polite of Albuquerque called them; those at the train station would more likely have called them "lungers." Their kind had been coming to Albuquerque since before the turn of the century, hoping to find a cure for tuberculosis in the frontier settlement. By 1915, 2,500 of the town's 11,000 residents were "chasing the cure."[24]

Many arrived in such desperate condition that they did not survive the first few days in the hot, dry air; others lingered for weeks or months before finally losing their battle with the white plague. But many others found something like the health they were seeking in the desert town a mile above sea level. Of the 18,000 people living in the Albuquerque area in 1928, thousands were "lungers" or recuperated "lungers," and thousands more were members of their families. Each year 350 to 500 new patients arrived—so many that it was said that the two sources of employment in Albuquerque were the Santa Fe Railroad and tuberculosis.

Richter had passed through the area in 1912 on his western trip from Cleveland, but his memories did not prepare him for what he would experience when he stepped into the bright light and heat of the station platform. The trip had taken six days, the train clacking and swaying its way through the East's farms and forests, across the Great Plains to Denver, and then south into New Mexico. With Harvey propped on pillows, they had watched the changing scenery outside their stateroom window. To Richter's surprise, northern New Mexico was much less barren than he expected, with flowering bushes and small pines dotting the hills and mesas, and further south he found the rolling desert broken by the mountains in the distance, the Sangre de Cristos, the Jemez, and the Sandias, all covered with the hazy blue green of piñon and ponderosa pine.

Albuquerque, he discovered that first day, was a western town of dusty roads and mixed houses, single-story adobes and bungalows of white clapboard and red brick. From the foothills of the Sandias, he could see the new skyscraper of eight stories prominently marking the business district and trace by the lines of gray-green cottonwoods the paths of the Rio Grande and the acequias, irrigation canals crisscrossing the valley farms and neighborhoods. Above everything, transfiguring the drab earth tones, spread an incredibly wide and brilliantly blue sky. Most of the newer homes were cottages with sleeping porches, designed and built specifically for the ever-arriving families of health seekers. These were interspersed among the other homes of Albuquerque, without restriction. Families with sources of income often rented these to be near relatives in the sanitariums. Families that had exhausted their capital often lived in these with the TB victim, their own private cure cottages.

Central Avenue ran through the middle of Albuquerque, from the university in the east to Oldtown in the west, near the Rio Grande. This was U.S. 66, the road that soon would carry the victims of the dust bowl from Texas and Oklahoma through Albuquerque to Arizona and on to California. In 1928 Central Avenue was for most of its length a quiet, sandy thoroughfare for local traffic, lined with so many private sanitariums that it was known as "san alley." Richter found Harvey a place at Sunset Lodge, just off Central Avenue on Gold Street, a modest, private facility for twenty patients. There Harvey would stay for over a year, attended by Dr. Leroy Peters, whose name Richter had brought from Saranac Lake as that of the most prominent of the lung specialists in New Mexico. Harvey would leave Sunset Lodge only once that fall, to visit several houses Richter was thinking of buying. Although she did not even step out of the car, she returned so exhausted that Richter did not consider asking Peters if he might take her out again.

Richter did not buy a house in Albuquerque; instead he continued to rent a small bungalow he found the first week, at 416 North Eleventh Street. Typical of Albuquerque homes built for health seekers, this single-story frame house contained four sparely furnished rooms and a sleeping porch facing west. One neighbor, Richter decided, was an "important personage" in her own estimation; he did not speak to her. Others were friendly enough, and there was something of a neighborhood life so that, everything considered, Richter and his daughter were soon well enough settled. But they were not comfortable, and when Richter and Vene visited Harvey midday for an hour, they talked of the new town and of their experiences exploring on its trolleys, but then they returned, often, to memories of Clark's Valley and Pennsylvania. Answering a letter from the Harrisburg banker Donald McCormick, Richter admitted that news from Pennsylvania gave them all "pangs of homesickness," adding that "my little girl plaintively mentions nearly every day that 'there is no place like Pine Tree Farm.'"[25]

Dr. Peters did not tell Richter until years later that, like Dr. Woods at Saranac Lake, he did not expect Harvey to live. He did warn Richter that, for there to be any hope for her, she must resign herself to many years in the Southwest. To a family already thinking of its time in New Mexico as a forced expatriation, this was not happy news. Nor could Richter take any encouragement in his carefully invested savings, which were already dwindling. The costs for Harvey's care were unexpectedly high, and so were living expenses for Richter and Vene. Days after their arrival in Albuquerque, Richter realized that $18,000 would not last them the five years he had expected, and no doubt this entered into the decision not to buy a house, but to save the principal for investment. He also delayed buying a car until November, finally choosing a used Chrysler similar to the Dodge he had sold at Saranac Lake.

Taking account of everything that fall, Richter could say that the best of their situation was that Harvey was in New Mexico, the most therapeutic climate for her, and that she was receiving the best medical attention available. The worst of their circumstance was that they were living on their savings, and he had overestimated how long they would be able to do so. Richter knew that to continue his work on his nerve theories, which he hoped to take up again, he had to supplement the interest from his invested savings. That meant writing short stories or perhaps a novel, he thought, and the pressure to write salable fiction grew when neither Dr. Collins nor Erd Brandt could interest a publisher in his "Nerve Energy and Its Management." Short stories written for the popular market seemed his only choice, and that meant stories of a kind he did not want to consider. To write such stories as those Erd Brandt had suggested violated Richter's ideas of inner evolution and his sense of his own life's purpose.

If his theories were correct, then he had a duty to explain them to others. But because such writing did not interest editors of magazines, reluctantly he turned to "stories that will sell, artificial fiction," for which he had "little interest except for the check, stories of youth and pep and criminals." He paid a high price in lost self-esteem, as he acknowledged somewhat melodramatically in his journal: "For what I have done, may God forgive me."[26] He wrote two stories that fall, "Sitting on Sally" in October and "Reprieve" in December. "Sitting on Sally" sold to *Farm Journal* in April; "Reprieve" was bought by the Munsey group of magazines, probably to be published in *Cavalier*, the magazine that in 1913 had purchased the first of his stories.

That fall Richter found himself increasingly troubled about his own health, and then his daughter's. First he had an attack of his "old enemy," a recurrence of the abdominal pain that the appendectomy had not cured. Later a nagging cough led him to worry that he too had contracted TB. At Harvey's insistence, Dr. Peters examined Richter on November 13. He found no signs of current activity, but there was, he reported, some scar tissue on one lung, signs of an earlier infection. This finding, of course, reminded Richter of the bar of bluish-white light he had experienced at Saranac Lake. Was this evidence that he had indeed experienced one of the interventions Cornillier's *The Survival of the Soul* had described? It was a hopeful thought that astral spirits had found him important enough to protect from tuberculosis, prodding him to continue his energy theories. But such speculation, unable to be confirmed, was only fleetingly encouraging.

By December both Richter and his daughter were suffering from bronchitis. He and Vene coughed through December and into January, months when the hazy smoke of cedar and piñon fires hung daily over Albuquerque, and Richter's bronchitis led to other complications including influenza and tonsillitis. Finally Richter agreed to a tonsillectomy, which was performed on the last day of January under a local anesthetic. He recuperated at Sunset Lodge, and because there was no place else for Vene to live, she too moved into the sanitarium for TB patients. Later Richter decided to remain with Harvey in the sanitarium. Of course that meant Vene did too.

Subject himself to so much ill health, it is no wonder that Richter summarized his first six months in New Mexico by writing in his journal, "I cannot be reconciled to this country. . . . What drab farms called ranches; what sordid adobe houses; what a cold bare outlook to the bare Sandias over the bald sand hills."[27] His journal does record numerous responses to the natural world of the high desert, but tied as he was to an alien landscape, to a "a life drab and hopeless," to "a sick wife and sick body,"[28] he felt the enchantment of New Mexico only fitfully. At times he responded with his old enthusiasm, especially in the spring. But the intensely bright sunlight and startlingly clear nighttime skies, full of the sharp sparks of stars, brought to him a sense of how large and cold a universe stretched out around him. His reconciliation did not really begin until late that spring.

By February 1929 May Achenbach, Harvey's sister and her closest friend, had arrived in the Southwest. Though also suffering from TB, May was in much better health than Harvey, well enough to work as a nurse at a local hospital. Her arrival may have prompted what was for Richter, given his hovering protectiveness over both Harvey and Vene, a curious decision. Perhaps it was for his health; more likely it was to find a place where he could write. Although he rented a spare room at Sunset Lodge as a study, he was not having any success writing there. Whatever the reason, he spent the month of May alone in a mountain cabin at Cedar Crest, a group of rustic cottages well above 7,000 feet in the Sandia Mountains. Richter called his cabin "Slabsides," the name John Burroughs had given his cabin above the Hudson in New York. There he spent his time writing, completing three stories among the ponderosa pines, the junipers and scrub oaks, the profusion of wildflowers growing from the soft brown earth. He wrote during the days listening to the chatter of birds, and at night, by kerosene lamp, to the scratching of mice and the flurries of wind sweeping slowly through the trees. For reading he had taken along Darwin's journals of South America and Algernon Blackwood's *Episodes Before Thirty*. Both were soon added to the collection of "his" books.

Richter's "Slabsides" was no hermitage. At Cedar Crest he met the first people who, like himself, preferred the wildness of nature to the conveniences of towns. He could talk to them easily. First he met the Dalbeys, who owned a ranch near his cabin, and the Tiltons, who ran the local store. Then he met the Sharps,

11. Vene rides a burro at the cabin at Cedar Crest in the Sandia Mountains, New Mexico, spring 1929. Richter named the cabin "Slabsides," after John Burroughs's cabin on the Hudson in New York.

who owned his cabin and lived in another near his. The Sharps knew the local countryside well and enjoyed showing it to a writer new to the area, looking for local color. He also met Edward Castetter that month. Chairman of the biology department of the University of New Mexico, Castetter was an expert on local flowers. With the Sharps, Richter went on various excursions that month, including drives into the Estancia Valley and to San Antonito, a village east of the Sandias, where he met Henry Schultz, the rug weaver Richter would later use as his model for the saint/seer in *The Mountain on the Desert*. On these excursions by car and on horseback, Richter found himself awakening to the "austere and bleak" landscape of New Mexico, its canyons and mesas, lonely but beautiful, its hills covered with the yellow-green bloom of chamisa. When Vene joined him at Slabsides after her school year was completed, he took her to Santa Fe and to Las Vegas, New Mexico—then a writers' colony—and to the Indian pueblos of Taos, Cochiti, and the numinously still Sky City of Acoma.

None of the three stories Richter wrote at Cedar Crest got further than Erd Brandt's desk. Brandt saw no chance for any, he wrote his client, because

Richter's stories, all set in the Southwest, betrayed that he himself did not have "any sympathy for any of these people," which was always "fatal."[29] The stories have not survived to verify that assessment, but it is likely that Brandt, later to demonstrate himself to be an especially appreciative reader of Richter's stories, was at least partly right. While Richter's feeling for the land was developing, he did not yet have the sympathetic identification with its people to be able to write convincingly about them. In his own terms, his inner evolution had not progressed far enough to allow him to understand the Southwest.

Richter did little writing of any kind after sending Brandt the three stories. His mind was more on his energy theories and on scientific evidence of an afterlife. One Scottish Presbyterian at Sunset Lodge, John Gardner, became a favorite sparring partner, Richter "bombarding [Gardner] with his psycho-energic theories" and Gardner countering these and Richter's other "anti-Christian" notions with Presbyterian doctrine as conservative and rigid as John Absalom Richter's Lutheranism. Richter pressed books about seances on Gardner, and the feisty Presbyterian made fun of these and also of Ouija boards, which had also caught Richter's interest.[30] Other than these ongoing disputes with Gardner, Richter spent his time idly, reading and exploring the countryside. Rereading Willa Cather's *The Professor's House* in early October, he lamented in his journal that his writing had "gone to seed." He had been doing little but sitting in front of a stock quotation board, visiting among the patients, and going to the movies. But Cather's novel reawakened his ambition: "I was alive again to the birthright I was trying to sell for a mess of pottage."[31]

More than a little of his time was spent worrying about Harvey. After almost a year in the Southwest, Harvey seemed hardly to have improved. To relieve the strain on her more damaged lung, Dr. Peters had tried thoracoplasty, a procedure to collapse the lung by injecting inert gas into the pleural cavity. When this did not appear to be successful, he recommended the surgical procedure of pneumolysis, burning the adhesions between the lung and the wall of the pleural cavity to allow the lung to collapse more completely. Peters had more than ten years' experience with these two procedures, having pioneered both in New Mexico, but pneumolysis was a difficult and lengthy surgery, under local anesthetic, and sometimes required more than one operation. Harvey had a first operation on September 17; she had two more before the year was over, each lasting more than three hours.

Before Harvey underwent the first of these operations, Richter made a long-considered move to increase his income from stocks. Until then he had bought stocks and bonds outright, making little on the bonds but gaining significant paper profits in stock appreciation in the still-bullish stock market. Enticed by this success, he sold his bonds and began buying stocks on margin. His thinking was that if he bought only the safest stocks and he kept his margins to 50 percent, he could purchase twice as many stocks, increasing his dividends and doubling his potential profits from market appreciation. The price for this was only a slightly greater risk than owning stocks outright, and in the extended bull market of 1928–29 investment houses not only encouraged such buying but lent the capital needed for these transactions. In effect the brokerages offered high-interest loans to investors, loans secured by the stocks themselves, which they kept as collateral. In this financial arrangement investors were betting that the stocks would appreciate faster than their debt grew on 8-to-10-percent loans. Banks and investment houses made a much safer bet, that the stocks would never drop so precipitously that they could not protect their investment by selling the stocks just at the point when the margins had completely eroded. A 50-percent margin meant that for Richter to be in danger of losing his stock, and therefore his savings, the stock's value would have to drop to half what he had paid for it. In the bull market of the late twenties such a decline was unthought of, and Richter purchased only high-quality stock. Even after a number of market dips early in 1929 and a more serious erosion in September, buying on margin was thought to be a sound investment practice. It would never be again after Tuesday, October 28, 1929, the day the market crashed.

Like thousands of others that night, Richter worked over the figures of what the stock market's calamitous fall had done to his investments. By midnight he knew that the unthinkable had happened: he had lost almost all his margin on almost all of his stocks. The day before they had been worth over $30,000; at the closing prices of October 28, his stock holdings totaled only $15,000. If he sold, or let the margin slip further so that his broker sold for him, he would lose all his savings. He would also lose all the money Harvey's sister May and his father John Richter had given him to invest for them.

Richter did not go to bed that night; even if he could have slept, he needed all the quiet hours to wrestle with the problem of just what to do when the banks opened in the morning. By daylight he made up his mind: he would ask the local bank to protect his stock temporarily, then he would write to friends to ask for loans to see him through until the market righted itself.[32] The bank trip took till mid-morning, for there were many others at the bank on the same errand. He spent the rest of the day crafting a letter to send to friends with capital. But first he sent a telegram to Donald McCormick, the Harrisburg banker, for he needed money quickly to protect his stocks. "I have been foolish in the stock market," the telegram began, and continued by asking for a loan on insurance policies held at McCormick's bank as part of a trust. It was a difficult telegram to send, and the letters that followed, to his father and his brother Fred, to his brother-in-law Art Achenbach, to Harry Hayden who had offered him the job with Handy Book Company, and to Charles Warfel, once a salesman working for him at Handy Book Company and by 1929 a successful businessman in California, got no easier to write as he typed to each the same story of his disastrous error. Each time he had to swallow the lump of pride in his throat. His only choice, these letters were nonetheless excruciatingly painful and damaging.

All but Donald McCormick responded immediately that they were sending the money or arranging for loans that they would co-sign, just as Richter asked. Asked the least and the only one offered collateral, McCormick refused. Outraged and devastated, Richter had no choice but to tell the Albuquerque bank that the bank he had dealt with for years had turned him down. To Richter's relief, the Albuquerque bank agreed to protect his stocks until he could himself borrow on his insurance policies, but even then he found himself forcing down his bitterness and writing a second time to McCormick. At the second request McCormick relented, but that would never assuage Richter's humiliation at having to write again to a man who had, without warning or reason, refused him.

As the story of the crash of 1929 and following bear market worked itself out over the next five years, Richter's good credit and reputation actually harmed him. He would have been much better off if he had been forced to abandon his stocks. But nobody could see that in fall 1929, when financial experts and bankers were all advising calm and patience for the inevitable return to prosperity. Even many of those who were wily enough to have gotten out of the market before the panic began got back in for the bargains, if not in 1929 then in 1930 or 1931, guessing that the market could not go lower. Those who did were themselves caught in the slide that would erode even the best stocks to a fraction of their 1929 highs. At the end of October 1929, Richter knew only that he was entirely without income, owing about $15,000 at 8 percent on stocks worth approximately that same amount. To recover his capital, he had to wait for the market to return, which could take a long, long time.

And losing all his money was not the worst of Richter's situation. Harvey's second operation to burn the adhesions did not allow the lung to be collapsed, and so in early December a third operation was performed. This operation did allow the collapse, Dr. Peters told Richter, and Harvey had once again gone through the ordeal without a murmur of complaint. But the next day Harvey's fever spiked to 103 and the day after that she was desperately close to death. Richter had few words to comfort his terrified and crying daughter, for nobody expected her mother to survive what turned out to be a week of raging fever.[33]

Nobody but Harvey. Later she said that she would have let go that week, simply given up her struggle, but she could not leave her family in such trouble.

Through most of his difficult times Richter relied on his journal as a place to vent his anguish and anger; the journal would be, as his daughter later described it, his wailing wall. But at moments of crisis with Harvey, Richter could not write in his journal; perhaps such times were too painful to record. After Harvey's third operation Richter abandoned his journal until late December, when his wife was finally out of danger, summarizing then the aftermath of her operation and the continuing slide of the stock market. Unable to afford Sunset Lodge, even for Harvena, he and Vene had moved to 720 West New York Avenue, a small house where he would personally nurse Harvey once she was able to leave the sanitarium. There his twelve-year-old daughter would have to take care of herself, for Richter would have to spend all his time with Harvey and the household, cooking and cleaning, saving what little time was left to write stories to sell to magazines. Vene was expected to help with the household duties—and with more than light cleaning and dish washing. One of her memories would be of washing the family's clothes in the bathtub.

In January the stock market rebounded somewhat, allowing Richter to borrow against his improved margins and repay some of his loans. The improvement made it possible for Vene to continue in a convent school, St. Vincent's, which was important to Richter, for he worried that Vene, shy and uncertain with children her own age, would not adjust easily to public school. If he still had the interest income from their lost $15,000, perhaps his small family could have scraped by. But whatever return his stocks brought went to pay his margin loans, and so he knew he had to write stories to sell to popular magazines, and write them quickly. Even before leaving Sunset Lodge, Richter made a second critical decision, as fateful as his choice to protect his stocks until they regained their value. At Harvey's urging he decided that, instead of trying to find a job, he would concentrate on writing stories. He allowed himself exactly a year, until November 1930; if by then he had not succeeded, he would give up the attempt and find a job. In the meantime he would borrow only to protect his stocks; the money they lived on had to come from his typewriter.

Just as soon as Dr. Peters would permit him, Richter took Harvey to their new home on New York Avenue. Although Harvey was still desperately ill—Peters was in effect giving up, releasing her to die at home with her family—

Richter was happy to get her into his own care.[34] He had relied on the best experts, and they had just about killed his wife. Now he would rely on himself and on his energy theories to restore Harvey. Each day he gave her "cocktails" of raw eggs beaten into orange juice. He rented a sun lamp for the exorbitant sum of $15 a month (their monthly rent, for a furnished home, was $50), and over Dr. Peters's objections he insisted that she take sun for a prescribed period each day—one minute on each side.[35] Although there was no dramatic recovery, little by little she did improve. On February 14, Valentine's Day, Richter recorded in his journal that Harvey had gained four pounds.

Richter continued to do all the nursing himself and he and Vene all the household chores, for there was no money for a nurse or a maid, and by early spring, when the market turned down again and no stories sold, sometimes there was almost no money for food. Richter wrote whenever he could, but primarily after Vene and Harvey were in bed each night. Like his first apprenticeship in his parents' home in Reading many years before, his family fell asleep to the sound of his typing. He began writing stories in November, immediately after he and his daughter moved to the house on New York Avenue. By Christmas he had sent Erd Brandt five stories; in January he sent two more, and in February, with Harvey at home to care for, he still managed to write a story and revise one of the December stories. By March he was desperate. None of the stories sold, and he was left with only pennies in his checking account. When he discovered a forgotten bank balance of $1.12 on the Harrisburg bank, he wrote a check for $1.00 and cashed it at the grocery story, bringing home a loaf of bread, a pound of butter, and a dozen eggs. At dinner that night sharp pangs went through him when Vene "asked gravely and for the first time in her life if she might have another piece of bread."[36]

There was no lamenting now that these stories were not what he wanted to be writing; his thoughts were on finding out what editors would buy at a time when businesses had little money for advertising in magazines. His own health, always closely watched and worried over, was not especially good that spring, whether from the strain of the long days or, as he fretted, from something looming much more serious. Thinking about the scars Dr. Peters had found on his lungs, he began keeping a record of his own temperature each afternoon. But he could not afford to be sick. Nor did he often admit, even in his journal, that the burden of it all, the growing debt, the daily household duties, the worries over Harvey and Vene, kept him in a state of melancholy, a "deep inner loneliness" as severe as any he could remember since his unhappiness in East Pittsburgh when he was sixteen.[37] Even depression was a luxury he could not afford. He cooked and cleaned, he cared for Harvey and Vene, and he wrote stories. When he could stand the suffocating restriction no longer, he slipped out to an afternoon matinee while Harvey slept, or took Vene for a late afternoon drive out onto the mesas.

The movies were primarily escapes, though Richter remained interested in how moviemakers told stories. The drives were escapes, too, but they were more than that; they became nurturing experiences and his primary source of pleasure. This was especially true when things looked blackest. Then his troubles seemed to sharpen his perceptions, making the countryside more inviting, lovelier. Desert flowers were brighter, the sky bluer, and cloud shadows scudding across the mesa more startlingly ominous. Even as his troubles piled up that spring, he could note in his journal, without any apparent sense of irony, that outside flowered "the loveliest spring" he had ever experienced.[38]

These outings would be all Richter had to look forward to as the months passed and Harvey showed no more improvement. In June he admitted in his journal that his wife was slipping from him and that there was nothing more he could do. All day she lay listlessly in bed, turning away from the food with which Richter attempted to entice her. Each afternoon her fever climbed to dangerous levels, and she looked "sallow, sad, in herself, like a woman who has given herself to religion."[39] One day she asked him to get for her several buckets of soil from Pine Tree Farm. She wanted to be buried with some of her beloved land below and some above her in her desert grave.[40]

Richter seemed not much better, looking so haggard that visitors thought that he too was an invalid. But he refused to see Dr. Peters again, unwilling to risk the effect that any confirmation of illness might have on him. Nor did he often let himself think about the grind that his life had become. By midsummer his afternoon drives were his only moments of freedom, and even the sight of the road north past the Sandia Mountains made him long to escape the worries and feelings of failure "written into the streets and the air of the city itself."[41] But each day he turned the 1926 Chrysler back to town, where his wife and daughter waited for him, and where the evidence continued to accumulate that the country was in a depression much more severe than that of 1920–21—when his stories had been almost unsalable. After its brief winter recovery the stock market spent the spring sliding downward. Public officials still advised patience, promising an eventual return to prosperity, but more and more people were finding themselves out of work. Isolated as it was from the rest of the nation, Albuquerque seemed less affected than many other places. But area ranchers were already beginning to struggle against debt, and eventually all but one of the local banks would be forced to close. Albuquerque was no place for an outsider to find a job, and the national magazines were buying very few stories.

Of the stories Richter wrote that winter and spring, only three sold, all stories in a series about a hard-driving mine foreman named Broady who had two-fisted answers for his job's toughest problems. They sold to *Blue Book Magazine*, each for $200, which brought Richter after agent's fees $540 for seven months' work—at a time when he was spending, still, more than $200 a month. Most of the stories Richter was writing were set in the Southwest, as stories of the summer before had been, and a number of these were, like the Broady stories, Richter's early attempts to write for a different class of magazine, the so-called pulp magazines, named for the poor quality paper these monthlies printed their stories on. In contrast to the "slicks" or "smooth-paper magazines," Richter's usual market, the pulps paid little for their stories, sometimes as low as one or two cents a word. But because their editors were not particularly concerned with originality, literary niceties, or even verisimilitude—only with action plots—good pulp writers turned out their yarns in a fraction of the time it took to write stories for the *Post* or the *American*. Some pulp writers made as much as $10,000 a year, Richter discovered from two local pulp writers, Paul Everman in Albuquerque and Ted Flynn in Santa Fe.

Everman and Flynn encouraged Richter to follow their example, helping him with plots and providing him with the names of magazines and editors. The pulp stories Richter wrote on their advice were declined by Erd Brandt, and so Richter found other agents. First there was Rosa Bake, who was Carl Clausen's agent for his detective stories. When after several months Rosa Bake had not sold any of his stories, Richter sent them to Sydney Sanders, who handled both pulps and smooth-paper stories. Having no more success than Rosa Bake, Sanders lasted only six months, but before he departed he offered a shrewd analysis of Richter's problem in getting sales. He was writing neither pulps nor slicks but something in the middle, relying on pulp plots but writing them in a smooth-paper style. In the same letter Sanders also offered a succinct summary of the story market. Simple wholesomeness would not sell any longer, at least not in the old formats, and simple wholesomeness was what Richter was writing, by and large.[42] Richter took this advice seriously, and he also took Ted Flynn's advice to try his agent, Marguerite Harper, who knew the pulp market well and, Flynn promised, would work hard to sell each story.

Richter's year to write was to end on November 1, 1930. Three months before his deadline, he recorded in his journal that in addition to his margin loans he was more than $2,500 in debt, with $20 in the bank and only $150 left on the margins of his stocks.[43] Although Harvey had recovered slightly, she was still bedridden and her care required most of Richter's time. A month before the deadline he had not sold anything but the three Broady stories to *Blue Book*. On October 11, two days before his fortieth birthday, Richter set for himself a new plan. He and Harvey would simply forget the $15,000 they had lost and work just to get themselves out of debt. First, he would borrow another $1,500 from friends, which was itself no easy task. Second, he would write pulp stories and smooth-paper stories so that he made $175 a month profit. If he could borrow $1,500, he could own outright, at their depressed prices, some of his best stocks held on margin. If he could sell $175 in stories, he would be able to make his interest payments on all his loans—almost $70 a month—and his family would be able to live, though penuriously, in Albuquerque. When the stock market rebounded, he would sell the stocks for something close to what they had been worth before, and that would be enough to get him out of the debt that had become increasingly a psychological burden as the interest on his loans mounted inexorably.

The prospect, however unlikely, was all Richter had, and for that reason it was worth the new humiliation of asking friends and relatives for money. Three turned him down, but four others did indeed lend him more than $1,500: his brother Fred borrowed $600 and sent it to him; his brother-in-law Arthur Achenbach took out another $500 loan for him; a friend from Harrisburg borrowed $400 from his children's bank accounts and sent that; and Charlie Warfel, one of those Richter had repaid the previous January, again sent him $500 as a personal loan. To Richter's surprise, one other man also came to his aid, the president of the Albuquerque bank from which Richter had been borrowing small amounts each month to protect his stocks. Richter had never met George Kaseman, reportedly the richest man in New Mexico, when he wrote to him asking him to do personally what his bank was on the verge of refusing to do further, continue to protect his stocks. One of a number of blind letters Richter sent out that fall asking for advice and help to protect his stocks (others went to such notable people as Cyrus McCormick and Owen Young, chairman of the board of General Electric), it sets out Richter's own sense of his situation, summarizing his business successes in Pennsylvania, his "independent scientific research," his reasons for buying stocks on margin, and his efforts to right himself since the crash. At letter's end he asks:

> Shall I sacrifice my holdings now at their pitiful panic prices, leaving me with heavy moral debts and little chance to continue the biggest work I

felt I was doing in my life? Or shall I borrow more from my friends and hang on? We have gone through a living hell for nearly a year. I don't mean the fact that I have been obliged to take care of my wife with my own hands, do the housework in addition and write stories far into the night. That was a pleasure. It was something I could do. I mean the worry, the fear, the realization of my terrible financial mistakes. Tonight when I came home from the bank I found that Mrs. Richter had been out of bed on her knees on the floor praying for nearly the entire time. We are almost crazy not only with our own trouble but the trouble we have caused others. . . .

I do not for a moment mean to intimate that you have any responsibility in my dilemma. But sometimes when our own powers fail and we are helpless to do more, we turn blindly to a stronger hand. If I ever needed a friend and counselor, I do tonight. If you can somehow see a way in which to guide me through this terrible experience so that I can escape the heavy, bitter penalty of losing my stock before my debts are paid, I earnestly promise you that the work still to come from a hand thus freed will help you to believe some future day that your effort may have been worthwhile.[44]

Kaseman agreed to help. He would protect Richter's stocks with his personal loan whenever the bank decided it no longer could.

Having borrowed the money, Richter then had to find markets for his stories. Writing in late October to Marguerite Harper, Richter summed up his resolve baldly: "I will do anything for checks."[45] At least he was looking up to better times, Richter thought, even though he was starting over with practically nothing but a few stocks bought with other people's money and some others held on dangerously thin margins. When the November deadline arrived Richter ignored it and kept on writing. But new trouble awaited in unanticipated places. In November, Harvey's sister May, her only close friend in Albuquerque, entered the hospital for what was supposed to be a simple surgical procedure. A week later she died of peritonitis. Richter was barely back in Albuquerque from accompanying May's casket to Chicago when word came that Arthur Achenbach, Harvey's favorite brother and Richter's good friend, had died unexpectedly from blood poisoning that had begun as a slight infection in his nose.

Not even Harvey's equanimity could stand two such blows. She was devastated, and so too was Richter—both at the loss of May and Art, and then at

Harvey's severe setback following the shock. A week after Arthur's death, Harvey told her husband that it was time to name her pallbearers. Richter did not try to talk her out of this formal acknowledgment that she was preparing for her own end; he only asked that she not name any of his friends. He owed them all too much already.[46]

THREE

Christmas 1930, like Christmas 1929, was not a time for family celebration, and Richter's low state of mind was raised only slightly by the arrival of Christmas checks for $50 each from his father and his brothers Joe and Fred. He put these checks into a savings account in Vene's name, a buffer against the next emergency. Marguerite Harper wrote that she had succeeded in placing one story, "Bull Pup Brown" with *High Spot Magazine* for $85, the lowest sale price he had received since the depression of 1921. The new year began and Richter continued as he had for months, nursing Harvey, sharing with his daughter the household chores, and writing whenever he could. He created a work schedule for himself, the first of many: Monday through Friday evenings he would write a weekly story, Saturday he would type and mail it, and Sunday he would do the heavier housework and catch up on errands and mail. On this schedule he was primarily writing pulp stories, but writing as well stories he thought might sell to the smooth papers, to work himself back into the better markets. As little as he liked writing popular stories, he liked the pulp westerns even less. And this antipathy was not helped by knowing that he was not good at them, though with Paul Everman's and Ted Flynn's help he was learning to craft stronger, more action-packed plots. Flynn was especially encouraging, visiting Richter and Harvey in Albuquerque, introducing him to other writers in Santa Fe, writing him long letters about the pulp markets.

For contact with other writers, Richter relied primarily on the mails. Taking his cue from Norman Reilly Raine, who had struck up a correspondence by writing to congratulate Richter on a story, Richter wrote to other writers whose stories he came across in magazines. In this way he began a number of correspondences, several of which he continued for decades. In the lonely days in Albuquerque, his letters to Omar Barker; Bill Adams of Dutch Flat, California; Kyle Crichton, a New Mexico writer editing for Scribner's in New York; and others, were chances to exchange practical information about markets and story rates and to commiserate about the weak magazine market.

Richter wrote daily through the winter and spring, finishing a story about every ten days. He was not able to keep to his schedule of a story a week, but he was pushing himself as hard as he could, and he was also pushing Harper for evidence that she too was working hard. He sent her requests for market information, for detailed summaries of what editors had said in rejecting stories, for the lists of magazines that had seen and rejected each story. He did this politely, but increasingly insistently, for he had reached the point, he wrote her, where it was either "get in a minimum of $200 a month or starve."[47] If he was thinking at all of his energy theories and his ideas for another book about them, he wrote nothing about these in his journal. His mind was on stories and sales, especially when Harper began to place his stories. By spring she had sold four pulp stories and three smooth papers. Although one of the pulps brought only $65 and the others less than $100 each, the smooth paper sales were more like earlier sales: *Liberty* bought two, "The High Places" and "The Heart of a Horseman"—both westerns—for $600 each, and *Country Home* took "Saddle Brothers" for $350.

But though he was selling at the rate he told Harper he had to sell or starve, he was not yet breaking even. Long before June he had been forced to use the $150 he had put into Vene's account, and he had borrowed against the few stocks he had bought outright with borrowed money—meaning he owed twice for the same stock. Most months he was signing personal notes to his landlord for half the $50 rent. In May Richter gave up the house on New York Avenue and moved his family to a cabin high in the Sandia Mountains. They moved to save money on rent, and they also moved to avoid the extreme heat of the desert summer, hoping that in the thin air Harvey would breathe more easily.

By the end of June Harvey and Vene were as fond of their cabin as Richter, enjoying the warm afternoons and cool nights, the trees and flowers, the songs of a hermit thrush. June also turned out to be Richter's best month ever for story sales, with Harper writing regularly to report acceptances that finally added to $1,200. They stayed at the cabin through the summer and fall, long after the other summer residents had returned to town. Vene went to school by car, over an hour's drive each way, traveling with the children of the Dalbeys, neighbors who lived in a house built for cold weather. They stayed because they had no money to move back into town, despite the year's sales. And they stayed because all three of them found the cabin in the mountains the happiest place they had been since Pine Tree Farm—even after the nights got so cold that the fireplace could not warm the cabin. They also stayed because, for the first time since coming to Albuquerque, Harvey seemed to be improving. Both she and Vene gained weight during the summer, and both seemed to keep their vigor even as the temperature dropped and the days shortened. Harvey held out for Christmas in the mountains, but in early December the family finally returned to Albuquerque. Vene was more and more unhappy about the long daily drive to school, and the temperature at night that high in the mountains sometimes dropped close to zero. To keep warm they had to push together two of the three beds and pile all their covers onto them.

Back in Albuquerque, Richter tallied up his year. He had written thirty-three stories, and fifteen had sold. In a time of extremely tough story markets, when magazines were finding it so hard to attract advertising that most were cutting back on size (soon even the *Saturday Evening Post* would be reduced from 210 pages to 102), his success rate was unusually good. Better yet, in a year when he had expected to rely primarily on pulp stories, he had made a number of sales to better magazines. These accounted for $2,800 of the $3,700 he grossed for the year, by far his best year ever.

The new home they rented reflected the family's optimism. It was the nicest home they had lived in during their time in the Southwest, with hardwood floors and a bright new kitchen and bathroom. It was also the most expensive, which Richter began worrying about the afternoon he rented it. Pressing Harper once again, he urged her to renewed effort. "We're flat," he wrote.[48] And they were, because he used the extra income that year to pay back loans and to buy school clothes for Vene, her first since coming to Albuquerque. He kept back nothing for a cushion, gambling that he could keep the sales coming.

Early Americana

O N E

For Conrad Richter the worst of the depression years was not the life of privation, but rather the continuing, even daily assault of that life on Richter's self-esteem. He could get by with a single threadbare suit. Many did. He could see Vene go off to school in clothes cut down from her Aunt May's wardrobe. He could stand by as his daughter divided a Milky Way candy bar in half, then sliced the half into thirds, one bit for herself and one each for her mother and father, the day's treat. He could put off paying the milkman and the landlady for another week, and he could write letters explaining to his creditors why he was unable to pay even the interest on money he owed. He could even endure the daily worry about how Harvey would hold up with less food and much more trouble than was good for her. After all, he had no choice. But throughout the weeks, months, and finally years of poverty, his heaviest load was not that his wife and daughter were deprived of normal comforts but that they were deprived because of his foolish mistake. His gambling in the stock market had gotten them into such a mess, and his efforts to extricate them only got them deeper and deeper into trouble. By February, 1932, Richter was $10,000 in debt, almost entirely money he had borrowed to protect stocks that had declined in value to only $2,000.[1]

To combat his sense of failure, Richter set for himself a rigid rectitude, built on his promise to himself that he would someday pay back all the money he had borrowed. While many others found relief in the courts, Richter refused to consider bankruptcy: the legal fees would just add to his debt, he said, because he would still have to pay back all his creditors regardless of what a court decreed.[2] This rectitude was not limited to his financial dealings. It pervaded his dealings with people, his impeccable propriety a carapace against the opinions of others. Even after he was reduced to a single business suit, he wore it whenever he left the house. Always secretive, Richter withdrew into an obsessive privacy during the depression, sometimes with unexpected effect. Ashamed that he was writing pulp stories, Richter ordered his daughter, a child of thirteen in 1930, not to tell anyone he was a writer. Vene took this injunction literally, and when neighbors asked what her father did for a living she stood silent, giving no answer at all. The rumor this may have led to, that Richter was a bootlegger, would have caused trouble if they had not lived so frugally that, though neighbors might repeat the rumor, few could actually believe it.[3]

Inside his home, Richter seemed to Vene little changed from how he had seemed throughout her life. If the day's writing went well and he was happy, he whistled tunes and sang hymns. If the writing went badly, he was glum and irritable, finding fault with everything. In his own way he doted on his daughter, even smothering her with care, though at times he was intensely critical of her, projecting onto her his worries about his own inadequacies. When Harvey's health began to improve, Richter was able to spend more hours each day working on his stories, usually writing at the dining room table. He worked best when he felt his family around him, and, surprisingly, he enjoyed having Vene play the piano while he worked. When writing, he expected both Harvey and Vene to be ready to help with plots or to listen to him read a section of a story, but otherwise he expected Vene and her mother to live their lives at an attentive hush so as not to disturb him. He was in a desperate battle for his family's welfare, and every bit of his energy and much of his wife's and daughter's needed to be turned to his stories. His fixation on his writing was utterly single-minded, much too concentrated for him to see other human needs, even those of an adolescent daughter. Vene would not be allowed to have a friend stay overnight until she graduated from college.[4]

After two years of sunlamp treatments and daily cocktails of orange juice and eggs, Harvey was finally declared by Dr. Peters to be out of danger. Although she still spent much of her time in bed, she moved about the house for several hours each day, helping with the cooking and cleaning. When friends visited, they found her reclining on a sofa in the living room, her husband hovering solicitously nearby.[5] As her health improved, Harvey joined her husband and daughter for their afternoon drives out onto the desert. On those trips Richter would make a bed for Harvey on the back seat of the blue Chrysler, propping her up with pillows so she could enjoy the view as they followed old wheel tracks across the mesas, losing themselves in the enchanting desert wilderness.[6]

For all the errands of ordinary life, Richter went out alone or with Vene, and on these outings he continued to depend on a public self, a manifest personality, as he had since Cleveland. But in Albuquerque he was not a young man with a promising future; he was a middle-aged man who had lost everything in the crash. In his dealings about town he tried to show himself to be sensible and self-controlled, down-to-earth yet sophisticated, modest but quietly confident. He kept special notebooks to coach himself on his demeanor in public, reminding himself before social gatherings to control his tongue, admitting after visits that he had talked too long or too effusively, bragged of a recent sale or compliment, confided too much or been too eager to please others.[7] Be reserved, he told himself, be pleasant but cool, expecting no favors. And when thanking others either in person or in letters do not be excessively grateful, for then they would think they had done enough and rest on that assumption.[8] He drank almost no alcoholic beverages, not because he believed in prohibition but because more than a taste of wine disrupted his sensitive nervous balance.

Typically people were more generous in their appraisal of Richter than he was of himself. Although he thought of himself as an unhappy combination of shyness, excitability, and hypersensitivity, others found him to be a likable fellow and a pleasant companion. Wherever they lived he made friends among his neighbors, and the friends he made were loyal ones, often for life. He was at his best with ordinary people, least on his guard, relishing the sharp local expressions and the friendly, easygoing ways of the common folk of the Southwest. A man of enthusiasms, he shared these eagerly once he began to be comfortable in a friendship, and with trusted friends his sense of humor came to the fore, as did his talent for mimicry. When amused, his face contorted in a comic grimace, laughing soundlessly. Even at his stiffest and most formal, talking to officers of the Albuquerque National Bank, Richter convinced people that he was what he genuinely was, a man of unimpeachable integrity. He was a risk worth taking, one his bank—even after every other bank in town had closed its doors in failure—continued to take. Slender and handsome in his suit and tie, he seemed more a businessman than a struggling writer.

Richter was never so fully convincing to himself, however. Against the ideal construct of what he wanted to be, what he actually accomplished was always a disappointment. But if he announced to himself over and over again that he was a failure, remarkably he never accepted that conclusion as his own personal doom. In what was a curious and lifelong habit of mind, Richter's acute despondency over his past errors would catalyze an equally intense resolve that the next regimen, the next plan for self-improvement, would bring him success.

In spring 1932, Richter decided to return to the cabin in the Sandias. It was to be a haven for his family until the story market improved, for Harper was able to sell only a few stories to pulp magazines in the first months of 1932. To make matters worse, stock prices dropped again and again. When March interest payments came due Richter had no money to pay them or the rent, and he was two months late on the milk bill. Then Harvey suffered a setback—and Dr. Peters took Richter aside to tell him it was caused by too much worry over money.[9] But though sick once again, Harvey had not lost her pluck: when Richter came to her on Easter eve, apologizing that he had been unable to find any flowers for a dollar, Harvey retorted that she did not want flowers, she would much rather have a beefsteak.[10]

The stock market's continuing slow collapse, the falling off of his story markets after such a strong spring and summer the year before, and Harvey's illness: these made 1932 the darkest time of the depression for Richter. Although he was to owe more money before his financial fortunes turned, he would look back on this time as when he had most felt "forgotten by God and man, or in disfavor with both."[11] Though uncharacteristically hyperbolic for Richter, perhaps this journal entry was not hyperbolic at all. After two years of writing pulp and popular stories, Richter still thought of such stories as unpleasant necessities. If he could just turn out pulps quickly or work his way back to selling stories to the better magazines, he could return at least occasionally to what he thought of as his real work—writing about nervous afflictions and the evolution of consciousness. But caught in an economy spiraling downward, all he could see before him were unending days writing stories he did not care about. He had no time to give to his theories and no time to develop a project he was then turning over in his mind. This was, he wrote to Joseph Collins, a new way of introducing his ideas to the average reader, one growing out of his experience in the Southwest.[12] Thinking about this project in spring and summer of 1932, he wrote some sketchy notes about "a Book for Your Life Work," a "Western Bible" that "might not get much attention at first but . . . that readers would come back to again and again."[13] If such a work indeed provided a better way to communicate his theories, then his coming to the Southwest would not be a "catastrophe" but "an unconscious pilgrimage."[14] His life again would take on meaning. But without relief from his debts, he could not pursue this work of explaining the ways of God to man.

Richter, Harvey, and Vene returned to the cabin in April. Hoping to arouse Marguerite Harper to his own sense of urgency, Richter wrote his agent that they were forced to the mountain cabin to save money.[15] That was in fact one reason, but another was that Harvey was eager to return. Even though Vene would have a long ride to school each day, Harvey believed they were all much happier in the mountains. By mid-April spring had arrived in the Sandias, with early flowers already in bloom and afternoon temperatures reaching 75 degrees in the shade. At night they could sleep on the porch, looking out through the shadows of pines and cedars and into the crystal stars of the desert sky.

Richter's blue Chrysler was battered but still running, allowing him to make regular trips to Albuquerque and occasional ones to Las Vegas, San Antonio, and Santa Fe to gather "color," authentic detail for his stories of the Southwest. He spent his happiest days in libraries and county court houses, losing himself in the yellowed documents and newspapers printed on paper carried by wagon train from the East. He also took pleasure in visiting old-timers who told him stories about the settling of the plains. He was on just such a visit to an old rancher in Quay County when he encountered a vista of the grassland that had once stretched across the desert, before the range was overgrazed by cattle and broken up by plows. It was like "a sea of grass," he remarked in his journal. Several years later, looking for a title for his first novel, he came across these words.[16]

In Albuquerque his best sources for color were Herbert Hardy and his wife Lou. A silver miner and rancher in his early manhood, Hardy had a precise memory for interesting details and a storyteller's ability to string them together, making him a treasure to Richter. So too was Judge Botts, retired from the bench but still active, sharp of mind, and happy to share his legal expertise about early land disputes between cattlemen and farmers. After visits to the Hardys, Judge Botts, or to any of his other sources, Richter recorded his information painstakingly in notebooks. The thickest of these was the one on "color" about the Old West; another that grew into a tome was a writer's dictionary of authentic language of the period, listing words and their usages as he heard them from old-timers and read them in early newspapers. From these Richter drew the rich detail to create the sense of the past and the salty western speech of his characters. There were also notebooks of story ideas, kernels for stories gleaned from accounts of actual experiences, one notebook for pulps and another for smooth-paper stories. Sitting over his collected material or reading accounts by participants in the individual adventures that made up the settling of the West, he felt most intimately the lives those early settlers had lived.

He was happier reading and thinking about the past than he was writing about it, which typically went agonizingly slowly. Plotting a story always took several days, even when writing pulps, and usually he found the process so difficult that he called on Harvey and Vene to help. When finally he was sure of his plot, he wrote each story in pieces, first a section by hand, then a typed version to read to Harvey and Vene. From their responses he would decide whether the section needed further work before going on to the next section, and when a section needed more work it often meant a problem with the plot and the need to worry out a new version of that. When he had completed all the story sections, he would rewrite the entire story at least twice more, reading each version to his wife and daughter. If they said good things about the story and seemed genuinely enthusiastic about it, then he would mail the story to his agent. Otherwise, he rewrote his story yet again.

When the writing was going well, he wrote everywhere, even sitting in his car out on a mesa. When the writing went slowly, he often suspected that the place where he was writing was to blame. He believed he could sense on first entering a house if he would be able to write there, feeling "the yeast of living" from former residents, a "human emanation" on which his writing fed.[17] Some houses were lucky for writing, as their first home in Reading, Pennsylvania, had been. He had sold several stories written there, including one to the *Saturday Evening Post.* Others were just unlucky, it seemed. A third reason for returning to the cabin in spring 1932 was that Richter had growing doubts about the Stanford Street house. Although he had written stories there as easily as he had at most other places, only four pulp stories sold. And he had discovered that the three previous families who had lived there, all from Pennsylvania, had all left the house in disastrous circumstances—two families after deaths and the third after declaring bankruptcy.[18]

Richter's hope to change his luck by changing his surroundings did not turn out well. Harper wrote infrequently to say she was working hard for sales even though the market was especially dry that year. But she gave suspiciously few particulars of what editors had rejected which stories or what they said in declining them. When she wrote that she was giving up her Manhattan office to work from her home, Richter began to look for a new agent, writing letters to Erd Brandt of Brandt and Brandt and to Kyle Crichton, the New Mexico writer working in New York for Scribner's. Although the mountain spring gave Richter and Harvey day after day of happy experiences, filling his journal with descriptions of the natural beauty surrounding them, he was increasingly upset about the trickle of sales. By the end of May these totaled only six pulp stories and one smooth-paper story, and the smooth-paper story Harper did sell, "Her People of the Patch," sold at the lowest price *Liberty* had yet paid—$400, $200 less than the magazine had paid a year earlier. He wrote daily, completing a story about every ten days. But though he was writing stories that he, Harvey, and Vene thought were better than the stories of the previous year, his sales lagged far behind.

In May Richter began to worry again about Harvey. It was not that she grew worse, only that she did not improve from her setback in February as she should have with the coming of warmer weather. While her tuberculosis was officially recorded as arrested, Richter lived with the fragility of her health. Any change could upset it, he knew, even changes in the weather. Certainly it would be affected by a pregnancy. In June Richter sent Vene off to an overnight Girl Scout camp. When she returned she found her mother in bed and a nurse taking care of her. Her mother would be better soon, Richter told Vene, she need not worry. He did not tell her that while she was at camp a doctor had come from town to perform an abortion. Nor would he ever tell her.[19]

The procedure was of course a medical necessity; Harvey was not physically able to carry a pregnancy to term. But the decision was no less harrowing, nor her recovery any easier for the knowledge that there had been no alternative. Trying to keep his own delicate balance, Richter worked at his writing as best he could, pressing Harper for sales or at least information. As with other crises concerning Harvey, he kept his feelings locked within him. The only betrayal of the intensity of his feeling came in a letter to Harper sending a story with the title "You Don't Understand": "I've got to get some money," he wrote, "I've simply GOT TO."[20] When he wrote a week later, he again had control of his voice, recapturing the amiable formality he kept throughout their correspondence. He would not tell Harper or anyone that he had lost his chance for a second child, on top of all his other losses. He set himself back to work writing stories, hoping for sales of any kind.

Just at the time when Richter was focused on Harvey's emergency, a letter arrived from Paul R. Reynolds, a well-known New York literary agent. Richter had dealt with Reynolds briefly in 1915, when Reynolds had sold one story and the second serial rights to "Brothers of No Kin" before declining "The Laughter of Leen" as an unsalable war story, thus ending their relationship. Now he wrote to say he had read a Richter story in *Liberty* and to ask if Richter needed an agent to represent him. One register of Richter's state of mind was that he let Reynolds's letter sit unanswered for almost two weeks. He did write to ask Kyle Crichton for advice, who responded sensibly that though Reynolds was well known as a fine agent for selling to the better magazines, he was uninformed about pulps and probably unable to sell them effectively. But before Crichton's answer arrived Richter had written to Reynolds, laying out his needs and as much about his personal circumstances as he confided to anyone. When Reynolds answered, Richter liked the candor of his reply, which only promised, it seemed to Richter, what he could actually deliver. Although the gamble was a long chance, and certainly not the safest choice if Reynolds, like Brandt and Brandt, could not sell pulps, Richter decided to take it. He liked Reynolds's tone, and he liked that Reynolds sought him out, placing some extra burden on himself to find sales. But perhaps most of all Richter was encouraged by the timeliness of Reynolds's letter.

Could Reynolds's letter be a sign? he asked himself. Did its arrival at such an unhappy moment, when his mind could not really focus on his writing, mean that fate or God or whatever force intervened in men's lives was finally sending relief, after his years of failure and distress? Richter was still predisposed to believe that such outside help could happen. He had not forgotten Cornillier's *The Survival of the Soul*, in which a spirit from the astral confided that on occasion spirits did indeed intervene in lives, attempting to influence personal evolution. Furthermore, he continued to wonder if other events in his life were not instances of such intervention. During the first fall in Albuquerque, when Richter was deciding to buy a car, he explained in his journal his reasons for choosing the used Chrysler: it was a serviceable car; the dealership would give him an extra $200 off; and just at that moment a garage to keep it in became available. Were the price reduction and the garage simply coincidences? Perhaps. To Richter they were possible signs, bits of persuasion from the astral to lead him into a choice he otherwise might have missed.

There were other such events earlier in his life, and many later, that Richter would think of as possible influences from the astral. Although instances of Richter's interest in the occult occur as early as 1912, when he was twenty-two years old, this line of thought seems to have become prominent during times of his deepest distress. The death of his mother was one such time, and it was during this period that Richter read *The Survival of the Soul*. Richter pursued the ideas of *The Survival of the Soul* as many pursue astrology: if he was not wholly convinced and committed, he was nonetheless infatuated and even unwilling to disbelieve, especially in difficult times. On such occasions he scrutinized every untoward event or even normal happenings as potential omens or imperfect communications. In Albuquerque, Richter began to take notice of the red traffic lights at intersections that delayed him as he went about his errands, becoming especially attentive when driving to the post office to mail a story to his agent. He often recorded how many times his errand was interrupted, either going or coming. Red lights suggested, he speculated, that he was being warned not to count on a sale. A trip with all green lights perhaps meant that the story would be unimpeded on its way to publication.

In January 1932 Richter began a special notebook, writing on its cover "A Record of Dreams, Signs, Etc. To Examine Later to See if Any Prove True," a log of possible instances of communication from the astral. In this notebook of 150 pages and more than a thousand entries, many items are summaries of his, Harvey's, and occasionally Vene's dreams; others are songs, often hymns from his father's churches, snatches of tunes he found himself humming, whistling, or singing. When he could remember them, he wrote the song's words in his note-book; when he could not, he taxed his memory to bring them back. Although he wrote little about whether these signs turned out to be true portents, Richter entered items regularly for decades.

Out of context, Richter's fascination with the occult may seem an idio-syncrasy, a foible not very significant to his writing. Within the context of his family's collection of shared experiences with the supernatural and his own care-ful reading of work such as Cornillier's, his attentiveness to signs is more under-standable and more significant. His mother's vision of dignitaries visiting his cradle, the family belief that friendly spirits shared Aunt Lizzie's house, Harvey's visitation by her mother at Vene's birth—all these were a family legacy of inti-mate congress with the spirit world. So too was Harvey's story of her sister Alma, who as she was dying of tuberculosis promised her best friend Margaret Yocum that she would always be with her: thereafter when Margaret sat on her family's porch, the rocking chair next to her would begin swaying.[21] The stories from his past, the attempts to establish contact with his mother at seances, the "hits" and "misses" he recorded at these sessions—this background moved quickly to the foreground in times of trouble. Then, too, there was the experience with the mysterious blue light at Saranac Lake, followed by Dr. Peters's remark a few months later that one of his lungs showed scars from a healed tubercle. Never wholly believing but always wanting to believe, Richter lived in a daily aware-ness, a deliberate wariness, alert to any possible sign of help or warning. So too did Harvey, who shared his preoccupation and was if anything even more con-vinced, sometimes experiencing "bubbly" sensations inside her that seemed to portend coming good news. Reynolds's letter was just such an event, an item for Richter's notebook of dreams and possible signs. Years later Richter began a special page of that notebook, writing at the top of the sheet "To Try to Examine 'Providence' in Our Lives—To See If Results Were Good, Bad or Both." Immediately below this he wrote "Reynolds's letter out of the clear sky."

On June 30 Richter airmailed to Reynolds the story he had just finished, "Henry's Blood of the Tsars," and by the end of August he had sent Reynolds six more stories. In July Reynolds wrote that he was taking one of these stories, "A Little Lower than the Angels," personally to the editor of McCall's; but a month later he had to report that McCall's had rejected the story and he had not been able to place any of the others. How Richter was bearing up against these disappointments would be revealed in his journal for August 20, 1932: "Black, Blackest Yet: No story has sold for four months except one in June for $54. . . . I have insurance due in a few days. School starts in Albuquerque and we cannot think of moving in for Vene to start it. We owe Dalbeys around $200—interest to everyone for six months."

Later that same day Richter returned to his journal to write another entry, about what he would call "the mocking nature of fate." In it Richter lays out the crux of his argument with God: if there was a plan of life, an evolutionary pro-cess, why did not the powers overseeing this evolution of consciousness intercede in ways that would demonstrate their active concern? Why did so much of what happened seem random, or—worse—deliberately teasing and bedeviling? Unable to believe as his father did that man was simply too humble an instrument to comprehend the meaningful whole of God's creation, Richter would struggle with the problem throughout his life, hoping that such a noble plan would ulti-mately reveal itself and fearing that the idea was the chimera of his own dreaming. If he could never calm his grappling spirit into an accepting faith, neither did he allow himself to slip into the despair of what for him was the ultimate nightmare, a vision of himself as a mind without sponsorship amid Russell's "secular hurryings through space." But that terror was never far away.

TWO

Richter and his family remained in their cabin at Sandia Park even later than they had the year before, living frugally. On Christmas Day they departed for Tucson, Arizona, pulling a used trailer behind their Chrysler. In the lower altitude and more moderate winter of Tucson they hoped Harvey would fare better than she did in the coldest months in New Mexico, and they may well have chosen to make the move because of the impending closing of the Albuquerque schools. The school board had run out of money.

At the end of 1932 times were at their worst in the Southwest, as they were in most other areas of the country. In November Richter joined with the rest of the country in electing Franklin Roosevelt president, his only vote for a Democratic presidential candidate in his life. Although uneasy about what seemed to him Roosevelt's reckless proposals, his vote was a protest against a privileged financial community and the "rich who have fattened like octopuses" by protecting themselves with inside knowledge during the stock market failure. He blamed them for what happened to him, but he also blamed himself, as he wrote to a friend: "I have been hard hit at the hands of these swollen rich the past several years. It was, however, my own fault for trusting or believing them."[22]

In Tucson the family found a small, pleasant house on a narrow street near the campus of the University of Arizona. The winter there did turn out to be milder and the food cheaper than in Albuquerque, and the local schools remained open for Vene, which were all to the good. But Harvey suffered another relapse, and in spite of his pleasant daily walks on the university campus Richter could not settle comfortably into the new environment. He missed New Mexico, he wrote Paul Everman, and though he had made the acquaintance of George Maddox, a retired army colonel who wrote poems for the *Atlantic*, he missed his writing friends in Albuquerque and Santa Fe.[23] Just as soon as Vene's school year ended, they packed up the trailer and said good-bye to the friends they had made, including Colonel Maddox, who soon thereafter initiated a correspondence that continued for over thirty years. When they arrived at the cabin at Sandia Park, they still owed $100 to the Dalbeys for the previous year's rent and several hundred dollars to Carter's store.

During the first days at the cabin, Richter was in especially low spirits, calling the first hour of his day "zero hour," the time when he awoke again to his troubles. It reminded him of the first days after the death of his mother, awaking from sleep into renewed pain, feeling "heavy, hopeless beyond words."[24] Nonetheless he would climb out of his depression to write each day, and Reynolds sold several of the stories Richter sent to him. In September there was just enough money to rent a house at 305 North Carlisle Street, at the northeastern edge of Albuquerque. Beyond their house North Carlisle turned into wheel tracks across the sandy mesa. Vene reentered school, and Richter settled down to his daily writing, broken by visits to early settlers for color, drives on the mesas, and meetings of Hammer and Tongs, a discussion club he was invited to join. Composed primarily of a few faculty members of the University of New Mexico and several prominent professional men, Hammer and Tongs met twice monthly to discuss topics in politics, science, and the arts. Dean Matthews of the Episcopal Cathedral evidently was responsible for Richter's invitation, Matthews having come to know Richter when the writer visited him to gather color. Pleased to be invited among such successful men, Richter overcame his misgivings about his shyness. Each meeting a member read a paper, and this meant that Richter would eventually have to speak in public for the first time in his adult life. Nonetheless, he attended and participated modestly, enjoying the breaks from his solitary regimen of writing.

If Richter counted on story sales to cover the extra expense of living in Albuquerque, he was disappointed: he sold only three pulp stories during the remainder of the year. By November Richter was desperate enough to be casting lines, once again, in every direction. He wrote letters to prospective agents, including Erd Brandt of Brandt and Brandt. He wrote Dr. George St. Clair, head of New Mexico's English department, to propose himself as a tutor for students who wanted to learn to write stories.[25] Two weeks later he wrote to another stranger, the president of the United States, asking his help in finding work. Shortly thereafter he wrote to Charles Kettering, chairman of the board of General Motors, and to Harold Ickes, Secretary of the Interior, making the same request. In reply he received only pleasant refusals. But Charlie Warfel, the former salesman for the Handy Book Company who had become a successful businessman in California, was much more encouraging. Warfel wrote to say he occasionally needed a good manager when his debt collection service had to replace officers of companies that had been badly run. If Richter were in California, he'd be on the spot when such an occasion came up again.

After years of struggling in New Mexico, Richter found the thought almost irresistibly inviting. Winter was coming on quickly, and their latest house, drafty and heated by ineffective space heaters, would not keep them warm. Unwilling throughout their difficulties to spend money on himself, Richter had only a few remaining pieces of clothing which were wearable: a light suit, a few shirts, two pairs of shoes, some old stockings, a hat, and a light coat. He was selling only pulp stories, and these were increasingly difficult to write, taking him just as long to complete as stories for better magazines.[26] Late in November, his exasperation with a pulp story, "Cotter's Saturday Night," led to a fight with Harvey. (These angry and utterly unsatisfying confrontations with his wife were common enough so that a single word had come to summarize them in his journal: "Trouble.") Unable to work out a plot, he asked for his wife's help and did not get it. That led to harsh words and sullen silences. "At least," he griped in his journal, "she's refusing outside to do any of those things which inside she has been refusing to do all along."[27] It was his "darkest day yet," and in such darkness California seemed a faint light at the end of a long tunnel. "California beckons," he wrote in his journal, "yet we stay because Vene wants to finish school here and there is so much color I haven't gathered."[28]

On December 5 he concocted another plan to turn out stories on a schedule, but a week later he admitted that his writing had faltered and he was again discouraged. His unhappiness and consequent irritability led to another angry row with Harvena, described in his shortest journal entry of the year: *"Blue Again. Trouble. No sales."*[29] The next day a letter arrived from Paul Reynolds saying that, though *Short Stories* had taken "Cotter's Saturday Night," it had reduced his rate to a cent and a quarter a word. That afternoon Richter sat down to write letters to Charles Kettering and Harold Ickes, near the point of abandoning what had stretched into a four-year effort to live by his writing. But his spirits improved with a night's sleep. His next journal entry began, "Black, yet Happy. Wrote 3,000 words. My big day despite felt terrible. Last night read 'Northern Gold' and 'Hell's Fire Hogan' [early pulp stories]. Was amazed how I have improved since then." Later in the entry came an explanation for his change of mood: "Harvey is now determined we shall win out and is doing something about it."[30] By this Richter meant, evidently, that his wife was offering more than just encouraging words. The next evening Harvey stayed with him at the supper table until after 10 P.M., working out the "trickiest" plot Richter thought he had ever tried.

The key to writing successful stories, Richter decided, was to get each story idea entirely plotted before he began to write. To accomplish this he relied heavily on his wife and daughter, testing out his ideas on them and then taking their thoughts back to the dining room table to work out an improved plot. He relied on Vene especially, whose reading was growing increasingly sophisticated as she studied classics in school. Vene was already writing accomplished poetry: Dean Matthews read one of her poems at that year's Christmas Eve service at the Episcopal Cathedral in Albuquerque, and another poem appeared in the *New Mexico Quarterly*. The family's single luxury for Christmas that year was to print one of Vene's poems as their Christmas card. Richter took the poem to the printers on December 18, and then he and Vene went to the mountains to cut a Christmas tree. The next day a copy of *Liberty* arrived with several letters praising a story that had appeared in the same issue as "Hoofbeat, Heartbeat." There were no letters about Richter's story. That afternoon at the bank his voice broke as he explained to Fred White, the vice president, that he could not make his interest payment. He had to walk away to save himself from breaking down even further.[31]

On December 22, the family began yet another plan, with every household activity arranged to accommodate Richter's work schedule. It was another grab at a straw of hope. When Richter picked up his Christmas cards from the printer, he discovered a significant misprint: the word *wreath* had become *wealth*. Was the printer's error a sign? At any rate it improved the family's spirits. So too did an encouraging letter from Paul Reynolds, saying the sparse sales were simply a consequence of the reduced market and that together they would succeed "if we both do our best."[32]

Richter began plotting a new smooth-paper story, "Valhalla," on December 29. This story was to be about an aged ranch hand whose yarns of the past are too tall for everyone but a young boy, who does not understand the reasons for conflict between his friend and his family. Telling the story from the perspective of an unknowing boy was a new narrative strategy for Richter, creating problems first in plotting and then in writing. These false starts he shared with Harvey and Vene, but with a notable change: he carefully kept to himself his worries about not being able to work the problems out, and by January 4 he was sure he had his story.

Richter worked on "Valhalla" all that day, to the last minute before the evening's Hammer and Tongs meeting. There Richter joined the discussion more vigorously than usual, bringing in part of his energy theory to explain "God's use of War, etc." Evidently his attempt did not go well. It was "a poor effort," he wrote disconsolately in his journal, concluding that his ideas were of no interest to the other members, who would only "smile and consider me a sort of nut."[33]

The next morning Richter was too "full of regrets" about his participation the preceding night to do much except brood over his error, though as usual he found a way to see his humiliation as a lesson. It was, he told himself, "a failure for me except that it taught me what I must not do."[34] He must keep his ideas to himself until he could present them in writing in his Western Bible.

Over the next several days Richter worked fitfully, replotting and rewriting a story that seemed to him to be more difficult to work out than any other. He read all he had written to Harvey and Vene on the evening of the tenth, noting carefully Vene's enthusiastic comments and Harvey's more reserved ones. Feeling worn down, nervous, and "not tired so much as dazed" after each writing session, he worked on, containing his worries. When Richter took an afternoon break to drive out onto the mesa, the sight of freight cars along a railroad siding tricked him for a moment into believing he had somehow escaped his problems: "I was somewhere far from Albuquerque, and I could have cried with joy and delight."[35]

Richter completed his first draft of "Valhalla" on January 15, writing the final two thousand words that afternoon. The next day he returned from the bank "very blue," but he kept his feelings to himself and succeeded finally in a substantial revision, "cutting, cutting," repeating to himself "I can do it" and "I must believe."[36] The next day he decided the middle of the story needed more interest and rewrote that. After two more days rewriting, on the night of January 18 he read the story to his family and recorded the responses: "When I was finished H[arvey] said it was marvelous. Vene said she was stunned for the first time I had read one of my stories. . . . Tears were in both H[arvey's] and V[ene]'s eyes at end."[37] Typing the story, he found himself still satisfied with it. Here was a story he was proud he had written, for it exemplified the values of the West rather than caricatured them, as he had to do in pulps. He mailed "Valhalla" on January 22, slightly more than three weeks after he had started it.

Although it did not ultimately sell to a better magazine than *Blue Book*, the best of the pulps, Richter was right that he was making progress in his writing. "Valhalla" was tightly constructed with clear, precise characters and convincing dialogue, as were all his recent stories, and its incidents were if not wholly realistic at least well enough prepared for so that the growing intensity of the story was not disrupted by implausible events. If its conclusion slipped into sentimentality, the focus and feel of the story, even hours after reading, remained sharp, as Harvey and Vene reported. But though it was a deftly conceived and constructed story, professionally crafted, it did not quite have that something which, when Richter finally found it, would stir readers into immediate and empathetic identification. It missed, but it just missed.

Two days after mailing "Valhalla" Richter was still enthusiastic enough about his story to put off writing a pulp story and to try instead a tale told him by an elderly woman in Albuquerque. The summer before, Red Dow, a laundryman who delivered to homes at Cedar Crest, had encouraged Richter to talk to his mother, Isabel McAtee Dow, who had known Billy the Kid. Having heard that claim before, Richter expected little when he visited Mrs. Dow, mostly as a courtesy to the laundry deliveryman who had talked so enthusiastically about his mother's stories. As Richter suspected, she had little to offer about Billy the Kid, but among the anecdotes Mrs. Dow shared that day was one about her own experience traveling with her adolescent brother across a vast expanse of dangerous country. Richter immediately saw in this the possibility of a good story. That thought remained with him, and on January 20, while finishing "Valhalla," he again visited Mrs. Dow and had her retell her story.

Here was a story to test his newfound ability to create mood, and he set to work with the tools he had learned writing pulp stories, starting immediately with a sense of impending danger: "For two days the leathery face of Asa Putnam had been a document in cipher to anyone who could read the code." But this would be no pulp story, relying on fistfights and shoot-outs to energize a wooden plot. This time he would create a real place and put real people within it, allowing them to live in a world where ordinary living made choices unusually consequential. To get to her wedding, Asa Putnam's seventeen-year-old daughter Nancy Belle would travel two hundred miles—five days by wagon—across a lonely, desolate wilderness, despite signs of an Indian uprising. That would be the obstruction of the story, the two hundred miles of desert with its threats of wind, storm, and Indians separating Nancy Belle from her marriage. What gave the story its special meaning was the unstated acknowledgment of each character that, as dangerous as such a desert journey was, the trip was only reasonable for Nancy Belle to make: it was a choice of ordinary living.

Richter made this story different from the usual western tale by making it a woman's story, told from Nancy Belle's perspective. Another writer might have told the story from the perspective of Rife, her younger brother. Perhaps Richter would have himself, not trusting his sense of a woman's world, but Mrs. Dow gave him the story and Mrs. Hardy helped with details that a woman would see and remember. In the West that Richter imagined, sitting over his notes of old-time western ways, women endured as men did. Their hardships and dangers were essentially the same, though often men chose to keep the details of the danger from their wives and daughters. Oddly enough, stories of frontier women had seldom been told and so had not yet been turned into triteness.

Two days before Richter began writing "Early Marriage" Paul Everman died of tuberculosis. The following day Richter visited Mrs. Everman and then, trying to put aside his sorrow, visited the Hardys for color. That evening he settled in his mind that he had his plot, but the next day he worked exceptionally slowly, writing a single page over and over again. The day after he managed three more pages, one each in his writing sessions of morning, afternoon, and night. Hoping he had his beginning, he read the four pages to Harvey and Vene. "Both enthusiastic," he noted; "Eyes of both shining."[38] Stimulated by their reactions, he completed thirty-five pages of draft by the end of the thirtieth. But then he wilted: "I could think of snatches of what I wanted to say. But I couldn't say it on paper except thinly."[39] He seemed to have lost all the energy reserves he needed for his writing. Then came a second setback. Paul R. Reynolds, Jr., in partnership with his father but not normally corresponding with Richter, wrote with a list of rejections for several stories and concluded by commenting that he thought the atmosphere of "Valhalla" "almost ran away with the story,"[40] making it hard to follow. Although Reynolds added that his was "just a personal reaction," Richter was crestfallen. Unable to write, he spent the day typing his handwritten draft of "Early Marriage."

Finishing up that evening, Richter still thought he had a good story in "Early Marriage," even though its growing suspense did not lead to an action-filled climax and though the full reality of the danger, because it was withheld from Nancy Belle, was implied rather than dramatized. He read his draft to Harvey and Vene, noting carefully Harvey's criticisms. The opening scene with father and daughter was not strong enough; there was not enough suspense for the Indians; the girl herself was not vivid enough. Even so, Harvey said, it was better than "Valhalla" and had a better chance of selling to the *Saturday Evening Post*. Vene agreed, exclaiming that it was the "most real story" she had ever heard, the best chance for the *Post* of any story her father had done. By all means he should insist that Reynolds send it first to the *Post*, even if the extra wait meant she had to walk to school because they had no money for the bus.[41]

Richter awoke the next morning with an unexpected inner sense of confidence: his "old eternal fear, worry over money," had "vanished." Although the rent was already days overdue and they had only enough money for food for another two weeks, he was "neither frantic nor distracted." Was this, he asked, due to an inner satisfaction from writing a story that was "so near to my heart that it generates a wall of confidence"? Was it inner strength from physical and mental discipline and from "keeping things to myself"?[42] Or was it simply the energy released to the body by a subconscious mind already anticipating that bad news was coming? The rewriting went steadily forward until a final version was ready to send to Reynolds. On Tuesday Richter gave Harvey the story to read herself, and later recorded her reaction. She said it "moved her more than any story I had written, excepting 'The Bells of San Angelo' [which would never sell] and 'Early Marriage' was more tensing and stronger."[43]

The word Harvena chose to describe his story, "tensing," was one Richter had begun to use about his writing—though he meant by it a part of his process rather than his product. Tensing was the special, concentrated focusing of his own energy that Richter needed to create the intimate and sharp immediacy of a story's core, the ineffable presence to be found only in the best stories he knew. He was sure he had achieved such a presence in "Brothers of No Kin" and believed he had come close in other stories. Now he felt this immediacy in "Early Marriage." It came from mood, which he was learning to create, but it was more than that. It came from his precise description of the landscape, a true expression of the acutely vibrant beauty he himself experienced when at his unhappiest. It came from his admiring portrait of ordinary people whose lives demanded of them more than ordinary character. And it came from an unexplainable instinct for the right relationship, as when Nancy Belle prays, after her marriage vows, entangling her memory of her father in her love for her husband. Somehow his concentrated focusing, his tensing, gave his story the special quality he had been trying so long to achieve. As he read it, his story lifted from the typewritten page.

"What I Believe It Is," he entitled the second part of his journal entry for that Tuesday, trying to explain his feeling of strength and personal power. "I believe it is my keeping things to myself, building up energy to strong reserve cells, self-control in saying things—plus physical reserves." Here he spoke in the language of *Human Vibration;* later he elaborated anecdotally: "Half a dozen times today I silenced myself from saying an enthusiastic—and even once or twice an unpleasant—needless thing. . . . Strong men who accomplish—scheming men—men with that driving power—say little or nothing about their intentions, feelings, and affairs. Perhaps that is the cause of it."[44] Whatever the source, he felt that strength in himself as he read "Early Marriage."

The feeling lasted only until Wednesday, when he was listless after mailing "Early Marriage" to Reynolds. Harvey said it was the first time he was ever blue after mailing a story; normally he was "set up." The story had taken him only two weeks, a week less than "Valhalla" or "Stuff of a Ranger," and the writing had gone so well he was reluctant to put the story away. Could he create another such story and another such storytelling experience? And once he let go of this story, would the weight of all his troubles descend upon him again? For sure he could not keep from worrying about money. On February 9 he detailed in his journal just how heavily those worries lay upon him. Under the title, "Fate, the Ruthless Herder," he compared himself to a steer being turned repeatedly toward the chute leading to a slaughterhouse. Premiums for two of his insurance policies were soon due, and if he could not find a way to pay them he would lose a last chance to get his family out of debt. He could see only one solution, a horrible one: "If I wait too long H[arvey] and V[ene] will have barely enough to pay my debts when I go. We have barely enough for two weeks more. Lately I have been keeping things more to myself and this leads more to decision. I believe if I had not practiced confiding everything with H[arvey] for the last 5 years, I would have either succeeded or passed out before this. I said to myself this AM, 'This is a matter of your own. No one can advise you. You must see it through yourself. You lost the money and you must pay for it.'"

Richter would sink even lower into despair before finishing with his journal that night. Under the title "Fate, the Pervert," he listed the ways "fate" had repeatedly undercut his efforts. The first of these had to do with his story writing, how smooth-paper stories sold when he had decided to concentrate on pulps, how two agents in December had promised much better sales and then not delivered for months into the new year. Perhaps the most poignant entry, the most deeply felt, had to do with his daughter: "After three years of unhappy, friendless, unsatisfying high school for Vene, she suddenly achieves success and happiness and friends and now we cannot see how we can keep her here the last four months before she graduates." And almost as painful: "Having never accepted anything without paying it back with interest, for four years I have been under the humiliation of being unable to pay my notes to friends, even the interest, and being obliged to use their gifts to live."

Not yet emptied of his anguish, Richter continued with another passage, "Was Christ's the Hardest Cross?" contrasting the cruel victimage of crucifixion with that of a man forced to suicide as fate "stands aside and grinningly watches, draws you to it." Out of this deep despondency Richter began a new project, a "Depression Journal" he intended to send to the *Atlantic Monthly* as the record of a man forced to suicide. He spent hours gathering appropriate entries from his journal, typing them almost verbatim from his handwritten pages until the process itself became restorative. Once again finding in this record of his worst moments a pride in his own perseverance, he ended the day "ashamed that today I was so discouraged and rebellant [sic]." Two days later he made what he termed in his journal "A Bargain with God": if God would just allow him to earn freedom from his debts, a moderate income, and health for his family, he would promise to continue his evolution by self-discipline. Instead of relying on Harvey and Vene to share his problems, he would keep to himself his worries and failures. And he would accept the whole burden of writing, no longer complaining to Harvey or Vene. His first step would be self-containment, "holding back confessions of weakness, worry, confidings of sudden hope."[45]

Richter worked for the next several days on "Gramma Grass," a pulp western. The writing went slowly, grudgingly, because Richter could not gather any enthusiasm for his story. He wrote no further comments in his journal about his bargain, but he had plenty to contain besides his exasperation with the story, for the landlady came to warn him that his family might have to vacate the house, and in addition to owing for the rent he was behind in payments for milk, gas, and the telephone. By February 16 he was down to $10 for groceries and $20 from Harvey's father he was keeping as a reserve. To Richter, it seemed more and more that fate was indeed ruthlessly herding him to a dark passageway.

THREE

February 16, 1934

This AM came a thick letter from Reynolds. I felt a clip inside, which usually means a check attached. But when I opened it eagerly it contained (1) letter from Reynolds not thinking much of "Early Marriage" (2) rejection from Short Stories saying "Mountain Man" was trite (3) rejection from Argosy saying "Stuff of a Ranger" didn't measure up (4) letter from Argosy (in answer to mine) saying it didn't want any more Singing Jim stories. . . .

I do not think I was ever so blue. I couldn't borrow from [a prospective lender] because I couldn't tell him I expected any sales. I didn't. I was completely sunk. I told Harvey I was a failure and asked if she would mind much if I ended it all which would give her $21,000 and enable her to pay off my debts. I didn't see what I could do except try to get a job that would keep us and then write for smooth-paper magazines only evenings, etc. But where should I get it? I felt Kaseman was through with me—he felt he had helped me enough. I have tried writing so many [possible employers] and did not have one hopeful reply. Perhaps I could dig up something humble here but after living here these years writing stories and being known as a writer and then going to humble work tears me apart inside. Then I felt it so keenly since I am going to the Hammer and Tongs Club and these successful men consider me as one of them. What would they think of me?

I sat here at my little green table for an hour unable to work when the bell rang. "You answer it," I called to Harvey. "No you do," she said. I thought it was the donut women, but when I opened the hall door, I saw what looked like a uniform. . . . It was the telegraph boy. He asked, "Are you Conrad Richter?" I was afraid to ask him to wait to know whether to tip him or not for fear there would be nothing to tip him about. I tore it open, saw Paul Reynolds name and then the utterly incredible news that the *Post* had taken "Early Marriage." I cried and Harvey grew hysterical— she had been so fine and brave all AM—I never saw her better. I had to go to bed to noon. Tears kept rolling down my cheek. I felt so sad. Never before had anything affected me like this. Now, I think, I realize the terrible thing we are up against. Before, when a story sold, I felt our troubles were over—everything would sell now. But now I know another sale will be just as much of a miracle and it sobers me, saddens me. Then I thought of all the others in the world who need telegrams like this.

The Sea of Grass

ONE

Lying in bed until noon, elated by his success and distraught at
the difficulty of ever accomplishing it again, Conrad Richter
had no presentiment that his desperate apprenticeship was over.
With "Early Marriage" he had found his voice and his subject,
and—as sales to the *Post* were to demonstrate—he had found
his audience. Over the next ten months Richter wrote only five
stories, but each sold, at increasing prices, to George Horace
Lorimer, editor of the *Saturday Evening Post* and the *Ladies' Home
Journal*. Richter never completed the pulp western he was struggling to write on the morning of February 16, and he never again

attempted a story for the penny-a-word magazines. He wrote with only the *Saturday Evening Post* in mind, and the *Post* editors responded by buying every story he submitted for more than the next decade.

But even after an unbroken string of six sales to Lorimer, Richter was little more confident that he could craft another story from the raw material of his notebooks. Each had to be extracted bit by bit from his imagination, and this process was attenuated by his worry, each time, that his imagination was failing him. Only after weeks of worrying over a plot would Richter finally begin to write. By spring 1935 Richter had come to think of "Early Marriage" as a model for successful stories, an illustration of the right combination and arrangement of story parts. Like "Early Marriage," each story had to rest on an authentic experience, true to the lives of the ordinary people who had settled the frontier, and each needed a single story obstruction, some dramatic obstacle to a duty or goal. In "Early Marriage" the authentic experience is a journey to a wedding, and the obstruction the two hundred miles of dangerous wilderness the bride must cross. Only with such an obstruction, Richter decided, could he create the vivid reality of frontier life as he imagined it, dramatizing the natural heroism of his characters—a humble, unmindful stoicism in accepting their lot without bitterness or complaint—and contrasting the roughness of their lives to the austere beauty of the land. As with "Early Marriage," he wrote and rewrote each story, attempting to achieve what he thought of as "a pure style"—simple, graceful but not literary, taut yet flexible—a language supple enough to convey both the internal tensions of the story and the evocativeness of ordinary life. Because "Early Marriage" did all these, capturing in an authentic story the heroic in the ordinary, the beautiful in the mundane, Richter returned to it frequently when he was in plot trouble, making notes to himself about how it was constructed. Following his model, Richter learned to pare away from surface descriptions and dialogue almost all mention of physical danger, instead finding ways to suggest how sensitized his characters were to all that was hidden beneath what the eye could see. As with his own heightened responses to the natural world, especially intense in times of deep unhappiness, the perceptions are so vivid exactly because the senses are heightened. Richter's frontier women feel but do not name the dangers they can never entirely forget are lurking beneath the rough but serenely beautiful landscape, the chamisa, the Indian paintbrush, the cloud shadows scudding across the mesas.

Two weeks after receiving the telegram announcing the sale of "Early Marriage" Richter was still unsure of his next story. Each day he plotted and replotted "The Long Drouth," trying to find the right combination of character and event to repeat the miracle of his sale to the *Post*. The final version of "Long Drouth" (published as "Long Engagement" in the *Post*) took only ten days of actual writing, but almost a month of plotting and false starts. Of the two months "New Home" took from first thoughts to mailing on May 11, more than half was spent plotting. "Frontier Woman" took nine weeks through the intense heat of Albuquerque summer afternoons, and Richter labored another ten weeks on "The Square Piano," begun at the cabin in the Sandia Mountains and finished after Vene began her classes at the University of New Mexico. The final story of 1934, "Buckskin Vacation," the most difficult and time-consuming, was also the one most interrupted by other events before Richter mailed it in early December. As with the others, Richter spent the majority of its eleven weeks of actual work searching for the combination of character, story, and setting to repeat what continued to seem his miraculous sales to the *Post*.

Subjects were never hard to find. His notebooks were full of kernels for stories, culled from old newspapers and books and from his conversations with the Hardys, Judge Botts, and his list of old-timers who told him stories about the settling of the West. His trouble began when he had to invest an authentic experience with enough plot conflict and suspense to support his evocations of place. "Nothing else," he wrote in his journal, "but a powerful obstruction with strong emotion flow will breathe life into all the color and detail I use."[1] Typically Richter found his conflict by juxtaposing the actions of settlers to the starkly beautiful but unforgiving landscape they count on for sustenance. Although the land forces accommodations on the people who settle it, some choices are based on ideas of how things should be, ideas brought with them from the fenced-in pastures and civilized communities of the East. These settlers have left behind their homes and relatives, but they have not abandoned their values. They can homestead in sod dugouts miles from any neighbor, and they can learn to live in a deliberate wariness of any change across the wide expanses of desert; but there are limits to accommodation. How else to explain a father's acceptance of his young daughter's decision to cross two hundred miles of wilderness during an Indian uprising, except that he agrees with her that keeping faith with one's promise to marry at a certain time and place—matters of convenience in the East—outweighs the risk that she and her brother must take?

These stories are built on contrasts between the ideas of order that inform the settlers' dreams for the future and the realities imposed by the new environment they have come to make their own. Among these ideas is a code for behavior between men and women, a code based upon assumptions of woman's vulnerability and fragility. Having brought women into so unwelcoming a place, men have compacted to protect them from dangers and even from the knowledge of dangers. Although Nancy Belle Putnam of "Early Marriage" is two years older than her brother Rife, Asa Putnam walks his son out of Nancy Belle's hearing to instruct him on his duties in taking his sister to her wedding. Later a settler passing on the trail stops his wagon and again walks the boy off, out of the hearing of his older sister. Further in the journey Rife follows their example, choosing not to acknowledge what his sister has guessed, that he has discovered the grisly remains of an Indian attack on a cabin. Only a boy, he "must bear a man's responsibilities and tell a man's lies,"[2] his sister understands. And though women like Nancy Belle participate in the silences, accepting that some subjects are not to be discussed, they carry just as heavy a burden in their unspoken knowledge of dangers imminent and latent. In all six stories these codes are evident and significant; in the best, "Early Marriage" and "New Home," the consciousness of a young woman living through a dangerous experience is the heart of the story.

For each story Richter chose a different moment in the lives of women pioneers, all part of the same larger story, that of westering. The hope for new life and land, the acceptance of danger and privation, the often enormous personal costs of loneliness and isolation: only the most stalwart could bear these hopes and suffer these burdens. These were new stories of the West for the readers of the *Post* and *Ladies' Home Journal*, decidedly different from the paradigms of westerns that had been ritualized and stripped of authenticity in the pulp stories of derring-do Richter had himself written. Danger is primarily latent, violence seen only in its aftermath, and conflict is more often than not internal. But these stories are different in more than just their avoidance of overt action. After more than two decades, Richter had finally found a subject commensurate with the one he happened upon in "Brothers of No Kin." In these stories of women pioneers of the Southwest, Richter's imagination and sympathetic identification with the feelings of his characters allow him to portray movingly a different life, and thus a different reality. These were truly new stories.

"How could you?" one reader wrote to ask, meaning how could he, a man, know so much about the feelings of women.[3] It was not a question he could answer, except to say that his women characters were as he imagined them, reading old documents and listening to memories of women and men who had lived through those days. In truth he knew well only a very few women, and knew intimately, now that his mother, his Aunt Lizzie, and his Cousin Beth were dead, only his wife and his daughter. There was perhaps a single addition. When Richter moved with Vene from Sunset Lodge to West New York Avenue, they found themselves next-door neighbors of the family of Joaquin Garduño, a medical doctor from Mexico City. Vene became best friends with Lucille Garduño

12. Harvena Richter looks at Sadie Garduño, who would be a model for both Lutie Brewton in *The Sea of Grass* and Doña Ellen in *The Lady*.

and spent so much time in the Garduño home that she came to call Sadie Garduño, Lucille's mother, Cita, short for Mamacita. Richter himself found much to admire in Sadie Garduño, and Harvey, quite possibly, at least a little to worry about. The child of a Scottish sea captain and a Mexican shipowner's daughter, she was warm, gracious, high-spirited, and pretty. In the year that they were neighbors she developed a special friendship with Richter, a friendship that did not go unnoticed. Vene would sense in her mother a hint of coldness toward Sadie Garduño, and in Dr. Garduño, some years older than his wife, the slightest suggestion of jealousy.

Some time later, after the Garduños had moved from New York Avenue to the country club district of Albuquerque, a Garduño relative wondered in Vene's hearing if Richter and the attractive and spirited Mrs. Garduño were not more than just friends.[4] To this perhaps mean-spirited speculation there is no hint of an answer, and it is the only whisper of such a kind about Richter to survive him. With another man, the circumstances would make an assignation seem more possible—a handsome man with an invalid wife, an attractive and welcoming neighbor. And Sadie Garduño was exactly the kind of woman Richter was most attracted to. Like his mother as Richter remembered her, Sadie Garduño was always poised, at once welcoming and distant. Like Harvey as Richter recalled her in the days of their early courtship, she had a special warmth in her eyes. But however inviting the circumstances, nobody who knew Richter well would have thought such an affair probable.[5]

Richter later acknowledged Sadie Garduño to be a model for one of his most memorable portraits, Lutie Cameron Brewton of *The Sea of Grass*,[6] and she was certainly the primary model for Doña Ellen in *The Lady*. But that would be much later. While the women of Richter's first *Post* stories have qualities he admired in Sadie Garduño, these qualities are those he had singled out earlier in his life, a kind of idealized version of womanhood he had urged on Harvey in their early years of marriage. In his first stories of frontier women, his models most obviously were his mother and his wife. Or rather, his model was a personal ideal of womanhood, emphasizing constancy and self-control, for which he had his memories of his mother and the daily presence of his wife.

Even as Richter established himself as a regular contributor to the *Post*, other possibilities began to distract him from his pursuit of stories that George Horace Lorimer would buy. First, Paul R. Reynolds, Jr., the son and business partner of Richter's agent, began a campaign to persuade Richter to try writing a novel. "Reputations are built on the long story, not the short one,"[7] Reynolds, Jr., wrote in summer 1934. Reynolds, Sr., was less optimistic, cautioning that, though his son was essentially correct about the prestige of novels, first novels were problematic for a short story writer. Because novels took so long to write and brought returns only on actual sales, they were, he warned, "a big gamble, and there is no way of getting out of it."[8] As a less risky alternative, Reynolds, Sr., approached the *Post* editors about a serial story in two or three parts that could later be published as a short novel. Although Lorimer had a strict policy against advancing money for stories, Reynolds thought that the *Post* might commit itself to a serial on the basis of a first part. Before the end of August, Reynolds reported that he had received some encouraging words from Thomas Costain, the *Post*'s New York story editor. But with no corroborating expression of interest from Lorimer, the risk seemed too great. Instead he chose to concentrate on what seemed still a tenuously held connection to a primary story market. If his success continued, later he would have time to think about a novel.

He did think longingly about a change of scenery, spurred by another alternative to story writing. In May Paul Reynolds reported overtures from the Fox Film Corporation, which offered to send Richter a train ticket to Hollywood for talks about writing a script. Richter was eager enough about this possibility to buy a new suit for the trip and to be disappointed when, without explanation, the ticket did not arrive. "That's the way those people seem to be built," Reynolds wrote to Richter, summarizing the fickle behavior for which the movie corporations were already well known.[9]

Even if a trip to Hollywood had led to an offer, Richter could not have accepted without much agonizing. He was of course attracted to the high wages movie corporations were reputed to pay writers, which seemed the only way he would ever escape from the $10,000 debt hanging over him. And California itself continued to be a magnet. Especially in the early stages of a story, when he spent day after exasperating day reworking plots, he thought that a change of scenery would energize him. And the lower altitude of southern California and its warm dry climate might be helpful for both Harvey's and his own health. But then there was Vene. Seventeen years old, she was at the beginning of the dangerous years for tuberculosis. Although his daughter showed no signs of the disease, Richter worried, as he had about Harvey twenty years earlier, that the symptoms might appear at any time. Would she be better off in California or New Mexico? Richter did not know, but the point was moot. Vene had already enrolled in the University of New Mexico for the fall. With his debts he could not afford to send her anywhere else, nor could he think very seriously about being far away from her, even though the comings and goings of his teenage daughter sometimes disrupted his writing. Richter looked forward to sharing Vene's college life, anticipating vicarious pleasure as his daughter undertook an experience he regretted missing. (He would, in fact, read the texts for many of her courses.) He was also more than a little interested in his daughter's social life at the university. Having watched her blossom socially during her senior year of high school, he and Harvey both hoped for Vene a happier time on campus than they had been able to offer her during their years of poverty. Vene's Aunt Emily wrote to encourage her to join a sorority, preferably her own, Phi Mu, and Mary Dalbey at Cedar Crest, another Phi Mu, promised that Vene would receive a bid.

When sorority bids arrived in September, Vene announced to her parents that she had to choose among three, including Phi Mu and Kappa Kappa Gamma, the one she finally chose. Kappa Kappa Gamma was also the most expensive, which worried Richter; and he worried, in his habitual and lifelong substitution of his own feelings of inadequacy onto his daughter, that Vene would not be happy with girls of a higher social class than she was used to.[10] He also worried about her extracurricular activities. Early in her first semester Vene began writing a weekly column for the *Lobo*, the student newspaper, and soon thereafter she was named an editor for the *Mirage*, the campus yearbook. Did she have the self-discipline to write a column successfully? Would all her extracurricular activities use up too much of her energy and affect her grades—or increase her suscepti-bility to tuberculosis? These became daily worries as Vene brought home her stories of campus life. It was all so distracting to his writing that in November, badly stalled on "Buckskin Vacation," Richter suggested that Vene move into the Kappa house to live. He could not afford the expense, but neither could he afford any longer the daily interferences with his writing.[11]

In October Paul Reynolds wrote with the unsettling news that Thomas Costain had resigned from the New York office of the *Saturday Evening Post* to take a job at the Fox Film Corporation. Knowing that Costain was a promoter of his stories, Richter worried that his sales to the *Post* and *Ladies' Home Journal* were over. What the next several months disclosed, however, was that his real champion at the *Post* had been George Horace Lorimer, the prime moving force at Curtis Publishing Company. Lorimer continued to buy every story Richter sent him, either for the *Post* or for the *Ladies' Home Journal*, and at increasing prices. Costain's departure turned out not to be a loss but another opportunity—and distraction—for almost immediately after his arrival at Fox, the movie studio was again asking if Richter would come to talk about writing for motion pictures.

This time they sent the ticket. Wearing the suit he had bought months before, Richter made a brief trip to Hollywood. But his conversations with Fox came to nothing and were for Richter so disspiriting that when Costain called a few weeks later to ask him to return for another discussion, Richter was not easily persuaded to go. After a series of misunderstood telegrams and telephone calls, Richter finally agreed to make another trip to talk to Warner Baxter, the director of *The Cisco Kid*, about writing a sequel to that movie. Richter's decision came shortly after Vene had moved into the Kappa house and while he was stuck on "Buckskin Vacation," and his worries about Vene's college expenses undoubtedly spoke to him more persuasively than Costain did. Already seven weeks into the story and still without a satisfactory plot, Richter had even canceled his evening newspaper so that it would not take time away from his writing. The problem with "Buckskin Vacation" was his usual one, the lack of a

sufficiently powerful obstruction. The story was "too thin—not epic or important,"[12] he worried in his journal. And day after day of reworking brought little
result. Had his power to create stories vanished as suddenly as it had come?
Unable to write stories, he could not possibly keep up Vene's Kappa dues or pay
her tuition. Although he had mixed feelings about what college and sorority life
were doing to his daughter, tempting her, he grumbled, to be "high hat and
risque,"[13] he nonetheless saw that her poise had improved—for Richter always a
critical matter. He did not want her to be denied a college experience as he had
been.

Richter committed himself to write a sequel to *The Cisco Kid* for $1,000, with
the understanding that if Fox chose to make the movie they would pay Richter
$3,000 more. Prodded by his promise that he would start on the sequel just as
soon as he finished the story he was writing, Richter finally settled on a plot for
"Buckskin Vacation." It seems more than coincidental that the story he crafted
had more scenes with cinematographic possibilities than were usual for his
stories. Although "Buckskin Vacation" was the least promising of the stories he
had attempted since "Early Marriage," Richter turned this slight narrative of a
young woman's thwarted plans to elope into a visually interesting story of some
drama and pageantry. There is, as well, another notable feature of this story:
Richter's portrait of a young woman does not fit the models of the women in
earlier stories. Although she too has the fiber to withstand hardship, disappointment, and danger, she is a younger, less rustic, more delicate version than
Richter's stalwart settlers, a young lady refined by a year in a women's seminary
in Missouri. In truth, she shared many characteristics with Vene at the beginning
of her life at the university. Sending Vene to the Kappa house might lessen his
daily distractions, but it did not remove the complex feelings he was discovering as his only child took her first formal steps away from him. Rosalie Potter
in "Buckskin Vacation" is no more Vene Richter than Nancy Belle Putnam in "Early
Marriage" is Harvey or Lottie Richter. But Richter's feelings for his daughter
invested this story of a young woman's first independent adventures with its
emotional core. As with his first successful story, "Brothers of No Kin," Richter
had found a way to explore his own emotions through the distancing device of
storytelling.

The day before Richter mailed "Buckskin Vacation" to Reynolds, he read the
story to his wife and daughter. Later that evening he recorded their bright predictions. In especially good humor, he continued his journal with a brief reflection on his daughter, concluding happily that Vene that day had been "the best
I have seen her for several years. Composed, enjoying home and old things like

stories, so glad, she said, she could come back and feel them, her real self."[14] Richter's pleasure in his daughter's response to his story was compounded by Paul Reynolds's letter on December 13, complimenting him on another "remarkably vivid" picture of the people and country, and by a telegram a week later: "Lorimer buys Buckskin Vacation for eight fifty. Merry Christmas."

T W O

Writing continued to occupy the major part of Richter's days in the months thereafter, as it would almost without break for the rest of his life. About this regimen he was always to have mixed feelings. Regularly he protested in his journal that he was only happy when alone with his work, but such comments were often occasioned by some social disappointment. Even when his writing was going well, he remained as restless and dissatisfied with himself in Albuquerque as he had been at Pine Tree Farm. Christmas night 1934, after a day of writing capped by an uncomfortable visit in the home of a friend, Richter wrote an emphatic journal entry about his—and his family's—private and public lives. They would be happier, Richter wrote, if they accepted a simple truth about themselves: they were queer people, not at all congenial with society and its falseness. Being queer people, they would be much better off, all three of them, if they simply told others frankly that they were queer. Instead of apologizing or trying to pretend they were not, they needed to be proud of their queerness. At least he had his work, he wrote. But though Richter knew that his work gave him a more solid accomplishment than most people he met, that accomplishment was never itself sufficient. At some level, his concentration on his work seemed an acknowledgment of failure, a retreat from something that, after all, he still wanted. No amount of mental struggle had allowed him to overcome his "cursed shyness," as he had named his self-consciousness. Forty-four years old, he was still unable to accept himself as he was, no matter how emphatically he named his limitations and renounced the parts of life that these limitations kept from him.

This sense of disappointment in himself may well have been a primary impulse behind a theme that increasingly asserted itself in his fiction about the Southwest. In these stories, Richter's first settlers live more vital lives and are more vital people than their children and grandchildren would be. Some years later he stated this belief more explicitly, first in an article in the *Atlantic Monthly*, "That Early American Quality," and again in "Individualists Under the Shade

Trees," his contribution to a book of essays, *A Vanishing America,* in which he contrasted modern Pine Grove to the Pine Grove of his childhood.[15] Although Richter makes no overt references to his energy theories in these essays, clearly they are behind his argument that the diminishment of vigor is a result of a life of greater ease. It is hardship and struggle that build energy reserves and their by-products, individualism, self-assurance, constancy, and temperance; what America had experienced had been a process of "thinning, declining, civilizing," and his own family served as his best example: "My father was not so severe as my grandfathers. The rugged old American breed was declining." That decline continued to his father's sons: "The blood has thinned out, and I for one can say it has not been to our advantage."[16]

Richter's notion of himself as a more anemic version of his father and grandfathers seems to have been the basis for his renewed efforts in 1935 to make himself more like these men he admired. Like many of Richter's choices, the impulses behind it were twofold, both inner- and outer-directed. While he sought to make himself a better person by his own standard, a self he would be more content with than the imperfect self he regularly criticized in his journal, the effort was nonetheless one that would be judged first not by his own feelings but rather by how his improved self was acknowledged by others. He needed the good opinion of others.

On January 2 Richter completed and mailed his synopsis for a sequel to *The Cisco Kid,* a treatment he titled "Hand on His Heart." The next day he began to turn his treatment into a story for the *Post,* as he had been encouraged to do, only to put it aside when Julian Johnson of Fox wrote to say that, though Richter had the character of the Cisco Kid just right, his story was "trite and unconvincing" and that he should wait for further word from Johnson and for a visit from Irving Cummings, the sequel's director.[17] Like the rail ticket a year before, no visitor or letter arrived, making it impossible for Richter to complete the treatment or put it away as a failed experiment. Fox's admission that they had abandoned the project came only after Richter prodded Thomas Costain, the ex-*Post* editor who had persuaded him to write for Fox.

A year later Richter noted in his journal that he wrote "Smoke Over the Prairie" to prove to Fox that he could write a story with an epic sweep.[18] In fact, he had completed the story before writing Costain about the disposition of "Hand on His Heart." Richter began "Smoke Over the Prairie" as a story about a young woman's plans to marry a construction engineer for the coming railroad. The story's obstruction is the refusal of her father, the powerful owner of a freight line, to allow his daughter to marry an employee of a railroad that will compete with his overland freighting wagons. But what began as the daughter's story, another story from a woman's perspective, evolved in to a story from the point of view of the father. A giant of a man in taming a wilderness, Frank Gant is on his way to becoming another out-of-luck teamster, losing place and prestige to the westward march of civilization. His problems with his daughter are only a late, dramatic moment in a seemingly inevitable sequence of events, a tragedy of progress.

The story had enormous appeal to Richter. It was about just the kind of character he most admired and longed to be, and it gave him an opportunity to dramatize his understanding that such men had not survived the first era of western expansion, an ironic result of their own success. His longest and most complex story—a compressed novel, he would call it—"Smoke Over the Prairie" took less than two months to write. As with "Early Marriage" a year earlier, after mailing his story he was despondent for the rest of the day.[19]

It is difficult to say how much Richter's sense of his own inadequacy contributed to the emotional energy he built into his portrait of Frank Gant, and it is equally difficult to assess its effect on "As It Was in the Beginning," the story he spent the next four months writing. Like "Smoke Over the Prairie," this was the story of a strong male, though a much younger one, and it became in final form another compressed novel. (In effect it is three discrete stories, the first of Foard Hudspeth's decision, out of his fevered thoughts while suffering through an illness, that he needs a wife; the second of his bartering with a Comanche chief to obtain the release of a young white woman held in captivity; the third of what happens after he discovers, once he has secured the woman's release, that she will not marry him simply because he has bought her freedom.) Although it is impossible to know just how fully Richter's sense of self-worth was invested in this story, his journal and personal notebooks tell a complicated story of corresponding struggles inside Richter, his struggles to get this story plotted and written in an acceptable final form and his struggles to model his own behavior on that of characters he was celebrating in his stories. It would be another chapter in the ongoing story of Richter's wrestling with his own feelings of inadequacy.

Richter began "As It Was in the Beginning" in early April. Six weeks later he was still worrying out its plot. In a matter of hours he could go from enthusiasm over his latest idea to despair that what he had written was worthless, would never sell, and did not deserve to. In one of the typical ironies which led Richter to exasperated declarations that the gods were meanly toying with him, at a moment when he was hopelessly struggling he received a letter from Paul Reynolds saying that the *Post* editors were eager for another story and wanted a thousand-word personal statement to print with "Smoke Over the Prairie."[20] That he should go stale at just the time when his years of hard work were beginning to be rewarded seemed the cruelest of life's jokes on him, and his bargain with God to discipline himself seemed another joke, one he had perpetrated on himself.

Running concurrently through the journal entries about his writing problems would be an account of his health problems. That spring Richter again was having trouble with his eyes, suffering through bouts of hay fever and conjunctivitis. These were compounded by blurred vision, nausea, and extremely low energy levels. (On May 5 he described himself in his journal as looking "like a Kentucky mountaineer with the hookworm.") Sometimes, he complained, he simply could not gather enough energy to concentrate on his writing: "there is a kind of blur, not so much in my eyes as in my brain, detaching me from what I see, giving me the impression I am already inexorably removed from that life and living in another world of dim, vague existence."[21] He was also worried about his heart; often at night it behaved erratically, fluttering and missing beats. Was his inability to get his story started affecting his health, or were these health problems the reason he was unable to write effectively? He did not know: "Sometimes I think it is the altitude, sometimes nerves, sometimes the strain of being in an unfinished story for more than two months."[22] Reaching for help for his stalled story, he got out "Early Marriage," writing extensive notes on its formula. A brief while later he got out "Smoke Over the Prairie" to use as another model, anatomizing it as well. Although the sheets of notes are undated, this would probably have happened after his copy of the *Post* containing "Smoke Over the Prairie" and his personal statement arrived on May 28 with the strongest endorsement yet from George Horace Lorimer. For the first time Richter found his name on the cover of the magazine.

As he filled notebooks with outlines for stories, he filled others with page after page of self-assessment and advice, writing lists of things to do and to avoid doing. As can be inferred from some of the specific pieces of advice he offered himself, his efforts at self-discipline were primarily aimed at changing the way he was seen by others:

> never raise your voice
> speak without hesitation or hurry
> end sentences and interviews firmly
> no exaggeration
> don't emphasize when speaking
> confide nothing

> never say "fine"
> look people cool and direct in the eye
> never think a weakness
> never complain
> never criticize
> never compliment yourself[23]

On one sheet Richter writes, "I am not important even after a little success. The moment I get the mistaken idea I am important and expect to be treated as such, I am dropped." On another sheet he addresses specifically his problems with Harvey and Vene, attributing their collective unhappiness to his "hard heart." On a third he pursues this idea further, blaming himself more comprehensively: "My ego causes all our troubles, either as a hard heart, lack of responsibility, defense, evasion, silence, self-righteousness, dishonesty, misstatement, whitewashing, laziest way—anything to support and protect itself, the ego. . . . The only cure is an humble and honest heart that knows it doesn't know but wants to find out and accomplish success."

Certainly Richter's unhappiness with himself influenced the stories and characters he was creating. Both Frank Gant and Foard Hudspeth are men like his grandfather E. S. Henry, men with strength of will sufficient to be content within themselves and consequently admired or secretly envied by others. Their choices are inner choices, unaffected by others because they have earned through hardship an inner trust that they rely upon. Richter seldom felt such inner confidence, most notably after reading his journals from the darkest times of the depression, and even then his recollection of his own stamina lifted him only momentarily. More often he felt it vicariously in his characters. And therein lay the rub. As fictional creations, both Hudspeth and Gant were, of course, dreams of Richter's imagination—and it was exactly because of this that they were for him least satisfying. For if they were models, they were also escapes and, he decided, impediments to self-improvement. Imaginatively living the lives of favorite characters kept him in "an inner dream existence," drugging "normal efforts for improvement."

But as harshly as he judged himself, he would not lower his expectations. To make himself more like his heroes, he asked God for assistance. He experimented with his prayers, changing his tone and manner, trying supplication and also forthright assertion. He prayed to God and to "the Gods" and, recalling Cornillier's hierarchy of spirits, he prayed to the highest powers able to hear him. On another undated page he offered this thought: "I have no longer any faith in waiting until God works us out of our difficulties—which means drifting, putting troubles aside and thinking of less unpleasant things. Instead I have faith that God will only help me if I face our troubles and figure out the best way to overcome them—which means thinking and saying each step of accomplishment quickly and definitely."

Richter completed "As It Was in the Beginning" on July 9. Returning from mailing the story, he noted in his journal that the traffic lights split evenly, three reds on the way to the post office and three greens on his return home. This mixed signal was verified ten days later when Lorimer wrote to say that he wanted to buy "As It Was in the Beginning," though he recommended a change in the story's last scene. Unhappy but compliant, Richter took the rest of the day to rewrite the ending, discouraged that he "had to add something unnatural," determined to make it as natural as he could.[24]

Three days after word arrived that the *Post* would publish "As It Was in the Beginning," Richter bought the new Chevrolet he had been contemplating for months as "something to help keep up self-respect."[25] Two weeks later he arrived with Harvey and Vene at Laguna Beach, California, where they rented a house overlooking the ocean. For Harvey and Vene, Laguna Beach was to be their first vacation through all the years of the depression. For Richter, California was another place to write, perhaps a place to spur his energy and creativity into more efficient storytelling. Perhaps as well, surrounded by so many signs of successful people, he would be helped to remake himself into something closer to his characters. The family planned to stay at least until fall, when Vene would return to the University of New Mexico; and if Laguna Beach turned out to be a comfortable place for Richter to write, he and Harvey thought they might stay on longer. But like the spring in Tucson, the sojourn in southern California was only briefly and intermittently a happy time. In the evenings the damp came in from the ocean, chilling them and worrying Richter about Harvey's and Vene's health. ("The only way [California] makes you feel younger," he wrote a friend, "is to give you the sensation of having your clothes perpetually wet.")[26] And though he continued to write daily, working on the plots for a story and two novels, he could settle into none of them. As he wrote Johnny Gardner, California "is no place to work. Everybody is having a good time living—just loafing and listening to the radio and going to movies and exclaiming over the stars and telling each other what a wonderful climate they have when they may not have seen the sun for a week or two and the airplanes roar so loud you think they will hit the roof and you can't even see them."[27] By September they were all three ready to return to New Mexico (Vene announcing she hoped never again to see an orange grove), and they considered themselves lucky when their house on Carlisle Street, where Richter had written all his *Post* stories, unexpectedly turned out to be available.

Although Richter completed no stories in California, he did accomplish some important preliminary writing. One story he worked on, titled "The Trees," was the beginning of what would become his second novel. The other, with a working title of "Early Americana"—a title he would transfer to his next short story—was the combination of two story ideas that he would expand into his first novel, *The Sea of Grass*. The first was the story of a mine owner's wife who disappears from a rough mining community, leaving behind her two children. As Richter later explained to Ruth Laughlin Alexander, this particular idea kept recurring to him: "whenever I went over my notes for something to write about, her tragic figure and story intrigued me more than anything else in my files."[28] The second was one that a source for color, Agnes Morley Cleaveland, had urged him to write. The daughter of a northern New Mexico rancher—and later the author (urged on by Richter) of a book about her life, *No Life for a Lady*, Cleaveland pressed Richter to "write the story of the cattleman-nester feud from the side of the big cattleman who was always pictured as a great villain."[29] Combining these two, Richter outlined a novel about the conflict between a cattle baron and settlers intent upon farming his range and the disappearance of the cattle baron's wife, leaving behind her children.

During his time in California Richter also had his first meeting with Paul R. Reynolds, Jr., who turned out to be a tall, thin man, not as young as Richter expected (he was thirty-one), with a reddish mustache, a slightly pockmarked face, dark brown eyes, and a habit of averting his eyes when talking. Richter was not impressed with the younger Reynolds, whose manner seemed to him affected and not particularly welcoming. They talked of a possible novel, as Reynolds had been urging, and Reynolds reported that the *Post* editors were interested in seeing a serial from him. But Richter still worried about how he could support his family for the year and a half he estimated a novel would take him. Reynolds and his father had been trying to interest a publisher in a collection of Richter's stories, but with no success: Scribner's, Houghton Mifflin, Harcourt Brace, and Little, Brown had all declined. Although every one of them was eager to see a Richter novel, all replied that books of short stories were seldom profitable. Nor were they willing to offer more than a token advance on a first novel. Without substantial royalties or an advance, Richter was stymied on the novel. He had whittled away at his debts, but he still owed more than $10,000. With his creditors less and less patient as his stories appeared in the *Post*, Richter decided he had no choice but to put aside his ideas for novels and write another story.

Once the family was settled again at 305 Carlisle Street, Vene announced to her parents that she had decided to study medicine—alarming her father, who envisioned his daughter losing her health in ill-lit laboratories. He immediately set himself to talk her out of it. Back at his typewriter, Richter took up the story that would become his first novel, thinking to write the first part of "His Cattle on a Thousand Hills," his working title, as a separate story to sell to Lorimer. But his plot would not come: ideas for a climax seemed cheap, Harvey and Vene "unencouraging," and the project "hopeless."[30] By the beginning of October, he was "frantic" over his inability to work out the plot—at one time so desperate as to suggest taking Vene out of school to join him in a "factory for stories" to pay off debts and put some money ahead. Then Vene "could go to be a doctor if she liked."[31]

Sometime after midnight on October 2, Richter gave up on "His Cattle on a Thousand Hills" and began listing on the laundry board in the kitchen his ideas for other stories. First he listed one about life in "an oldtime bank with Western color." A second was his idea about Pennsylvanians pioneering into the virgin forests of Ohio, which would become *The Trees*. The third was the "incident of doling out in an Apache raid of who was to shoot whom," in which men draw cards to decide which woman each of them will have to shoot if Indians overrun their outpost. The last seemed the best: "The sub-ideas for it flowered fast and soon I had half the laundry board full of them."[32] When Harvey and Vene showed interest the next day, Richter set out to turn his ideas into a plot. He began with Laban Oldham as a buffalo hunter, a plainsman with no thoughts at all of giving up his freedom for the young woman with black hair at a trading outpost. After several days trying to create a plot from such a beginning, Richter decided he did not have enough sympathy for his character and so was indifferent to the story. Next he tried making Oldham a younger man, just eighteen and so eager for the life of a buffalo hunter that he pays little attention to Chatherine Minor until he draws the queen of hearts, her card. Vene thought this particular idea "insipid," and Richter dropped the story to return to "His Cattle on a Thousand Hills" for half a day. Having no breakthrough with that plot, he returned to "Early Americana," as he had now titled the story of drawing cards, and struggled through several more days of plotting and replotting.

Eventually he hit upon the key to this story, the human feeling that would make it the most evocative of his stories of the West. It is not Laban's emotions during his night of waiting or his relief when help arrives; rather it is his unexpectedly happy memories of his parents' homestead, ten miles away across the Staked Plain. Returning from two days beside the campfires of the hunters, Laban enters the kitchen to sit with Chatherine as she mixed sourdough leaven into flour, a room feeling "as snug and pleasant as the dugout at home," where he can "close his eyes and know that either his mother or Chatherine Minor must be there."

The story did not come all at once—they never did—and Richter struggled through days of plotting and writing. He created the scene of Laban at home with his parents, listening at night as his mother's breathing caught up with his father's and passed it. Then he wrote the eerily evocative description of Laban's ride to Carnuel, and then the beautiful and terrible description of Laban's ride into a cañada at nightfall to discover the mutilated bodies at the Hedd homestead. In their early versions these scenes were all so rough, unfinished, and unsatisfyingly narrated that often Richter was discouraged and thinking about other plots. Writing to a friend he summarized his exasperation: "a man will do a great deal to get money to live and eat and writing a story is carrying that great deal to its fartherest [sic] extremity."[33]

On October 17 Reynolds reported another mixed response from a publisher, Alfred Knopf. Like the others, Knopf was wary of a short story collection but interested in seeing a novel—at least interested enough to question Reynolds about how long Richter would need to write a novel. Later Knopf himself wrote to Richter, speaking candidly of the realities of book publication during the depression but concluding with the hope that Richter understood that he would not be talking with Reynolds and writing at length if he were not "most decidedly interested."[34] A week later there came a telegram from Alfred Knopf— "Due Albuquerque noon plane tomorrow. Stopping overnight solely for the pleasure seeing you. Please leave message Alvarado [Hotel]"[35]—putting Richter into a dither of nervous anticipation. The next afternoon Richter found Knopf a more congenial companion than anyone would have predicted, and the meeting became the beginning of what to many would always seem an odd friendship. The two men could hardly be more different, a shy, nervous, almost reclusive writer and a New York publisher with a taste for expensive food and wines, flashy clothing, and big city sophistication. Knopf was exactly the image of "country club" mentality Richter had found so off-putting in New York City a decade earlier. Perhaps Richter's later speculation was right: Knopf stopped by Albuquerque because the reports from Reynolds and his son made Richter seem so odd and so difficult that they piqued his interest. At any rate, Richter met Knopf and drove him to Santa Fe to visit the poet Witter Bynner, with Knopf talking all the way. Richter had met Bynner earlier, but he had not met Frieda Lawrence, who was visiting Bynner when they arrived. Frieda Lawrence turned out to be "a big stout German hausfrau who part of the time told how she made biscuits and part of the time indulged in ultra modern conversation, all in a broken tongue, and yet rather likable withal."[36] In his journal that night, Richter had his usual regrets about having been too friendly and talking too much, wishing he had not told Knopf he was in debt and that he wrote only four or five stories a year. When they met again the second day, Richter's fears were some-what allayed by Knopf's cautious optimism about both a contract for a short story collection and for a first novel, though the question of a sizable advance remained a critical problem. Richter agreed to send Knopf a brief summary of the novel he had in mind.[37]

Energized by Knopf's visit, Richter pressed forward on his story with little vacillating. On November 28, Thanksgiving, he wrote the last 1,500 words, and the next day, before dinner, he read the story to Harvey and Vene. Both were in tears when he read the scene in which Laban, after asking Chatherine to marry him, listens to her breathing as it catches up to and passes his own. Just after mailing the story on November 30, Richter remembered to his astonishment that an astrologer a month before had warned him that November 30 and December 9 and 10 would be especially bad days. Writing a note to himself in his journal to watch the dates, he admitted that his nervous tension was high, worrying that Lorimer would reject the story. That tension was heightened by Richter's indecision over an offer Paul Reynolds had made, which arrived the same day Richter read the finished story to Harvey and Vene. Probably at the instigation of Alfred Knopf, Reynolds suggested that since the *Post* was inter-ested in a serial by Richter but unwilling to pay by the installment, Reynolds himself would advance Richter $750 for each completed section of a serial story, up to $3,000.

THREE

On December 6 word came from Paul Reynolds that the *Post* was buying "Early Americana" for $1,400. The same day a letter arrived from Alfred Knopf reminding Richter that he was waiting for an outline of a novel. Richter could never expect a more auspicious set of circumstances: a magazine editor encour-aging him to write a serial, a publisher eager for a novel, an agent willing to pro-vide funds to allow him time to write a long story. But still he would not commit himself. Writing to thank Reynolds, he said he would probably accept this "sporting" offer but needed to give the matter more thought. Perhaps this was another illustration of Richter's secretiveness born out of low self-esteem, his not wanting others to know his actions for fear he would later have to admit he had failed. But in fact, as at other times of life-changing decisions—his months putting Mrs. Miller off about her offer to become her secretary; his backing away, repeatedly, from writing as a full-time occupation, despite the encouragement of the Pagets and Harvey; his slow answer to Paul R. Reynolds during the summer of 1932—he had difficulty making any decision at all.

After writing to Knopf that he would put off a novel until he had written several more stories,[38] Richter then picked up again the pieces of "His Cattle on a Thousand Hills," the combined story of the range conflict between cattlemen and farmers and a wife's abandonment of her husband and children. Was it a short story or a novel he was writing? He could not say. Almost two months later, just two weeks before sending to Reynolds this manuscript, which would become the first part of *The Sea of Grass,* he was still undecided whether he was writing the beginning of the novel he had outlined in California or simply a story that could stand on its own.

One thing he was sure of, and that was that his portrait of Lutie Brewton was decidedly—and dangerously—different from his other portraits of frontier women. In a reverse of what had happened with "Smoke Over the Prairie," Richter found his story slipping away from Colonel Brewton's troubles with nesters and moving toward the disastrous choices of his unhappy wife. Would Lorimer accept a story that more than hinted at adultery? Richter knew George Horace Lorimer would not welcome such a subject into his magazines, which he thought of as repositories of wholesome values. But Lutie Brewton's story generated for Richter an intense emotional energy. Never able to rest easy in his wife's love, never wholly able to shake free from his childhood fears of abandonment, Richter felt this story of infidelity and desertion resonating deeply within him. Always sensitive to the sound and sense of his characters' names, he could not have missed the closeness between Lutie, the name of his central character, and Lottie, his mother's name. He was flirting with his own repressed feelings.

Richter's portrait of Colonel James Brewton does not appear to have been charged by his feelings for his father. Richter later described Brewton as a composite of people, drawn from men he had read about and several he had met. Judge Botts figures in the colonel's character, as does Ed Sargent, a New Mexico cattleman who at one time controlled Chama County, and Robert Putney, another cattle baron. Richter knew Putney only in old age, after he had suffered reverses. Seeing him on one occasion in the Bernalillo County Courthouse, where Putney was called to testify, Richter responded to "his dramatic entrance, the power in his great, ruthless, almost dissolute face, and the look of scorn he gave the courtroom, filled with men who had come to New Mexico in tamer and easier times than he." The experience "gave power to the image of the Colonel" as Richter crafted his story.[39]

Lutie Brewton is also a composite as Richter created her at his desk in January and February of 1936. A woman from New Zealand whom Richter met in Albuquerque contributed to Lutie's social grace and charm, as did Sadie Garduño, his neighbor at West New York Avenue. "Not a little of Lutie was drawn to life from her," Richter would write, adding that she was "as difficult to describe then as now, impulsive, intensely personal, full of gay animation, intimate fun, talk and laughter, quite lovely, with the faint sad melancholy of the Spanish waiting to appear on her face at any moment and as suddenly to vanish."[40] A third acquaintance figuring in Richter's portrait of Lutie was a woman Richter had known for only a few days during his adventure into the silver mining territory of Idaho in 1912. The wife of a wealthy and prominent resident, she had been kind enough to a young man visiting that Richter was startled and dismayed, several years later, to discover that one day she had simply vanished from a place she hated, boarding a train and never returning, leaving behind two sons. The story was strong enough in Richter's mind that when he sent Willa Cather a copy of *Human Vibration* in 1926, he inscribed it "To Willa Cather, whose Lost Lady I knew very well, but her name was not Marian Forrester."[41] During his stay in California he was reminded of the disappearance on receiving a letter from Wallace, Idaho, from a reader of his stories in the *Post*. In his reply Richter asked if the woman had ever returned. She had not, his correspondent reported.[42]

Richter returned to his notes for "His Cattle on a Thousand Hills" on January 1, 1936. That same day he took a room at the El Fidel Hotel, hoping he could there carve out another story quickly or find his way into a novel. Five days later he gave up the room, noting that his cost for it was $10.50, which worked out to about a cent a word for what he had written there. At home he continued to write daily, taking time out to visit the Hardys for color and to look for another house. His father John Richter, finally retired from the ministry, was coming to visit. Richter hoped to find a house with an extra bedroom so that his father would not have to stay in a hotel. When he found a home that met his needs, just across the street from the university, he worried about paying a higher rent, $65 a month rather than the $45 they paid for the house on Carlisle Street.

Throughout January letters passed back and forth among Richter, Knopf, and Paul Reynolds, Jr., about Knopf publishing a collection of Richter's short stories, and on February 1 a contract agreement was concluded. Knopf would publish Richter's frontier stories as *Early Americana* and he would have first option on any "long story" Richter had accepted by the *Post*. During the negotiations Richter kept at work on his story, choosing critical incidents to dramatize Lutie's personality and present her actions sympathetically. A key decision was his choice of a first-person narrator, both a shrewd and a curious selection. Like "Early Americana" and "Smoke Over the Prairie," his story is told retrospectively, by an old-timer looking back with admitted nostalgia. But this narrator is one who as a child has reason to resent and even despise Lutie Brewton. An orphan in the custody of his Uncle Jim, Hal Brewton knows he will be sent East to a boarding school as soon as Lutie arrives to marry his uncle. But despite the resentment Hal feels when she arrives, he is also attracted to her—in part a response he shares with the other inhabitants of Salt Fork, a community's acknowledgment of so unusual a sight as an Eastern lady, and in part the natural tug on an orphan by a maternal presence. That attraction colors Hal's story, as do his memories for an era long past, and he makes no claim to be an objective narrator.

Lutie as Hal sees her is both appealing and enigmatic, warm and sympathetic to Hal yet full of a feverish intensity that unsettles him. But if (as some commentators have suggested) there are likenesses to Hester Prynne in Lutie's marriage to an older man and attraction to a younger man who is not worthy of her, Richter's character study is far less a psychological exploration than Hawthorne's. This is a story told from the outside: Hal can describe but not explain Lutie's attraction to Brice Chamberlain; he can admire but not fully understand the colonel's steadfast refusal to acknowledge, in the face of overwhelming circumstantial evidence, that his wife has betrayed him, that his second son is in fact the child of his enemy, that her departure from his home was less an escape from unhappy surroundings than a flight to a secret lover.

Richter and his family moved into the new house at the beginning of February, taking time, as always, to clean the Carlisle Street house so that they left it in better condition than they had found it. Still, he kept at his story, working at night after his wife and daughter were asleep. Soon after the move something happened that he could not simply work through. Two years earlier, while he was writing "Early Marriage," his friend and fellow writer Paul Everman had succumbed to tuberculosis. This time a writer friend was murdered, and in circumstances that made Richter, however irrationally, worry that he was to blame.

For several years Richter had encouraged a young writer named Carl Taylor, as Paul Everman had encouraged him. Just weeks earlier, he had helped Carl secure permission from his English publisher to publish a section of his book on the South Seas in *Cosmopolitan*. That sale earned Taylor $750, his first sizable sum of money in years, and the temptation of this cash evidently lay behind Taylor's murder by his Mexican houseboy. Nobody but Richter would have seen himself as culpable in this turn of events. He had tried to help a friend, and then the horror of mischance got into the event. It took Richter over a week to climb out of despondency, and when he did return to work on his story, he was still feeling outrage at the unfairness of Taylor's death, brooding about what, if any, signs of intelligence and compassion could be discerned in a world of such horrors. The houseboy had shot Taylor in the back and then shot him again while he lay on the floor protecting his face with his arm. The second shot had been at point-blank range, directly into Taylor's face.[43]

Over the next month Richter worked to complete his story, thinking through the patterns of his plot and also of the unfathomable motivations of humankind. How could one understand such a murder or predict that an ordinary houseboy could think such thoughts? How could the husband and children of Lutie Brewton understand her unhappiness or her betrayal and abandonment of them? "This story is going to be long, long" he wrote in his journal on the last day of February, still thinking that he might be able to offer it to Lorimer as a separate submission. The next day Richter began planning another section of his story. That section would take him another 10,000 words, he thought, and he discussed with Harvey and Vene his idea of submitting the initial chapters of his story as the first part of a two-part serial—knowing that Lorimer especially disliked and almost never bought two-part serials. It was Vene who suggested that "His Cattle on a Thousand Hills" would not be an appropriate title for the expanded story, and they all three agreed that "The Sea of Grass," a description from Richter's journal, was a better choice.[44]

Richter completed the first part of *The Sea of Grass* in the second week of March, reading it to Harvey and Vene and recording their reactions in his journal. Vene raved at his success, calling it the best he had done, but Richter thought his wife was "plainly bluffing" and "trouble ensued—terrible."[45] He mailed the manuscript to Reynolds on March 13, his daughter's nineteenth birthday, and waited eight days for the telegram from Paul Reynolds, Jr., that Lorimer would pay $1,500 for that first part, with the understanding that there would follow a second, concluding section. After the telegram arrived from Reynolds, Richter's writing was done for the day. Instead he waxed the floors of the kitchen, the hall, and his writing room; then he went to town to buy shoes and a suit, his first shoes since spring 1933 and his first suit since the one he had bought to visit Fox Film Studio in spring 1934. When Reynolds's confirming letter arrived, it began "Mr. Lorimer writes us that as we know he heartily dislikes two-part stories but he is going to make an exception in your case."[46]

Quickly Richter got down to writing what he expected to be a concluding section. But orphanage, abandonment, and the secret unknowable interior of a heart were matters Richter could not conclude either decisively or quickly: these were the critical, irrational terrors of Richter's own childhood. And as an adult, to be lost, to be left alone, without help in a frightening world, these were matters intimately associated with his own anxieties about God, about a universe empty of meaning. By early June Richter had written not one but two additional parts for his novel, each about the same length as the first. The second is the colonel's section, telling the story of the loss of the range to the disastrous farming of nesters, with Brice Chamberlain, the smooth young lawyer with Washington connections, once again slipping away from a confrontation with his enemy. Lutie is present in this section only as a significant emptiness in the lives of her family, and she remains missing from all but the concluding pages of the third section, which is named for her younger son, Brock. Unsure of his father and deserted by his mother, young Brock grows into the best and worst of his feral nature, all natural feeling unmitigated by the hard lessons of self-restraint. Rebelling against his father, he moves to town and later takes the name of Chamberlain, seemingly intent on forcing Brewton to deny him. In the end he murders a man and is then fatally wounded when he refuses to give himself up to a posse. Word that he lies dying in a nester's cabin, shot through the lung, sends Chamberlain off by train in the opposite direction, his final betrayal, and brings Brewton riding across the prairie to his dying son's side.

In this tragic novel of victimage, weakness, and uncontrollable emotional forces, Jim Brewton remains true to himself and to others, protecting his son and his wife's reputation as best he can. Inexplicably his constancy is paid for at a high cost, for while unbroken by his burden, Brewton is nonetheless exhausted by it. Like Ebenezer Straint in "Brothers of No Kin," he has taken on himself the burden of a loved one, and his body shows the result of his suffering. When Lutie returns for her son's funeral, looking no older than the day she boarded the train for Denver, she finds the colonel haggard and spent. But he still holds on to his beliefs: the tombstone he orders reads "Brock Brewton, Son of Lutie Brewton and James Brewton." And about his returned wife, he says to

Hal, "Have you noticed how young she looks, Hal? . . . It was a hard thing for a lady to go through. But she's one in a thousand, Hal. No one else will ever be like her."[47]

The ambiguity of Colonel Brewton's remark, apparently deliberate on Richter's part, has been all but ignored. Just what was the "hard thing" for Lutie—her years alone, her return for her son's funeral, her discovery of the consequences of her weakness and selfishness? For the inattention to this ambiguity Richter is responsible, by creating through Hal so admiring a portrait of Lutie Brewton. Although a necessary vehicle to validate the colonel's constancy, Hal's perspective makes it all too easy to ignore Lutie's critical flaws. An orphan living on a ranch with men, Hal falls immediately under the thrall of Lutie Cameron; and even though he knows she is to blame for his exile to the East, as alien to him as the West is to Lutie, he is incapable, once in her presence, of resenting the unhappiness she has brought to his life. He is a boy in need of a mother. Writing in old age and admitting that his story is the nostalgic recollection of one who regrets the lost life of the early settlements, Hal Brewton does not seem to have made the connection between the story of Lutie Brewton's betrayal and desertion of her family and the consequences of the coming of the second wave of westering settlers. For all the attractions of civilization, the second wave of immigrants brings with it the worm of disillusion for the original order Colonel Brewton and his kind created out of wilderness. Brewton and his kind are heroic; however sympathetically the colonel chooses to construe his wife's behavior, Lutie Brewton and her kind are at best only sad.

Richter mailed *The Sea of Grass* to Reynolds on June 13, noting in his journal that the envelope had taken thirteen airmail stamps, just as there were thirteen letters in the title and in his name, and that he had mailed the first part of the typescript on March 13. Thirteen was for Richter a special number, not necessarily unlucky, and the convergence of so many thirteens encouraged him to think positively about the novel's chances. Nonetheless he had his doubts. The sections of *The Sea of Grass* he then was sending to Reynolds were twice as long as the first, requiring, he supposed, the *Post* to publish his story as a three-part serial. Typing out the final version, he experienced his usual last-minute jitters. There were terrible fights with Harvey when he thought she was bluffing about her interest in his readings, and when he read the typescript to the Hardys, he suspected that Mrs. Hardy had not really been enthusiastic—though the next day she had called to tell him that she had dreamed about his story and he was not to change a single word. Mailing his typescript, he could not quite make himself believe that George Horace Lorimer would ever publish his story; and if he did publish it, Richter worried, it would do his magazine harm.[48]

The *Post* evidently had no such worries. Only a week after Richter submitted the rest of his serial, word arrived from Lorimer that the *Post* wanted to take the second installment as a second and third part, but that the story needed two changes. Readers would want to know where Lutie had been, Lorimer wrote, and they would want to know just what, after her return, her relationship was to be with Colonel Brewton. As with earlier requests for changes from the *Post*, Richter was incensed but trapped: he had no practical way to proceed but to accede to Lorimer's request. Gathering color from St. Vincent's Convent[49] (where Vene had first attended school in Albuquerque), Richter rewrote the conclusion to explain Lutie's whereabouts during the missing years as a retreat into a convent, and to suggest the possibility of her permanent return into a settled if not happy life with Colonel Brewton. The writing took him a week of concentrated effort, during which he maintained an unusual regimen. For however long the revision took, he decided, he would stay away from Harvey's bed. As he explained his decision to himself, the issue was wholly physiological, a garnering of energy to concentrate on his writing. He had done so just once before, writing the final section of "Smoke Over the Prairie," and then too he explained his decision as a corollary of his theory about human energy: people with low energy levels must use care not to exhaust themselves in large energy depletions.[50]

When he was finally finished, Richter decided that the new ending for *The Sea of Grass* was in several respects an improvement over the old, though he continued to prefer to keep the mystery of Lutie's missing years. Writing to Reynolds, Richter listed the minor differences between the serial the *Post* would publish and the typescript he was submitting to Knopf, noting that he preferred "blurring the end a trifle" for book publication.[51] Later he would consider more substantial changes, but he finally put these aside so as not to embarrass Lorimer. The *Post* had been so supportive of him that they deserved treatment in kind. He would not publicly question its editorial judgment by markedly changing the ending when the novel was published as a book. That was, he thought, simply a matter of fair play.[52]

George Horace Lorimer paid another $3,500 for the revised second and third parts of *The Sea of Grass*, bringing the total for the serial to $5,000. Only after receiving the check from Paul Reynolds, Jr., did Richter accept that the sale was final. The day the check arrived he finally shared the news with his brother and sister-in-law, Fred and Emily Richter: "Have smelling salts ready! Stand side by side each so you can catch the other when you fall! And when you recover, open a can of Schlitz for the occasion! I've sold my first serial." With typical modesty he undercut his accomplishment, adding that the serial was "not a long one, just three parts," and then concluded with the news he was happiest to give his brother: "I'm enclosing a check that I hope will liquidate the principal of my debt to you and some time in the next year I'm hoping to clean up the accumulated interest."[53] With the Fox money he had paid off completely two of his debts; with *The Sea of Grass* check he would pay at least part of what he owed on eleven more, reducing his total debt to about $8,500. Perhaps the royalties from his short story collection, *Early Americana,* would let him whittle away at more of the debt. And if Knopf accepted *The Sea of Grass* perhaps it would sell well, or even sell to Hollywood.

eight

Something for Myself

ONE

On August 1, 1936, Conrad Richter received word of a highly
favorable review of *Early Americana* in the *New York Herald Tribune*.
Hearing that his photograph appeared with the review, he commented to himself, wryly, "I am a little overwhelmed with my
importance." Two days later Richter was startled to discover a
large display of *Early Americana* in the New Mexico Book Store.
Instead of elation, he reacted with alarm that his friend Jim
Threlkeld, the store's owner, was staking so much on his book's
success. When Richter told Threlkeld that he felt badly that the
store might be stuck with so many copies, Threlkeld offered to

bet him that he would sell all the books in the display and another twenty-five before Christmas.

Some days earlier Alfred Knopf had written that the stories in *Early Americana* held up beautifully—and that he was delighted with everything about *The Sea of Grass* except its brief length. "I am more sure than ever that you belong on my list," Knopf concluded.[1] When Reynolds wrote with the details of the contract Knopf was offering, he reported that Knopf had commented to him that the novel was "very fine and favorably compared to Willa Cather's,"[2] which to Richter was high praise indeed. But the contract made the soft words seem preparation for hard bargaining, calling for only a $500 advance and for first refusal rights for Richter's next two books. Richter was unhappy about both conditions, but after an exchange of letters with Reynolds, who advised him that Knopf could probably be pressed either into advancing more money or tying up fewer books, Richter signed the contract as it was. He would agree to the small advance, he wrote Reynolds, because he wanted only what his book actually earned. As for the commitment of future work, he wrote to Knopf that "you have staked something on me and my plans, I think I should stake something on you and yours."[3]

As the reviews of *Early Americana* came in, Richter found himself in some discomfort, disbelieving the substantial number of good reviews and dwelling on the few that were less favorable. He was also upset by both Harvey and Vene, who were making his life "miserable" saying he was ruining *The Sea of Grass* with last-minute corrections to the galleys.[4] With both *Early Americana* and *The Sea of Grass* to worry about, and reports from Reynolds and from Gerald Adams, Reynolds's Hollywood agent, that all the major movie studios were eager to get a copy of *The Sea of Grass*, Richter was able to work only fitfully on "The Simple Life," a short story for the *Post*. Then another worry cropped up. Rereading Willa Cather's *A Lost Lady*, Vene discovered a number of phrases that were surprisingly like descriptions in *The Sea of Grass*. Because *A Lost Lady* was also about a woman who abandoned her family, the coincidental similarities were too close for Richter's comfort. Writing to Knopf to ask for the manuscript back, he explained evasively that "several changes have come to mind that I should like very much to make before it goes to the printer."[5] Then he wrote to the *Post* with the same request, offering to pay the cost of late changes in proof.

Two days later Gerry Adams called to convey an invitation from Metro-Goldwyn-Mayer, the premier motion picture company in Hollywood, for Richter to visit their studio to discuss writing for them. Although he had long since learned to be wary of Hollywood overtures, a week later Richter took the overnight train to Los Angeles, steeling himself for two days of interviews and discussions. Once checked into the Beverly Wilshire Hotel, he wrote to Harvey that he had paid the extra train fare for a sleeping berth and accepted the expensive room reserved for him, even though he was not absolutely sure that the studio would pay his expenses, because he was determined not to lower his confidence by doing anything cheap—at least not until after his discussions at MGM. He had even taken a cab from the railway station, passing up the trolley, and gone straight to Bullock's Department Store to buy a new suit for his interview.

Armored in his new double-breasted suit, Richter met Edwin Knopf the next morning at MGM. The half brother of Alfred Knopf, Edwin Knopf, Richter gathered, headed the writing section at MGM. With him was Kate Corbaley, in charge of story development. To Richter's mind, the meeting did not go well. Although the dark, portly Knopf was "very pleasant" and both Knopf and Corbaley exclaimed extravagantly about *The Sea of Grass*, it seemed to Richter that they really had "nothing sure" for him to do, "jumping from one thing to another" until Richter was left feeling "bewildered and humiliated." To lower Richter's spirits further, when he returned to the Beverly Wilshire the elevator boy tried to send him to the front desk to be announced. For Richter the bell-boy's mistake was telling. The new suit was clearly a failure, he wrote Harvey, and so were his discussions at MGM. Expect him home soon.[6] The next day Edwin Knopf kept Richter busy with more meetings, Richter speaking again to Kate Corbaley and to Clarence Brown, the director of "Ah, Wilderness!" who was then directing a film starring Clark Gable and Joan Crawford. Brown was interested in developing the movie possibilities of a story about Abraham Lincoln. Did Richter think that he could work on a script about Lincoln? At day's end Richter telegraphed Harvey that he had been offered "a modest four-month contract"; MGM would pay him $500 a week to write a treatment of Honore Morrow's story, "Benefits Forgot."[7]

Although almost certain that Alfred Knopf had had something to do with his brother's overtures, Richter felt he owed an explanation to the man to whom he had committed his next two novels. Reminding Knopf of his heavy debts, Richter wrote of the MGM contract that "I felt that I could not be fair to my creditors, fine and patient as they have been, and turn down the offer."[8] To his agent Adams he put the matter less politicly: "I should be willing to go through hell to get my debts paid." Recording this remark in his journal, he added another comment to himself: "I must not be surprised if fate takes me up on it."[9]

September 21, the day Richter began work at the studio, Gerald Adams called with the news that MGM had agreed to pay $15,000 for the movie rights to *The Sea of Grass*. After paying his agent's commission, Richter would have in hand $13,500, $5,000 more than what he owed creditors. For the first time since October 1929, Richter slipped out from under the grinding burden of debts he had no way to pay. For the first time in seven years his thoughts about the future did not automatically begin with a first necessity of getting out of debt. When the check for $13,500 arrived, Richter immediately began paying his creditors, eleven in all, and in each case Richter refused adamantly to accept any accounting that might be thought to favor him. In spite of his father-in-law's protests that his small checks on holidays and birthdays were meant to be gifts—and similar protests from his own father and brothers—Richter insisted on adding in every contribution and repaying them all, with interest.[10] When the Albuquerque National Bank offered him a reduced rate for his long-term loans, adjusting the interest to reflect the changes in prevailing rates over the depression years, Richter refused. He had borrowed the money at 8 percent; that was what he would pay.[11]

The check arrived on October 9, three weeks after Richter began his four months' contract with MGM. By then Richter had completed a preliminary synopsis to share with John Considine, the producer of "Benefits Forgot," and on October 5 he had met with Considine and others to discuss it. It was good work, quite acceptable, Considine told him, but then Considine continued by listing ways it could be made better. Upset, Richter nonetheless kept his own counsel until late in the meeting. Then he suggested that, if his work were not up to their standards, they need only tell him; he was not earning more in Hollywood than he would make writing his own stories. Then why, Considine asked, had he come to work for the studio? The joke was on him, Richter confided: he had heard about the easy money to be made writing for pictures but so far he was working harder for MGM than he had for himself.[12]

It took some stretching of reality to claim that writing stories had ever earned him $500 a week, but otherwise Richter's statement was an accurate description. Determined to produce work of high quality, he kept the same long hours writing for MGM as he had always done, working six and often seven days a week, in morning, afternoon, and evening sessions. It did not help that he did not have, even after weeks of work, a very good idea of just what a "treatment" should look like. Nor did it help, especially after the conference with John Considine, that he wrote acutely aware that he had to please people other than himself. Hesitant to ask questions that might have embarrassing answers, he had waited until the first conference before asking Considine whether he was actually on the payroll. Then it came out that nobody had thought to inform him where to collect his checks. There were three waiting for him.

Although Richter was assigned an office at MGM, Considine granted him the unusual accommodation of writing at home. Thereafter Richter avoided the studio, working daily at the small, unpretentious house he rented for $70 a month on Lankershim Boulevard. Vene lived there with her parents, having decided to defer her college course work in favor of piano lessons in California. For most of the fall Richter's father stayed with them as well, both before and after surgery to remove his prostate. Vene served as her father's secretary and typist; she also played the piano for hours on end—sometimes at her father's request when his writing was going badly.[13] When he completed a section of "Benefits Forgot," he had Vene type copies and deliver them to MGM, so that he did not have to go to the studio. Unsure of protocols, he had Vene type two copies, one for Considine and one for Brown, so that neither would be insulted by receiving a carbon copy.[14]

Late in October Richter visited the set where Clarence Brown was directing Clark Gable and Joan Crawford. Richter admitted he was happy to have experienced this, a treat for a tourist, but there was always something unsettling about the studio, a "tremendous oppression" he found hard to lift. Driving to the studio, he enjoyed the first part of the trip, the journey through an area of small houses with ordinary people along the sidewalks. But as he drove through Beverly Hills the imposing homes bore down on him. He would tell himself to "brace up" and to lift his spirits so that when he arrived at the studio, he would not appear to others as insignificant as he felt.[15]

At MGM all signs remained uniformly positive, if Richter could only believe them. Shortly after Richter had given the first section of "Benefits Forgot" to Clarence Brown and Considine, his agent Gerald Adams reported that Brown had said in conference that Richter was "one of the highest grade writers ever to work there."[16] Considine telephoned to say the treatment was "swell" and that they were "on the way to a big picture." Clarence Brown, he confided, had even read the treatment twice.[17] All the flattery was nice to hear, but it was only talk, after all, and only Hollywood talk, which Richter deeply suspected. By the middle of November Richter had written half his treatment for MGM. He continued to write at least ten hours daily, with work sessions interrupted only by visits to his father who was in the hospital recovering from surgery. When Richter submitted the second installment of "Benefits Forgot," Considine called to say he was "tremendously interested" and awaiting the third part, and that Brown was

13.   Richter walking the streets of Los Angeles during his time screenwriting for Metro-Goldwyn-Mayer, fall 1936 or 1937.

eager for the third part too.[18] Ten days later Gerry Adams stopped by to report that Richter was now considered "tops" at MGM and that the studio had decided to put off all discussion of the film until the treatment was completed, just to allow Richter to work in his own way. Always an agent, Adams suggested that Richter could take six months to complete the project, rather than four, and then ask two weeks vacation when he finished. To a man who had grown up in Pennsylvania Dutch country the idea was preposterous, and Richter dismissed both the report and the reporter. "I don't believe him," he wrote. "He doesn't lie, just doesn't know the facts."[19]

Early in December Richter carried the completed third section of the typescript to the studio, going to see Edwin Knopf, as Knopf had requested, and picking up several waiting salary checks. After the usual pleasantries Knopf informed his novice screenwriter that he had decided not to invoke the studio's option for a second contract if Richter did not want one, adding that he supposed Richter would want to leave just as soon as his current contract was completed. Listening to the studio executive, Richter was unable to decide if he was politely being dismissed or if he was really being offered the option to stay or leave as he chose. Under these circumstances Richter could not offer to continue, nor could he walk away with any sense of closure. Neither courted nor fired, Richter left the meeting unhappy with himself and with Knopf, Considine, and Brown. If he did not really want another contract, he at least wanted the chance to say no.

And he still owed MGM several weeks' work. On December 4 and again on December 8 Richter met Considine, Brown, and others for conferences on his completed treatment. Having been given the latitude to work out the story in his own way, Richter was now obliged to listen to pragmatic professionals scrutinize it for its picture possibilities, and then to rewrite. A primary topic at these meetings was whether the movie should incorporate the human details Richter had added to the original story to enrich it and give it more emotional meaning. Clarence Brown argued against most of these, with Considine siding with Richter's treatment, against Brown. Later Considine told Richter that he thought "Benefits Forgot" was the best script ever handed in by a new writer at the studio,[20] but such compliments were of little help as Richter set himself to revise in ways he did not believe appropriate.

On December 9 Richter made another trip to the studio, a trip with no apparent purpose other than to give Edwin Knopf and Considine another opportunity to offer him a contract extension. They did not. Three days later, after seeing two especially disappointing movies, Richter left the theater "cursing the stupidity, the cheapness, the unimaginative low monotony of pictures" and praying that "when I finish here, I shall never touch pictures again."[21] Richter's next trip to MGM, December 22, turned out to be an especially unhappy one. First he discovered that his studio office had been given to another writer and he assigned a less prestigious one. Then he had a meeting with Alfred Knopf's wife, Blanche, an active participant in the Knopf publishing firm, and to Richter's mind their conversation went painfully badly. At home that night, his promise to God was too much to keep. He must accept himself as a peasant, he told his wife and daughter, and not try any longer to be anything more. He should plan his life so that as much as possible he did not have to meet people, only to write to them. Two days later he decided once again that his primary problem was a low energy level and high rate of expenditure. "The lack of [energy] makes me testy, hard (my effort of will to keep up despite no energy), helpless to be warm and pleasant despite all my trying, makes me dislike people and places, makes me feel grievances."[22]

Believing himself discarded by MGM, Richter nonetheless worked daily on the revisions he had promised. When Considine suggested that another writer could complete the changes, Richter replied simply that he always finished what he started.[23] When *The Sea of Grass* arrived from Knopf, Richter carried autographed copies to Edwin Knopf, John Considine, and Clarence Brown, accepting their congratulations and thanks with his usual modesty. At the studio, Richter sensed he was being treated differently and he assumed the change came from rumors that he was being dropped. But just two days later, January 6, Gerald Adams reported to a surprised Richter that he and Paul R. Reynolds, Jr., had met with Edwin Knopf, and that Knopf wanted to offer Richter a contract for $9,000 to do a treatment of Harvey Fergusson's novel *In Those Days*.

When Richter explored this offer with Knopf on January 8, he began with a disclaimer and a statement of gratitude: "I told [Knopf] I wasn't soliciting him for any work, that a few months ago I had come to Hollywood with my debts whittled down to $8000 and now I had $12,000 in the bank and debts paid, only spending a thousand dollars since here, and as a result I felt deeply indebted to him and the studio and would try to do something for them before I went back [to Albuquerque]."[24] Edwin Knopf entered into the spirit of the meeting with his own confidences, telling Richter that his "agents came in pairs like gendarmes" to warn him that the sensitive writer needed special handling. By day's end Richter had agreed to think further about the Fergusson project and to extend his work on "Benefits Forgot" until the end of the month. The day had provided just the confirmation he needed. He could now close out his Hollywood experience without feeling that he had failed himself or let others down.

On his last day Richter met briefly with Edwin Knopf to tell him he was putting aside the idea of an immediate continuation at MGM but would accept with gratitude Knopf's offer to return to MGM whenever he wanted to. Richter liked the portly, dark-complected half-brother of his publisher, and he was grateful for what he now saw as Knopf's very decent treatment of him throughout his months at MGM. Perhaps, he thought, it was Knopf who had drawn the tougher assignment, having to deal with a writer unpracticed in Hollywood's ways. Leaving the studio behind him, Richter drove out through the mansions of Beverly Hills, back into the comfortable, modest community along Lankershim Boulevard. Once home, he took an Alka-Seltzer and treated himself to the rare pleasure of an afternoon nap.

TWO

On February 8 *The Sea of Grass* was officially published. When Blanche Knopf wired to ask if Richter would sign some first editions of *The Sea of Grass*, he wired back: "Shall be very glad to autograph the copies. Has anybody bought any?"— a line Knopf released to the wire services along with the advance sales figures— over 10,000 copies.[25] Richter had not liked the jacket Alfred Knopf chose for his novel, but Knopf obviously did, from his letters, and Richter kept his thoughts for his journal. He was happy with the book otherwise. Like *Early Americana* it had been designed by W. A. Dwiggins, who did all Cather's books, and Richter knew Knopf had assigned Dwiggins to the books as a favor to him.

Curiously, Richter and Harvey made no firm plans to leave California. Vene had talked her parents into extending her leave from the University of New Mexico, attending instead the University of Arizona for the spring semester. Uneasy about Vene's health, Richter and Harvey had agreed with the understanding that Vene would take a light course load and fill her days with horseback riding, swimming, and tennis. They talked of returning to Albuquerque or making the long drive back to Pennsylvania for the summer—their first return in nine years. But Richter was worried about Harvey, who seemed to have lost ground during the last months in California. Could she withstand the long trip? And what of her health there? Any decision was deferred until after February 8, the publication day of *The Sea of Grass*. Without outwardly admitting it, Richter was waiting for his novel's first reviews before deciding whether he would go to Albuquerque, Pine Grove, or a place where nobody knew them.

In the days before publication Richter saw a series of psychics, attempting to allay his worries about the future. None of these sessions prepared him for the news that the *New York Times* Sunday edition did not review his novel and the *New York Herald Tribune's* review dismissed it as a rewriting of *A Lost Lady!* "Said it Before but Never True Till Now: All is Lost" Richter entitled his journal entry. Picturing the ugly aspersions that would pass among Paul Horgan, Erna and Harvey Fergusson, Kyle Crichton, and other New Mexico writers, Richter knew immediately that he could not go back to Albuquerque. Then his thoughts took a characteristic turn, from his own problems to those he might be bringing on others: "Chiefly I feel sorry for Alfred Knopf—and humiliation for being the means of causing him this slur on his name and publishing."[26] After several days brooding over the first reviews, Richter wrote to Paul Reynolds, instructing him to "wait for the remainder of the advance check until enough books may be actually sold to cover it."[27]

On Valentine's Day Vene left for the University of Arizona. The next day Richter read a painful review in the daily *New York Times,* which also called attention to the similarities to *A Lost Lady.* A letter did arrive from Jim Threlkeld, owner of the New Mexico Book Store in Albuquerque, saying he liked the book and it was selling well. Heartened by that news, for a while Richter and Harvey thought about going back to New Mexico. Unable to decide, they moved from Lankershim Boulevard to spend a week by the Pacific, renting a hillside home with large windows looking out onto seals playing in Three-Arch Bay. There Richter experienced a supernatural event equivalent to the visitation of the blue light at Saranac. Kneeling in prayer at the window seat in the dining room, Richter looked up to see "golden chords running down to different parts of the sea, like fine golden search-lights. . . . It was almost as if the earth was being held in place by these ethereal or gravity currents or whatever they were, suspended from the stars."[28] The experience was an intensely pleasurable one for Richter, and each night he returned to pray at the window, anticipating a recurrence. Given his inclination to see possible signs from the astral in any unusual event, Richter would certainly have wondered if there was some meaning in this vision. If he thought it a reassurance at a time when prospects for his novel seemed so disappointing, the connection was insufficiently definite to buoy Richter's hopes. Shortly thereafter Richter and Harvey decided that it would be prudent to spend the spring in Banning, California, on the edge of the desert. One reason for choosing Banning was that the warm dry sunshine would be good for Harvey; a second was that in Banning nobody would recognize him as the author of *The Sea of Grass.*

The novel's reviews were far from uniformly negative; many positive, even enthusiastic reviews spurred book sales, and by early March the novel had climbed onto the best-seller lists in five of ten cities, leading the list in Chicago and Washington.[29] Although there had been no letter from Alfred Knopf, which Richter awaited with dread, he was enough recovered to begin plotting two stories. One was entitled "The Dominant Eighth," about a Mexican boy's inherited traits from an Anglo grandfather. The other, seemingly more promising one was a story growing out of Richter's reading of Henry Howe's *History of Ohio,* an anecdote about children becoming lost in the deep forests of wilderness Ohio. Once again it would be a disappearance, a separation of children from their parents, that caught Richter's imagination. At first he decided that his story would be about a father's hatred of the trees surrounding the family cabin, a sea of trees, in which he had lost his favorite daughter. By March 20, Richter had settled on this idea, if not a plot. It is curious that, following the attention by critics to parallels between *A Lost Lady* and *The Sea of Grass*, Richter found himself recalling Willa Cather's formulas for successful plots, deciding that for his novel to be a powerful story he needed, as Cather had taught him, a strong central character.

Why then, of all times, did Richter find himself dwelling on the models of a writer he had been accused of copying? Of course he did not believe that he had plagiarized Cather. He had not reread her novel, apparently, since he had carried it home to Pine Tree Farm. But with reviews calling attention to the likenesses, after he had changed some of his phrasing to remove what Vene had thought to be dangerously close echoes, why would he turn to Cather as a model? The answer seems to be that he did truly aspire to write like Cather. He admired her characters, her plots, her ways of telling stories. He valued the things that she valued in her fiction: her simple, direct narration; her evocation of the intimate relationship between characters and the land. He knew almost nothing about Willa Cather herself and showed little curiosity in her. But reading her novels he felt the true sensations that came only from writing that was real. It may well have been important to Richter that she was notably successful, perhaps the only American writer who could make a best-seller out of a slender novella. He was out of debt, but he had to stay out. And as *The Sea of Grass* slipped down and finally off the best-seller lists, Richter discovered book sales were very much an issue—especially after he decided, on March 20, that he was not going to write a story for the *Post* but a novel about pioneers westering into Ohio. That same night he decided it was time to change his prayers. Until then he had prayed nightly for *The Sea of Grass*. Thereafter he would ask God's help for his new novel.

At Banning Richter and Harvey settled into another modest, quiet neighborhood, renting a white clapboard house with green shutters and a yard full of evergreens, shrubs, and almond trees, which by early March were in bloom. They liked the town better than any other they had seen in California. As Harvey's health improved, they exchanged their afternoon drives into the desert for walks along the quiet streets of Banning where, as he had hoped, Richter retained his anonymity. Much of the spring Richter read Howe's history and copied notes for his new novel. Occasionally he put Howe aside and picked up "The Simple Life," the story he had begun many months earlier, before Hollywood. He began, too, a story that would grow into *Tacey Cromwell*, another novel of a strong woman. By the time he had completed note-taking from Howe, he had decided that he had more than one novel in front of him, perhaps a trilogy. Excited by the idea of his book, he felt, reading Howe, the sensations of early

Ohio life rising up to him from Howe's history. He was apparently unconcerned that his longest sustained work was a 30,000-word novella.

When he finally finished taking notes on the 900 pages of Howe's first volume, Richter found himself elated to begin what he anticipated to be the hardest part, the plotting of "The Rawhide Knot," as he was then calling his novel. "I am glad tonight to have gotten back to my writing," he acknowledged in his journal. Though "appalled" at the thought of the work before him, he knew that nothing else ever quite satisfied him: "I have no respect for myself when I loaf, do not write, put it off with subterfuges of taking notes, etc."[30] As always, the initial plotting went slowly, making him feel the awful demands of work that came wholly from his own imagination. Often a day's plotting and writing would be erased by ten minutes reading the next morning. At other times, Richter would go to bed worn and discouraged, listening to trains in the distance and envying all those whose jobs allowed them to repeat the same act over and over again. Then in the morning he would find that his despairing feelings had "matured into a determination to [write], and the morning hours were clear and keen."[31]

On April 26 reviews arrived from a clipping service, some praising *The Sea of Grass* extravagantly. Perhaps because of these, he thought, he found himself changing his plans for the new novel:

> I felt that I wanted to do The Rawhide Knot differently—more real as I imagined in the first place—but in a different way—one small incident after the other, each with a number as a chapter, each significant, not running into the next but standing much alone as a brush stroke here and a brush stroke there and when looked at as a whole, there is a story. It would mean that I should not have to stoop to the artificialities of plot, the bending toward this, the bringing in of explanations, the making every thing fit, preparing the ground which always takes up so much room and makes it fictional—just the incidents as they occur in life— something happens to us this year, something next, something ten years further on and these three incidents together one after the other are more important than all the rest of the life.[32]

That day at lunch he shared with Harvey his idea: each chapter a separate incident, each "something beautiful and different," such as a chapter of "little children weeding the garden and talking in low tones of the person buried under it for a hundred years." Then, he explained, he could go on with the person, developing one scene and then another until in the end there would be "a succession of fragments that would be far more real and artistic than a perfect photograph."

While "the currents were turned on," Richter explored with Harvey the possibility of transferring his story from frontier Ohio to the Southwest. That thought sustained itself only briefly, but while the idea was on them the couple began to talk about Albuquerque. Banning was still pleasant, and they were, all things considered, well settled in a comfortable home. Richter was not yet so restless he had to move on, and Harvey would regret, she said, leaving the California desert country. Housing was always hard to find in Albuquerque, but Harvey was well enough to travel, the spring sandstorms had passed in New Mexico, and, as they both knew, he had written almost all of his successful stories in Albuquerque. Perhaps his writing was spurred by the drabness of Albuquerque, as Harvey suggested, so unlike Banning with its lush green orchards and lawns. "If only we had a sign," Richter exclaimed to Harvey—anything to help them see what they ought to do.[33] That sign came on the first day of May. Coughing himself awake, Richter turned on his bedside flashlight to examine the phlegm in his handkerchief and discovered blood on it. By morning the blood was only a brown splotch on his handkerchief; it had come, he decided, from his throat rather than his lungs, as the blood had when an Albuquerque doctor had talked him into the tonsillectomy. That day a Banning doctor agreed with him about the source of the blood. What he really needed, the doctor said, was less work and more relaxation.[34]

Richter and Harvey packed that day and left the day after for Pennsylvania, with Harvey resting on the back seat of their Chevrolet, propped up by pillows. By then Richter had decided against setting "The Rawhide Knot" in a western locale, and so a trip East would give him needed color for the story. A stay in Clark's Valley would also allow him a chance to hear again the quaint speech of his former neighbors. Relishing the surprise of suddenly appearing at the homes of family and friends, the couple arrived with no notice, settling into a rented house in Dauphin, Pennsylvania, before their relatives knew they were back in the East. The stone house overlooking the Susquehanna River was just four miles from Pine Tree Farm, and within short Eastern miles were relatives and old friends—some of whom, like the Minskers, Richter counted on for color for his Ohio book. Vene arrived from Arizona soon after her parents moved into the Dauphin house.

As he and Harvey had hoped, Dauphin turned out to be far enough away from Pine Grove and Reading that visitors could be kept to a manageable level, though on Sundays, he warned Alfred Knopf when his publisher asked to visit, "the place is bound to be plastered with sundry and inescapable relatives."[35] Answering letters from the *Post* staff, Richter wrote Graeme Lorimer on June 9 that he was putting on a sweatshirt and "laying down in front of me" the short story he had started in Hollywood, "The Simple Life." As for accepting an invitation to visit the *Post* staff in Philadelphia, he wrote Wesley Stout that "I've sat down and dined with chaps out in my adopted country who had killed from seven to thirteen men, but what's that to sitting down with a ring of *Post* editors about me?"[36] Richter's letter to Stout began a summer of often quite funny exchanges between the two, Stout cajoling Richter into traveling to Philadelphia and Richter sidestepping his requests. He was also putting off Alfred Knopf and Paul Reynolds, Sr., whom he had still not met in person. Each time Richter came to the point of setting dates to visit, he fell back on his cautionary notes to himself in his journal. He was best on paper, he reminded himself; he was a shepherd's grandson, better off leaving personal appearances to those who had the right talents and energy supplies.

Early in August Richter sent a new story to the *Post*—not "The Simple Life" but rather a chapter from his novel, an account of a backwoods wedding that might, Richter worried, be too raw for the *Post.* When a reply came, however, it was not the story's rude characters but its lax plot that caused the editors concern. In an unusual two-page letter that demonstrates how much care the *Post* was taking with Richter's feelings, Wesley Stout urged Richter to rework the story. As submitted, Stout wrote, he was afraid the story would disappoint Richter's audience.[37] A letter from Paul Reynolds, Jr., the next day offered to send the story elsewhere, but Richter almost immediately decided to revise, explaining in his journal a rationale that is a window into his way of constructing things. He would rewrite, he told himself, to keep the *Post* connection—so that later, when he was once again penniless, he would not have to reproach himself for having made too little effort to keep an important market.[38]

After several days revising, Richter wrote Stout that he did not like any of his attempts. Nonetheless, he would come to Philadelphia, as Stout had repeatedly requested. In his journal, Richter explained the story's problem: he had written it as a chapter of his novel, writing in his new manner. To sell it as a short story to the *Post,* he had to rewrite it in precisely the ways he had promised himself he would not do. That discovery came out of what was evidently an exceptionally difficult period, a time when Harvey, entirely out of patience with him, finally accused him of infantile behavior—a charge that sent him into a stomping, cursing rage. This may well have also been the moment when Richter threw a fork at Harvey which, to his horror, struck her tines forward, puncturing her forearm.[39] Contrite beyond his usual after-argument remorse, Richter that night reminded himself, yet again, that his troubles with his writing and with Harvey were all from the same source, his failure to keep things within himself: "I am convinced that most if not all of my troubles, in my work, wife, and child, come from not keeping my promise to God, from failing to contain complaints, criticisms, compliments, enthusiasm, plans, hopes, good things but mostly bad. This always keeps me from a happy married life and a strong and likable personality myself."[40]

When Wesley Stout's telegram arrived the next day, with Stout offering to help work out a solution during Richter's visit, Richter had already decided on a new approach. He would have his heroine tell the story from her deathbed. A day later he boarded a train to Philadelphia, finally to meet George Horace Lorimer, the man who had pulled him from a bleak life writing pulp westerns. On the train ride back to Harrisburg, Richter found himself deeply disappointed. Not that the day had gone badly: with the exception of missing George Horace Lorimer (who, Richter would later discover, was suffering through the late stages of throat cancer), he had met Graeme Lorimer and met again Erd Brandt and Wesley Stout, and he had heard extravagant (Richter suspected fulsome) praise of his talent. He was simply too modest, Stout had told Richter; he could sell his stories to any number of magazines, but the *Post* could not replace Richter.[41] But Richter was depressed. It was not so much that the staff's treatment of him seemed so much soft soap, a compensation for refusing his story. It was that the *Post* had seemed so ordinary—just ordinary offices and ordinary men. The locus for so many years of desperate hoping, the *Post's* editorial offices had turned out to be just offices. He returned to Dauphin to tell Harvey that the editors of the Curtis Publishing Company, the men who for so many years had held the keys to his escape from poverty, were not the giants he had made them out to be. His disappointment did not keep him from rewriting "The Rawhide Knot." Early in September he had the story back in Stout's hands, and this time the *Post* bought the story for $1,400. Sending the story to his agent, Richter specifically asked Reynolds not to raise his asking price to the *Post*.

The New York trip turned out for Richter decidedly better than his visit to Philadelphia, with Richter meeting Paul R. Reynolds, Sr., on Tuesday, September 7, and Alfred Knopf the next day. To keep up appearances, Richter checked into the Biltmore Hotel on Fifth Avenue, which he remembered as one of New York's posh hotels. From there he went to meet Paul R. Reynolds. Tall like his son, Reynolds had the formal demeanor of a Boston Brahmin, which in fact he was, but a soft-spoken manner somewhat at odds with the large, imperious signature with which he ended his letters. At seventy-three, he was the dean of New York literary agents, having invented the occupation by first representing foreign writers' literary interests in the United States. Richter liked Reynolds enough to enjoy their lunch at the Century Club, ending the day pleased with his agent and with himself. He had held up well. The next day Alfred Knopf carried the wooing further, taking Richter to lunch with a high-powered group of editors and publishers at the Jewish Athletic Club. That evening they dined at Knopf's Manhattan apartment, with a French maid serving. Afterwards Knopf took Richter to see *You Can't Take It with You*, the hit at the Booth Theater, then on to the Twenty-One Club to talk until well after midnight. In the early morning hours the two men parted at a corner on Fifth Avenue. Afterward Richter sat for a long time in St. Patrick's Cathedral, calming his rushing thoughts until he would be able to sleep.[42]

Richter told both Reynolds and Knopf about his verbal agreement with Edwin Knopf to return for another stint at MGM, observing that perhaps that fall was the time to do it. His savings were being depleted quickly, Richter admitted, and then there was another worry. Richter had heard of a novel about life in early Ohio, which meant that another novelist might already have written his story. Knopf offered to get an early copy of Mead Winnegerode's *The Black Forest* from Farrar and Rinehart, its publisher, and then offered some advice. Richter's problem, he summarized, was that so far his novels did not pay enough to support Richter, and so he was obliged to earn added money either by writing for magazines or pictures. Because pictures promised more money, Richter should write to Knopf's brother "and make no more fuss about it."[43]

A week later when Gerry Adams called with an offer from MGM, Richter and Harvey were already packing to head west, and Vene had just left for the University of New Mexico. Richter accepted Edwin Knopf's offer of $750 a week for four months, deciding with Harvey that they would use the money to buy a house and a car and to provide for his father.[44] Once again they drove a leisurely route across the country, heading south to Florida and then west to New Orleans, arriving in Los Angeles before the middle of October. Because Harvey knew about the Beverly Wilshire Hotel only from her husband's letters, Richter insisted on staying there until they found a place to rent. When MGM agreed again to allow Richter to write at home, they looked for a house in the San Fernando Valley. By the beginning of November they had broken two leases and moved into a third home, each further to the east, trying to escape the smoggy air that spread each morning across the valley. Richter was sufficiently worried about Harvey's health to think of breaking his contract with MGM; finally, however, he cautioned himself again that if he did burn that bridge he might later regret it.[45]

At MGM, Richter's head was not turned when former colleagues and acquaintances welcomed him back effusively. That was simply Hollywood, Richter understood, where hyperbole was the coin of the realm. Richter secretly hoped that MGM would assign him to *The Sea of Grass*, though he had heard that Harvey Fergusson was already at work on it. After declining several possible stories MGM offered, thinking them all "low-grade stuff," he agreed to write a first treatment of Kenneth Roberts's *Northwest Passage*, a novel he did not especially admire but thought he could turn into a script. Everywhere people congratulated him on his assignment to a major studio project. But Richter's sense of unease began to grow almost immediately. First Hunt Stromberg, the movie's producer, put him off for an appointment for days and then let him sit in an outer office for over an hour. Next a clerical error delayed Richter's check for two weeks. On October 23 Richter was startled to read that George H. Lorimer had died. A year earlier Lorimer had written to urge him not to stay long in Hollywood; now that letter seemed a warning. And just a year before, Richter remembered, he had seen Dalton Trumbo, a pallid little fellow, waiting impatiently outside Knopf's office. Knopf had ignored Trumbo and seen Richter first. On the day Lorimer died Richter had been standing in exactly the same place in Knopf's office when Trumbo swept in with his waxed mustache and a box of candy for the staff. He ignored Richter. That was the day after Richter read in the local trade newspaper that all his work on "Benefits Forgot" had been jettisoned. Perhaps these were clues to his fate, Richter wondered in that evening's journal entry. Already he regretted trading in his Chevrolet for the used black Packard that he was to pick up the next day.[46]

A week later, packing for the second move in as many weeks, Richter wrote himself a truculent reminder about Hollywood: "When I am away and need money, the unpleasant things about Hollywood fade away and I remember how new and sparkling it is and how fast I made money." But working on a story he did not care about actually did him physical harm: "to write about what is given me—and in Hollywood it is someone else's choice—I must tear myself in half to get up the power to write about it for a few hours—then do it all over the next day."[47] Waking each morning he discovered that his chest hurt him, and so did his eyes. Keeping at such a pace for months at a time was unthinkable.

On November 6 Richter handed in his first treatment to Stromberg, then went home to wait for a conference with the movie's producer. When no call came, he telephoned and then visited Stromberg's office, discovering that Stromberg remained tied up with another picture. One day Richter picked up the revised script of "Benefits Forgot," which listed Bradbury Foote's name with his for credit, and while his Packard was being washed he walked up the street reading the new script. By the time his car was ready Richter was beside himself. Foote had ruined all his work, deleting many of his additions and changing others so that they were flat and meaningless. He did not even want his name on the script, he told Harvey and Gerry Adams that evening. But they convinced him to control his feelings until he had talked to Knopf, arguing that he could damage his standing with the studio. Then before he could see Knopf, Richter received a phone call from the Academy of Motion Picture Arts and Sciences, saying Bradbury Foote was demanding sole credit for the script. Richter saw immediately that an already bad situation had become even worse: because he had not immediately repudiated the script, anything he did would make him look even more foolish.[48]

That Tuesday an angry and resentful Richter had his talk with Edwin Knopf, a meeting Knopf delayed for more than two hours while Richter waited outside his office. Not having seen Knopf since his return, Richter in his choleric state of mind entered his former friend's office to find him looking "fat and dark and sure of himself." Knopf did not really believe that he had wanted his name off the script, Richter could see, but Knopf did agree, finally, that with Richter feeling as he did it was best to accede to Foote. Richter penned the telegram to the academy carefully, though he did not expect anyone in Hollywood to read it with such care: "Glad to tell you there will be no need for arbitration. If treatment were as typical of my work as it is based on my treatment, I would fight for credit. But since it is definitely not and Mr. Foote feels entitled to sole credit, please give it to him."[49]

Briefly Richter thought again of breaking his contract, writing in his journal that, if Vene were not coming for Christmas, they could just pack and leave. As an expression of his contempt he would leave behind his last several paychecks, which he had not yet picked up. So far he at least had been able to contain himself, though he was "blue, but desperately, silently blue," and unable to fathom why Stromberg had kept him idle for a week unless it was because Stromberg's interest in him had been undermined by the "Benefits Forgot" fiasco. By November 16 he could stand the waiting no longer, calling Stromberg's office and pressing for an appointment. That evening Stromberg's secretary called with a Thursday morning appointment, then on Thursday called twice to put the appointment off until later in the day. Finally Richter met Stromberg late Thursday afternoon, surprised that he was kept waiting only half an hour beyond the appointed time.

The studio had decided against Richter's treatment, Stromberg told him, and had already assigned it to another studio writer. The problem with Richter's treatment was that Richter had decided to add stronger human motivations to the original novel, to hold more interest and to make the individual scenes matter a little more. Like Clarence Brown the year before, Stromberg disagreed that the added interest was necessary. Later, Stromberg promised, they would all meet in conference to thrash out the outline for a final treatment. Richter's ideas would get a hearing then. What was he to do in the meantime, Richter disconsolately asked. Enjoy the California air, Stromberg replied—and have no compunction about doing so.

"All in all," Richter later wrote, Stromberg "turned out to be quite princely and grand despite my obstinacy in refusing to see that the book had enough interest as it was."[50] But rather than accepting his vacation as an opportunity to rest or to take up his own writing, Richter found himself feeling "useless"; later he would revise this description to "nervous and worthless." Taking money without working made him feel "like a cheap cad," and he resolved not to pick up any of his checks until he had done something to earn them.[51] Then Adams visited to pass on the news that Knopf was delighted to have gotten Richter back to Hollywood—because Stromberg was so pleased with Richter's writing. Richter found himself without an explanation for such odd behavior by the studio bosses, complimenting him extravagantly but then discarding his work. "It is very funny," he wrote. "I can't make it out."[52] Perhaps they were just easing him out, he thought, choosing this way to rid themselves of him.

The next day, a Sunday, Richter drove Harvena to the desert for the better air. That evening, tired from the driving, he took a peppermint for quick energy and got down to a new outline of the novel he was again calling "The Trees." His new beginning would start with a strapping young girl, Sayward Luckett, first establishing her strength and character, then contrasting her to the other members of her family. Two days later he was far enough into his writing to remind himself that he needed "to think and feel in words"; only that allowed him to write expressively and meaningfully.[53] Late in October Alfred Knopf had kept his promise to send an advance copy of Mead Winnegerode's novel about Ohio, and by the end of an evening's reading Richter knew that Winnegerode's was an entirely different story from his own. Once he actually began working on *The Trees*, he began talking to Harvey about getting away from Hollywood just as quickly after Christmas as they decently could. That did not mean, of course, that he looked forward to being let go, but after more days without word from Stromberg he began to make his plans based on what seemed more and more likely to be his dismissal from MGM. He continued to pick up his checks, but he did not cash them.

When the promised story conference materialized early in December, Richter felt himself "shamed" when others said they needed a story that was more real. Stromberg even compounded the insult, announcing that they did not want a formula story.[54] In a private conference with Stromberg, Richter could no longer contain himself, answering Stromberg's question as to whether he could write the dialogue for the picture by telling him that he should know the worst, that practically nothing from his earlier "Benefits Forgot" script had survived a second writing.[55] From his meeting with Stromberg, Richter went to see Edwin Knopf, waiting two hours for him to return from lunch. Richter's journal entry summarizing the meeting (which he titled "I PROBABLY KILL MYSELF AT MGM") betrays just how mixed his feelings had become, how unsure he remained of his place in Hollywood, and how deeply suspicious he was of others' motives:

> The first thing Knopf said was, "What's the matter? I never saw you so up before." I told him to expect Stromberg calling him up and cutting me off, that I had told him the worst about me. I accused his good words and arguing for me to have kept me on so far, and he forgot himself to reply, walking up and down the room, that he had told Stromberg that any time he didn't want me he had a dozen things he could put me on. He gave me a copy of "The Young American" to bring along but when I read it tonight I realized that it is by far the cheapest thing ever given me, that he probably knew I wouldn't do it and expected me to give up. I recall the gleam in his eye when I answered his question why I was so up by saying I was closer to New Mexico. . . . [H]e said, "You would stay longer if you had something to do?" but I didn't like the gleam in his eye. I told him the four best pictures I had seen and that none of them were MGM. Afterward I realized it might have been the Liver Extract pills I started taking last night. I didn't give a damn.[56]

If Richter's agitated journal entry accurately portrays Knopf's manner in that meeting, Richter's conclusions about Knopf's motives seem far more negative than what is reasonably inferable—as Richter himself immediately acknowledged in his next paragraph, a single sentence, reflecting his dismay at his own anger: "Reading the above tells me that Hollywood is no place for me if it makes me write like this."

Spurred by such exasperating experiences, Richter was moving, in his lifelong conflict between aspiring to succeed in other people's terms and craving an inner, personal sense of self-worth, toward a break with the Hollywood enticements of money and prestige. He was not being profitably used by the studio, he was quite certain; and except for the weekly checks he was getting nothing of value from the experience. Hollywood took from him his free will as a writer, making him a "studio slave" to other people's ideas. When he put aside his Hollywood worries for *The Trees*, his mind carried him so far from Hollywood that he was "a little stunned" and even found it hard to start. But then he would think of the Minsker family of Clark's Valley, his primary model for the Lucketts. Putting the Minskers on the march out of Pennsylvania and into the deep forests of Ohio, "with John Minsker shouting 'boop, boop' or imitating some thing of the time" as he had done when leading his family on berrying expeditions, these thoughts carried him back into the rich story resources of Howe's history.[57] Late in November, at about the time he had returned to the opening of *The Trees*, Richter had read Steinbeck's *Of Mice and Men* and found himself with mixed feelings. The story was not his kind: Lenny's repeated questions to George, his pleas to George to tell again about the farm, seemed "very much like moving picture talk, like Wallace Beery." Yet when he compared Steinbeck's style to his own in *Early Americana* and *The Sea of Grass*, Richter was "amazed at how poor and sweet [his own] was." And Steinbeck's sentiment, though not quite convincing while Richter was reading, remained when the book was done, its "harshness" and the "rough character of the men . . . left a deep memory of being real and true."[58]

That observation led him to reconsider his own narrative style: "I must be simpler, much more detail[ed]. My plots are good enough perhaps. It is the writing that dresses them up too much, strains too much for effect. There should be not too much effect aimed at all. Now I have the feeling of real characters in the Steinbeck book while a great deal of the poor stuff I felt while reading is gone." Other writers, too, were potential models for a less contrived style: "Frost should be my study as well as Cather. . . . The plots, the story part, seem all right when I go over them—but the writing is too artificial, sketchy, soaring, over-doing the effects I want to make. I NEED MORE SOLID, STARKER, TRUER WRITING AND STORY AND CHARACTERS."[59]

But first he needed to finish with Hollywood. Perhaps as a gambit to keep Richter occupied until Stromberg was available for *Northwest Passage*, Knopf suggested to Richter that he spend his remaining time developing a fresh story, of his own choosing. This Richter took up immediately, hoping to complete the project by the end of the year. Hoping, too, that his original idea would bring him some vindication in Hollywood, Richter worked long days at his desk, broken irregularly by fights with Harvey. On December 14 two arguments in one day led to a lengthy meditation and self-reproach in his journal. Once again he told himself that he must try to accept Harvey as she was, to change himself instead of pointlessly trying to make her see her weaknesses. These were unchangeable, hereditary, and had to be "left to God." His own weakness should be his first concern—his inability to stand alone, keeping his thoughts and feelings to himself. As for his wife: "I am convinced that so long as I expect any comradeship and understanding from H[arvey], I shall get a stone as I did twice today and two thousand times in the last twenty-two years. Holding my own counsel will soften that stone but I am a fool now if I let it deceive me. The entire A[chenbach] family is like that, solid and firm and cool to the hand and brain."[60] Christmas Day Richter broke his regimen of daily writing sessions, allowing Harvey and Vene to talk him into relaxing before a traditional turkey dinner. After an evening drive to the Pacific, Richter returned to his desk to read Robert Frost and to write in his journal: "Reading Robert Frost and thinking of my own crowded style, I wish that I would write it in the simplest way and go on to other thoughts and things. The moment a writer fills a sentence too full, he is writing too much for the reader."

Before completing his assignment in Hollywood on January 19, Richter had a final opportunity to perplex Edwin Knopf. When he had not finished his original treatment by early January, Richter wrote Knopf to ask that he be taken off the payroll and allowed to finish on his own time. Knopf declined, replying by return mail that, while he liked Richter "well enough to do almost anything you ask me," he could not agree to such a request.[61] The two men met briefly on Richter's last day, Knopf stepping out from a meeting to talk with Richter in his secretary's office. There Knopf offered that he was sorry things had not worked out well with Stromberg. But Richter was not, this time, angling for another contract; he had had his fill of Hollywood. He could not write for committees, and he was simply unable to understand a system that could be so wasteful as to allow him to sit idle at $750 a week. At the end of their conversation Richter reminded Knopf that he had cashed none of his checks since November and would not do so unless Knopf was satisfied that Richter had met all MGM's expectations. When the man in charge of MGM's 125 writers assured Richter that he was happy with the work he had done, including the original treatment, Richter deposited the checks in his savings account and prepared to put Hollywood behind him. This time he and Harvey would not wait a day longer than necessary.

He did not escape, however, without experiencing what seemed a final insult. Alerted by a studio friend, Richter went to see Twentieth Century Fox's new movie *In Old Chicago* and discovered that Fox had stolen his scene of a buggy race against a train, the climax from his "Smoke Over the Prairie"—a story Fox had considered but rejected just a year earlier. A day later he saw Wallace Beery in *Bad Man of Brimstone*, made from a plot he had helped another studio writer to develop. The writer did not even receive writing credit for the film, Richter noted in disgust. Perhaps it was just as well, he remarked in his journal. The movie was only another Hollywood western, full of hocum and misinformation about the real West. "I am terrifically ashamed for having sold myself to these penny cheapsters," he continued, men "whose chief ability is their glib confidence in themselves and ability to scheme and swagger."[62]

THREE

Richter and Harvey left early on January 26, 1938, driving to Tucson for a brief stay and then on to Albuquerque, where Richter picked up almost immediately the novel he knew he needed to write next. He had already written about Sayward Luckett's thoughts on her deathbed in "The Rawhide Knot," the story he had sold to the *Post*, but he intended to put aside that manner of telling her story. There would be no fiction in Sayward's story. This was not for Hollywood and not for the *Post*, and not even for popular sales. It was for himself, his own accomplishment—written out of all he had learned, all the mistakes he had made in writing stories for other people. There would be no screaming for effect. Chapters would be built on simple feeling, and they would have emotional meaning from direct events, narrated in the language of the time. He would write a chapter every two weeks or so, he promised himself, and by the time of Vene's graduation from college he would have 20,000 words written, a third of the 60,000 he planned. Perhaps he could salvage 5,000 to 10,000 words from the previous summer's work, but only if he could be absolutely sure that his earlier writing would fit his reaffirmed conviction, expressed in the terse shorthand of his journal, that all the book must be about "humble lives with spirit meaning."[63]

In Albuquerque Richter and Harvey rented a house at the corner of Cedar and Los Lomas, an expensive house that Richter was not sure he could write in. There he settled into his daily schedule, breaking off from writing to take late afternoon rides with Harvey and then returning evenings to his desk. Before March he was having trouble with hay fever, and later Vene sprained her ankle in a fall while horseback riding and had to spend weeks at home. His real problem, however, was not his health or Vene's interruptions but the incidents he wanted to turn into chapters, which once again were stubbornly resisting his storytelling. He would write an incident from one perspective and then, dissatisfied, he would write it from another. Unable to decide which version would, on revision, yield the emotional meaning he wanted, he turned to Harvey and Vene for help he did not believe they could give him. He did need their encouragement, and when Harvey was not enthusiastic, his next journal entry inevitably registered the result: "trouble."

On February 11, after a week of plotting and note transcribing, Richter began a new first chapter, "writing and rewriting nearly a thousand words over and over again but finding it unconvincing." That evening he relaxed by paging through his loose-leaf book of notes for color, hoping for inspiration. Another night he reread his stories from the *Post*, trying to find the right voice for the story of his pioneer woman. Something was happening to him, he conjectured: "I am not excited any more when I read my stories. I am much depressed. They are shouting at top-of-voice. I want to do something more simple. And to be interesting and gripping a simple novel must have very real and absorbing life." Richter finished the journal entry with two paragraphs about recent signs and symbols perhaps portending success writing in the house on Los Lomas and Cedar, where the street address—643 North Cedar—added up to thirteen. Thirteens had been "scattered all the way from California to Albuquerque," where he and Harvey discovered the town full of license numbers in the thirteen hundreds. "Now do these things mean anything?" he once again asked himself.[64] There would be no quick answer. He decided his plot lacked enough emotional energy, just as he had believed about *Northwest Passage* and "Benefits Forgot." Reading Frost's "Home Burial," with its charged emotion beneath the blunt words of Frost's New England farmer, Richter thought of a new beginning, a chapter he would call "Bread," the story of Sayward's mother, dying of tuberculosis, craving real bread to eat. Quickly he wrote by hand over a thousand words, feeling himself moved all through the writing. This was, he hoped, a seminal moment: "Of course it is very rough and probably indecipherable but I shall try to get it in shape still in pen tomorrow. At least now I feel that I have my characters. I have feeling for them."[65]

As a gray, windy February passed into a bright desert spring, Richter worked doggedly through a series of colds and bouts of hay fever. For help with his woodsy family, he got out his journals from the Pine Tree Farm years, which led to another self-assessment. "I HAVE BEEN SUCH A FOOL," he began his entry for March 3. Imitating the nature writing of John Burroughs, he had managed only "a stiff, unnatural, and self-conscious style," and he had missed his real subject: "I tried to be eloquent, draw analogies, dilate, and usually over nothing, and all the while I lived in a valley filled with human drama and authenticities. . . . When I wrote of even the most ordinary things and wrote in simple words of simple honest observations, what people looked like, when a tree bloomed, it has a dignity and significance. . . . Best of all was when I noted and simply described people as they looked, walked, talked, and what they said. The people were real, rich, mellow, authentic. They are always literature."

But such admonitions did little to spur on Richter's writing. Soon he was again lamenting, in entries which always, when he looked back, made him ashamed of himself, that "All is lost!" He had chosen the hardest possible novel to write, about people he could not know. He was "plodding too much, writing too slowly, and adding, padding."[66] Not until May 3 could Richter report that finally, after months of writing far away from Hollywood and its influences, he was able to "see things in words," the first necessity of his writing. With that important change came the ability to see some humor in his situation. Writing to Erd Brandt, he reported that his new novel would not be of interest to the *Post*—and he was throwing away most of what he wrote anyway. His latest try "was moving chiefly through the enthusiasm of my wife and daughter who scheme up nice things to say to keep me from tearing things up, no doubt being afraid I might get to the curtains and carpets."[67]

As Vene's graduation drew near, there were family talks about her future. Richter discouraged his daughter from graduate school in literature and a career in teaching, urging her instead to think about journalism, the path he had taken into professional writing. Recalling one of his own ideas from a decade earlier, he suggested she return to Pine Grove and restart the weekly newspaper. With that to support her, she might in time learn the ways of the Pennsylvania Dutch and central Pennsylvanians to become the Robert Frost of the region. Reluctantly, Richter and Harvey allowed Vene to join Lucille Garduño and her family for a summer in Mexico City, with the understanding that afterwards she would go to Columbia University in New York City to study journalism.

Richter's own plans remained indefinite while he tried to interest Harvey in an experiment. Richter's idea was to buy a trailer to pull behind their Packard. Then they could travel freely, stopping as they would, even renting a house for a few months each time they wanted. And they could also pack up and leave without the usual bother, and without the need to decide in advance just where they were going. Although Harvey did not take to the proposal easily, thinking as she must have about her loneliness in new places and the discomfort of cramped quarters with a restless husband, by June she was ready to try the experiment. Placing an order with the Anderson Coach Company, the two drove to the factory in Michigan to pick up a twenty-four foot trailer, black with a silver roof. From Michigan they drove to Ohio, stopping at libraries and historical societies for Richter to gather information for his trilogy. By early August the trailer was settled into a quiet spot in Clark's Valley, near Pine Tree Farm, where Richter dammed up a creek for a private swimming hole.

They stayed in Pennsylvania until October, Richter gathering notes from conversations with John Minsker, Petey Meyers, and others in Clark's Valley who still evoked the old speech and values of pioneer life. Vene was by then returned from Mexico, residing in the International House in New York City. Having applied too late to be admitted to Columbia's journalism program, she had succeeded in enrolling in two of Columbia's writing seminars in fiction. Once Richter and Harvey were satisfied that Vene could get along without them, they departed for Tucson. Richter was reluctant to leave just as the trees were beginning to turn, but he was eager to get to a place where he could write. He could not write in Pennsylvania where there were so many distractions, and he had decided that he would never be able to write in a trailer.

In Tucson the house Richter and Harvey rented had a noisy oil burner that shook the house, but outside there were huge cacti, and each morning a covey of quail came to drink from a pool beside their patio. Knowing few people in Tucson and having no close neighbors, they found themselves as isolated as they had been, years earlier, in their cabin in the Sandia Mountains. That suited Richter perfectly. By the end of the third week in Tucson Richter had written two chapters. Surrounding himself with his writing, he wrote almost without break except for errands to the store and post office and the afternoon drive with Harvey. At Harvey's insistence he put away his typewriter for Thanksgiving, but he spent part of the day reading and sorting his notes. Taking the day off had been a mistake, he commented cryptically in his journal: "Nervous. Blue. I get nothing from loafing. Only work counts." Two days later he began "The Little Tyke," about Sulie's becoming lost in the woods, which had been from the beginning the most emotionally charged incident Richter planned for his book. Although the story of Sulie's disappearance was intensely moving for Richter, he kept his prose simple, deliberately writing shorter sentences than in *The Sea of Grass*. Before Christmas he had written fourteen chapters and was working on "Genny's Wide, Wide World." Worried about a fire, Richter carried the manuscript with him each time he left the house. When he took Harvey to see a movie, he put the manuscript into his briefcase and carried it into the theater, just in case his car was stolen.[68]

In mid-April when he had completed the first draft of the last chapter, Richter looked back over months of intensely concentrated writing, often accompanied by bouts of pain. In January, moving a daybed onto the porch for Harvey, Richter suffered a hernia that made walking and even sitting painful. Several doctors insisted the tear needed to be surgically repaired, but he put them all off and relied for temporary relief on a truss. Then he decided some of his pain was caused by varicose veins in his scrotum and was alarmed to have this condition diagnosed as an infection in his prostate. Remembering his appendectomy in Harrisburg, he dreaded the thought of undergoing general anesthesia. Despite the pain, he decided that he had to put off any operation until completing his novel. It took so long for him to get himself into the desperate "tensing" his best writing came from that he would not chance breaking his writing regimen while he was in it.[69]

Hearing about her father's troubles, Vene offered to come from New York to help care for him, but Richter insisted that she stay to complete her writing seminars at Columbia. Although he had not read her stories—and had asked not to read any until something was published—when he wrote Richter often offered advice about story writing. When letters from Vene arrived, he and Harvey would take turns reading them aloud to each other, rereading each several times. Usually Harvey replied, but when Vene wrote to describe her cheeks rosy with good health, her father immediately wrote back to warn her that flushed cheeks were the first sign of tuberculosis. She was "at a bad age," she must remember—and also remember that susceptibility to TB was part of her inheritance. She must rest daily, bundle up against the cold, and eat raw eggs mixed with orange juice.[70]

In part what kept Richter pressing on his novel was his hope of being able to complete it before having to break into his last $2,000 in savings. It would be only a few months before Vene's New York allowance, the monthly check to John Richter, and their own household expenses wiped out the money they had saved from the two contracts with MGM.[71] Once Richter suffered the hernia, selling the trailer was a foregone conclusion. It was a luxury they could not afford, although they could not sell it for anything close to the $950 they had paid for it. But regardless of his fears of slipping into debt, Richter did not waver in his commitment to writing that "would not yield anything to fiction." He would not fall back on his *Post* tricks for generating emotion or for tying things together neatly; instead he relied entirely on simple events honestly seen in words to achieve the critical emotional core for his story.[72]

In February he had extreme trouble writing "Out on the Tract," the chapter in which Genny, abandoned by her husband, suffers a nervous collapse. In March, approaching the last chapters, he found himself stymied trying to turn "The Rawhide Knot," his *Post* story of Sayward's marriage, into "It Came a Tuesday," his penultimate chapter. Read after the eighteen other chapters, his *Post* story now seemed "loud and fictional" and not at all "slow and convincing" like his new narrative. Repeatedly failing to find a way to rewrite it brought him to the point where he was "blue almost to tears," his confidence almost crushed. Finally he abandoned the exterior description of the wedding, which made the incident too farcical for the rest of the novel, and concentrated on Sayward's thoughts and on her ordinary actions, "real things, like making supper."[73] In the completed chapter he kept nothing from "The Rawhide Knot." Late in March he wrote the final chapter; immediately he began revising, starting at the beginning, pressing himself to finish before his money ran out.

Even with his money worries, Richter refused to promote his new novel. When Wesley Stout visited, Richter deflated all Stout's talk of sending the new novel to his magazine, saying that his novel would not make a serial for the *Post*.[74] He wrote Alfred Knopf not to expect a best-seller, that there would probably not be enough sales to warrant his continuing with the trilogy.[75] To Paul Reynolds he wrote that his novel was unlikely to interest Hollywood, that it was an experiment, something for himself, unlikely to find a wide audience.[76] Twice in March he wrote Gerry Adams not to encourage MGM or other studios, and in April he wrote to Edwin Knopf, who had left MGM to produce for Samuel Goldwyn, that Goldwyn could not get a big movie from *The Trees*, there being no part for Gary Cooper, Goldwyn's premier star.[77] Not even to his brother Fred would he let his guard down, telling Fred not to expect much, the book being "ordinary."[78] Secretly he must have hoped that his novel was so good that others would see that he had done more, not less, than novels that usually sold for serials and for movies. But he did not share this thought with anyone except perhaps Harvey.

On April 2, Harvey wrote an especially revealing letter to Vene: "The long strain of his novel, together with these various illnesses (you're not to tell anyone) have lowered Daddy's morale so much that he worries about everything more than ever and especially about you." She might well have acknowledged that her own emotional underpinnings had been weakened: on May 3, an especially virulent argument left Harvey hysterical, her legs numb and seemingly paralyzed, exclaiming that she could put up with no more. Terrified that his wife was losing her sanity or perhaps even her life, Richter pressed Harvey to forgive him. It was all his fault; if she would just get better he promised to take care of her always, just as she was, without criticizing or trying to change her. He promised as well to keep his compact with God to contain his emotion, to say nothing.[79] In the aftermath of this horrific experience, Richter's own health gave way in a "black wave of nerve weakness."[80] Over the next days he suffered extreme pains in his heart and at night heart palpitations and bouts of intense, profuse sweating that left his sheets soaked. Doctors whom Richter consulted all said what others had before; his heart problem was a nervous condition, related to overwork and overworry. On May 11, a week after the terrible trouble in which "Harvey nearly died," they left Tucson. He had not finished his rewriting, even dropping a chapter mid-revision. But Harvey's health and his own outweighed the unfinished novel. They needed to escape.

A week later they were back in Albuquerque, renting again 1617 Los Lomas, the house where Richter had finished writing *The Sea of Grass*. Before the end of the month he was back at work on chapter 11, "Corpse Candles," and before Vene arrived in mid-June Richter had given over half the chapters to a typist for final copy. Reading proof, Harvey did not seem very enthusiastic—about which Richter kept his disappointment to himself—but the typist was eager for new chapters so he could read more of the story, and Richter was temporarily elated. By the end of the month, when the last chapters were being typed, Richter's habitual worries descended. On rereading, his chapters seemed dull, not at all the vital story he had believed himself to be writing. Hearing that Erna Fergusson had given a party for Paul Horgan, Richter decided that he and Harvey must get out of town before the book came out, to be far away from their laughter at his failure. Driving to the post office to mail the typescript on July 1, Richter had to slow his car to a crawl to avoid red lights at intersections. His novel for himself was accomplished, even if the *Post*, which had ignored his warnings and asked to read his typescript, decided to turn it down.

Unable to remain in Albuquerque while he awaited the *Post* reply, Richter took Harvey and Vene on a trip to Colorado. When they returned on July 16, the letter he expected awaited him: as he predicted, the *Post* could not use his novel. It was undoubtedly a fine novel, Erd Brandt wrote, but it did not have the "necessary drive of story" for a serial.[81] Richter believed he had been forewarned: in Denver he had looked up at an intersection to see two street names together—"Stout" and "Downing."[82] Over the next month *Woman's Home Companion, Cosmopolitan*, and the *Atlantic* declined *The Trees*, all for reasons much like the *Post*'s. Even before these rejections came in, Richter was again allowing himself to think about writing "wooden claptrap" for Hollywood. Edwin Knopf was earnestly pursuing him, sending telegrams promising that if Richter came to work for him, the movie's producer would always be available. Later he wrote to say that Richter could even stay in Albuquerque to work through the initial draft of a Gary Cooper movie and sent three proposals for Richter to consider, "Black Gold," "Vinagaroon," and another about Judge Roy Bean. But Richter thought the offer—$750 for an initial plot and $3,000 for a fuller treatment—insultingly low. The day Blanche Knopf's telegram arrived exclaiming that *The Trees* was "superb," Richter telegraphed Gerry Adams to reject the contract.[83]

In a letter a week later, Blanche Knopf exclaimed herself "enormously enthusiastic" about the book and projected a later publication than usual because it was "important to have enough time on a book as fine as this to do all the necessary promotional work." But then she made two suggestions: that he dramatize the "interior monologues"—an expression Richter did not know—and rewrite the marriage chapter to make Sayward's motivations clearer.[84] With or without the changes his wife suggested, Knopf wanted to exercise his option to publish the novel, and without any intercession by Reynolds raised the advance to $1,500. To Blanche Knopf, Richter wrote as polite a letter as he could, given his seething outrage at her presumption. He did not agree that dramatizing more events would improve his novel (in truth she was asking for exactly the book he had worked so hard not to write) but if she would send her thoughts about Sayward's marriage he'd consider them. Soon, however, he ruled out even modest changes to "It Came a Tuesday." Leaving Sayward's feelings a mystery was exactly his point. Some human motivations were simply not fathomable, and Sayward's attraction to Portius Wheeler was one of them. In this she was like Lutie Cameron of *The Sea of Grass*, whose feelings were unknowable even to her family. And she was like Harvena Achenbach, standing on a porch in Pine Grove on a humid August day in 1914. She was like Conrad Richter, meeting Harvey's eyes for the first time and hearing her say she was thinking of him. Such feelings were ineffable.

Through July and August Gerry Adams reported persistent interest among Hollywood studios to see Richter's new novel. Reluctant to put his novel into any studio's hands, he responded that his price would be $50,000 for the whole trilogy; later he acquiesced to ask $35,000 just for *The Trees*. Such bravado was undercut by Richter's worries about money as the magazines publishing serials one by one rejected his book. Although he had told himself from the beginning that his method for writing *The Trees* would make it unsuitable for serialization, the *Post*'s rejection affected him deeply. He had written his very best work, compromising nothing. But instead of writing a better novel, he evidently had written a worse one. Only Blanche Knopf was enthusiastic.

When Germany invaded Poland on September 1, world events pushed aside Richter's personal worries, and he spent the day next to his radio, listening for news. Worries about the war in Europe stayed with him throughout the fall, a counterpoint and even a corrective to his worries about the upcoming publication of his novel. His personal worries were alleviated when the *Post* made "a fine offer" of $7,500 for Richter's next three-part serial.[85] Then on November 6 Alfred Knopf announced that the Book of the Month Club had chosen *The Trees* as a dual selection, enclosing with his letter a first royalty payment of over $4,500. Even before the *Post* had bought for $1,750 the story Richter worked on intermittently all that fall, "The Simple Life," Richter had written to Gerry Adams to tell him that *The Trees* was not for sale to a movie studio.[86]

Before the winter weather settled into Albuquerque, Richter had taken Harvey and Vene to San Marino, California, where he could research his next serial at the Huntington Library. That Christmas they regretted not seeing the snow of the East, but they had much to be thankful for—especially when they remembered their Christmases during the years after the crash of 1929, and even their last Christmas at Pine Tree Farm, when Harvey's health was so clearly slipping. They were all reasonably healthy, their bank accounts were at least temporarily full, the new novel would be out in the early spring, and already there was a new project for Richter to work on, with a promise of easy publication. But the war news from Europe nagged at Richter, and then, just before the New Year, came the disquieting news from his brother Joe that John Absalom Richter had taken to his bed and simply refused to get up.

Nomads

O N E

On January 17, 1940, the telegram Conrad Richter had been dreading arrived. From Edna, Joe's wife, it said simply, "Dad failing fast." By noon Richter had boarded the Santa Fe Chief for the three-day trip from California to Reading, Pennsylvania. As the train crossed the rolling plains of Kansas a second telegram was delivered to him, this one from Harvey. John Richter was dead. Outside the clacking, swaying train, Kansas shivered through its coldest weather of that winter.

Fred and Joe Jr., Joe's oldest boy, were waiting for Richter at the Reading train station. At the funeral home Richter was upset to discover that his father's mustache was gone, then dismayed to learn that John Richter had shaved it off several years earlier. Richter was also struck by his father's appearance in the coffin—by the "peculiarly bitter look" to his mouth.[1] Was this expression a sign to him from the astral? Did it register his father's first reaction as he passed from this life to the next? That bitter look would continue to haunt him.[2]

On Sunday there was a memorial service in Reading, and on Monday morning a funeral in Pine Grove. In his first letter to Harvey, Richter commented that he preferred the second service; he liked the Pine Grove pastor's reserved manner, less professionally up-tempo than that of the minister in Reading. But far more comforting than either service was the story of Lily May's dream. Edna's severely crippled sister, Lily May had lived in an upstairs bedroom of her brother-in-law and sister's home for most of their marriage. John Richter visited her there often, and the two had become close friends. At 11:30 P.M. on January 17, Lily May awakened crying, remembering vividly a dream of John Richter coming to her and saying, "Good-bye, I must go now, Lily May." Minutes later the hospital called to say John Richter had died.

"A peculiar thing," were the noncommittal words with which Richter began his relation of the episode to Harvey. But after his few brief sentences narrating the event, he confided that the experience offered him more hope than all the prayers, hymns, and reassuring words of the eulogies: "It meant more to me," he wrote, "than any part of the services."[3] Spurred by Lily May's dream, Richter wrote in his journal of his hopes to be again with his father and his mother, thoughts leading him to assertions that were never quite wholehearted beliefs. In the days before his father's death, Richter prodded himself in his devotional notebook to remember Cornillier's *The Survival of the Soul*, in which souls in an afterlife communicate with loved ones still alive, telling himself: "read this again. Think and believe this."[4] But he was unable to give himself over completely to his own advice, writing in his journal what may have been the most anguished question of his adult life: "Does my mother love me after she is dead? Nobody knows."[5]

Back in California, Richter found himself suffering through grief he awoke to each morning. For a time all music was painful to hear, reminding him of his father's exuberant singing.[6] Soon he was making appointments to see psychics and attempting to establish contact with his father and with his mother.[7] And once again he was reading his well-thumbed copy of Cornillier. When he discovered that Cornillier had written a sequel to *The Survival of the Soul*, Richter set out to acquire it. A book service found *The Prediction of the Future*, translated into

English by L. E. Eeland, but the book turned out not to be a sequel. A letter to Eeland in England elicited the news that Cornillier, over eighty years old, was living in Normandy; but Germany's occupation of France meant that Eeland was no longer able to contact the aged artist, and Eeland knew nothing about a sequel.[8] Writing himself to Cornillier, Richter announced that, after years of gathering information about survival, he had found no other account that impressed him so deeply: "I am Pennsylvania Dutch. My people have been in America for many generations and there is a certain slow and stolid blood in me that ponders and checks and rechecks very carefully. In no other study of an after-life but yours have I found such practical, matter-of-fact details that add up to conviction."[9] In a second letter to Eeland, Richter confided his intention to write a Western Bible, a project that had gone without mention in his journal for several years: "My last two novels have had a very fortunate reception over here, and my hope has been to climax them with one on the riddle of existence. Indeed much of my fiction has been planned to this end—to secure a public that would buy and read at least one book on this subject."[10] No reply came from the French artist, but in his efforts to verify that souls did indeed survive death Richter was prepared to rely on another Pennsylvania Dutch trait, persistence. He wrote Cornillier just after the Allied invasion swept across Normandy in 1944 and again in 1946, at the end of all hostilities.[11] Only when the third letter brought no response did Richter accept that he would hear no more of the young model who predicted her own death and promised to communicate from the astral. His interest in the topic did not wane, however, nor did he give up his plan to write his own Bible.

A month after his father's funeral, Richter finally put himself in the care of a surgeon for the hernia operation he had avoided for more than a year— agonizing to the last minute over which of several surgeons he would actually allow to perform the operation, then regretting his choice when postoperative shock from the anesthesia kept him hospitalized for almost three weeks and in bed for over a month, a time when his quicksilver temper was at its worst. Although he had been warned that full recovery could take as long as six months, he was not prepared to find, weeks after the operation, that the double hernia repair left him in more discomfort rather than less. Curiously, he scheduled his operation to coincide with the publication of *The Trees*, which was officially released on March 1, 1940. Recovering in his hospital bed, Richter received congratulatory telegrams from Alfred and Blanche Knopf and from Paul R. Reynolds, Jr., who had become Richter's primary agent as his father, approaching eighty, gradually withdrew from the agency. Harvey read him excerpts of reviews

14. Portrait of Conrad Richter, *circa* 1940.

as they came in. In the main these were highly favorable, complimenting his evocation of pioneer life through the speech of early settlers. This time no reviewers suggested debts to Willa Cather; rather, the critics treated him with the respect due an established writer. That point was underlined just before Richter was released from his hospital room when he received an invitation to join P.E.N., the international association of writers. He gratefully accepted.

Beginning with a half-page ad in the *Times Book Review*, Alfred Knopf mounted an ambitious advertising campaign for *The Trees*, spending $5,000 on advertisements that announced *The Trees* as "a book that comes once in a lifetime" and on the unusual marketing ploy of having statuettes of Sayward distributed to forty of the largest booksellers. Well promoted, *The Trees* climbed steadily up the best-seller lists. Then Gerry Adams brought a $25,000 offer from Fox Film Corporation for the movie rights to the novel. For a family who had lived desperately on the edge through five years of the depression, $25,000 was an almost irresistible offer—enough money to replace the savings lost in the stock market crash, more than enough money to buy and furnish a home comfortably in Albuquerque. And for a writer who was never confident that his next story would sell, the offer must have seemed like a God-sent insurance policy—perhaps even the security Richter believed he needed to write his Western Bible. But Richter worried that a film adaption of *The Trees*, especially if it turned out to be the usual Hollywood fare, would ruin Sayward's story for him, making it impossible for him to continue the trilogy. With his novel apparently selling well in bookstores and over 100,000 copies already sold through the Book of the Month Club, Richter again decided that the movie rights would not be for sale until he had completed the rest of his pioneer woman's life.[12]

About a month after the publication of *The Trees*, Knopf's advertisements stopped. Soon afterward *The Trees* slipped off the lists, causing Richter to regret at least momentarily his quick refusal of the Fox offer. Making his disappointment all the more painful was that the novel paired with *The Trees* as a Book of the Month Club dual selection, Richard Wright's *Native Son*, continued to sell well. Alfred Knopf saw the circumstance as unusually bad luck, writing to Richter that *Native Son* turned out to be one of those rare books that "just sweeps everything before it," with the result that "while *The Trees* got immensely favorable notices, it was in almost every case played down by literary editors in favor of *Native Son*."[13] *The Trees*, Knopf predicted, would nonetheless last as a perennial seller, one of the books bookstores reordered as a matter of course. Knopf's prediction might well have satisfied the disappointed Richter had he not discovered that Knopf had transferred most of his stock of the novel to the Book of the Month Club. To Richter's mind this could mean only that Knopf, despite his declared optimism for future sales, had given up on the book.

Richter was just as upset that he had received no advance warning of his novel being paired with Richard Wright's. When the Book of the Month Club promotional material arrived, Richter discovered a picture of the African-American novelist handsomely attired in a suit and tie, and below this the old *Post* picture of himself lounging on horseback—a photograph not even appropriate for his novel. "I hold Knopf's alone responsible," Richter wrote in his journal—adding that he resented deeply his being associated with a Negro writer of a sensationally lurid novel. "[Knopf] compromised me for five thousand dollars," he concluded indignantly.[14]

While *Native Son* continued atop the lists, Richter grumbled in his journal about Knopf and about Reynolds, who Richter suspected had participated in keeping the Wright information from him. But his primary worry was not his association with somebody else's novel, but rather why his own did not sell more quickly from booksellers' shelves. Even as he blamed Knopf for abandoning the sales campaign, he also blamed himself for the book he had written. The qualities he had worked so hard to achieve—the novel's accumulating sense of pioneer life, its leisurely pace, its careful evocation of authentic language—just the accomplishments that had made the novel something for himself and not for sales—these became the culprits, the reasons his novel failed to attract a wider readership. Although he had written his novel telling himself that it could not become a *Post* serial or much of a seller, the book's modest success was a larger disappointment than he had anticipated.

Alfred Knopf seemed to agree about the reasons for the novel's limited sales. Musing over why *The Trees* had not matched the sales of Marjorie Rawlings's immensely popular *The Yearling*, to which critics had repeatedly compared Richter's novel, he offered an analysis matching Richter's own: "I think you must reckon the archaic language which you deliberately adopted a commercial handicap. I don't question its artistic advisability mind you, but I think you must reckon on the sacrifice involved. I think also that *The Trees* suffered rather from lack of action and story, and gave the reader not enough narrative to bite into and something of the impression of being an overture rather than the main show." Earlier in the same letter, however, Knopf reminded Richter of the "enormous" sales through Book of the Month Club (eventually topping 200,000), and he made his feelings about a sequel as clear as he could, writing that "it would be tragic" if Richter abandoned the story he had begun in *The Trees*.[15] In his next letter, countering Richter's continued discouragement, Knopf insisted, "I think you are all wrong about *The Trees*. . . . Go on with whatever you want to write, but don't abandon for good Saird and her people."[16]

Despite Knopf's continued support for a sequel and several equally strong letters from Blanche Knopf, who urged him not to abandon "a grand and important work,"[17] Richter remained unconvinced, dwelling on the 14,000 copies sold through stores. Would there be a sequel? Richter's reply to Blanche Knopf offered an answer that may have struck her as simply an evasion, but which may equally well be read as a candid acknowledgment of Richter's reliance on guidance from above: "If I am really to do the series, I am sure I will."[18]

In early May Richter had recuperated sufficiently to set out across the country, driving from California to Pennsylvania in leisurely days of short drives and long rests, sharing the driving with Vene. Once in Pennsylvania Richter rented again the stone house in Dauphin, overlooking the Susquehanna, where he planned to write the serial he had promised the *Post*. The story of a German indentured servant in pre-Revolutionary America, the novel was tentatively entitled "The Dutchman"—soon to be called *The Free Man*. Although he had worked productively at the Huntington Library, gathering details about daily life in colonial America, exasperations over *The Trees* had poisoned his efforts to plot out the first section, getting his young protagonist from Germany to America. Further distracting him was the European war. Reading the daily newspaper and listening to the radio, Richter was outraged at what he believed to be his country's foolish neglect of the assault on liberty taking place in Europe. Although copies of the letters have not survived, later he was to remember writing newspapers and calling radio stations to complain about deceptive reportage that encouraged "America's incredible indifference to the great and growing Fascist menace."[19] Richter's feelings against Hitler and his forces were so ardent that one night he even found himself praying to God not to allow Nazis into heaven.[20]

At the end of June Vene departed for New York City, hoping to find a job in advertising or publishing. Richter actively encouraged her choice, but nonetheless her departure gave him something else to worry about. Through July Richter worked on the first section of his serial, describing the hardships of a sea passage by German and Swiss immigrants who had placed their faith in an unscrupulous sea captain. Although Richter intended *The Free Man* to be a moral tale about the high but justified price of freedom, he worried that a book with a German protagonist would make him seem at least indirectly sympathetic to Nazism. That concern and his nagging pain from the hernia, recurrent troubles with his prostate, and the discouraging sales of *The Trees* kept him anxious and despondent. Daily his mind was drawn away from his story to the events in Europe, where by the middle of June Paris had fallen and the French surrendered. Writing to Johnny Gardner, his friend from Sunset Lodge in Albuquerque, Richter admitted that he was "nearly a nervous wreck" over the happenings in Europe, and he worried that they betokened even more cataclysmic events to follow. "A wave of frightful consequences seems to have come from the astral," he warned his old friend.[21]

Perhaps prompted by Richter's unhappiness over the marketing of his novel, Alfred and Blanche Knopf made a special visit to their author, staying overnight in a hotel in Hershey. Accustomed to the Knopf visits in Albuquerque, stopovers on their flights east or west, Richter was surprised and flattered to discover that they were making a trip just to see him, though dismayed that he would have to entertain them for most of a day. Richter entertained the Knopfs primarily by giving them a tour of the area, including trips to places from his childhood. A camera buff, Alfred Knopf took pictures at every stop along their drive. Among the photographs Knopf later sent to Richter were shots of Richter and Blanche Knopf leaning against the railing of the Millersburg ferry and several taken on the porch of the Dauphin home. One portrait of Harvena captures her special quality of seeming full of vitality and yet wholly at her ease. A photograph of Richter features a rather stern Richter sitting in a rattan chair against the stone wall of the Dauphin porch. Richter later would write to a friend that his demeanor in the photograph was simply annoyance at Alfred Knopf's intrusions with his camera: "[Knopf] carries a little Leica and keeps on using it. Just as we would get interested in a discussion, he would lift it up and snap it at me. It irritated me, as you can see, but Harvey and Vene like [the picture] and say it's very typical of me—what do you think of that—and they say it is not irritation at all but righteous literary anger."22

When August arrived and the first section of his novel still lay unfinished on his desk, Richter decided that he could not write the serial in the East. He needed to return to Albuquerque, and if he could not write the serial there he would put it aside for another story, one set in the West. There remained the problem of Vene, who had not found a job. But though he worried about leaving his daughter alone in New York, he worried too about Harvey's health and his own. The year to date, he wrote Fred, "had been a frost for us, ill health and little or nothing done."23 His own sickness and Harvey's, the war news, and other distractions had kept him from writing the serial, which after almost a year's work he might have to abandon. He had to get out of the East.

When they arrived in New Mexico, the country seemed brown and barren, and Albuquerque a dry, dusty western town. As word spread of the Richters' arrival, there was a flurry of welcoming visits and invitations from their old Albuquerque friends, from Dean Matthews of the Episcopal Cathedral, from Matt Pearce of the university's English department, from the Stromes, the Welches, and many others. At the end of September, browsing in Jim Threlkeld's New Mexico Book Store, Richter picked up a copy of Erna Fergusson's *Our Southwest*, just published by Knopf. That evening he verified what his first quick look had indicated, that he was the only New Mexico writer not to be mentioned. He counted on nothing better from Erna Fergusson, whom he had long suspected of not liking him, but surely he had a right to expect his own publisher, a man who pretended to a friendship, to protect him from such a publicly demeaning oversight by one of his own writers.[24] On a different occasion, the perceived insult might have been put behind him after several days of resentment punctuated by flurries of anger, and it might even have catalyzed a period of intense writing. But this time the blow further loosened the props under what was an already shaky emotional equilibrium. Richter vented his anger directly and indirectly, first in his journal, as he had always done, but then—in a real departure from his efforts to keep his temper at least publicly in control—in letters to others. Writing to his daughter, Richter demonstrated that he had not escaped the narrow bigotry he so disliked in the Pennsylvania Dutch, commenting that his publisher, like the powers in Hollywood who had alternately flattered and belittled him, worshipped different gods from Richter and consequently could not be trusted. When Vene wrote that she was considering work in the garment trade, Richter answered with a warning: "the field is a tricky one, filled with crafty, scheming and cunning people, mostly Jews."[25] Even Vene was scorched by Richter's increasingly volatile temper when she chose that moment to ask that her evening clothes be sent to her from storage. Lecturing Vene about concentrating on her employment search, Richter announced that she would receive no evening clothing until she found a job.

Richter delayed just over a month before writing to Knopf, brooding over the injustices done him before crafting a bill of particulars of his grievances, spelling out Knopf's abandonment of advertising for *The Trees*, his transferring of his stock of the novel to the Book of the Month Club, and finally Knopf's publishing a book that publicly embarrassed Richter by excluding him. Then he waited more than another month before deciding that he would be cowardly not to mail it—and he did so on November 26. Sending a carbon copy to Paul Reynolds, Jr., Richter asked his agent to negotiate a release from his obligation to Knopf for two more short novels and two longer ones (a contract condition Richter had agreed to after Knopf had said so many complimentary things about *The Trees*).[26] For Richter the heart of his letter was not the list of grievances but the effect that those grievances, combined with his commitments to Knopf, were having on his writing: "These things naturally have shaken me in one who called himself my friend. Always the slowest of writers, the thought of laboring through four more volumes subject to the same conditions has stifled initiative."

When both Reynolds, father and son, visited Knopf to discuss a release, Knopf declined to name terms and said that he would write directly to Richter. When he did reply on December 30, Knopf communicated his personal sense of injury that Richter harbored such thoughts about him: "I have been living more time than I like to think with your letter of November 26th. This has shaken me considerably in one whom I thought a friend, and toward whom I have always behaved as a friend. It may be unwise, as many publishers feel, to become emotionally and sentimentally involved with authors, but in twenty-five years I have suffered as a result only twice, and yours is the second time." As for Richter's charges, all resulted, Knopf asserted, from misunderstandings. The advertising campaign for *The Trees* had exceeded all but one other book for spring 1940. Selling copies of *The Trees* to the Book of the Month Club was simply an industry courtesy; he would have expected copies from them if he had been running short. About Erna Fergusson's slighting of Richter, Knopf claimed no previous knowledge. Surely he could not be expected to see each book through the editing and publishing process. Knopf concluded his letter with the hope that author and publisher would wipe both letters "right off the record": "We can then go on as before, and as we should, doing our level best and a lot more than any purely professional relationship would require us to do for a man of whom we are genuinely fond and a writer in whom we have the greatest confidence and belief." Lest Richter misunderstand the "we" to mean the publishing house itself, Knopf reminded him that "you have a valuable and devoted friend in the firm in Blanche who has done for you, out of a full heart and a great belief, what she has attempted to do for very few authors who have come our way."

As Richter would acknowledge, Knopf's letter was a persuasive piece of writing; but to a man who for months had been living with the strain of acute grievances, the reply seemed only a clever deceit, making him the villain for secretly harboring resentments. If Richter's first letter had been cool and carefully polite, in the second he completely lost his temper: "What a cad you go on to make me out to be! Although I wrote neither you or Blanche or saw either of you after reading *Our Southwest* or learning of *The Trees'* third edition disposal, you say that I, who my family and friends say cannot hide my slightest feeling, 'corresponded' with you 'in a fashion that apparently left our friendship untouched' and broke bread with you and Blanche at Hershey all while nursing venom in [my] heart." Restating his grievances, Richter put his publisher on notice: Knopf should know that what had been accomplished in friendship and trust would thereafter be subjected to the closest scrutiny. He would be taken advantage of no more.[27]

After spending most of a year on *The Free Man*, Richter abandoned it in late October to take up the short novel he first entitled "The Lady of Brewery Gulch" and published as *Tacey Cromwell*. That fall in Albuquerque his heart began again to beat irregularly, especially at night. Doctors continued to attribute the arrhythmia to nerves—a diagnosis that did not satisfy Richter. Daily he kept a record of his health, and he would do so, as he had at Pine Tree Farm and at times in Albuquerque during the depression, for the next several years. In his visits to doctors he also pressed them for information about the aftereffects of sex. From his Pine Tree Farm days he had believed that sex for people with acute energy shortages was foolishly draining; now, just past fifty years old, he had decided that sex for people over fifty was actually detrimental to health. Women naturally understand this, he summarized in one of his health notes, but men foolishly continue, and the consequence to men like himself, men of low energy, could be severe. Although several doctors assured him that sexual relations once or twice a week was normal, Richter decided that for himself a sane regimen would be only once a month, and fewer times than that if possible. Men like him could not be wastrels of their energy, and sex was the most lavish energy expenditure. Often, he had discovered, it took as much as two weeks to build up energy reserves depleted by one brief time in bed with Harvey. He would even be willing to give up sex altogether, he reflected in one of his special health journals, except that sex was one of his few ways of initiating the "tensing" process that was vital to his writing.

In February Vene called with the news that she had at last landed a job, or rather the possibility of a job, in the advertising department of Saks Fifth Avenue, a triumph of persistence that had to please her father. Given an opportunity to meet the head of advertising at Saks, Vene made the most it by offering to work without pay until she demonstrated her value, an offer Saks took her up on. It was six weeks before Vene would be paid for her work.[28] Well before then Richter and Harvey had decided to escape the spring sandstorms by moving to Tucson, where several times he had been able to "tense" himself for periods of concentrated writing. This time was no exception, and he wrote another 20,000 words in Tucson before the summer heat drove them back to Albuquerque in June, where the high desert afforded cool mornings and nights. As with his two earlier novels, Richter began *Tacey Cromwell* with little more in mind than a plot conflict and a setting. The germ of his plot was one Richter knew to be a true story of the early West and one as yet untold, the changing fortunes of sporting house women and gamblers as civilization came to raw western towns. For a setting, Richter chose Brewery Gulch, a picturesque miners community in Bisbee, Arizona, where tiers of houses perched along the sides of a canyon. Richter had visited Bisbee in 1938, beginning then a notebook of "color" for a novel about life in the Gulch, filling its pages with notes on copper mining and mining towns, gambling and card cheats, town characters and vinegary "talk" appropriate for the Gulch.

Out of this notebook would come Tacey Cromwell, a reformed madam, and her common-law husband, Gaye Oldaker, a gambler from Tacey's former sporting house in New Mexico. Arriving in Bisbee, they move into a house on an upper tier of the Gulch, where they provide a home for Gaye's younger half brother Nugget, a twelve-year-old orphan. When another orphan, Seely Dowden, joins the household, the arrangement suits the residents of the Gulch well enough, the young girl having scrambled and scratched her way among the tiers of houses like a feral child; but the other side of town, Quality Hill, steps in to take both Nugget and Seely from a woman living with a man who is not her husband. For Nugget the foster home works out well enough, but for Seely, petted and privileged by the daughter of the town's richest man, the change spells disaster.

Richter wrote to Alfred Knopf that a major issue of the book was to be who was the better mother, the scarred woman who knows what could befall a willful young girl or the doting one who indulges the child's self-destructive behavior.[29] A second issue for Richter would be how differently the community treats a man and a woman who have, in effect, sinned similarly. Although in Bisbee it is unthinkable that Tacey be forgiven for her past life, Gaye is not even blamed. The shunned Tacey struggles to survive, while Gaye moves from gambling to banking and finally to politics, arriving at novel's end as treasurer of the territory.

In a clear departure from his usual method, while writing *Tacey Cromwell* Richter put off reading his drafts to Harvey. To Harvey this change was an indication of how well the writing was going, and she was relieved to escape the often impossible task of both encouraging and critiquing. Another explanation was that Richter's relationship with Harvey had changed since that moment in Tucson in 1938 when, trapped and desperate, her legs paralyzed, Harvey had ranted at her husband that she had to get away from him. Under ordinary circumstances thereafter she seemed still her old self, poised, unflappable, wry and fun-loving even in her restricted life. But when an argument arose she became much more openly defiant. "Her face hardens. Her eyes hate me," Richter exclaimed miserably at the end of one journal description of "trouble."[30] Several fights ended in Harvey reaffirming her intention to leave him or die trying. In February a disagreement that escalated into shouting led an alarmed Richter to warn himself that when he broke his promise to contain his disappointment in his wife and brought on trouble, the "hard, bitter, unforgiving, uncaring nature of the Achenbachs will come out . . . until she doesn't care what happens to Vene, or me, or herself." Shortly thereafter Richter asked Harvey to forgive him and to start anew, but soon Harvey was singing, loudly enough so that he could not mistake her words, "Will you walk into my parlor, said the spider to the fly."[31] A dispute in July was brought to an end only when Richter, after shouting himself out, again told Harvey that he was to blame for everything, pressing her to calm herself with some blackberry brandy.

One fight ended in a bizarre incident, to which Richter made several journal references but left no complete description. Much later Harvena Richter reported the incident to her daughter, who has summarized it as follows: "[My mother and father] were having a ferocious fight. Mother said they would have killed each other had not they heard a knock at the kitchen screen door. They found a snake—very gently, very kindly, as Mother expressed it—knocking its head against the screen door (it must have been somewhat erect in order to do this). It so shocked both of them, was so obviously meant to save the situation from disaster, that the fight stopped at once. The combination of the snake—a very powerful and deadly symbol—and the obvious kindness of the act—made an unforgettable comparison."[32]

By the beginning of June 1941, Richter and Harvey were back in Albuquerque, renting a house at 1617 Los Lomas Road. When Vene took her vacation from Saks, she joined her parents there, looking tall and smart in her sophisticated new clothing. By the time Vene arrived, Richter was far enough along with his novel to be plotting its conclusion, and he was counting on Vene's help to find an ending that was not "fiction." The blowup with Knopf had provoked Richter into a period of concentrated writing that the isolation of Tucson had continued. Other, more positive spurs helped extend the "tensing." Soon after returning to Albuquerque, Richter learned that his second novel had just missed being selected for the Pulitzer Prize; *The Trees* and Walter Van Tilberg Clark's *The Oxbow Incident* had both been recommended by the fiction nominating committee, but a dispute with the Pulitzer advisory board (over Hemingway's runaway best-seller *For Whom the Bell Tolls*) led to the awarding of no prize for 1940.[33] Earlier, Edward Weeks, editor of the *Atlantic*, had asked permission to include *The Sea of Grass* in an anthology to be entitled *Great Short Novels*, putting Richter into the company of Joseph Conrad, John Galsworthy, and Henry James.

While Vene visited, Richter worked out a conclusion for *Tacey Cromwell*, which, like the ending of *The Sea of Grass*, offered closure without resorting to fiction. The four principal characters have come together, but there is no suggestion of a perfect, or even an imperfect, resolution of the social differences and conflicting personal motivations that have separated them. In its depiction of human nature this novel would be for Richter a dark book, portraying people as isolated and uncaring, primarily because of their failures of imaginative sympathy—of "understanding." As a community, Bisbee is a closed, repressive system, recalling the novels of Richter's neighbor from Pottsville, John O'Hara. (*Tacey* would be Richter's only novel where social conventions become weapons for the ambitious and vindictive.) Richter's personal disappointments with his publisher and his agent, his pessimistic view of the maneuverings necessary for Vene to land a job in New York City, his upset at America's failure to accept its responsibility to confront the fascist menace—all these occupied Richter while he was writing his novel. Like the world Richter found himself living in, Tacey's world required wariness and a shrewd sense of human nature, and especially it required the self-discipline to guard one's thoughts and feelings. Writing to Vene the good news about Edward Weeks's anthology, Richter ended with his familiar warning, elaborated into fatherly advice: "Say nothing to anyone. Are you able to keep things to yourself—to contain them? So many things shouldn't be said."[34] In a later letter, after mentioning evasively that there had been "some friction with Knopf," Richter turned again to advise his daughter, still a neophyte to cosmopolitan life in New York: "I thought I felt from your last letter or two that you were going it a little too strong, robbing you of an undertone of strength and skepticism. Watch out! Be on your guard."[35]

By late September 1941, Richter and Harvey were back in Tucson. Richter was well into revising his novel when on December 7, 1941, the Japanese bombed Pearl Harbor, wrenching the United States into the world war—and pushing Richter deeper into the anxiety and emotional distress that had been accumulating since the death of John Richter two years earlier. With the coming of war came as well a number of smaller, more mundane worries. Richter had delayed buying new tires until they simply were no longer available, and his Packard, in its sixth year, was much too worn to last several more years. He quickly bought a new car, a Buick Roadmaster, paying a premium price for a disappearing commodity, then began worrying about gas rationing. How could he gather color if he could not drive? And how could he and Harvey travel for their health? Although he felt guilty of selfishness, he worried about how his small family could fare through difficult times. Could Vene get proper food in New York? Would her job be affected? Would the growing world troubles provoke her into a foolish overexertion, bringing on tuberculosis?

Working daily on his novel, Richter substituted the practical, solvable problems of rewriting, questions to which he could find answers, for the worries about the future that, as his anxiety increased, threatened his equilibrium. He took refuge as well in his thoughts about his childhood, protected by his mother and his father and by his Aunt Lizzie, who had reminded him repeatedly how lucky he was to have been born to such loving parents. But neither work nor nostalgic memories were a successful antidote for his increasing nervousness. By December his journal had become a daily record of his health complaints—general, sometimes cryptic comments about his stomach, his prostate, his heart, and his nerves. Just before Pearl Harbor he wrote more specifically, acknowledging his nerves were "so bad [that] it seemed things would burst or paralyze."[36] When he looked in the mirror each morning, he saw an aging face. In just the last year his mustache had begun to turn gray and his hair to thin and recede from his temples.

In late February Richter's nerves would not let him stay in Tucson. With Harvey reclining on the back seat of their new Buick, they started toward Bisbee for another view of Brewery Gulch. From there they planned a leisurely trip that would carry them to Florida and then, late in the spring, to Pine Grove. But driving toward Bisbee Richter's tautly strung nerves did not soothe, as they habitually did when he settled into the steady precision of long-distance driving. This time Harvey could not report to Vene that her father was ener-gized by the thought of new places. Instead, to his and Harvey's dismay he slipped further into depression, suffering a sense of alarm that would not go away. Nights especially were full of fears that quickened his heart and would not relent. The symptoms he remembered well enough: his emotions were slipping from his control, just as they had during the breakdown ending his first job in East Pittsburgh, when he was seventeen, and just as they had six years later, ending his job as a private secretary in Cleveland.

T W O

It is not possible to compare Richter's emotional troubles in spring 1942, about which he would write little in his journal, with those of his adolescence and early manhood, about which he did write retrospectively. The evidence is incontrovertible, however, that a distraught, increasingly dysfunctional Conrad Richter drove his wife (who had never learned to drive) across several states, over several days, to collapse into something like the condition in which he returned to his parents' home in White Deer Valley at the age of seventeen.[37] But this time there were no parents waiting to comfort and to care for him, only Harvey, his semi-invalid wife, and the professional services available to any vacationer staying in a Florida tourist cabin. Sick, frightened, and virtually homeless, Richter resorted to a desperate measure: he sought out a Christian Science practitioner. Richter had studied Christian Science while preparing to write *Human Vibration*, and although Christian Science thought and practice were built on a foundation that corresponded in significant ways to his own beliefs about the critical roles of the mind in directing and controlling one's energies, he had always been put off by what seemed to him the human side of Christian Science, the hyperbole in its claims and its indulgence in what to his mind remained a number of highly questionable beliefs. Desperate enough to put aside his skepticism, Richter sought out a Mrs. Spalding and later Margaret Jones, Christian Science practitioners who "worked" for people for pay by focusing their own good thoughts with their clients' to accomplish the healing therapy of affirmation. Mrs. Jones, Richter told Harvey, reminded him of his mother in her calming and reassuring manner, and as Richter found himself feeling better, and better able to work, he gladly attributed his recuperation, partial though it was, to Mrs. Jones.

As best he was able, Richter began working again on *Tacey Cromwell*, dictating his final corrections to a hired stenographer. Although his nerves were still badly frayed, a carefully restricted life of daily walks on the beach interspersed with short writing sessions brought him ever closer to the end of his novel. At first he attended Christian Science services with Harvey, who would soon become a convert to Christian Science. Later, he drove Harvey to services but himself attended only intermittently, often remaining outside in his car reading. He encouraged his daughter to explore Christian Science for herself and he carefully read Christian Science literature and continued to call on Mrs. Jones, but his disagreements with Christian Science remained, making him uncomfortable joining in the actual services.

On April 6 Richter completed the typescript of *Tacey Cromwell* to send to Reynolds. Several days later, feeling the healthful influence of a visit to Mrs. Jones, Richter decided with Harvey that, for their own sake, they needed to rid themselves of harmful negative thoughts, which meant they should forgive completely everyone with whom they had ever been angry. "There were only a few," Richter wrote, "but Knopf was one of them." Perhaps to exorcize these thoughts, Richter listed on a page in his devotional notebook the good acts of Knopf for which he had not given his publisher sufficient credit, and then his own errors in his dealings with Knopf. Among his own failings, Richter would list in quiet self-judgment, "my feelings against Jews."[38] Unable to escape the prejudices of his time, he was at least mindful, and ashamed, of them. Part of his regimen toward self-improvement was to rid himself of what he acknowledged as, in fact, his own failure at "understanding."

Alfred Knopf was evidently equally determined to be conciliatory, writing a glowing letter about *Tacey Cromwell* and offering a substantial increase in Richter's advance. He also agreed to cancel his option for two short novels remaining from the *Sea of Grass* contract, keeping only the option for two long ones. Paul Reynolds, Sr., wrote as well to express his admiration for the new novel, and collectively these letters helped Richter resign himself to his old professional relationships, however bound in he felt by them. By early spring Richter's nerves seemed sufficiently healed to allow him to return to Pine Grove. He was not entirely sure, however, that he was ready for a trip to New York City, even to receive an award. On March 2 the Associated Libraries of New York University had written to offer him their Gold Medal, intended "to recognize American authors who reveal new and distinctive talent in the field of imaginative literature."[39] To Richter's relief, the letter announcing the award also noted that, in keeping with wartime restrictions, the actual award ceremony would be modest and could be scheduled after his return north. But as pleased as he was by the honor, neither Richter nor Harvey was sure he was well enough for the strain of even a modest affair, and he worried that if he did not attend, the award might be withdrawn.[40] Twice on the day the letter arrived Richter drove to the telegraph office to send a night letter expressing his gratitude for the award but also his regret that he might not be able to receive it in person. Both times he returned with the telegram unsent, explaining to Harvey that he was simply not able to get the wording quite right.[41]

Back in Pine Grove, Richter and Harvey rented a cabin at Sweet Arrow Lake. All the other cabins were empty at the local summer retreat, making the long quiet days a helpful extension of Richter's convalescence. As the weather warmed, Richter rowed a small boat along the shore of the artificial lake. Richter did attend the award ceremony in New York, which occurred on May 20, though to the end neither Alfred Knopf nor Richter's agents knew for sure that he would actually make an appearance. Evidently the event went well, both the dinner with the judges and the award ceremony itself. But if the prize had been coveted, the experience rated only the briefest of entries in his journal, which read in its entirety: "wonderful time in N.Y., medal, dinner, etc."[42]

Once the chore of the award ceremony was behind him, Richter returned to the novel he had abandoned eighteen months earlier, the story of a German immigrant in colonial America. Just in case *Tacey Cromwell* did not sell as a serial or as a movie to Hollywood, he intended to complete that still fragmentary story to offer as a serial to the *Post*. As Richter rightly guessed magazines were reluctant to publish a novel that included scenes set inside a house of prostitution. First Edward Weeks, who had written Richter that he "urgently" needed a serial for the *Atlantic*, declined *Tacey*, explaining too elaborately that he did so for "practical, not puritanical, reasons."[43] The *Post* turned it down as well, saying more succinctly and perhaps more candidly that the story was "inappropriate" for the *Post*. One by one the other possible magazines declined the serial rights, each finding its subject, in the words of Paul Reynolds, Jr., "very difficult for a magazine."[44] Richter wondered if the change in editors at the *Post* might not signal a change in that magazine's interest in his work, but soon after rejecting *Tacey*, Ben Hibbs, who replaced Wesley Stout as managing editor, wrote to assure him otherwise. Sent the first part of *The Free Man* and a synopsis of the remainder, Hibbs bought the serial for $7,500, with a $2,500 advance.[45]

In Pine Grove, where Richter had not actually lived since his childhood, old neighbors recognized him on the streets, calling him "Connie" as they had when he was a child; and they invited him and Harvey to town affairs, church socials, and Rotary dinners. Surrounded by farms and orchards, Pine Grove offered ready access to fresh produce, eggs, and milk products and often to other commodities that would grow harder to find as the war continued. Later, when Vene was settled into a New York apartment, her parents would keep her supplied with eggs, which Harvey and Vene still drank with orange juice to guard against tuberculosis. But if Pine Grove and Sweet Arrow Lake provided an effective place for Richter's nerves to repair themselves during the war's first summer, Richter was soon restless there. With gasoline rationing limiting his travel, Richter used most of his allotted fifty-eight gallons for May and June to drive back and forth from Sweet Arrow Lake to Pine Grove and to make brief afternoon excursions with Harvey. There was no gasoline left for longer trips.

By the end of September Richter was eager to escape Pine Grove, proposing to Harvey that they try living in New York, where they would be close to Vene. They rented a modest room in Beekman Towers, on Forty-seventh Street, paying $35 a week for a corner room with cross ventilation and a view of the East River. Both enjoyed the time in the city, Harvey taking Vene with her on outings to museums and theaters, Richter venturing forth daily to walk New York's crowded streets and ride its trolleys. Perhaps the most important reason Richter proposed the sojourn in New York was to provide a haven where he could be inconspicuous when *Tacey Cromwell* was released. When that occurred on October 19, a week after his fifty-second birthday, Richter was relieved that he was not in

Albuquerque or Pine Grove, where he would be forced to pretend to be unaffected by the novel's dismayingly quiet critical reception.

In New York Harvey attended Christian Science services with Vene, bringing home Christian Science publications that all three read conscientiously. On occasion Richter attended services with his wife and daughter and felt the healing presence of others' good wishes. But Richter was still unable to accept Christian Science's attribution of all health to faith alone. His experience with Harvey during her most critical illnesses convinced him of the efficacy of vitamins, daily doses of sunshine, and a diet of high energy foods like eggs, liver, and sweet breads. Later, he would summarize for his brother Fred just how far he could, and could not, travel with Christian Science: "I'm a believer in mentally denying the bad and declaring the good, the infinite presence. The Scientists would never take me in, because I like medical diagnosis, then have a practitioner work on what is wrong. . . . None of us can live forever but a good practitioner buoys up the hope and courage while we are alive, and these things are often more important even to doctors than medicine."[46] Visiting Fred in Syracuse, Richter was unhappy at how thin and how gloomy his youngest brother had become, and he subjected him to a pep talk about proper diet, exercise, and garnering enough vitamin D from sunshine. Back in New York, he immediately purchased a sun lamp and sent it to Fred.[47]

Caught in the East by gas rationing, over the next year Richter and Harvey moved repeatedly back and forth between Pine Grove and New York.[48] During the summer they escaped to the cooler air of Hazleton and Williamsport, staying in each town's best hotel and only in a corner room with cross ventilation. In these rooms Richter settled comfortably into his regimen of writing, for there were no visitors and no calls to make, as at Pine Grove, and few enticements to take him away from his work on *The Free Man*. When the writing mood was on him, a brief daily walk and a trip or two to a hotel dining room was stimulus enough. Richter worked while Harvey read magazines and played solitaire. That was the pattern of their days, though for Harvey the sojourns in hotels were certainly monotonous and tedious. Without gasoline for their afternoon drives, she stayed in the hotel room except for dinner, which remained for them, in the Pennsylvania Dutch tradition, the noontime meal. For supper, Richter habitually ate alone, either in the hotel dining room or in a less expensive diner or restaurant near the hotel. He would order liver, sweetbreads, or occasionally steak, a high-energy entree that he would divide in two and then surreptitiously slip half into his handkerchief to take to his wife, back in the hotel room playing solitaire.

During this period Vene moved into her first apartment, a converted speakeasy on Grove Street that she shared with three other women from the International House. Later she would move with one of her roommates, Elizabeth Archer, into a first-floor flat on Commerce Street, by the Cherry Land Theater. A tall, slender young woman, Elizabeth Archer turned out to be an irresponsible roommate, arriving and departing with little notice and leaving the pieces of her life behind for others to pick up. Richter viewed his daughter's living companion nervously but not entirely negatively. Impressed by Archer's entertaining letters, he encouraged her to try fiction—as he had encouraged Johnny Gardner and others who wrote letters with flair. But he disapproved of Elizabeth Archer's flighty self-indulgence and her many romances, and he urged his daughter to find a more dependable roommate. An advantage of Vene's living arrangement, however, was that Elizabeth Archer was often gone from the apartment for extended periods, during which Vene habitually invited her parents to stay with her.

During his stays in Pine Grove, Richter volunteered for civil defense duty as an airplane spotter, and along with most other authors of best-selling books he agreed to allow special armed forces editions of his novels, for which he received only token royalties. When *Tacey Cromwell* was published, he wrote a special back-cover promotion for savings bonds, and when Alfred Knopf succeeded in placing *Tacey* with the Dollar Book Club—as another dual selection, with MacKinley Cantor's *The Happy Land*—Richter himself put $5,000 from that sale into savings bonds. All this Richter felt to be little enough for a cause he firmly supported and for which American lives were being spent. When Richter finished *The Free Man* Ben Hibbs accepted it as a four-part serial for the *Post*. Richter and Harvey celebrated with a two-week sojourn in Beekman Towers, during which he rewrote the ending of the serial, as Hibbs requested, to make more definite the marriage between Henry Free and the daughter of his former master. Rewriting, he also attempted to make their marriage more obviously symbolic of the union of German immigrants with English settlers in their shared fight to gain independence for the English colonies. He still worried that readers might find his story unpatriotic.

Back in Pine Grove Richter wrote a short story for war times, "The Good Neighbors." A slight story, more message driven than anything he had written since before the depression, "The Good Neighbors" suited the *Post* wartime policies for patriotic and uplifting fiction, and they bought without quibble a story demonstrating more than anything that Richter could slip into sententiousness even after almost a decade of better story writing. The same could be said of *The Free Man*, which after an effectively realized first section, the shipboard sequence, and some deftly comic characterizations of the Pennsylvania Dutch, slid further with each installment into the "fiction" of ordinary historical romance. Several *Post* readers wrote to complain that the editors had condensed the narrative too drastically, taking the marrow from the story. But in fact the editors cut Richter's manuscript only slightly. The parts readers missed from Richter's story were parts he had not succeeded in writing in what for him was a hastily finished work. Plotted out and drafted during his nervous collapse and completed during his recuperation, it was his weakest novel.

In the meantime Alfred Knopf had accepted *The Free Man*. For so short and so slight a story, Knopf was surprisingly complimentary to Richter, offering another large advance against sales even though *Tacey Cromwell* had sold only modestly. Throughout the editing and publishing of the novel Knopf would be curiously solicitous of Richter's thoughts about such matters as book design and jacket design, inviting suggestions and sending illustrations developed from Richter's ideas for the author to choose among. Given many opportunities to meddle, Richter took them all. That Knopf continued to solicit Richter's opinion suggests more than anything how earnestly Knopf wanted to keep Richter on his lists. The year before, Paul Reynolds, Jr., bluntly summarized what he saw as Knopf's continuing interest in Richter: "Knopf values you as a property very much which is the reason why he won't let you go. . . . He cares about two things: prestige and money, and he cares passionately about these two things. Selling books helps him get these two things; not selling them hurts him."[49] Evidently Alfred Knopf was looking forward to the book Richter was finally preparing to write, the sequel to his best novel, *The Trees*.

Ten

Nothing but Christmas

O N E

Later, while writing "Trees II," as Richter initially called his second novel about Sayward Luckett, he thought back on the three years spent writing *Tacey Cromwell* and *The Free Man* as a hiatus, a delay, even a series of blunders.[1] In his estimation neither novel had improved his reputation appreciably, nor had either made him much money. His second conclusion was not wholly accurate: although the royalties from book sales had been modest, income from the Dollar Book Club version of *Tacey* and from the *Post* serial of *The Free Man* allowed him to live comfortably during the war years. There was always sufficient money in various accounts for him to move at will from hotel to house rental to hotel.[2] But his reputation was the thing. When others complimented Richter on his recent novels and stories, often they asked when he would write the sequel to *The Trees*. That, others seemed to assume, was to be his real accomplishment.[3]

By summer 1943 Richter settled the matter, finally, for himself. He would return to Sayward's story, writing one long novel or two shorter ones, even though he did not know how he would support himself during the three years he believed he needed to write the sequel. For precisely this reason Richter spent two months on "The Good Neighbors," selling it for $1,750 to the *Post*. He thought again about quick money from Hollywood, proposing to MGM a "home front" screenplay set in White Deer Valley; but when MGM expressed no interest Richter dropped the matter, refusing to allow Paul Reynolds, Jr., to offer the synopsis to other studios.[4] Richter also continued to hope for a Hollywood sale from *Tacey Cromwell*. In fall 1942 Paul Reynolds, Jr., had reported that Hunt Stromberg of MGM was seriously interested in *Tacey Cromwell* as a major vehicle for Barbara Stanwyck. But when Stanwyck refused to play the part of a reformed madam, the deal fell through.[5]

Having no ready sources of money other than what he had accumulated in bank accounts, savings bonds, and deferred royalties, Richter decided that the only practical solution was to write chapters for his sequel and sell them individually as short stories. Harvey opposed the idea, reminding her husband that his attempt with "The Rawhide Knot" had twice resulted in over a month's lost time, the chapter having to be rewritten as a magazine story and then, a year later, reworked again to fit back into *The Trees*. But Harvey could think of no other means of producing income, except options taking Richter away from writing the sequel.[6] In July Richter began plotting, soon settling on a title, *The Fields*. In August Knopf published *The Free Man*, with a dust jacket modeled after a design proposed by Richter and jacket copy provided by his daughter. Reviews were mild but unexceptionable, and sales, once again, modest. Richter expected nothing more from a book he had written as a serial for the *Post*.

When "The Good Neighbors" appeared in the *Post* on October 30, Richter accepted compliments from the townspeople of Pine Grove as he met them in the barber shop, the grocery, and the post office. Earlier that month he had found the leather-bound red notebook in which, as a senior in high school, he penned his first notes as an aspiring writer. Struggling with the first chapter of his new novel, looking ahead to two, perhaps three years' work before him, Richter found little encouragement in the notebook: "I should be thankful for what writing success I have," he remarked in his journal. As he painfully reminded himself about his writing ability: "It was not a native talent but has been slowly built, grafted on the rest of me, bought in sweat, blood, and despair. Gradually as my taste in reading improves, I endeavor to write to that level. It goes terrifically hard, but I find that what I try to write is not something I have read anywhere else but is a sort of standard, if I may be forgiven for the word, in the back of my mind, that must be satisfied. I have, of course, known this latter all along, but I completely forgot with what little I started."[7] Reading this passage, one infers just how deeply ingrained was Richter's modesty about his writing. How, then, had he been able to keep up his spirits to continue, through the depression and thereafter, writing that went so "terrifically hard"? How was it that he kept himself from giving up, simply despairing of success, as he wrote month after month over a number of years? In his journal at night he had repeatedly exclaimed that the story he was writing just was not writable, or at least could not be written by him, and by morning he would again be ready to labor over the plotting, and drafting, and rewriting of a story he had no faith he would ever be able to sell. What brought him back to his desk each morning?

The answer seems to be that as real and pervasively affecting to Richter as his distrust of his own ability remained, he carried within him a contrary belief that he would succeed if he persevered; that he was special, marked, chosen. The evidence for his difference was the work he accomplished—and his ability to do that work. For Richter there was a satisfaction approaching a sense of personal identity in overcoming the difficulties and self-doubt, in discovering a new standard and then learning to meet it. Just as important, perhaps, there was difference, an identity, in his daily effort itself, hard as it often was, to meet a self-imposed standard. In an especially revealing journal entry, written during the first months of plotting his sequel, Richter sorted out for himself what, after all, really mattered to him: "Mother used to tell me to be more pleasant. H[arvey] has told me so. But it never gets me anywhere. I must just go ahead and do my work, get it done, and be sad or however you will. Let Alfred, Blanche, and Paul be as they may. Pay no attention to how they are. . . . Just be mildly interested or mildly uninterested, interested only in my work. If only I had always such quiet uninterest and strength as tonight. My work is all that counts."[8]

By late November Richter was back in New York at Beekman Towers, settled with Harvey into a favorite corner room on the twentieth floor, one with a balcony facing northeast and a window looking out toward the East River. Having undergone an unusually long period of poor health, Harvey arrived at Beekman Towers sick and unhappy. She was just blue, Harvey said, but her depression seemed more than that to Richter. "It is not the kind you can cheer up like Vene," he wrote in his journal. "She just looks at you with those red-rimmed eyes as if you are to blame for everything."[9] Believing her condition to be "mostly mental," Harvey attended Christian Science services regularly with Vene—Richter encouraging them both and willingly paying to enlist the prayers of Christian Science practitioners to help concentrate the positive effects of affirmation. When Liz Archer decided to take a lengthy Christmas vacation, Vene invited her parents to join her in her new apartment, a fifth-floor flat overlooking Washington Square.

During the several years of writing *Tacey Cromwell* and *The Free Man*, Richter had seldom picked up *The Trees*: he had "worked too hard on it," making it "too painful to read."[10] In January 1944, turning its pages after a day's work on its sequel, he found himself pleased with its slow, measured movement to the novel's end, where Sayward, a sturdy woman of twenty, is clearing away the trees closest to her cabin.[11] In *The Fields* Sayward would continue to be the center of his work, with the story told primarily in her voice. In five middle chapters, however, Richter shifted the narrative perspective to two of Sayward's children. From the eyes of Resolve, the oldest, and Guerdon, his younger brother, their father Portius Wheeler cuts an increasingly impressive figure as the backwoods "improvement" surrounding their cabin becomes the settlement of Moonshine Church and finally the incorporated town of Americus. But Sayward is the rock upon which the family is built. Once a strapping young girl, she has become, after years of heavy work and the birth of seven children, a tall, thick, imposing woman. Still very much a "woodsy," struggling even to write her own name, she is nonetheless the unquestioned head of the family. Even Portius, for all his eloquence and education, defers to her.

In *The Trees* Richter's model for Sayward had been the young au pair Johanna Kenngott and especially his wife Harvena. Writing *The Fields* Richter drew more on his memories of his mother, attributing to Resolve and Guerdon thoughts and sentiments about their mother that were directly drawn from his own memories of Lottie Richter. Like *The Trees*, the story would be essentially static; there would be no central conflict, no obstruction to be overcome, to carry rising action to a climax. Instead, incidents would play out over seasons, with Richter's rich evocation making the land a major character, pervasively changing lives. If his descriptive ability was not at first "a native talent," he clearly had mastered his craft, weaving the sound of pioneer speech into his narrator's voice. At book's end, Richter decided, Sayward would be surrounded by her family at a public celebration day, a woodsy who is too modest to recognize that her central position in the community is being acknowledged by her neighbors.

Early that January Richter found himself in the special frame of mind from which his best work came. In his January 5 journal entry he described it as "a dull, dazed, worn out physical feeling and yet the knowledge that I can sit down and write easily, naturally, know what to say and how to say it. . . . Whether my conscious is sufficiently dulled for my subconscious to dominate, I don't know. I rather think I am in the groove, dedicated, devoted, given up to writing." Five days later he decided optimistically to offer the first three chapters to the *Post*. Quickly the *Post* editors returned them all, with an explanation that seemed to confirm Harvey's worry: while beautifully written, none had a strong enough story to make it even a possibility for the *Post*. Erd Brandt did not even propose a revision, as he had with "The Rawhide Knot." Although the *Atlantic* would eventually buy one of these, Edward Weeks paid only $250, a fraction of what Ben Hibbs was prepared to pay and far less than Richter needed to subsidize *The Fields*.

By the time Reynolds reported the *Post* decision, Richter and Harvey were back in Pine Grove, living with Stanley Achenbach, Harvey's brother, in his home on High Street. Until the rejection Richter had been enjoying the winter in Pennsylvania, walking through the crusted snow and ice-skating on the old canal pond. After the *Post* news, the place of his happy childhood memories seemed ugly and drab, a town of rude young people who were "loud, Dutchified, unlovable."[12] It was Richter's old complaint against his Pennsylvania Dutch neighbors: "There is humor, hardihood, robustness, and peasant virtues among them, but no thoughts or feelings of spirit and beauty." And furthermore, they were not storytellers; they were not interested in human nature.[13] Only when Vene visited, as she did in late February, did the town brighten again into colorful life. Returning to Harvey and Stanley after seeing his daughter off at the railroad station, Richter ruminated despondently on the vitality that went out of Stanley's house when Vene left: "The light was gone . . . that invisible spirit and power which I could so plainly feel and almost see while and after [Vene] wrote her letter and talked writing had flown out of the cracks, and the old solid material atmosphere of the house was in control everywhere. Harvey alone does not produce this light anymore." Later that day Richter continued the entry, correcting his inclination to put too much emphasis on the energizing presence of Harvey and Vene: "It is not just the person; I do not feed on energy they produce. I once thought so. Now after today I know definitely it is the spirit produced, the atmosphere or plane of existence my mind steps into, of a home, of literary things, of a piano being played, especially by a child." The following day he added a sentence to this thought: "At the feel of a gentle household around, of kindred spirits, of the sound of a piano, of good writing and others writing and reading, my spirit freshens, feels more at home and can receive and function more freely."[14] In such an atmosphere he could write.

He could not write his best when Harvey was nurturing some hidden grudge against him. In both New York and Pine Grove, Richter's primary worry was Harvey's continued unhappiness. It was because she was unwell, he told himself, though he knew that her despondency came at least in part from his having had his own way in secluding her from her family and friends, forcing her to live in hotels and other people's homes, without possessions of her own. If she remained unhappy in Pine Grove, where she was surrounded by family and friends, it was because, he knew she believed, he often criticized her unjustly. When trouble came, Richter found himself alarmed at his wife's disclosure that her threats to leave were not simply expressions of anger. Even when they were not fighting, she told him, she still wanted to leave him and in truth was planning to do so when she could.[15]

As he had done years earlier, when trying unsuccessfully to talk Harvey into moving to a better climate, Richter asked his brother-in-law's advice. In 1928 Stanley's reply had been that Richter should ignore Harvey's wishes, not even to ask her about moving. He should sell the farm, pack up, and simply take her away. In 1944 Stanley's advice was equally Pennsylvania Dutch in its pragmatism. Richter was much too attentive to Harvey, he said, treating her like an invalid and spending too much time with her. He should have an office that he went to daily, leaving her at home. And he should take trips alone. It was Richter's business to go. Stanley would take care of his sister, taking her out twice a week while Richter was away.[16] Taking Stanley's advice, Richter decided to travel alone to Chapel Hill, North Carolina, thinking to explore the university town as a winter home for Harvey. But he would not leave his wife with his brother-in-law; while Richter was in North Carolina Harvey went to stay with Vene in her apartment at 31 Washington Square.

During his three weeks in Chapel Hill Richter enjoyed little but his walks on the campus of the University of North Carolina. Although he wrote daily, at the end of his stay he found he had done almost no salvageable writing. Chapel Hill was not a community where he could work, he decided, in part because he did not feel comfortable among Southerners. His writing may also have been affected by his increasing uneasiness about Harvey. Writing of her stay in New York, Harvey's letters were consistently upbeat, without any hint of missing him. Vene's letters added to his sense that the two were getting on well as roommates, eating and resting sensibly (in bed each night by eleven, Vene dutifully reported) but going out regularly to the theater, films, museums, and galleries. In Harvey's last letter, sent to Pine Grove and awaiting his return there, she announced that she would not be joining him for several weeks. It was too important for her to stay and continue helping Vene, who responded well to encouragement and simply wilted under criticism.[17] That her final comment was aimed at him was unmistakable, at his habitually critical manner with his daughter and his faultfinding with his wife. When he telephoned that evening, asking if Harvey did not want to return to see the spring foliage, she repeated her intention of staying in New York. Worse, she did not invite him to join him there. Was she really separating from him as she had threatened? Had she grasped this, her first opportunity to escape from him since the onset of her tuberculosis? After a sleepless night he resolved to drive immediately to New York. Arriving at Vene's apartment, he was immeasurably relieved when Harvey, startled by his unexpected appearance, ran to his arms.[18]

While in Chapel Hill Richter had received word from Paul Reynolds, Jr., about an offer of $5,000 for the film rights to *Tacey Cromwell*. Writing back immediately, Richter reminded his agent that they had set a firm price of $15,000, adding that he would rather go back to the Sandia Mountains and live penuriously, as in the depression, than accept so low an offer. But having rejected the offer and failed to sell chapters of *The Fields*, Richter did need to worry about money. Writing to Gerry Adams, Richter asked him to explore the option of another writing assignment in Hollywood. While he waited for a reply from Adams, Richter decided to abbreviate his workdays on his sequel, using his evening writing session to plan and then write a story for the *Post*. The process took some months, but by early September he had completed "The Flood" and sold it to Ben Hibbs. Encouraged that he had been able to make good progress on *The Fields* and at the same time write a story of the Texas frontier, Richter continued to reserve his evenings for another distinctly different story, a possible serial for the *Post*. Setting his novella in turn-of-the-century Pine Grove, Richter planned to draw on his childhood memories, thereby reducing the strain on an imagination already taxed to create all the characters and events of a pioneer settlement in Ohio. Unusual for Richter, he began his serial having already chosen a title, *Always Young and Fair*.

Richter would remember 1944 as a mixed assortment, much like Sayward's concluding comment in *The Trees*: "That's how life was, death and birth, grub and harvest, rain and clearing, winter and summer. You had to take one with the other, for that's the way it ran."[19] It was the year of the unfortunate trip to Chapel Hill, when Richter thought he was losing Harvey. It was the year Gerry Adams had tantalized him with the possibility of three months of writing for MGM, at $1,000 a week, only to have this come to nothing. But also in 1944 Susquehanna University, where his father had attended college and seminary, conferred on him an honorary degree. Richter's memories were in the main positive about the experience, though he had been nervous and unable to work for a week in advance. At lunch before the May ceremony Carl Carmer, who was also receiving an honorary degree, told Richter that he had primed himself for his own latest novel by reading *The Trees*. It was the year of D-day, the allied assault on the beaches of Normandy, and the year Richter again tried, unsuccessfully, to contact Cornillier for information about a sequel to *The Survival of the Soul*. In August 1944 Paul Reynolds, Sr., died. Months earlier, knowing his old agent's health was failing, Richter had sent him a copy of Cornillier's book.

In September 1944 Harvey discovered that her brother Stanley had married and was keeping it a secret from her so that she and Richter would not feel they had no place to stay in Pine Grove. That was exactly how they did feel, and they moved almost immediately back to New York. In November, perhaps prodded by Carl Carmer, president of P.E.N., Richter attended a P.E.N. dinner, albeit reluctantly. After making his reservations, Richter immediately regretted his rash act, succumbing to his anxieties. "I kicked at the bed . . . in my frantic desperation," he wrote disconsolately in his journal. "I was caught, caught." On seeing Somerset Maugham at the ceremony, Richter retreated to the entrance hall and had to be led by Harvey back into the gathering, where they lingered along a wall until most of the members and guests had gone into the dining room.[20]

After another Christmas with Vene, Richter and Harvey stayed on with their daughter in her Washington Square apartment. By the end of January Richter had finished three more chapters of *The Fields*, typing out his drafts on his portable typewriter. Mornings and most afternoons he wrote while his daughter was as work at Macy's, Vene having left Saks for the higher salary and, as it turned out, higher pressure of Macy's advertising department. Occasionally he would take an afternoon off for a movie or a play; Richter typically went alone to matinees while Harvey and Vene attended evening performances. While they were out of the apartment, Richter would settle into an evening's work on *Always Young and Fair*.

Early in February, Richter decided that he would publish the chapters he had already written as *The Fields*, saving the remainder of Sayward's story for a third volume, to be entitled *The Town*. Although Richter was as usual dismayed by the work yet to be done, the revising went quickly in Vene's apartment and in

Beekman Towers. Working "in high grind," Richter once again found himself experiencing chest pains at night, but more visits to heart specialists brought only negative reports and advice about relaxing from so much work. Living as best he could with his heart complaints and ongoing discomfort from his prostate, Richter nonetheless continued to enjoy excursions into New York's bustling street life, participating anonymously in the public fair that occurred outside Vene's apartment in Washington Square. On April 27 Richter delivered his completed typescript to Reynolds, then had lunch with his agent. Discussing the contract terms they would propose to Knopf, Reynolds suggested spreading the royalties out at a fixed amount each month, easing the writing of the third part of the trilogy. This Richter declined, slipping with a smile into an amused self-deprecation, saying only that he did not want to give Knopf an opportunity to "chortle" at him. Two days later, Richter alerted Knopf that his novel had been delivered to Reynolds, and as usual he described it modestly: "I wish you would tell Blanche for me that the second novel of *The Trees* which I promised in the summer of 1939 is now belatedly finished. Whether she and you may like it is something else. It is slow but, I hope, solid."[21] When he replied on May 14, Knopf's letter was far more enthusiastic than his author's: "I cannot exaggerate my admiration for what you have done. I think that this is a good cut above *The Trees* and represents a distinguished writer at his best." Soon Blanche Knopf was seconding her husband's estimate, calling *The Fields* "magnificent."[22] But such compliments held Richter's optimism only briefly. Waiting for the actual publication of his novel, Richter was unable to keep himself from the complaining and dark predictions which he had actively struggled to conquer for most of his life.

It is a mistake, however, to infer from these pessimistic journal entries that Richter's prevailing mood was one of despondency. On days when he entered his gloomiest predictions about *The Fields*, most of his time was spent working productively, and optimistically, on *Always Young and Fair*. On rare occasions his wife and daughter joined forces to accuse Richter of being too critical of everything, but they also knew the other, seemingly contradictory aspects of their mercurial husband and father, who just as often demonstrated to them his enthusiasm for life.

Concerned that the public sense of her husband was that of a stiffly reserved, even unfriendly person, in 1937 Harvena Richter began a journal of her own, a place to record the actions and emotions of Richter that many others did not see.[23] From Harvey's journal comes a portrait of a man who is generous and openhearted, one whose sensitivity to the feelings of others exacerbated his life-long shyness in public. As new friends came to know Richter, they discovered him to be friendlier and wittier, more outgoing and fun-loving, than they expected. He was intense, at times "nervy," but he was also gentle, affable, and deeply respectful of all living things. He was a man, Harvena would write, who carefully caught moths fluttering about the lantern light of their Sandia cabin to release them unharmed into the night.

From Richter's own journal comes evidence of his sense of humor. Although he took delight in creating Portius Wheeler, who with wit and sly irony passes amused judgment on the events, great and small, of a growing Ohio town, Sayward's iconoclastic husband is a personality different from Richter's own. Unlike Portius Wheeler's humor, which is public and turned outward on others, Richter's journal humor is habitually private, a subtle self-mockery. There is, however, a recognizable pattern to his humor. When Harvey read the second of two chapters from *The Fields* published in the *Atlantic*, Richter had this to say: "Harvey and 'The Nettle Patch.' She read it in the Atlantic without my knowledge and cried out to me her very real and enthusiastic delight that it was the best thing she had read since 'The Face at the Winder' [another chapter from *The Fields* published in the *Atlantic*]. She said it was 100% artistry and that no one could have done it but I. No one living today, she said. I told her she was my critic, my fan, my proof reader, my laundress, cook and housekeeper. What more could one ask, although one does at times."[24] The final clause is essential Richter, an ironist poking fun at his own unreasonable expectations. A similar example is Richter's final turn of thought when commenting on Christian Science: when healthy, Richter thought Christian Science "a bit beneath" him, but when he was sick "it was quite good enough, or almost."[25] It is the self-realization in the "or almost" that characterizes his journal humor, the delicate bite of satire turned inward. So too was his refusal to have Paul Reynolds propose royalty payments that would likely cause Knopf to "chortle" at him. In another instance, writing to his daughter Vene, he would say he was "half Christian Science" and then, after a pause, continue, "if there can be such a thing."[26]

T W O

Deep into his new novel, Richter escaped his worries about *The Fields* by re-creating the Pine Grove of his childhood in *Always Young and Fair*. In 1900 Pine Grove was a town where the ladies in their Sunday best always wore white, a town of two distinct classes, friendly but separate, a town where a child lived within the "support of people who loved you, as Aunt Lizzie did me."[27] It was a time when his grandfather Henry's "high silk hat looked perfectly natural, when everybody was an individualist refreshingly different from his neighbor and when a couple score of town characters kept it in perpetual serious entertainment and good humor."[28] In modern Pine Grove the de facto leader of the aristocracy was Augusta Filbert, distantly related to Richter through marriage. A small, doll-like woman in her seventies, Augusta Filbert lived alone in the family home on Tulpehocken, a large frame house with verandas and gingerbread detail. Entertaining Richter and Harvey occasionally, she had hinted broadly that she would welcome them as houseguests whenever they returned to Pine Grove. In May 1945 she formally invited them to live with her. Too frail to venture above the first floor, she proposed that Richter take up residence on the second. There he would have all the privacy he needed to write, and they could enjoy each other's company for dinner. As Richter knew, Augusta Filbert kept an excellent cook.

The prospect of privacy and dinners with Augusta led Richter and Harvey to accept the offer. Though deaf, Augusta Filbert was a dinner table delight with her tales of early town life, which Richter turned into entries in his notebooks for *Always Young and Fair*. His serial went surprisingly quickly, Richter spending his days writing on the second floor of Augusta Filbert's house or, carrying his typewriter with him, in hotels in Williamsport and Hazleton during the steamiest weather of that summer in central Pennsylvania. Living intermittently in Pine Grove, moving in and out of touch with the town's oldest families, Richter came to frame his own sense of himself as the consequence of an internal battle resulting from a hereditary conflict. On an evening when his confidence was in ascendancy, he described the inner struggle in his journal: "The artist in me has had a terribly long, hard and bitter quarrel with the peasant in me. Only at a time like tonight when it gets a little life and sustenance can it rise and dominate the peasant. But most times the peasant controls. I fear anyone of rank, of position, and even lesser ones. In a circle of writers I would be tongue-tied. I envy men like [Thomas] Wolfe, but tonight I could be with any of them, silent perhaps but equal and unafraid. Or is this the artist, too, [who] is so sensitive he is afraid of everything but the child, the poor and the lowly."[29]

Through the dog days of August Richter worked at his typewriter, typing reporter-style with two fingers, writing chapters only to discard them, taking time out to read proof for *The Fields* and the other matters of a writer's life that continued to arrive in the mail. As he anticipated, talk of another Book of the Month Club option came to nothing, and motion picture studio offers had been such chimeras that Richter gave little thought to a sale. He did allow Reynolds to place *The Fields* in a $125,000 competition sponsored by MGM, though he himself believed it had not "a ghost of a chance," and to circulate copies to the major studios.[30] His price for the screen rights would be $50,000, a high enough price to avoid the nuisance and upset of small offers from minor studios. On August 14, 1945, Richter took time off to celebrate V-J day with the rest of the country. That celebration was tempered, however, by Richter's horror and growing outrage at Truman's decision to drop atomic bombs on Hiroshima and Nagasaki. Just the idea of such a bomb was almost unfathomably inhuman; to have actually detonated two of them on top of civilian populations put humanity beyond the pale. What must the forces from the astral be thinking after such incredible destructive power was developed and then unleashed? Richter never forgave Truman for his choice.[31]

When in October he and Harvey returned to Vene's Washington Square apartment, Richter carried a completed draft of *Always Young and Fair*. He read it on October 26, then listened to Harvey and Vene declare it to be better than either *Tacey Cromwell* or *The Free Man*—Vene declaring that it had "a French quality of bitter truth." But his wife and daughter also voiced reservations, agreeing that it was a novel, not a serial, and so might not sell to the *Post* or *Atlantic*. It was also gloomy; it needed brightening. They talked longer over this story than ever before, staying up until 1:00 A.M. Two days after reading his story, with the "steam" building in him, the "pressure of energy, feeling" out of which he wrote, Richter described his thoughts while hearing a Tchaikovsky symphony on the radio, comparing its effect on him to what he was attempting in his latest novel: "I wanted to write the literary equivalent of such a symphony, a stream or streams of beauty, strength, life, mystery, mingling."[32] Five days later, completing a difficult revision in which he had to contend with time passing, Lucy Markle's increasingly odd appearance, and Will Grail's unwavering love for her—"trying to make these convincing and interesting"—a still unsatisfied Richter reworked the chapter yet again from several earlier versions. Richter finished his day with a journal entry announcing that the hardest part of writing was the discovery of form: "the arrangement of all the thoughts and words for interest, beauty, and emotion. Once I get it, to work it up and make it more nearly perfect, even compress or enlarge it, is easy for me for the eventual form is already there. . . . That unknown eventual form! It is what I seek, endlessly work for, feel for, struggle for, patch and putter and almost give up to get. What it is to be I cannot tell you. But once found, it is recognized as the one sought."[33]

On November 15 Harvey read the completed revision and pronounced it "grand," no longer gloomy but something Knopf and the *Post* would both like. As Harvey predicted, the *Post* quickly accepted it, though as a story to run complete in a single issue rather than as a serial. They offered $7,500—all they could spend, they told Paul Reynolds, for a single-issue story. At first saddened by the news from the *Post*, Richter quickly recovered. The sale, after all, freed him from worry about immediate income. To celebrate, he treated Harvey and himself to chocolate ice cream sodas.[34] Two days later Richter sent his agent a typical reply, expressing disappointment that the *Post* had not liked his story "as much as we like it," a questionable inference from Reynolds's letter. "But I am very glad for the sale," Richter continued, "because I wrote it to my highest standards, making no compromise to magazines, and it is extremely decent of the *Post* to have taken it."[35]

News of the sale reached Richter in the small fishing village of Riviera, Florida, where Richter and Harvey had decided to stay at least briefly to see Mrs. Jones, the Christian Science practitioner who had helped Richter through his emotional troubles in winter 1942. It was a "poor cracker colony," Richter wrote his daughter, and he advised Vene, who was to join them for her Christmas vacation, not to tell others where she would be staying.[36] Before Vene arrived for Christmas, Richter had decided to make another series of changes to his story before offering it to Knopf. Rereading, he found himself still dissatisfied with a plot that did not sufficiently build to a strong climax.[37] When he completed revising, his short novel of 21,000 words had been lengthened to 25,000, and his story had grown into one different from anything else he had attempted. It is closest to *The Sea of Grass* in its depiction of strong-willed and enigmatically motivated characters and what in Richter stories are always vexed human relations of love and marriage. But whereas *The Sea of Grass* affirms a way of life as it laments its passing, *Always Young and Fair*, for all its celebration of small town life and deft portraiture of its minor and incidental characters, exposes the emptiness of its primary characters' lives. Coming so soon after Richter's paean to Sayward, the contrast is unmistakable. Lucy Markle and Will Grail live in turn-of-the-century America and suffer from the twentieth-century woes of alienation and displacement. Having promised herself to a young man who does not return from the Spanish-American War, Lucy Markle cannot bring herself to abandon the memory of the dead soldier she did not love to marry Will Grail, the man she does. Intended to be a love story, Richter's novel has something of the foreboding inevitability of *Ethan Frome*, Edith Wharton's stark tale, which Richter had read (and been powerfully moved by) in August 1945, just before beginning to write his story of Pine Grove. The flux of feeling between Lucy Markle and Will Grail creates an unsettling tale, and a sad one, of frustrated love and engagement between two people who, because they are alive, cannot be constant and, because they are "modern," have nothing fixed upon which to orient their lives.

Always an appreciative reader of Richter, his agent Paul Reynolds seldom undertook the role of critic. On *Always Young and Fair*, however, he would identify a telling difference between *The Sea of Grass* and Richter's novel of the Spanish-American War. While both were done with "magnificent craftsmanship," and *Always Young and Fair* presented characters who were "just as real" as those in Richter's first novel, characters in *The Sea of Grass* were strong, vital, "able to withstand the misfortunes and tragedies of this world." In *Always Young and Fair* Richter was writing about "almost brittle people."[38] Even so, Richter's first attempt to write extensively out of his own personal experience was writing that promised much. Relying on memory, Richter evocatively re-created the Pine Grove of his childhood—a re-creation sufficiently recognizable to townspeople to provoke speculation about just who, among the town's former residents, had served as the model for each character. Furthermore, there was something to Vene's first reaction, that the novel had a French quality to it, an air of tragic inevitability which gives the story a wholeness Richter had not quite achieved in *The Sea of Grass*, his first novel of characters struggling with the dislocation of changing times and obscure inner compulsions.

As February gave way to March, Richter found himself increasingly dissatisfied with Florida. He and Harvey remained undecided about where to go: it was still too cold in the Northeast for Harvey, and though they talked of driving to the Southwest, Richter was unwilling to go so early in the year. Without admitting it, he was waiting for the publication of *The Fields*, scheduled for late March. On that day he did not want to be caught where people would know him. Completing *Always Young and Fair*, Richter packed the Buick Roadmaster and headed north, stopping overnight in Augusta, Georgia, then meandering to Henderson, North Carolina, to await the first reviews of *The Fields*. These were so full of praise for his novel that Richter could not stand to have Harvey read more than one or two sentences at a time. Without further delay Richter and Harvey drove to Pine Grove. The reviews were good; they could go home again. And then perhaps to the Southwest, where they had not been for five years.

Driving north toward Pennsylvania, Richter and Harvey discussed their plans for the future. Since 1928 they had lived in rented homes, sitting on other people's furniture, eating from other people's dishes, sleeping in other people's beds. It was time, Harvey urged, for them to find a permanent place for themselves. They needed to decide where they wanted to live, and they needed a home of their own. Richter was less sure, remembering how the maintenance of Pine Tree Farm, the last home they had owned, had interfered with his writing. To write his best he needed to keep himself free as possible from the distractions that owning a home inevitably brought on. Then, too, owning a home would tie them to one place. Released from the travel restrictions of wartime rationing, he preferred to move at will from place to place. His writing relied on the re-energizing he received from each move, and he counted on being able to escape from any locale when his writing began to go badly. Just then he was looking forward to a sojourn in New Mexico.

When a house in Pine Grove was offered to them, unexpectedly, for only $45 a month rent, they decided to settle in Pennsylvania at least until the weather grew cold in the fall. A large house on Tulpehocken Street, the Hess house could serve as a base from which they could travel in larger circles than the war years had allowed them. There was room for Vene to visit on weekends, and for Fred and Emily to bring their sons Skeeks and Eddie to stay overnight. Harvey would be near her brother Stanley and her sister Grace and could easily visit Clark's Valley and the Stricklers in Lebanon. Of course they needed to be careful of Harvey's health; to keep his wife from overexerting herself in the large house, Richter insisted that they hire a maid.

Moving in to the Hess house, Richter uneasily noted that the telephone number, 234, was a sequence and likely to prove unlucky.[39] That first worry would shortly seem prophetic as passing coal trucks rattled their windows late at night, disturbing Richter's sleep. Soon Richter was worrying about the ambiance of the house itself, that it was one of those houses in which he could not write. For decades the home of a medical doctor, it was still filled, Richter suspected, with the energies remaining from the doctor's hard, skeptical, scientific ways of thinking, so antithetical to his own nature that it affected his writing, and to Harvey's Christian Science that it affected her health.[40] Thinking Pine Grove's water was also a potential culprit, he began a practice that would continue throughout his years in Pine Grove, loading his car trunk with water bottles and driving out to fill them at mountain springs.

In six months at the Hess house Richter managed to draft only three chapters of *The Town*, the third book of his trilogy, and most of those chapters were written when he took Harvey away from the house, seeking relief from the summer heat in the higher altitudes of Williamsport and Hazleton. "This seems to be a season of preparation rather than writing," he wrote to himself on one occasion.[41] On another, trying to analyze why he had written so little at the Hess house, Richter decided that he was perhaps too comfortable in Pine Grove. No longer self-

conscious among its townspeople, he worried that he had lost his acute attentiveness to what happened around him. He was not seeing what a writer needed
to see.[42] It did not help his writing of *The Town* that *The Fields* climbed only
briefly onto the list of best-sellers, then slipped off. By midsummer Richter was
reacting with disappointment to his novel's mediocre sales, blaming Knopf for a
languid advertising campaign but once again blaming his novel as well. Even on
the day when he discovered that his novel was being proposed for the Pulitzer
Prize, he wrote in his journal that *The Fields*, like *The Trees* before it, was too much
a series of pictures; in *The Town* there needed to be more plot, more of a story to
engage readers.[43]

This dialogue with himself would be ongoing, even as evidence accumulated
that his reputation, following the excellent critical reception of *The Fields*, was
clearly on the rise. A laudatory essay by Bruce Sutherland appeared in the spring
issue of *New Mexico Quarterly*, the first article on Richter's work by a scholar.
(Richter had not actually read the article, only listened to sentences read by
Harvey, when he asked Vene to write for copies; he wanted to send them to
Reynolds and Knopf.)[44] In May Theodore Morrison of Harvard's English
department wrote to invite Richter to teach a writing seminar at Harvard or at
the Bread Loaf Writer's Conference in Vermont, which Morrison directed.[45]
June brought an invitation to address the Ohio State Archaeological and Historical Society. In July came news from Paul Reynolds of French, Italian,
English, and Australian editions of Richter novels; and in August a letter from
the University of Iowa wondering if he would consider serving as a writing
adviser at $3,500 a year.[46] Richter declined all the invitations except Morrison's
for Bread Loaf, and that he accepted on his own terms. He would not come to
teach that summer, but he would stop in for several days in August (he did not
tell Morrison specifically when) to get a sense of the place and how the writers
interacted with the participants. Although unable to participate formally, he
explained, he would make himself available to talk privately to students. His
sentence offering his services suggests just how uncomfortable he felt in posing
as a teacher of others: "should it happen that anyone at the conference might
chance to care to talk over his work or ideas for a novel or short story with me,
my time is available while I am there, and, of course, without charge."[47]

On August 19 Richter arrived at the conference in the Green Mountains of
Vermont. That first day he avoided lunch with fellow writers by slipping off to
town, prompting Morrison, at dinner time, to walk out to his cabin to meet him.
That evening he joined the after-dinner singing to guitar accompaniment,
blending his tenor with the voices of Wallace Stegner, Louis Untermeyer,

Graeme Lorimer, and others. Richter left for bed when the well-lubricated group turned to singing off-color songs. The following day he attended conference sessions but did not speak, saving his comments for his journal. To his mind the clinics were of doubtful help to aspiring writers, the students talking too much and listening too little to professional advice. "One or two good mentors or critics are invaluable," he wrote, "but a hundred and thirty one are much too many." The next morning he slipped away before breakfast, pausing in Ticonderoga to send Morrison a telegram: "Didn't get to see you to say goodbye. Many thanks for your hospitality. Worth the long drive to have known you all."[48]

That fall when the Kroeger house in Albuquerque unexpectedly became available, Richter eagerly agreed to rent the house on Los Lomas Road, beginning in mid-November. But when page proof for *Always Young and Fair* arrived from Knopf on October 5, Richter almost immediately announced to Harvey that his story was still not right. Despite Knopf's glowing comments about the revised *Always Young and Fair*, Richter decided his Pine Grove novel was still "too slight and tenuous and drawn out."[49] Recognizing the quite substantial costs he himself would have to pay to reset a large section of proof, Richter set out to rewrite the last three chapters. To do so, he put off his departure for Albuquerque.

The revision took a month of concentrated writing, the most sustained and focused writing Richter had accomplished since the publication of *The Fields*. Returning the proof and the rewritten three chapters to Paul Reynolds, Richter wrote apologetically, worrying that his late revision would appear foolish to Knopf's staff. But soon Reynolds was able to report that, though rewriting three chapters of an already typeset book would significantly cut into his royalties, everybody at Knopf admired him for what they saw as a principled decision. Better yet, they liked the revision. Knopf underlined just this in his own letter: "I have just read the new version of *Always Young and Fair* and think you have improved it enormously. Saying this is a sort of backhanded slap at all of us who thought the book so fine in its earlier incarnation. But now that I have read this new ending I realize, in a flash, how absolutely right you are and it is."[50]

Knopf followed his compliments with another sally about bookselling. *The Fields* had sold, to date, 14,000 copies—like all Richter's books, in the range of a modest best-seller. Because it had been published in its entirety in a magazine, *Always Young and Fair* would in all likelihood have a significantly smaller sale, no matter what kind of campaign Knopf mounted. As for "advertising, publicity, and the like," he concluded, "they honestly don't matter a tinker's damn." Richter simply had to trust his publisher, who had "been dealing at pretty close quarters with publishing, advertising and selling of books now for more than thirty years."

On November 19, 1946, at quarter to seven in the morning, Richter eased his Buick Roadmaster expertly through the streets of Pine Grove, taking the Suedberg Road to the gap in Blue Mountain. It was a cold morning, with an unusually heavy frost shining off the fields and scattered pines, reminding Richter of Pine Tree Farm in the wintertime.[51] Departing from Pine Grove, Harvey was uneasy about their decision to return to the Southwest. Having been in the East since shortly after Pearl Harbor, she was sure to miss her daughter, her family, and her friends; and their last sojourn in the desert had ended with Richter's emotional breakdown. But by Texas Harvey was writing enthusiastically to Vene that "everything western gives us a thrill,—the cottonwoods, tumbleweeds, piñon pines, cedars." On the drive into New Mexico, she wrote, the mesas grew "more gorgeous every minute, until at sunset Daddy exclaimed 'Now I'm in love with New Mexico again. Where else could you find anything so beautiful.'"[52] After nightfall, coming out of Tijeras Canyon to the east of Albuquerque, they were delighted by the clear white lights of the city. A town of 18,000 when they first arrived in 1928, it had become a sprawling city of 50,000.

On the four-day drive, Richter and Harvey averaged just under 500 miles a day. They would not drive so many miles again, Richter commented in letters to Paul Reynolds and Alfred Knopf, but he was nonetheless pleased that, though in his mid-fifties, he still had the stamina for such long-distance driving. He still had lots of work to do, and his return to the Southwest made him eager to get to it. As news of the Richters' arrival spread among their friends, once again visits and invitations quickly followed—Richter uneasy in advance of social gatherings but affably joining in the affairs and even enjoying himself, Harvey wrote to Vene. On Thanksgiving they declined two invitations to dinner, instead packing a picnic lunch and driving alone into the mountains. There they prepared a simple meal of bacon and baked beans, fried eggs, lettuce sandwiches, and coffee. Beneath the desert sky, with the wind sweeping in rushes high in the ponderosas, Harvey unpacked the picnic basket while Richter built a small campfire of piñon branches.[53]

The outing went so well that they chose to repeat it for Christmas. By then Richter was finishing "The Hound's Tale," a short story he had begun while waiting for the second set of proofs from Knopf, putting aside the three chapters of The Town that he had labored on for six months. Writing to his publisher to thank him for his extravagant praise of the revised novel, Richter warned Knopf that the third part of his trilogy would not come quickly. The Fields had failed to sell, Richter decided, because he had not paid sufficient attention to its plot, and correcting this fault would reduce even further his already painfully slow writing pace. In his letter Richter summarized his situation: "It is very difficult for me to tell a continuous story and at the same time show the development of a region as I am accustomed. It also takes a good deal of time. In the hope of bringing in some income at the same time that I slowly develop *The Town*, I am starting short stories for the *Post*. I only regret the time they will steal from the novel."[54]

The Town took as long to write as Richter had predicted. Begun in the early spring of 1946, just after the first reviews for *The Fields*, the third novel of his trilogy was not mailed to Paul Reynolds until the end of August, 1949. As always Richter's progress was erratic; as always his spirits rose and fell depending on his estimate of how a day's or a week's writing had gone. Along the way he set his novel aside several times, twice to write short stories, "The Dower Chest" (published by the *Post* as "The Last Man Alive") and "Yankee in Hell," both written for the income they would bring. Written during a period when Richter's ready cash was especially tight, "The Dower Chest" brought in a much-needed $2,000, the highest price Richter had received for a story. Other attempts to write for money, however, were not successful. "Yankee in Hell," an attempt at satire, did not sell, nor did "The Hound's Tale" or a remembrance of Carl Taylor, Richter's writer friend who had been murdered by his houseboy. That *The Fields* sold, finally, only a modest 14,000 copies made him press himself to make the third part of his trilogy a more vivid and dramatic story. The need for a change in his methods was even further emphasized when *Always Young and Fair*, published in spring 1947 to mixed reviews, had only a slender sale.

It was also in spring 1947 that MGM finally released its movie version of *The Sea of Grass*. Having committed its stars, Spencer Tracy and Katharine Hepburn, to the film, MGM promoted it with the ballyhoo accorded only major productions, including a premier at Radio City Music Hall. Warned by his wife and daughter about the changes MGM had made in his story, Richter slipped into a New York theater on June 19, several months after the picture first came out. Unable to watch Spencer Tracy and Katharine Hepburn, actors he admired, struggle through the artificial Hollywood western that MGM had made of his novel, Richter sat restlessly in the darkened theater, his hand shielding his eyes from the images on the screen.[55]

Long before he actually saw "The Sea of Grass," Richter was convinced that the movie would fail and that *Always Young and Fair* would not sell anything like the 25,000 hardback copies Knopf had predicted in his advertising brochure. Nor would *The Fields* accomplish a wish he had been keeping to himself, reflected in a journal passage where Richter puzzles over his future: "What am I to turn my hand to? . . . To go back to *Post* stories will be as hard as to write pulps in Albuquerque. Is there no divine guidance after all? Or is this the result of my not keeping my old promise of 'containment,' keeping back every word of weakness, confession or confiding, for I flew up in anger tonight but it only lasted for a little while. Or is this an answer to my prayer in Mexico whenever a redbird flew across the road ahead of us that my first wish was for health."[56] Another journal entry explains the enigmatic wish on a redbird, a folk superstition Richter had included in *The Fields* and would again in *The Town*. On the day the Pulitzer Prizes for 1946 were announced, Richter admitted that, though his first wish on seeing a redbird had been for health, his second was to win the Pulitzer Prize for fiction.[57]

With only three chapters of *The Town* written in a year's time, Richter seriously considered putting the novel aside. But some good news arrived just at the right time, in the form of a letter from the Ohioana Library Association announcing that, in recognition of Ohio's debt to Richter for "the beautiful way in which he has preserved, for all time, the spirit, folk-habits and language of Ohio's earliest pioneers," it was departing from its tradition of awarding the prize only to native Ohioans to present him with its Grand Medal for 1947.[58] The award was sufficiently momentous to Richter for him to agree to attend an awards ceremony where six hundred people would be present, and it prodded him, he acknowledged in his journal and in his acceptance letter, to continue writing his trilogy.[59] But when the promotional literature from the association arrived in the fall, Richter discovered that he was not, after all, to receive their Grand Medal; that would once again go to an Ohio native. Without explanation his award had been changed to a "Special Medal." Surprisingly, Richter expressed only dismay at the change, commenting in his journal that he was glad he had told only a few people about the award, escaping some public humiliation. He noted also that, since they had changed their minds about the annual medal, he could at least now, without pangs of conscience, decline to attend their dinner.[60]

Richter did agree to attend a meeting of the Pennsylvania German Society, which also wished to give him an award. Perhaps thinking that an appearance before this less formidable group offered him an opportunity to work on his lifelong failure to speak in public, Richter even prepared a one-page speech. When the time came for him to read it, however, he found himself surrounded by people standing and clapping. Unnerved by the ovation, he could only force out a few words of appreciation. He would not speak, he apologized, saying simply that the hour was late and that speaking was not his talent. "I lost my dignity, I think," Richter wrote that night in his journal.[61] Two days later he wrote to the Ohioana Library Association and asked to be excused from attending, sending a copy of the brief acceptance address he had written.

THREE

As Richter had warned Knopf, completing the story of Sayward Luckett and her family was to take almost twice as many chapters as *The Trees* or *The Fields*. While writing his longest novel Richter would sketch out five "streams" that he intended to run through the final novel of his trilogy. One of these was Richter's complaint that easier times had made softer people, a view that Sayward, as she ages, voices more and more insistently. A second was the continuation of Sayward's evolving response to trees, so that by the novel's end Richter's heroine's perspective has changed so completely that she has planted and tended trees around her new home and even protected them in her will. Another stream was to be the expansion of the town, its growing pains as it develops into the county seat of Shawanee County. The fourth was the growth and departure from home of Sayward's children and the gradual dispersal, then death, of Sayward's oldest friends and relatives. The fifth stream concerned Chancey, Sayward's youngest, "born sickly" and nursed by Sayward through as many nights as Lottie Richter had nursed her first son, Connie. Like Connie, the infant Chancey was not expected to live.

Richter hit upon the idea of Chancey one May afternoon while cleaning celery at the kitchen sink. Introduced into the novel to allow Richter the opportunity to describe the natural world as a sensitive child experiences it, Sayward's youngest child develops into a character who is both like and not like Richter— a complex combination of Richter's own childhood experiences and temperament and a voice to present views about progress directly antithetical to Richter's own. He is, at once, Richter's portrait of himself as a boy and young adult, and a portrait of how Richter might well have turned out had he been, like Chancey, influenced in different ways. Because he has a weak heart and slight constitution, Chancey spends his young childhood sitting by a window, looking out on the world rather than participating in the running and games of his older brothers and sisters. His two compensations are his ability to breathe into himself completely the sights and sounds surrounding him, experiencing an enchanting world with all his senses as his brothers and sisters, scurrying about in their games, are apparently unable to do. His second compensation is his ability to daydream himself into a perfect place, where he can play like other children and where the others inhabiting this world understand his thoughts without his speaking. He is so comfortable there in his imagined world, and so uncomfortable among his boisterous family, that he believes himself not really Sayward's child after all, she only raising him for another family, whom in his fantasies he calls the Ormsbys: for secret reasons they have left him with the Wheelers. Such sensory delight in the natural world is of course taken directly from Richter's childhood, memories that in adulthood—and especially after the death of his father—he would connect repeatedly with the famous description by William Wordsworth in his "Ode: Intimations of Immortality" of children arriving into life "trailing clouds of glory" from their heavenly home.

In adolescence Chancey finds a soulmate in Rosa, his half sister from his father's adulterous affair in *The Fields*, who is equally sensitive to nature's marvels and escapes as Chancey does into her own imaginary world. When the young pair discover their true relationship and Rosa, in despair, commits suicide, Chancey's anger at the cruel circumstances he and Rosa have had forced upon them leaves him a lonely, embittered man, advocating everything "modern" that promises to help insulate suffering people from a relentlessly harsh nature. The publisher of a pacifist, Copperhead newspaper, Chancey writes solemn editorials which go virtually unnoticed by others except his mother. There remains, how-ever, more than a little Richter in the grown Chancey. Chancey's attempts to speak out among a group of politicians gets him the polite neglect Richter painfully remembered from his own attempt to explain his theories at Hammer and Tongs. And after Rosa's death, Chancey the young searcher rejects the callous pieties offered under the guise of condolence by several different religions, including Methodism, Catholicism, and his father's "religion" of the body of the law. More comforting than any of these, Chancey discovers, is the curious ranting of an addled old man, who preaches something about the unity of all in God and gives Chancey two pages torn from a book by Emanuel Swedenborg.

Although she recognizes Chancey's suffering, Sayward offers her youngest son no advice, having discovered that the act of helping others, however good her intentions, as often as not only makes matters worse. It is a lesson she has suffered greatly to learn, but finally has by heart—and far better than Richter himself would learn it in his own life. On March 13, 1947, Vene turned thirty years old. She had lived for almost a decade in New York City, gradually working her way through the maze of New York advertising to ever more responsible, prestigious, and remunerative positions. When Richter and Harvey were in Pine Grove, she visited often, usually every other weekend. When they were in Florida or the Southwest, she wrote them regularly—bright, up-tempo letters, full of the news of work and New York friends and the city's entertainments. Richter and Harvey read these letters out loud to each other, usually more than once. During Vene's years in New York, there had been a series of boyfriends, some of whom Richter knew only by Vene's descriptions of them in her letters. Whenever Vene seemed to be growing serious about one, something invariably happened, including at least one instance of her father's meddling. On that occasion, Richter's sleuthing in a credit office uncovered some serious lies a young man was telling.[62] (Two years later, when the same young man telephoned Vene and asked to visit, Richter resolved not to leave the pair alone, writing portentously in his journal, "I feel evil in it."[63]) On another occasion, when Vene's vacation with her parents in Florida coincided with the end of another relationship, leaving Richter's daughter in tears, Richter worried in his journal about her not having found a suitable husband, then ended his rumination with a typical turn of thought. What if she had married, he wondered, and had, already, five children? What would have happened to Harvey's health then, and to his writing? Had fate been a factor, he asked, in his daughter's remaining single? Or, perhaps, had his attempts to guide her actually interfered in her life, bringing on adverse effects?[64]

Richter would pursue just this idea in a nonfiction article called "The Unaccepted Gift." In it Richter described how hard his friend Carl Taylor had worked, and how Richter had helped him work, to secure permission to reprint two magazine articles. Failing to see providence in the resistance of events, the two men had blundered into a success that quickly turned into Carl's death, murdered by his houseboy for a few hundred dollars in traveler's checks. In the article Richter only hints at what he had exclaimed openly in his journal immediately after his friend's death: because he had not guessed the larger purpose in events, his good intentions had killed his friend. However irrationally, he held himself responsible.

In The Town Richter has Sayward worry about her own refusals to accept the choices of providence for her children. The most poignant example, the one causing the most heartache, is her attempt to keep her son Guerdon, still a young man, in Americus. The result is a disastrous marriage, a homicide, and then Guerdon's exile and death far from home. It is a consequence Sayward blames on her meddling: intending to help her son, she has interfered with God's will and hurt him. More thematically significant are Sayward's attempts to ease the afflictions life has placed on Chancey. Having overprotected him, she watches him grow into a prideful and cynical man, unable to see beyond his own self-interest.

While writing *The Town* Richter followed a pattern of life that had continued virtually unabated since the early days of the Great Depression. Whether in Pine Grove, New York, or Florida, he lived with Harvey a quiet life focused always on his writing, interrupted by occasional visits to relatives and friends. Each year he added approximately 30,000 words to his novel. In Pine Grove he allowed himself afternoon rides and walks, often with Harvey; in New York he interrupted his writing for walks and ferry rides, with occasional trips to museums and the theater. In Florida he walked in the sun on the beach, fishing occasionally and strolling out after dark onto bridges, talking to others as they fished. As had happened while Richter was writing *The Fields*, over time he grew to resent the inattention of his agent and publisher, who to his mind had all but forgotten him. In truth, his sense of grievance against his agent and publisher, the months without any mail from either, brought him not discouragement but a kind of dispassionate resolve. In October 1947 he summarized his attitude toward both in words recalling ones he had used in 1943, early in his writing of *The Fields*. "What do Knopf and Reynolds matter?" he asked himself in his journal. "Once upon a time they did. Now all that matters is my work."[65]

As with *The Fields*, one of the most productive places for writing *The Town* turned out to be New York City, where Richter did much of the final rewriting. It was to help out his daughter, who worried that she would lose her lease on the Washington Square apartment if she sublet it, that led Richter to his most extensive stays in New York. In spring 1948 Vene returned to Pine Grove to recover from an illness brought on by her work. Much earlier she had left Macy's to become copy chief for Elizabeth Arden, a prestigious position that carried with it the liability of having to work with the notoriously difficult Arden. Eventually the daily pressure and tirades by Arden led to Vene's resignation. After working briefly as advertising director at I. Miller, Vene moved to Abbott Kimball, an advertising agency, and it was there, in an office without windows, writing copy for merchandise she did not see, that Vene's health deteriorated so alarmingly that her Christian Science practitioner finally telephoned her parents, recommending that they take her home to recuperate.

In Pine Grove Vene turned again to writing stories, much as her father had returned to write after his illness in Cleveland, and she would remain in Pine Grove through the summer and early fall—the period during which Richter was writing "Summer Sweeting," the chapter in which Sayward resists interfering in her young daughter's affection for an unworthy suitor. The experience for both Richter and his daughter was a difficult one. During those times when his daughter had "poise, presence," Richter would be encouraged and encouraging; when she slipped into what he thought to be procrastination and complaining, or when she refused to act on his suggestions for revising her writing, he would end up lecturing her as he had once, early in his married life, lectured her mother. On one occasion he reminded his daughter that she was only a quarter Achenbach and "could handle herself anywhere if she would recognize certain traits and tendencies frankly"—meaning her stubbornness and refusal to see her own weaknesses.[66] Finally Richter's relationship with Vene became so strained that he resorted to Christian Science affirmations, determined to will his daughter into his idea of her, rather than to talk her into it. When Vene announced that she wanted to go abroad to find work in Paris, Richter acknowledged that his attempts to dissuade her were failures: "Tonight after more trouble . . . I changed, kept quiet, said pleasant things. I cried to God, 'It's the only way. I find it out again. Help me to use it all the time.'"[67]

Vene sailed for England on October 6, a week before her father's fifty-eighth birthday, leaving her parents in possession of her Washington Square apartment. While abroad, Vene landed a job as Riviera correspondent for the *Herald Tribune*, the English-language newspaper circulated throughout Europe. Settled at France for at least a year, she encouraged her parents to join her. Harvey was eager to accept, but Richter, willing though reluctant for Harvey to go, claimed he could not take time from *The Town*. Clearly Richter's response was in part another instance of his personal timidity toward any new experience; without doubt, however, he was also thinking about finances, for income during the writing of *The Town* had dwindled to an average of less than $4,000 a year— several thousand less than Richter and Harvey were actually spending.[68] Even after giving up the Hess house rental and subletting Vene's apartment for that first winter, their cash reserves were so low that the week before Christmas they rented a cold-water cabin at $25 a week in Riviera, Florida. Shortly into the new year, when high season rates when into effect, they moved to an equally Spartan accommodation they nicknamed "Camp Junco."[69]

For the final two chapters of *The Town* Richter would create monologues of the thoughts of Sayward and Chancey, his primary characters throughout the last novel of his trilogy. In "The Witness Tree" Sayward is too old to live alone but still holding off her children who want to move her from the large house on Wheeler Street that Portius had outfoxed her into building. The chapter eloquently records the thoughts of an old woman, still more woodsy than not, whose mind wanders over the past and her friends from those times, all of whom are gone. Among the primary sources for this chapter were Richter's memories of his mother's last days, but they must also have included his visits with Augusta

Filbert, living alone in her large house on Tulpehocken Street, who was herself old enough to seem strange to others. "Queer," Richter called Augusta in a letter to Vene, but then corrected himself: "I shouldn't say queer but eccentric." As Richter explained to his daughter, "That's the way old people used to get."[70] Like Augusta, Sayward in her last days is living an inward life, slipping away from the present into memories of lost times and lost friends.

Chancey's chapter is decidedly less celebratory of life. As his mother's health deteriorates he loses his newspaper to bankruptcy, then discovers that the anonymous angel whose monthly checks have supported his press has been his own mother.[71] For Chancey, the discovery that she has been a secret benefactor turns inside out his assumptions about her, but he can no longer ask why she has underwritten a newspaper directly attacking her own ideas. She is no longer reachable on this earth, and Chancey discovers just what it means to "ponder his own questions and travel his own way alone."

FOUR

"Conrad, this is it," Alfred Knopf wrote Richter immediately after reading the typescript of *The Town*. "You have written not only a distinguished book but a popular one."[72] Paul Reynolds was just as enthusiastic, naming it the best of the trilogy and Richter's best novel ever. It would sell enormously, Reynolds predicted, perhaps 50,000 for the third volume of the trilogy and then another large sale for the trilogy in a single volume. And it would be more than just popular, Reynolds insisted. "You just don't realize what a fine piece of work you have finished."[73]

Buoyed by his publisher's and his agent's enthusiasm, Richter quickly turned out a short story for the *Post*, "The Boy He Was." Then he took up his notes for the book he had been planning for over twenty years, his Western Bible. If *The Town* sold as well as Knopf and Reynolds were predicting, the time could finally be right for him to share his theories with his readers. But first "The Boy He Was" engaged more of his interest than most stories for the *Post*, for it was a story that was important to Richter in two distinct ways. The first of these Reynolds caught immediately when Richter sent it to him; it was an "idea story," as Reynolds disapprovingly called them, and he once again advised Richter against such stories, which seldom sold.[74] In this case the message was a warning about atomic bombs: a scientist made famous for his part in creating the atomic bomb is magically transported back into his own childhood where he discourages himself as a child, "the boy he was," from pursuing science, urging him instead into medicine.

Happily for Richter, Ben Hibbs thought differently. The editor of the *Post* and general editor for Curtis Publishing wrote personally to Richter to say the story was splendid—"as fine as anything we have bought during the eight years I have been editor of the *Post*."[75] He paid Richter $2,000 for it, and then demonstrated—by the introductory lead he added to the story and by a change of title—his understanding that the story could not be summed up as simply a "message" delivered by a man to himself as a boy; it was at least equally about the experience of finding one's long-dead parents. Just beneath the new title, "Dr. Hanray's Second Chance," he added the following: "Perhaps when you were young you underestimated your father. What would you give to live in the past for an hour and try to make amends?"[76] Clearly Richter would give a lot. Asked by a *Post* editor for background information about the story for its "Keeping Posted" column, Richter disclosed that the genesis of the story was his trips to White Deer Valley, once with his brothers Joe and Fred, and again—the day after Hiroshima—with just Fred. Searching among what was left of his childhood home, turned by World War II into an army reservation for manufacturing explosives, Richter was hoping for some signs of his own past: "Now as I came back to the valley I looked for the wagon shed, the stable and the blacksmith shop, and they were all gone. Really what I knew in my heart that I looked for the most were some living traces of my parents—of my mother in the terrible shack of a defaced parsonage and of my father in his boarded-up churches and along the valley roads he used to travel day and night making the rounds of his charge and people."[77]

For its "Keeping Posted" column the *Post* preferred a lighter fare and chose instead Richter's accounts of his misbehavior with his brothers, quoting the local blacksmith who had said of them: "Those damn Richter boys. They're wild ones. I won't let my Howard associate with them." But for Richter the message of his story was also the message he saw in the ministry of his father, John Richter, traveling about the quiet valley preaching peace on earth without any possibility of foreseeing that his beloved valley would be turned into a place devoted to war and destruction.

Visiting other homes from his early adolescence brought equally intense feeling, too private to reveal except in his journal. Returning from a drive to Tremont to see the parsonage where he had once lived, Richter wrote, "If only I could go in and find Mother there," and "I could almost believe Mother was there."[78] But as much as he wished to reexperience the sensations of his boyhood, he could do so only, and imperfectly, through his fiction. This sense of longing led to Richter's lament, from his journal of October 20, 1947, that he had lost more than the actual moments of the past, he had lost his boyhood sensitivity to the world around him: "Every morning waking up in bed was creation, a golden something far more than a base metal. Today in bed my body dimly remembered and tried unsuccessfully to reach that fluidic state in which it responded delicately to a hundred and one slight sensitive things that escape me now, things in the air, in the light, in yesterday, in today, in tomorrow. The log lies in the same beautiful glade in the woods where the tree stood. The same moon comes at night, the mist in the rain, the dawn and the deer to drink, but I cannot feel or respond to them any more." An even more plaintive cry came from his thoughts of what awaited him in an afterlife: "My mother and my father, my brothers and Aunt Lizzie and Beth and Henry I may meet in another world, but that inexpressibly rare childhood with all its characters and background and tender feelings, never."[79] Written immediately after completing the third part of his Ohio trilogy, *The Town*, "Dr. Hanray's Second Chance" was Richter's third attempt to re-create in his fiction a particular place from childhood. Like "The Good Neighbors" and *Always Young and Fair*, this story would be part of Richter's preparation for a second trilogy, novels about his family and his life. It also registers his fascination with the idea of a return as an adult into the world of one's childhood, an idea he would pursue again.

The Christmas season in Pine Grove was uncomfortable for Richter, and especially so when he was not hard at work on a project. On December 24, 1949, he wrote one of his emblematic journal entries, summing up his belief that time away from his writing was misspent. Perhaps he remembered the Thanksgiving in Tucson when, after promising he would not write that day, he had gotten out all his notes for *The Trees* and spent the afternoon restlessly rearranging them. "Only work counts," he had concluded that brief journal entry.[80] Perhaps he remembered the occasion when, living with Stanley Achenbach, he had acceded to Harvey's request to take a week off after finishing a chapter. "That week went quick," Stanley remarked, when he caught his brother-in-law bending over his typewriter the very next day.[81] "My work is all that counts," he had said in 1943, while writing *The Fields*; "All that matters is my work," he echoed in 1947 as he struggled with the middle chapters of *The Town*.[82] With *The Town* in his publisher's hands, "The Boy He Was" sold to the *Post*, and his Western Bible and family trilogy on his mind but not yet sufficiently developed to allow him the release of a day's writing, he wrote his last entry for 1949. Written in capital letters, suggesting that Richter intended the entry as a title for a paragraph he did not write, the three words were left by themselves to sum up his day. They were "NOTHING BUT CHRISTMAS."

eleven

Putting Away Toys and Pawns

ONE

Just before the new year Richter put New York, his agent, and his publisher behind him and set out for Albuquerque, where he had rented the Laraway house at 1617 Los Lomas Road. There he planned to work on his Western Bible, the book he had been preparing to write for over a decade. Richter now saw this book as more spiritual and much less psychological than *Human Vibration* and *Principles in Bio-Physics,* written more than twenty years earlier.[1] In his new work he planned to introduce desert scenes as symbolic settings for dialogues between a teacher and several pupils, discussions about the nature of humankind's relationship to God and about the evolution of human consciousness. Such a book might not sell well at first, Richter anticipated, but if *The Town* sold even half as well as Paul Reynolds and Alfred Knopf predicted, that would provide the necessary income. During the months preceding the publication of *The Town*, it seemed that God might be providing Richter the opportunity he had long desired. Finally he would have his say about spiritual evolution.

So much depended upon the success of *The Town*. A good sale meant he and Harvey could buy a home in the East or the Southwest. And a substantial sale would enable him to write without interruption not only his Western Bible but perhaps another of the books that were "a must to write." One such book was to be a novel about reincarnation; another, entitled "The Gifts," the story of a girl who discovers that her prayers come true. Then there was Richter's planned trilogy based on his own family; toward these he had gathered hundreds of pages of notes. He also had plans for a book about Shakespeare, perhaps a novel, based on his private belief that Shakespeare was lame, and another about Jesus' life. But these, he guessed, could not be written without trips to England and the Holy Land,[2] and he did not believe these were trips he would be given time to make.

In January 1950 Richter was approaching his sixtieth birthday; looking at snapshots taken in Texas during their drive to New Mexico, he saw himself an aging man with gray, thinning hair, looking "glum, shabby, and old."[3] Undeniably he was growing older: his health was not good, especially his heart, and he knew that his years to write were limited, as was his energy to continue his writing regimen.[4] He needed at least another twenty years to accomplish the most important books on his list.

On their arrival in Albuquerque, Richter and Harvey were surprised and upset to discover that the Laraways had enclosed Harvey's sleeping porch and redecorated with furniture neither liked. "Don't unpack," Richter announced to Harvey. "I can't write here."[5] But once they set to work moving furniture into new locations and getting their own rugs onto the floors, the house became again a place where they could be comfortable. On January 22, 1950, less than a week after settling into the Laraway house, Richter began to outline his Western Bible, telling himself that he needed to write simply, avoiding psychological terms. For a brief while he called his book "The Mountain"; a month later, thinking that this title would remind readers of Thomas Mann's *The Magic Mountain*, he settled on *The Mountain on the Desert*. January had not been an easy month, with worries over Harvey's health and his own, followed by the arrival of lackluster promotional material for *The Town* from Knopf and then disappointment with the dust jacket Knopf had chosen for the new book. That month the newspapers were full of the escalating tension in Korea, leading Richter to worry that a war with the Soviet Union was imminent. Should a war break out, Pine Grove could be a haven as it had been during World War II.[6] Prudence suggested that they buy a home in Pine Grove, and that, if *The Town* did not sell, he put aside his Western Bible to write another serial.

Worrying about a Russian preemptive attack with atomic weapons, Richter took time away from his energy theories to write a nonfiction article, which was a kind of addendum to *The Town*—another warning about humanity endangering itself in its search for pleasure and ease. The article would also serve as something of an introduction to the Western Bible. In Richter's theory, human evolution, because it is the will of God, is inevitable; but individuals have some choice in how that evolution occurs. Either people gain higher consciousness through self-discipline and self-denial or the "powers that be," what his spiritual leader in *The Mountain on the Desert* was to call "the Hand," would visit terrible suffering upon them, forcing humanity, both individually and collectively, to undergo trials from which it was possible to come to a higher understanding. Seeing the imminence of "the Hand" in a looming third world war, Richter decided to speak out directly. Calling his essay "The Changing American" (a title that Edward Weeks of the *Atlantic* would replace with "That Early American Quality") Richter elaborated the conviction of Sayward Luckett in her dotage— that the pioneers with their strength and distinctive individuality had given way to people of lesser, weaker character. The essay was not meant to be literary, Richter wrote to Weeks. According to Harvey, in its early drafts it was "all complaint," a criticism that upset Richter but led to changes making the essay more a celebration of earlier ways and less a jeremiad against present ones.[7]

On April 24, 1950, publication day for *The Town*, Richter was not feeling optimistic about world events or about his personal circumstances. "It was no use," he wrote. "I couldn't go ahead with [*The Mountain on the Desert*] while this awful vacuum of no home of our own pressed upon me, with the desperate need for money, with a probable war coming and no place to live." Nonetheless, two days later he was recording another day spent planning his new book, commenting simply that he could not stay away from it. On May 1 confirmation arrived from William Cole at Knopf that the reviews of *The Town* were "all wonderful"; enclosed with Cole's letter were several representative reviews, including Orville Prescott's from the *New York Times*. Hearing Harvey read only a few sentences from these, Richter had to escape outdoors, where he watered the lawn for an hour to calm himself.

In spite of the good reviews, actual book sales, once again, put *The Town* only briefly onto the best-seller lists. Writing to admit to Richter the book's disappointing sales, Knopf declared himself "heartbroken"; with the letter he added an encomium about the novel from a Chicago bookseller, which ended, "Feeling that way, why do I find it so difficult to sell?" Weeks later, forwarding a testimonial from the director of the Indiana Historical Bureau, Knopf added the best words he could about sales: "I haven't, alas, any really good news for you. *The Town* jogs along quietly, but I think it is making real friends as it goes. Its failure to catch on in a big way has been, as I told you, my great disappointment of the year."[8]

It was for Richter the old quandary. Once again he found himself with notebooks full of ideas for books and little prospect of the financial support he needed to write them. He had counted on substantial sales from *The Town*; moreover, he had anticipated offers for film rights to the trilogy, offers that might easily have been for much more than the $25,000 he had turned down for just *The Trees*. But no offer came from Hollywood, which was all the more puzzling to him because the books he planned to write, connected either directly or indirectly with his theories of human evolution, were all, Richter believed, part of his private compact with God. Given a chance, his work could serve to mediate, to bring together meaningfully two seemingly antithetical explanations of human significance. At one extreme was the Darwinian depiction of humans as passive recipients of natural selection; at the other extreme was an active, interventionist, and mystical apprehension of divinity in each self, which had found its most popular expression in Emersonian Transcendentalism and in a more sectarian way in Mary Baker Eddy's Christian Science. Richter saw *The Mountain on the Desert* as the book that would succeed in reaching all the way across this seemingly unbridgeable gulf.[9] Sometime earlier he had put his idea another way to his friend Dean Matthews:

> I am only dimly beginning to see that the God Jesus spoke of may be not so much a personal God as a principle, Who sends rain on the just and the unjust, and that our yielding all to Him is simply to let ourselves into harmony with this principle, which is all power and all powerful, which, being Life, is nearer to us than breathing, and by which all things are made new, not in any religious sense necessarily but in a biological and living sense, for God is love, spirit, biology, and life. In this I think the Christian Scientists are ahead of us, and if there were a religion that combined these primitive teachings of Christ with the beautiful liturgy

and warm feelings of the Protestant churches, I believe it would sweep the world. I know it would be a religion I could wholeheartedly join and work for.[10]

Richter's Western Bible was intended to describe this God of "love, spirit, biology, and life" and to explain how, "in a biological and living sense," individual lives were part of His plan. But how could he complete his book without income?

One June morning Richter set out for Socorro to attend a conference on rainmaking. As intellectually curious at sixty as he had been at twenty, he still looked for such opportunities to learn what he could about scientists and their methods. It was a hot day, and the main road crowded. Turning at Los Lunas onto the old road to Gallup, deserted for thirty miles, Richter rediscovered the New Mexico he used to know, "leisurely, lazy, uninhabited." Writing to Vene, who would remember the solitude and loneliness, the taste of air that had blown over hundreds of miles, he described the tamarisks blooming in the sandy banks of the Puerco, the desert larks springing into flight, sounding their shrill, lonely cry. Then he ended with a brief paragraph, bringing himself and his daughter back to the present: "I have not been too well which was why I took the morning off. Mother says to tell you that you will find us both older. We thought to find the fountain of youth out here, but it's not for us."[11]

Vene arrived in Albuquerque on June 24. After a year in France, where she had capped her journalistic feats by interviewing Somerset Maugham and Henri Matisse, Vene had spent the intervening months in New York, freelance writing for the *New York Herald Tribune* and the *Christian Science Monitor*. The day after her arrival the news spread across the front page of Albuquerque newspapers that South Korea was undergoing a massive assault from the north. Uneasy about the escalating cold war with the U.S.S.R., distrusting Truman since the atomic attacks on the Japanese cities of Hiroshima and Nagasaki, Richter suspected that they were witnessing the advent of another world war. He worried about Vene returning to New York, a target like Hiroshima or Nagasaki. To Richter nothing in the modern world seemed more unbearable than the idea of atomic holocaust. That fall he would summarize his sense of the world's condition to Charlie Warfel: "We live in the most terrible age the world has known, when at a moment's notice the whole population can be subjected to experiences which our forefathers never dreamed of."[12] During such a time, working on his Western Bible was for Richter an act of faith, an assertion of life's meaning. People were not simply creatures struggling in a chaos or victims of geopolitical machinations;

they were part of a plan, a purpose, and his *The Mountain on the Desert* would help reveal that meaning. And he was prepared to do even more. One can imagine the astonishment of Paul Reynolds on receiving from Richter, his client who would not participate in book signings, instructions not to say an unequivocal "no" to a request from Colston Leigh for Richter to undertake a lecture tour, but rather to "put him off while keeping him interested." Only one subject could coerce Richter into public speaking: the world's increasing danger of atomic holocaust brought on by the deterioration of individual strength of character. "Should the need arrive," he wrote, "to speak out for early America in person, I should try to do it, poor speaker as I am."[13]

On July 22 Richter read Harvey and Vene the first six chapters of *The Mountain on the Desert*. Encouraged by their responses (Harvey said hearing the chapters was therapeutic for her, like reading Christian Science literature)[14] Richter continued on with chapter 7, in which Henry uses a desert sandstorm to illustrate the relation between the limited "life energy" of the material body and the evolution of the soul toward God. During the same time he was also advising Vene on a short story. Rewritten twice, both times with large doses of fatherly guidance, "The Wedding Dress" was finally accepted by the *Post*, Vene's first major story sale. Ill with a headache and fever, Vene sobbed when she received the news. Now she could return to New York, she said, with a real success to show for her summer.[15] Vene had wanted to return East in August, but her parents persuaded her to stay on until early autumn. On October 1 Richter saw his daughter off at the Albuquerque train station; two days later Richter and Harvey themselves left Albuquerque to become, as he had written to a friend, "homeless wanderers, as usual."[16] That these words may communicate some yearning for a more settled life is suggested by Richter's decision to ask his brother-in-law, Stanley Achenbach, to keep track of houses for sale in Pine Grove and to alert them if anything suitable came on the market.

Departing from Albuquerque, Richter and Harvey's first destination was Mexico City, Mexico. In spring 1947 they had made a brief excursion south of the border, and that experience encouraged Richter to think of Mexico as a place where they could spend the winter months. The trip turned out well, with Richter and Harvey enjoying much of their travel and finding themselves generously treated when Harvey suddenly took ill. Yet despite Mexico's picturesque landscapes, comfortable accommodations, and friendly people, Richter soon decided that he could not write in Mexico, no matter how cheaply they might live there. Mexico's "spirit and color" felt wrong for his work, and the poverty surrounding them was just too appalling. He would not improve his own standard of living at the expense of others, and he could not live among such desperately poor people without himself making sacrifices to alleviate it. On the drive back to the United States, Richter's car malfunctioned, the Buick becoming locked in second gear. Richter suspected that the stuck transmission might be a sign to discourage him from returning to Mexico.[17]

Crossing the border at Rockport, Texas, Richter sought out a garage to fix his car and then the post office, where his mail was being held. Richter and Harvey planned to stay in Rockport only briefly, but the owners of the tourist cabins where they stayed turned out to be pleasant company, and the wife, Connie Hagar, an expert bird-watcher who was eager to share her knowledge. Earlier Harvey had written Vene that they would soon leave Texas for Florida, where she could meet them for her Christmas vacation. But by late November her parents' letters had become more vague about their plans. What they did not tell her was that a letter from Stanley Achenbach had arrived, describing a house that was to be auctioned in Pine Grove. They could not be sure whether their next destination was Florida or Pine Grove, and would not know until December 2, when they would find out whether they had bought a house or not.

The whole experience was to be an exceedingly curious one, especially for a couple as cautious of financial matters and as hesitant about major decisions as Richter and his wife had shown themselves repeatedly to be. And for a novelist who more than once had found himself unable to write in a house he had rented, the prospect must have been more than unsettling. Stanley's letter briefly described the Sheidy house at 11 Maple Street, a large, attractive house—stucco with a green tile roof—on a quiet side street off Tulpehocken. To his mind it was the nicest house in Pine Grove, and he urged them to come see for themselves.[18] In a quick exchange of letters that followed, Richter commissioned Stanley to bid on the house for them, though neither Harvey nor Richter remembered exactly which house was to be auctioned. They themselves, Richter wrote his brother-in-law, were not able to fly to Pine Grove for the auction.

There was, in fact, more than enough time for Richter to drive to Pennsylvania. Having recently made the trip from Pine Grove to Albuquerque in four days, Richter could easily have covered the distance from Rockport to his hometown and had days to spare. Instead, he and Harvey relied on Stanley's descriptions of the house and his reports of conversations with Pine Grove townspeople and a local banker to establish the likely price range of the house. But even with Stanley's full descriptions, Richter was planning to bid on a house he had not seen. Stanley Achenbach must have been surprised, perhaps even disconcerted, by his brother-in-law's request. Harvey may have been as well.

Even Richter offered no explanation in his journal about why he was trusting such a decision to another person. One possible reason was that the proposition itself seemed so unreal: there certainly was something a bit fantastic about sending Stanley instructions not to go beyond $17,500 in his bidding, and until the end, no doubt, Richter did not really expect his bid to be the winning one. An equally tenable reason was that, by staying in Rockport, Richter did not have to face a bout with his oldest enemy—shyness in public. If he returned to Pine Grove, Richter would not have been able to bid for himself on the Sheidy house, or even stand in the crowd at the auction. In all likelihood he could not picture himself walking Pine Grove's streets on the days before the auction, making a spectacle of himself as people gossiped about his interest in the house. There was as well one other explanation. By remaining in Texas, Richter was refusing to interfere in the work of providence. If he was to have the house, then he would have it. It was God's decision.

Shortly after 4 P.M. on December 2, Harvey answered the telephone to hear her brother Stanley's voice, telling her excitedly that they had bought the Sheidy house. The winning bid had been $16,000. The consensus in Pine Grove was that they had made a very good buy.

Richter and Harvey remained for almost a week in the guest cottage in Rockport, Texas, while Richter finished rewriting chapter 4 of his Western Bible. On December 8, rather later in the morning than they usually began their journeys, Richter and Harvey drove away from the Hagar cottages and headed toward Pennsylvania. Early in the afternoon of December 14, they arrived in Pine Grove, driving slowly past 11 Maple Street then hurrying on to Stanley's house to get a key. Their new home was from the outside an impressive house, a house that a doctor or judge might own, and Maple Street a quiet side street, still paved in brick. An alleyway separated their new home from its neighbor on one side, and an empty lot on the other side reached all the way to the corner. Once inside, the new homeowners found the rooms larger than they anticipated, despite Stanley's thorough descriptions. Some of the hardwood floors needed refinishing, there were water stains on old wallpaper, and the back porch was badly in need of paint. But the house felt immediately right to both of them. There was even a second-story porch that could be screened in for Harvey.

By the second night Richter and Harvey were camping out in their new home, sleeping on a borrowed studio couch and a spare mattress. Before Christmas they had sufficiently furnished 11 Maple Street so that Vene could come for the holidays. At the bank, Charlie Hikes congratulated Richter on a good buy, saying

15. Eleven Maple Street, Richter's home on a quiet street in Pine Grove from 1950 until 1968.

that such a house could not be built in 1950 for less than $40,000.[19] It was a bargain even with the added cost of repairs and modifications, which kept a carpenter busy all winter and spring. After the Christmas holidays, Vene returned briefly to her Washington Square apartment, then returned to Pine Grove for the winter. Vene's return was probably at Richter's urging, for the new home offered Harvey endless opportunities to overextend herself and she quickly did so, endangering her health. Vene may well have returned to Pine Grove reluctantly, for she was leaving behind a new friend, a photographer named Jack Haggerty, she had begun dating. In Pine Grove Vene shouldered most of the responsibilities for setting up the household; she also wrote another short story, "Shawnee Raid"—again under her father's hovering tutelage—and sold it to the *Post*.[20]

In spite of the hammering and sawing of the carpenter, Richter succeeded in working steadily on *The Mountain on the Desert*. On April 14 he mailed to Paul Reynolds the typescript, as well as a somewhat defensive letter reminding his agent that it was a different kind of book, a "labor of love": "Lately I have felt that if I didn't do this book soon, I might never do it, so I took a year and a quarter off to write it. I don't regret an hour of it. To me it's the most important thing I have done, but that's a personal matter, and I have no hope that you or Alfred or the critics will agree with me. Just the same, I had to do it."[21] The 165-page typescript Paul Reynolds read during the next week was a Socratic dialogue between Henry, an ascetic weaver living in a mountain hermitage, and four students from the nearby university. Collectively the thirteen individual chapters build toward the overarching messages that energy alone is the stuff of life; that all life is encompassed in the gathering and spending of energy; that human consciousness expands and rises toward the light—toward "God"—only by an increased capacity for energy release, allowing a person to see and feel differently and thereby shed lower orders of understanding; and that the higher levels are obtained either through self-imposed stoicism or by hardship imposed by the hand of fate. As Henry explains to the young men from the university, it is human nature (what Henry calls the "racial self") to crave ease, but humans grow only through experiences that strain energy resources, through which new energy channels are developed. According to Henry, a primary purpose of individual experiences that increase energy release is the process of turning hate into love, or in the terms of Richter's earlier discussions, raising consciousness to new levels of "understanding," which in its ultimate form is a sympathetic identification with all life. "Hate is the raw evolutionary material of love," Henry explains in chapter 12. Returning to the idea that higher understanding comes when increased energy flow allows the soul to shed lower understanding, he continues, "Love is only the sublimation of past hates."[22] And the characteristics achieved by the higher self? Humility is one; others are goodness, wisdom, compassion, joy in beauty, and finally that condition of the soul allowing it to experience intimations of immortality.[23] In the final chapter Henry returns again to the evolutionary nature of the process he has attempted to explain, suggesting a metaphor that may well offer the key to Henry's—and Richter's—sense of the experience of living: "In theory we grow spiritually to get nearer the light. In reality we do it to get away from darkness."[24]

On April 23 Paul Reynolds answered Richter with a carefully worded letter; the best he could find to say after reading *The Mountain on the Desert* was that it was "very interesting" and "done with a good deal of skill" and that he wished his father, Paul Reynolds, Sr., had lived to read it. About publication and sales, Paul Reynolds was highly tentative: "What its sales possibilities are is a matter I wouldn't have much opinion about," he wrote, adding that, while religious books had gained in popularity, those that sold well appealed to the emotions rather than the intellect, and Richter's was "much more a book dealing with philosophy." He was "quite dubious" that Knopf would understand the book or be able to sell it. Shortly thereafter Reynolds forwarded to Richter the first response from Knopf, verifying his prediction about the predisposition of the publisher. In a note to Paul Reynolds, Knopf candidly announced his dismay at the prospect of publishing such a book. Although declaring himself "perfectly willing to publish it and do the best I can for it if he insists," Knopf believed Richter would be making a mistake to publish the book, and he himself "would not be doing right by him as a friend and publisher" if he did not warn Richter that loyal readers who bought this book "would be disappointed if indeed not permanently alienated."[25]

In one of those coincidences that Richter often suspected to be signs from the astral, Knopf's warning was offset by some wholly unexpected good news. Knopf's letter arrived on May 6; on May 7 Richter and Harvey decided at the last moment to accept an invitation from Vene to spend several days at her apartment. Just an hour after their arrival late that afternoon, a telegram was delivered to Richter at 41 Washington Square. From Grayson Kirk, vice president of Columbia University, it announced that *The Town* had been awarded the Pulitzer Prize for fiction. To Richter, the fortuitous arrival seemed providential: although his presence in New York was unknown to anybody, somehow the message had been delivered to Vene's apartment, where he had done much of the revising of *The Town*. By arriving at Vene's, the telegram allowed his small family to share together the moment's euphoria.

When he returned to Pine Grove, Richter set out to answer each letter and telegram that awaited him there. The writer who often complained that he received so little attention was for once inundated, as he explained in one of his replies: "I have received more letters and telegrams than I can easily answer, and the town here had taken [the award] to heart. I've been congratulated in the house, on the telephone, at the front door, in the back yard, in the car, on the street and in stores and business places. Some of them are people who have never read a book and probably never will. It's Pine Grove, not I that really got this thing, and that lets me slip gracefully out of the picture. They wanted to have a welcoming committee and a public banquet waiting for us but my brother-in-law said I'd never attend and that put an end to that."[26] The letter giving him the most pleasure came from a Pine Grove soldier in Korea. Hearing late at night on Armed Forces Radio that Richter had won the Pulitzer, Sgt. Norman Clements had gone down the row of bunks, waking up the Pine Grove soldiers to share the news with each of them.[27] But the communication he would treasure beyond all others came in a dream four nights after receiving the award. In it his mother was leafing from page to page through a book. When she got to the final sheet, Richter could read clearly what was written there, in Lottie Richter's handwriting: it was "adoringly."[28]

Although delighted by the recognition his novel was receiving, Richter saw the prize as less a reward for *The Town* than encouragement to revise *The Mountain on the Desert*.[29] The Pulitzer Prize, he decided, was God's method of prodding him to persevere with his book, regardless of Knopf's reluctance to publish it. Just as soon as he finished responding to the congratulations, he set out to revise what he continued to think of as his most important book. In his prayers one evening, Richter asked God whether he should take *The Mountain on the Desert* back from Alfred Knopf, who would publish it only reluctantly. The next day Harvey, ever more optimistic about such matters, advised her husband with her bright matter-of-factness that had delighted and exasperated Richter from their first meeting. Of course he should stay with Knopf—and stay with him all the way to the Nobel Prize. For Richter such words were almost too audacious to be spoken aloud. He could not allow himself to even think them, writing in his journal a comment that registers twice, at beginning and ending, Richter's deep inner modesty and also his deeply held convictions about his energy theories: "[Harvey's ambition] astonished and saddened me a little. I have a prize now I never expected to get. The other is unattainable, but if it were to be got, I should not sacrifice the welfare of the *The Mountain on the Desert* for it, if I knew what was the book's welfare."[30] For the moment, he decided, the book's welfare lay in his own hands, and he asked Reynolds to retrieve it from Knopf and return it to him.

By the middle of June Richter had rewritten several chapters, enough to share with Harvey and Vene. Neither was optimistic. Vene thought Henry the mountain philosopher was still too preachy and the book's plot insufficiently developed to keep readers interested. Unprepared though he was for Vene's criticism, Richter took her opinion with surprising equanimity, commenting in his journal that he had not been upset by his daughter's comments: rereading the chapters himself, he was sure of them; they stood up.[31] But when, a week later, Harvey offered much the same evaluation to another rewriting, going so far as to suggest that he lay the book away for a year, Richter was unable to weather the second criticism. Reluctantly he set it aside. Later he would say that it was not Paul's or Alfred's inability to appreciate what he had written that had taken away his confidence about *The Mountain on the Desert*; it was Harvey's and Vene's.[32]

But if his working draft was put aside, Richter's thoughts about his energy theories and humankind's special, if not always knowable, relationship to God were not. While revising his book Richter had begun to sketch out three projects, an article, a short story, and a serial for the *Post*. Although all were intended to rebuild his bank balance, his topics were chosen for their fit with ideas he was pursuing in his Western Bible. First Richter wrote a narrative about the exploits of Colonel Boquet, one of his early American heroes, who had led a small expedition deep into the wilderness to quell an Indian uprising and to negotiate for the return of captive women and children. It was Boquet's higher order of understanding about the enemy, his stern self-discipline, and his close command of his troops that allowed him to succeed honorably, without the massacres and reprisals that had resulted from previous expeditions against the Indians. After completing the Boquet article, Richter immediately began "The Children of Light," a short story in which he wrote overtly about another of his personally held beliefs, that in the lives of people there are signs which foretell the future—if people only understood them. In "The Children of Light" the late return of a champion homing pigeon, injured during a race, prefigures the return of its owner, a bomber pilot downed behind enemy lines. Richter's original story, evidently, focused on the connection between the two returns; but the *Post* asked for revisions deemphasizing the possibility of the supernatural event and later cut even the revision, further shifting the story away from the significance of the bird's return and onto the steadfast faith of the pilot's wife, who waits after everyone else has given up the flier for dead. In what for Richter was a final insult, the *Post* changed his title to "The Marriage That Couldn't Succeed."

Long before Richter sent "Children of Light" to Paul Reynolds, Richter was plotting a long story that grew out of the narrative of Colonel Boquet's march, the return of the women and children who had been taken in Indian raids to the frontier village of Carlisle. What would happen, he asked himself, to a young man raised as an Indian when he was forcibly returned to his white parents? Telling the story of such a boy offered opportunities to contrast the two cultures, as the boy struggles against a way of life he cannot understand or accept. Two days after sending "The Children of Light" to Reynolds, Richter used his morning writing session to begin "My Enemy, My Son," the story that would become his best-known and most widely read novel, *The Light in the Forest*.

By August Richter and Harvey had been in Pine Grove for eight months, and Richter was restless. He needed to get away, he told himself; if need be he would go alone.[33] Late that month he talked Harvey into a visit to Fred and Emily Richter at Syracuse, New York, and when he finished "Children of Light" in September, he interrupted his writing regimen to take Harvey to visit Vene, who was spending the late summer working as a newspaper reporter at the seaside resort of Watch Hill, Rhode Island. There in a vacation home near the beach the two found themselves questioning their decision to own a home in Pine Grove. The house had turned into a burden: it was too big, too imposing for their modest taste. Both of them worried about the expectations that other people would have of them, living in such a house, and Harvey admitted to feeling the weight of furnishing and maintaining it.[34] Temporarily released from the responsibilities of home ownership, Richter wrote well at Watch Hill, completing the fourth chapter of "My Enemy, My Son." In this chapter True Son and his cousin Half Arrow puzzle over the curious ways of the white settlers, who selfishly collect things for themselves rather than sharing, as Indians do. Why did these people build large houses in which to keep their things and then build barns to store even more, making themselves slaves to their possessions? The question elicits only puzzled laughter from the Indian boys; and their creator apparently had no better answer to offer. When letters arrived from Albuquerque offering three different houses for rent, including the Weils', Richter saw this unusual circumstance as another sign pointing him back to the desert city. Reluctant to sell their Maple Street home after owning it less than a year, his solution was to rent it for eighteen months and return to the Weil house in New Mexico.

Before her parents left for the Southwest in December Vene brought Jack Haggerty home to Pine Grove to visit. When her parents were vacationing in Watch Hill, Vene had asked if Jack could stay in the house she had arranged for them, belonging to the newspaper's owner. But Harvey felt she could not invite somebody into a house where they themselves were guests, a choice Vene found overfastidious and hurtful. Neither of her parents were sympathetic to her, she charged in the argument that followed, an accusation Richter carried with him for at least the rest of that day. "Sad over Vene," he began that night's journal entry. Earlier that month he had visited his brother Joe's home and found himself, as usual, surrounded by the happy cacophony of Joe's children and grandchildren. How starkly different Vene's homelife had always been. "We have never given her a fair chance," Richter admitted unhappily. Recalling that last visit to his brother's home, he added, "Joe and Edna would have given her a great deal more opportunity. The fault is ours."[35] Arguably it was Richter's when Jack Haggerty visited Pine Grove. Although Richter had found Jack Haggerty to be an agreeable houseguest, making himself easily at home, nonetheless early Saturday Richter had insisted that Vene take her friend out of the house while he put in his morning on "My Enemy, My Son."[36]

T W O

Back in Albuquerque, Richter found once again that the house at 1421 Los Lomas Road was a place where he could write, and he worked steadily through the winter. Late in April Richter completed his first draft, fourteen chapters, and began immediately to revise. By the time Vene arrived on May 12, Richter had revised over half of his novel, and a month later he had finished, including a new ending for his story. Once again he had fashioned a final scene that would leave some readers unsettled, wondering what would happen to the young man who was unable to live in the world of either his biological or adoptive parents. As readers had written Richter to ask what was to become of Lutie Brewton, Tacey Cromwell, and Chancey Wheeler, many would want to be told just what lay in store for the young man who, after his anguished plea to know, "Who then is my father?" is left with neither a white father nor an Indian one. For these questioners, Richter had no resolution to offer; though he was writing a serial for the *Post*, he was not writing "fiction," as he had years earlier come to term the plot manipulations that allowed the tidy resolutions many readers preferred. True Son's question came from deep within Richter's own past, and it included not only his own mixed feelings about his father, John Absalom Richter, but his long struggle to affirm his connection to a seemingly unknowable God.[37] After Richter had spent more than two years, and failed twice, to write his most important book—the book he believed he had been led, and even prepared, to write—True Son's anguished question might well have been equally his own.

Mailing his novel to Paul Reynolds, Richter noticed that the traffic lights were almost all green, a good sign. Nothing else seemed encouraging, however, and by June 19 Richter had slid into his characteristic postcompletion angst. That day Vene left for Watch Hill, where she would again work for the summer newspaper and also on a novel. In the fall she planned to return to her Washington Square apartment and enroll as a degree student in New York University's graduate program in English. Later the same day neighbors complimented Richter on his story in the *Post*. Still upset because his title had been changed, Richter had not bought a copy of the issue, but he was interested to see how the magazine had illustrated his story. To his dismay, he discovered that the illustration was not of pigeons at all, but rather of a wedding ceremony. Awaiting the *Post's* decision about "My Enemy, My Son" and preparing to return to the book that had already defeated him twice, the illustration left him feeling "sickened and degraded." That night Richter suffered what he described as his worst bout ever of heart palpitations, brought on, he supposed, by worry that *The Mountain on the Desert* and his spiritual novels were to be denied him.[38] Preparing himself for the *Post's* rejection of "My Enemy, My Son," Richter considered cashing Liberty Bonds bought during the war to repay the $1,000 advance he had received for the serial. The next day he was acknowledging further his feeling by writing "I

DREAD THIS WEEK—the mails—from three sources, Paul, Alfred, and letters from *Post* readers," meaning in the last case he dreaded that letters would not come. Driving to a movie theater that evening, Richter found himself repeatedly stopped by red lights, and by the next morning he was telling himself that he was resigned to his novel's failure. Even Harvey's report of one of her bubbly sensations did not cheer him before the telephone call from a Western Union operator: the *Post* was indeed buying the serial, for the sum of $17,500. Stunned, Richter asked the operator to repeat the amount. Hearing the figure for a second time, Richter went immediately to find Harvey and tell her the news, exclaiming "You old bubbly, you!"[39]

The next day Richter would write Alfred Knopf to make sure his publisher understood that he had not given up on *The Mountain on the Desert*: "Fortunately, the *Post* has taken 'My Enemy, My Son' and at a very good price. I can now get to work on revision of the book you don't like but which I'm sure someone will." That the book was more important to Richter than ever, he acknowledged in a comment recalling a theme he had introduced in chapter 4 of "My Enemy, My Son" and would carry through to the novel's final paragraph: "The last years I have become more and more interested in non-material things. I belong to no church and subscribe to no one creed. There is no fear of what's to come in it, as I don't think the most hardened criminal has anything to fear, except the longer road he has to travel. Material things just don't mean so much to me any more. They fall away, slough to unimportant pieces. Some will think I'm failing, some that I'm just putting away toys and pawns. Any reader can take his choice."[40]

As Harvey confirmed to Vene, the sale of "My Enemy, My Son" was a tonic for Richter, improving his health and raising his morale. "I haven't seen him so relaxed in years," she ended.[41] In the wake of the good news, Richter agreed to put away his typewriter until after a visit from Fred and Emily, who were to arrive July 1. During the visit he served as a tour guide for his brother and sister-in-law, taking them to an anthropological dig along the Rio Grande, to the ancient Indian pueblo of Acoma, and then—to escape the desert heat in what was the hottest summer on record in Albuquerque—high into the Sandias for a picnic lunch, where the two brothers and their wives loafed away the afternoon, sleeping on picnic tables.[42] Richter did not return to *The Mountain on the Desert* until July 11, first addressing Vene's criticisms about his mountain philosopher's tendentiousness and the story's lack of sustaining plot. He would make his weaver—renamed "Michael," his own middle name—a more mystical and enigmatic figure, and he would have the student visitors puzzle among themselves over what Michael's sayings might mean.[43] With these changes in mind, Richter began a third version of his Western Bible.

Late in July, after considering a number of alternative titles for his *Post* serial, Richter finally decided on *The Light in the Forest*. For Richter the new choice seemed more likely to sell books, perhaps reminding readers of *The Trees*.[44] Alfred Knopf accepted the change as an improvement but objected to Richter's proposal to add two final paragraphs to his acknowledgments, meant once again to press Richter's message about the dangers of losing freedom to the conveniences of modern civilization. Such sermonizing would "actually weaken the strength of the appeal," Knopf argued.[45] But Richter was adamant, and the final two paragraphs remained—and at the book's beginning, not at the end, as Knopf also proposed. Perhaps Richter's contention with Knopf over the preface spurred Richter to finish a short story begun in Pine Grove. After completing his latest revision of the first part of *The Mountain on the Desert*, Richter turned to "The Hole in the Wall," a futuristic story meant to extend further his message in the preface of *The Light in the Forest*, that "in the pride of our American liberties, we're apt to forget that already we have lost a good many to civilization." The result was more parable than story, but despite the heavy-handed didacticism, the *Post* bought Richter's "interesting sermon," as Erd Brandt described it, for $2,500, publishing it as "The Sinister Journey."[46]

Richter finished his story in a tourist cottage in Mesa, Arizona, where he hoped Harvey could finally overcome, in the warmer air and lower altitude, the cough that had persisted throughout the summer and fall. In December Richter's restlessness took him and his wife to an apartment in Catalina Hills, above Tucson, Arizona, where he worked on the second section of *The Mountain on the Desert*.[47] A month later Richter once again put his major work aside, accepting a commission from *Holiday Magazine* to write an article on Albuquerque, Santa Fe, and Taos. Although Richter did not explicitly note his reasons for delaying, the key to his decision can be inferred from his journal: he was unable to concentrate on his theories while Harvey continued to cough. Throughout January 1953, Richter recorded hopefully each improvement in Harvey's health and state of mind, only to write later that she had slipped back into sallow depression. Worrying about Harvey, Richter found his own health deteriorating into various nervous afflictions, most frighteningly an ache in his chest he had not experienced since his breakdown in Pittsburgh.[48] Unable to accomplish any work on *The Mountain on the Desert*, Richter reluctantly admitted to Harvey that it seemed he was just not meant to write it.[49]

By the time Richter had finished "Three Towns I Love," the article for *Holiday*, Harvey's cough had finally disappeared; the color was back in her cheeks, and she was again in that difficult period when she felt as if she had energy for everything. A rosy-cheeked Harvey succeeded in cajoling her reluctant husband into a trip to California, writing to her daughter that she did so to give him a needed respite from his work. The impetus for the trip was an unanticipated windfall, the sale of *Tacey Cromwell* to a film company. Offered $5,000—the sum he had rejected angrily several years earlier—Richter was happy enough just then to accept $6,000. Returning from California, Richter stopped off again in Mesa and Phoenix, then drove on to Santa Fe and Taos to gather details of color to add to his recently completed article. On May 4 they drove out of Santa Fe into a snowstorm, driving east until they arrived in Camden, Missouri, where they settled in to wait for the publication of *Light in the Forest*. Writing to Alfred Knopf, Richter commented that he planned to remain "buried in the Ozarks," where he would not have to see the reviews. "Indeed," he admitted, "that's one reason I'm here."[50] A second reason was to pass some of the time before the end of the lease on 11 Maple Street, Pine Grove. On June 5 the home would be theirs again, and evidently they were both eager to return to Pine Grove. When the family renting 11 Maple Street offered $20,000 to buy it, Richter and Harvey gave the proposal only a cursory consideration.

When the reviews did find their way to Richter, they were, with a single exception, highly favorable. Vene called to tell her father that the *Saturday Review of Literature* was putting him on its cover. When she called again with news of more reviews, she invited her parents to stay with her in Washington Square, an offer they quickly accepted. While in New York Richter saw his agent and publisher, meeting Reynolds for the usual lunch at the Century Club. Lunch with Knopf turned out to be more entertaining. Returning from the occasion Richter would write amusedly of his editor that Knopf was "more impressive, commanding and oriental than ever, like a potentate with slaves and courtiers around him."[51] When Reynolds called with an offer for the movie rights to *The Light in the Forest*, from Walt Disney Studios, Richter rejected the $2,500 offer out of hand, countering immediately with $15,000. By the next morning Richter had lowered his asking price to $7,500, accepting Reynolds's warning that Disney never paid large fees for movie rights. When the deal was completed, Richter was to receive $7,500 divided into three installments and spread over three years, money Richter thought of as funds to underwrite *The Mountain on the Desert*.[52]

On June 5 Richter and Harvey moved back into 11 Maple Street. Sleeping that first night on the second-story porch "seemed grand," and the town quiet,

16.   Vene poses with her parents in her apartment in Washington Square, 1950s. Photograph by Elliot Erwitt.

"like a village."[53] When Vene's courses ended for the year, she joined her parents in Pine Grove. By July 13, when word arrived from Knopf that *The Light in the Forest* was already into its third printing, Richter had established a new, abbreviated writing schedule: mornings were reserved for writing followed by afternoon walks or drives with Harvey. Regularly he would drive out to mountain springs and fill up gallon bottles with water. In the evening there were visits from relatives and friends, and visits to return, and dinners with Augusta Filbert, frail and deaf but still for Richter a delightful conversationalist. Talking with Augusta, Richter would keep his pocket notebook out, to write down choice comments. When she offered some particularly tart observation, something he anticipated she would not like for him to record, he would hold that thought until she said something else, less testy or provocative, and then write the first comment under the guise of recording the second.

When the summer heat made the upstairs hall uncomfortable for his writing, Richter moved his desk downstairs to the dining room, where it would remain. Late in July Fred and Emily visited, recalling their days traveling together in the Southwest, their afternoon sleeping on picnic tables in the Sandias. Then the Stricklers visited, bringing their boisterous laughter into 11 Maple Street. At Anna and Mary Boyer's, Richter met a young writer of humorous verse, Richard Wheeler, a slight, bearded man who "like most humorists looked solemn and the part."[54] Richter immediately liked the young man's modest manner, and soon thereafter he drove out to Swopes Valley to visit Wheeler in the rustic cabin the writer had built for himself and where he lived without electricity or running water. Soon they were taking walks together.

After months of indecision about buying a new car to replace his worn-out Buick, Richter bought a used car, a 1950 gray Cadillac, paying $2,600 less $350 for his Buick. Although he had chosen the used Cadillac to save the price of a new car, he worried that his neighbors in Pine Grove would decide that he was wealthy and begin treating him so.[55] Writing to his brother Fred about a planned trip to Syracuse, Richter admitted laconically that he had "come home with a car Friday," but he was careful to explain that it was used and careful to leave out that it was a Cadillac.[56]

When Paul Reynolds visited Pine Grove that fall, Richter introduced him to Richard Wheeler and another writer he wanted to do something to help, the wife of Charles Hikes at the local bank, who wrote under her maiden name of Julia Truitt Yenni. Daily he walked to the post office and town stores, and when the weather was mild he would linger for a while on the bridge over the Swatera Creek, watching the water slip silently by. Mornings were reserved for rewriting *The Mountain on the Desert*, and on occasion afternoons as well. On October 21, having pushed himself especially hard, rewriting and retyping until four in the afternoon, Richter asked himself a basic question: "WHY DO I PUNISH myself on these pages that will never amount to anything—only do me harm if published at all? The answer is that I must. Bad, indifferent, obscure, they are my life work."

December found Richter and Harvey in West Palm Beach, where they planned to stay until at least the beginning of March. As had become Richter's winter pattern, he worked only a few hours each morning on *The Mountain on the Desert*, spending the rest of his day walking on the beach, taking Harvey for drives, and passing hours in conversation, pocket notebook in hand, with whoever chanced by. Occasionally he would fish from a pier or rent a boat to join the anglers in the tidewater bays. In January Vene planned to join them for her winter break from New York University, and there was some discussion of inviting Jack Haggerty as well. Knowing that Jack's new photography business was still struggling, Richter did ask Harvey whether their invitation ought to include an offer to pay his way. Harvey opposed this idea, and no such offer was made. For whatever reasons, Jack did not make the trip with Vene.

Almost immediately on arrival, Vene fell ill with the flu, and then a week into her stay came the terrible news that Jack Haggerty was dead: a stomach ulcer had perforated, killing him. Although of course Richter had nothing whatsoever to do with Jack Haggerty's fatal illness, Richter could not keep from thinking that, had he just paid Jack's way to Florida, things could have turned out differently, and the unhappy event became another instance when Richter worried that his lack of sufficient sympathy had played a part in the affair. Soon Richter was remembering the two failures that were still most painful to him: he had refused what turned out to be his mother's last request to him, to return with him to Pine Tree Farm, and the last time John Richter had visited he had placed his father in a hotel instead of inviting him to stay in his home. He had not wanted the upset of having Jack Haggerty in the house, as he had not wanted his father, and so he had not pressed Haggerty to come. If he had only sent him train fare, his act might have saved Jack's life.[57]

The Florida sojourn, that year, was disappointing for Richter. He finished a draft of his book, as he had hoped, but the weather was often too cold to allow him time outdoors, and his overall recollection of the stay was that it had been a dreary time.[58] Once back in his hometown, his early enthusiasm and buoyancy brought on by a change in surroundings soon dissipated into unease and complaints about pains in his chest and feeling "low" and "tired." "Why am I so often like this in P[ine] G[rove]?" he asked himself. Perhaps it was an "aura of sadness" associated with childhood memories, his continued close association with the place from which his parents and many others were gone, and where those who still remained were "like old reeds soon to be laid by the wind. It was all so near, the houses where they lived, the streets they walked, the churches they went to and now the cemetery they lie in where we must follow."[59]

In June Vene returned to Pine Grove for the summer, ready to begin writing her novel set in Watch Hill. Arriving, she announced to her father that, though she hoped to talk over some problems of plot with him, she did not intend to let him read and comment on her actual drafts. It was not a story with which he would sympathize, she said; she did not add that her story had evolved into the tale of a marriage's dissolution, and that the novel's protagonist, the woman who decides to abandon her marriage, was modeled on her mother.[60] Richter did allow Harvey and Vene to read parts of *The Mountain on the Desert*, which they had criticized sharply in its earlier version. When he read the last chapters to them in late July, they were much more appreciative, calling it "solid and real" except for chapter 10, which was too pious and metaphysical, and Michael too much like the old, preachy Henry.[61] In a week Richter was ready to read the chapter again, and that time his wife and daughter agreed that it was greatly improved. With that his last draft was finally completed, well over four years after he had begun it. Without delay Richter mailed it to his agent.

Although Richter immediately began another writing project, an article on Pennsylvania commissioned by *Holiday Magazine*, his mind remained with his most important book. When Reynolds sent back a retyped copy without a cover letter, Richter interpreted his agent's silence as evidence of bad news, and, as he typically did when awaiting his agent's judgment, jumped to the worst conclusion. "I have written a dud," he lamented in his journal.[62] That was not, precisely, what Paul Reynolds would say when he wrote on August 20. Though declaring Richter to be "a really great novelist" and he himself unable to judge the merit of a book such as *The Mountain on the Desert*, for Reynolds the bottom line was that it would be a difficult book to sell: "There is a very real philosophy or point of view toward life in your novels but the public reads them because the books hold them and move them. I think it's going to be very hard to get people to read *The Mountain on the Desert*."[63] From his publisher Alfred Knopf, Richter got a commitment to publish his book, but one that Knopf was obviously unhappy about: "I will shortly be sending Paul a contract for *The Mountain on the Desert*. I would be less than candid if I pretended to any great enthusiasm for this book because you know how I feel about it. On the other hand, as I think I told you earlier, since it means a great deal to you, I will do my best for it."[64]

Even before Knopf's letter arrived in late September, Richter was writing in his journal as if his book had already been published and had failed to find an audience: "I've given up on *The Mountain on the Desert* and feel better," he wrote on September 15. "It's a real satisfaction to have given it all I had. I really never expected much success for it while I was writing it. It turned out more than I expected. I put more thought and heart into it and I can in a measure forget it and get to work." But putting aside his most important book would not be easy, especially because Richter was not able to separate his sense of himself from the success of his work. Reading F. O. Matthiessen's *The James Family*, brought home by Vene, Richter came across John Dewey's remark that William James, the philosopher of pragmatism, had escaped from academic deadening because of his lack of a formal education. The thought led Richter to his own circumstance, to a way of thinking about himself which deflected his deep disappointment that his latest attempt was again found wanting. Had not his own limited education—and even his personal physical condition of limited energy and wasted nervous energy—resulted in his being "more responsive to life and to live and lively ideas"? To Richter, those untutored feelings seemed a kind of compensation. If too ill educated to engage others convincingly in a philosophical or scientific argument, he nonetheless had his compensatory strengths, his ability to see things and ideas directly, which made him the novelist that he was.[65]

Working by day on his article for *Holiday Magazine*, Richter brooded in his journal at night, where it was often not easy for him to think about compensatory strengths. The actual publication and public reception of his book was still many months away, but Richter continued to assume the worst. Again and again he returned to journals from earlier years, telling himself that he was "consoled" by their "crudity" and "childishness," as if their failings settled incontrovertibly that Richter's efforts to enter into the world of ideas had been futile from their beginning. On one evening he wrote, "The writer of such journals couldn't possibly be a philosopher who discovered anything new"; that being the case, he continued, "I have no grounds for disappointment at the reception of my book . . . no occasion to be depressed by my status as a writer."[66] On another, after reading entries from his journal for 1937, he continued the subject with a refrain from earlier moments when, just before a book's publication, his confidence typically ebbed to its lowest: "Strangely [the journal entries] didn't depress me. Rather, they made me feel that I have probably got more than my writing, both the writing and the writer, deserved."[67]

But such expressions were reserved for Richter's evenings; each morning he was again at his desk, and by the end of September Richter was ready to read his article on Pennsylvania to Harvey and Vene. It was, he commented to himself, better than he had hoped, and then he cautioned himself to remember that he was, at the moment, feeling well, and his good health made things read better than they really were.[68] Immediately after mailing the piece, he turned to an even briefer article he had promised several times to the editor of the *Writer*, a magazine for aspiring poets and novelists. Entitled "My Friend with the Hard Face," the essay returned to a favorite theme, the potentially positive effects of adversity. In it Richter would describe his own early days in Albuquerque, stubbornly writing story after story when there seemed only the faintest hope for success.

THREE

Early in December Richter completed a set of corrections to *The Mountain on the Desert* and set out with Harvey for Florida. For the 1954–55 winter they decided to try Gainesville in central Florida, a university town that would provide Richter opportunities to attend lectures and concerts. Moreover, the campus of the University of Florida offered pleasant walks, and the countryside surrounding the town a number of possible drives and places to explore. With no callers to distract him, Richter was soon writing what he thought of as an expediency, a serial for money. Despite the change of scenery, he was still unhappy and restless, worrying about what he saw as his declining reputation and—even more troubling—his reduced ability to work as he had in the thirties when adversity had struck its hardest. No longer could he write in three sessions a day, staying up long after his wife and daughter had gone to bed.[69]

Just before the new year Richter began the first chapter of his new novel, tentatively entitled "The Deadly Lady." Writing to Vene on New Year's Day, he commented that he had the first chapter of his "little book" almost written and that, though his ambition for this story rose no higher than another serial for the *Post*, nonetheless ideas were coming to him. "It won't be a world beater perhaps, but a new and deeper theme has come into it." That "deeper theme" would be the spiritual growth of the novel's central character, Doña Ellen, whose struggle with the consequences to her own rash action brings to her a higher level of understanding. His story might be only a serial for *Post*, but it was informed by the ideas of *The Mountain on the Desert*.

By March Richter was preparing to return to Pine Grove, but he delayed his departure for the chance to hear Robert Frost speak. Throughout the stay in Gainesville, Richter had put off introducing himself to Harry Warfel, a professor of English at the university, waiting until the end of his stay in Gainesville to reduce Warfel's opportunities to intrude with invitations. Although Warfel was the brother of Richter's longtime friend Charlie Warfel, Richter probably would not have contacted him at all except that Alfred Knopf, discovering where Richter was spending the winter, had urged him to seek out a man whom Knopf was sure he would like. Richter did like the affable English professor, who seemed as energetic as his brother and persuasive enough to talk Richter into putting off his return north until after a campus visit by Frost. Warfel planned a dinner party for Frost and wanted to give one for Richter as well. Richter was at the point in his career, Warfel exclaimed, when people should come to him and not he to them, adding that Richter was enough of a name that he could go about from college to college, doing nothing but giving each the honor and pleasure of his presence. Such talk Richter found "astonishing," he wrote his daughter, but nonetheless a pleasant change from his sense of writing in anonymity: "Really, he amused me but at the same time gave me pleasure and a kind of relaxation, relief that perhaps in all these clouds there must be a little moisture."[70] Richter declined both the dinner in his honor and Warfel's invitation to the Frost dinner. He did attend the Frost lecture, but, when Warfel sought him out from the seat he had chosen well back in the auditorium, Richter refused to move to the front and sit among the dignitaries. It was enough for Harvey to meet Frost and shake his hand, Richter said, and he would not be persuaded.[71]

Loading the car the next day, Richter was interrupted by a phone call from Archie Robertson, the English department chairman, who said that Frost, on hearing Richter was in town, had asked especially to meet him. Thus pressed, Richter agreed to a meeting and spent what apparently was an entertaining hour listening to Frost hold forth. "As is his custom," Richter later wrote, "he does most of the talking, going on and on, rambling while others respectfully listen because of his age and position."[72] During the visit Richter asked Frost if he would read his latest book if sent a copy. Frost agreed and offered to send one of his to Richter, though, Richter noted, he did not ask for an address.

Arriving in Pine Grove, Harvey was delighted to find their home warm and waiting for them, their housekeeper Annie having spent two days, unasked, preparing the house for their return. Awaiting the publication day for *The Mountain on the Desert*, Richter continued to work daily on "The Deadly Lady." He was alternately eager and edgy about the approaching publication day. The preceding fall he had promised himself that, once the book was actually submitted, he would allow it to make its own way, he would leave its success to God.[73] But however wise this advice, clearly it was advice which he was unable to take. When advance copies of *The Mountain on the Desert* reached him on Good Friday, Richter was dismayed by the dust jacket, a stylized representation of a mountain rising above a plain, then upset by his own writing in the volume. Passages that previously had been strong suddenly seemed to have "evaporated," and collectively his ideas "seemed like old stuff said importantly by someone of small stature." His only compensation, Richter thought with bitter whimsy, was that at least he would be "spared letters from neurotics and hypochondriacs."[74]

Working on "The Deadly Lady" every morning at his desk in the dining room, running errands each afternoon, visiting Augusta Filbert and taking walks with Richard Wheeler, Richter continued his Pine Grove life, waiting for May 9, publication day. He planned to escape to Vene's New York apartment, avoiding contact with people who knew him until after the first reviews were published. But when May 9 arrived, there were no reviews at all, not in the Sunday papers or in the dailies the following week. Two weeks later, Knopf wrote to acknowledge what by then Richter had discovered for himself. There had been no reviews because no review copies had been sent out until after the official publication day. Enclosed with Knopf's letter was another from Bill Cole, profusely apologizing for the error, which was, he said, his fault.[75] Richter was not convinced. To him it seemed more likely to have been an error of commission rather than omission, Knopf's effort to bury a book he had already predicted would damage Richter's reputation.[76] Also upsetting to Richter, he received no word from people whom he knew had been sent advance copies at his request, readers who normally responded quickly. "UTTERLY NO MAIL," Richter lamented on May 24. "I have just published what I thought my most important book and nothing comes in." The next day he returned to the subject in his journal: "I had thought that my work had truth behind it and God beneath it. One can take the silence of men if you feel that God is with you, but I felt now that what I had labored over meant nothing to Him. . . . All the good omens I imagined were coincidence, including [our sojourns in] Sandia Park, meant nothing. I felt sick."[77]

His first dismay settling into despondency, Richter experienced his characteristic increased sensitivity to the sights of the world around him. One evening walking up Mifflin Street, Richter found everything "looking more sharp and clean and beautiful" than since the days of deepest poverty in Albuquerque. "I had forgotten," he noted wryly, "that cans, jars, rolls of toilet paper could look lovely and wonderful."[78] The bright, fresh look of the physical universe is in fact an index of just how devastating a blow Richter had taken. He had counted on God for the success of his book. He had even prayed, just as it was becoming clear that his book had been dropped into a void, for God to judge his work and reward it appropriately: "If the book is true, let it come into its own. If it is untrue, let it perish."[79] Apparently it would perish—and for Richter, its failure meant one of two alternatives. One was that his theory had been delivered to an uncaring, insentient universe, that what he conceptualized as God had failed him by not hearing him. If not that, then perhaps he had made a disastrous mistake in presuming a kind of covenant between himself and God when God had entered into no such agreement. As devastating as the second interpretation was for a man who had pursued an idea for decades, who had believed that many of the events of his life, including the years of illness and poverty in Albuquerque, had been providential, preparing him to write his Western Bible, nonetheless Richter chose the second. It was simply unthinkable that he was alone, unsponsored, that the answer to his question "Then who is my father?" was silence. Richter could not accept such an answer. It was altogether too bleak.

On June 5 the first review finally appeared, a dismissive and apparently hastily written five paragraphs by Joseph Wood Krutch in the *New York Times Book Review*. Reviews that followed were more considered, and several, including one by Paul Jordan-Smith in the *Los Angeles Times* and another by Edward Wagenknecht in the *Chicago Tribune*, were highly laudatory. Richter gathered quotes from the best of these, hoping to prod Knopf into advertising his book, which had an extremely disappointing sales distribution of only 1,570 before publication, and another 604 in the four months following.[80] If there was a bright side for Richter, it was that by July he had begun to receive testimonials from readers, some from friends but others primarily from people whom he did not know, people who wanted to tell him how important a book he had written.

Through the summer Richter persevered with his serial for the *Post*, reminding himself in his journal to focus on how his main character experiences events, not the events themselves, and to bring in more dialogue to make his story alive.[81] When he completed the first draft, Richter took Harvey and Vene to Syracuse to visit Fred and Emily in their new home, a brick ranch house on several acres above the city. On their return, all three agreed that Maple Street in Pine Grove was not where they should be living. Either they should move away from Pine Grove entirely, or build a new home, as Fred and Emily had done, above the town and away from its noises and noxious fumes. Two days before Vene departed for Watch Hill, Richter asked Harvey's nephew Bud Achenbach to put 11 Maple Street up for sale. Evidently Bud did not take Richter's request seriously, telling his brother-in-law about a mother and daughter who had twice asked him to sell their house and then cried and refused to sign when he brought offers from buyers.[82]

Late in November, with cold weather setting in, Richter closed up 11 Maple Street for the winter and headed south. Harvey preferred to go straight to the Southwest, without the detour through Florida, but Richter thought that trip overtiring for Harvey. He may have been thinking of himself as well. Intermittently he had complained of his heart, and he was looking forward to the warm sunshine and the simple life in a tourist cottage. By their departure Richter had rewritten all but the final, climactic chapter of his novel. He had also settled on a final title, *The Lady*. Although he had continued to receive occasional letters about his Western Bible, his own reflections about *The Mountain on the Desert* had all but disappeared from his journal—its failure to find more than a small audience acknowledged if not yet accepted.

With *The Lady* so close to completion, Richter was already making notes for an autobiographical novel about his childhood with the curious working title of "Death and Life." It was to be, he promised himself, another important book based upon his energy theories. On Christmas Day 1955, Conrad Richter decided it was time, once again, to pray for help. If he could just be granted the health and strength to persevere until its completion, he promised God "to write the novel DEATH AND LIFE with tolerance, understanding and encouragement to all religions." *The Mountain on the Desert* might have failed to reach more than a negligible audience, but Richter was not yet giving up. Holding himself to his own standard and his own ideas, closer himself to the steadfast conviction he created in characters such as Colonel Brewton and Sayward Luckett than he would ever allow himself to acknowledge, he continued to plan out his spiritual books. If he could not find readers for *The Mountain on the Desert*, then he would offer his theories through his stories. Those theories were still his life's work.

The Closed Door

O N E

On February 11, 1956, Conrad Richter wrote Alfred Knopf that his latest novel was on its way. "It's the first I've done in what for want of a better word I'll call the tradition of *The Sea of Grass*," he commented. Set in the high desert of the Southwest as *The Sea of Grass* had been, *The Lady* like the earlier novel is built on the disastrous consequences to actions taken by an aristocratic, charismatic woman. In creating the character of Doña Ellen Johnson y Campo, Richter drew on his memories of his neighbor from New York Avenue in Albuquerque, the vivacious and mercurial Sadie Garduño, just as he had in creating Lutie

Brewton. This is not to say that *The Lady* is a retelling of *The Sea of Grass*, or that Lutie Brewton and Doña Ellen are two versions of the same character. In *The Sea of Grass* the elegant Lutie Brewton charms the rough frontiersmen of Salt Fork, but her gentle arts are without effect on the vast desert, a looming presence that frightens her. In *The Lady* Doña Ellen is entirely at home in the same country that unnerved Lutie Brewton. Heir to the immense landholdings of the Johnson y Campo family, she is also heir to the social codes of those who have claimed and held by force huge tracts of the desert, codes that include the unquestioned right to defend one's own property. When a cattleman is shot to death while driving his herd across her land and deliberately destroying her private garden, her neighbors assume Doña Ellen fired the rifle, even though her brother takes responsibility for the shooting.

Although her behavior is defended by her family and other landowners, Doña Ellen's rash act brings on more bloodshed, including the murder of her brother and the disappearance and presumed death of her husband and son. For Doña Ellen these events initiate a spiritual journey, one in which she comes to terms with her personal culpability. When she attempts to change the circumstances that brought on the enmity and killing, she is, ironically, made more vulnerable to the predations of the man responsible for the loss of her brother, husband, and son. In the novel's crisis, Doña Ellen must decide either to pursue a personal revenge against her enemy or to leave him to a higher justice.

Composed entirely while Richter was under the spell of *The Mountain on the Desert*, awaiting its publication and then recovering from the public's indifference to his philosophical theories, Richter believed he had not invested himself in *The Lady*. It was written as a serial for the *Post*, for money, the kind of writing Richter thought of as "craft"—needing to be done well, out of pride in his workmanship, but not to be considered in the same light as his important books, both those written and those planned for the future. When the *Post* bought his serial for $20,000, Richter did not record the event in his journal. Neither did he mention Knopf's sale of *The Lady* to the Reader's Digest Condensed Books for $75,000, half of which came to Richter. What he did note, but later, was that the combined sales meant he was financially secure for at least the next four years.[1] For once he could take some time to decide which of his important books he would write next.

After another winter in Florida, Richter and Harvey returned to Pine Grove in mid-March 1956. Vene visited her parents the first weekend after they were back and brought with her what must have been astonishing news. In January she had written that a friend, the poet Harry Roskolenko, was planning a trip by motor scooter from Italy to India, sponsored by the new magazine *Sports Illustrated*. In Pine Grove Vene announced that Harry Roskolenko had asked her to marry him and join him for at least part of the trip, and she had accepted. In just a few weeks she would embark for England, there to marry and then set out on an extraordinary wedding journey through Italy, Yugoslavia, and Greece. The picture Vene painted must have been difficult for Richter—his daughter jolting along foreign byroads in a contraption like a motorcycle sidecar but pulled behind a motor scooter. Richter and Harvey had not met Harry Roskolenko, knowing him only from their daughter's description of him as a voluble and energetic New Yorker, short, stocky, Jewish, forty-eight years old and something of a psychic.[2] Because Harry Roskolenko was already abroad, Richter and Harvey were not going to meet him before the planned marriage. Evidently there was no discussion at all of Richter and Harvey traveling with Vene to England for her wedding.

Vene's expedition could not help but evoke from Richter a flood of concerns. Was travel by motor scooter dangerous? Were the roads of Yugoslavia and Greece safe for travelers? Would she be able to eat properly and not overtire herself? And what of Harvey? What would be the possible effects on Harvey of Vene's madcap jaunt? When Harvey's winter cough took a turn for the worse, Richter said he believed it to be caused by her worry about Vene. But once again Harvey confounded her husband, announcing that just the opposite was true. She was excited by Vene's daring adventure and eager for it to begin. "If I can only live through her visit abroad," she exclaimed,[3] and left for New York to help her daughter prepare for her wedding and trip.

Richter joined Harvey and Vene in New York on May 1, the day before Vene sailed on the *Ile de France*. Visiting his daughter's cabin, Richter was spurred to think, perhaps for the first time, that he and Harvey might themselves consider a transatlantic voyage, and he even began clipping notices of sailing dates for other ships.[4] Back in Pine Grove, Richter and Harvey waited eagerly for word from Vene. The first letter from England brought news Richter would have received unhappily: Vene and Harry could not marry in England because of the long residency requirement, but Vene had decided to continue the trip regardless. Then came a letter from Genoa, confirming that Harry Roskolenko had bought his three-wheeled Vespa scooter with a rear-mounted passenger car and that on Saturday, May 19, the two were off for Padua, then on to Venice and Trieste. Soon Vene's letters and cards carried the exotic postage stamps of Yugoslavia, as Harry guided the Vespa through Slovenia to Ljubljana, on to Zagreb and Belgrade, then south through Nis and Skopje and finally into Greece.

Before Vene arrived in Athens, which was to be her final destination, she sent her parents a cryptic message that her next address would be Istanbul. Harvey wrote immediately, asking for an explanation of her change in plans. "Interested— not to say worried," she concluded her letter.[5] The answer reached Pine Grove on June 19; Vene had decided to continue on with Harry as far as Iran. She was off by boat to Istanbul and then on to places Richter and Harvey had to search for in an atlas: the Turkish cities of Bolu, Kizilcahamam, Sungurlu, Trabzon on the Black Sea, Erzerum, Agri, and finally Dogubayazit on the Iranian border, where Vene would wake in the morning to see a snow-covered Mt. Ararat. For Richter and Harvey, such places must have seemed at the very boundaries of the civilized world. Thoughts of roving bandits, murder, and white slavery alarmed them both.[6] When there was no message from Vene for a longer period than usual, their anxiety overflowed into desperate telephone calls and telegrams to the U.S. State Department, asking for embassy and consular personnel to find their missing daughter. The cablegram Richter sent to Vene in Teheran reduced his fears to the briefest possible message, revealing to strangers the least he could of his family's private matters: "What's wrong wire collect. Family." Even more economical—and exasperatingly uninformative—was Vene's reply: "OK sailing 14th." Vene's cablegram came from Teheran. Eventually Richter received an explanatory letter from his daughter, describing her entry into the capital of Iran in a U.S. army convoy, Vene riding in one truck, Harry another, and the broken-down motor scooter in a third. Rather than return to Italy for passage home, Vene sailed from Greece. The change in plans meant that Vene escaped being aboard the *Andrea Doria* when it sank off the coast of New York.

Vene's miraculous escape from all possible kinds of harm was the theme of a letter to Johnny Gardner, with whom Richter was still sparring about religion twenty-five years after Gardner, convalescing from tuberculosis in Albuquerque, began pitting his bedrock Calvinism against Richter's theories of human evolu- tion. On this occasion Richter used Vene's adventure to illustrate the benefits of a Christian Science practitioner. Without telling their daughter, Richter and Harvey had commissioned Mrs. Doolittle, who had successfully "worked" for Vene on other occasions, to help her through all the unanticipated pitfalls of traveling through foreign and possibly quite dangerous lands. "You will probably smile," Richter wrote his friend, but he was certain that Mrs. Doolittle's prayers were an important factor in Vene's returning safely, bringing with her "miraculous stories" of help from unexpected places, "of safety in dangerous regions," and finally of her last-minute change of plans which brought her home on a Greek liner instead of the *Andrea Doria*.[7]

Although Richter's letter to Gardner does not mention Mrs. Doolittle's efforts on Harvey's behalf and his own, journal entries during the late spring and early summer suggest that there was reason for him to have considered enlisting her aid. Beginning in January, while still in Florida, nighttime anxieties had again begun to break into Richter's sleep, leading him to seek medical help and— much to Harvey's displeasure—to accept a prescription for thorazine to help him sleep. (Evidently the drug proved only modestly successful, for in March Richter asked his daughter to locate a record player with a special feature, good sound reproduction at very low volume. His thought was to relieve his night-time anxiety by keeping the player by his bed and, when awakened, playing novels on records at so low a volume that they would not disturb Harvey.)[8] Even after Vene's safe return from Turkey and Iran, Richter's nerves remained a problem, leading him into actions he might well have avoided at other times. Once in early August, when he had no letter from Vene for a week and was unable to reach her by phone, Richter called the building superintendent and insisted that he check her apartment, to break in if necessary. When Vene returned she found her front door damaged by the forced entry of the police and the building super sitting in her living room, guarding her belongings. Richter paid to repair the door.[9]

Throughout 1955 and 1956 Richter was intermittently exchanging letters with a writer of popular westerns and Hollywood screen scripts, Frank Gruber— a correspondence Gruber had initiated by writing Richter to ask him to join the Western Writers of America.[10] Like Carl Clausen many years earlier, Gruber prodded Richter to think about stories and novels as products to be marketed, telling tales of his own various dealings with Hollywood and sending page-long lists of potential foreign markets. Unimpressed by Gruber's writing, Richter never-theless enjoyed Gruber's verve and may have envied his unembarrassed audacity in promoting himself. In one letter Gruber announced his expectation to finalize a $50,000 movie deal for a novel he had not yet written.[11] In another he described his method in dealing with Hollywood, sitting down in studio conferences and outyelling the others around the table.[12] But just as the Claussen advice to write "bacon bringers" had quickly run up against Richter's internal standards, so too did Gruber's. When it came to the actual marketing of his latest novel, once again there was a limit.

Early in fall 1956 Alfred Knopf wrote Richter a letter clearly meant to deflect a meddlesome writer from interfering with Knopf's plans for the new novel. In it he announced that the sales division was more excited about *The Lady* than any previous Richter novel but added that his staff believed it needed to market the book without interference. Knopf enclosed the proposed promotional narrative, professionally crafted to attract readers with promises of powerful forces clashing in a range war and a beautiful woman beset by "crisis after crisis."[13] Harvey and Vene liked the material, but to Richter it "read like a cheap western," as he said in his reply to Knopf; certainly the proposed promotional material was "expert copy of its extravagant kind" and it might sell more books, but it did not accurately reflect his novel, which was not about "melodramatic types" fighting for control of the open range but about something quite different: "The clash is not between a symbol of Mexican feudal life and new American ways," Richter wrote; that was "old movie stuff." Rather, "what the copy calls clash is due to the novel's theme, the spreading evil consequences to a family of a single act of violence and the subsequent dramatic consequences of acts of non-violence and restraint."[14]

That summer and fall Richter put off making a decision on his next major project, temporizing with a short story the *Post* would publish the following year as "The Iron Lady." He also wrote a personal narrative for *New Mexico Magazine*, entitled "New Mexico Was Our Fate," and returned again to the article he had started for the *Writer*, "My Friend with the Hard Face," also autobiographical of the depression years in Albuquerque, which he submitted and then withdrew, deciding it was too confessional. On January 2, 1957, Richter noted in his journal that he had started to write his "prayer novel," the story of a young girl who discovers that her prayers come true, titled "The Gifts." In each chapter the girl would be enticed to use her power to help and then witness the consequences. Although most of the incidents Richter included were wholly imagined, many of the characters in the novel were based on people Richter had known, including Dean Matthews of Albuquerque's Episcopal cathedral and Dr. Leroy Peters, Harvey's doctor in Albuquerque. For the climax of his novel, Richter planned to retell the story of Carl Taylor, the writer who was killed by his houseboy.

Journal entries in January suggest the early writing on "The Gifts" was slow and recursive, with Richter lamenting that "there is so much writing, making up, to do . . . so much story to cover, explain, join, arrange."[15] Increasingly the sixty-six-year-old novelist worried about the effect of such concentrated effort on his health—intermittently warning himself to limit his work to two pages a day, never to attempt more than a morning's work, and never to work more than four or five days a week.[16] On March 30 the *Post* began its four-part serialization of *The Lady*, with Knopf's publication in book form following soon after. Reviews were generally good, acknowledging the novel as the mature work of a senior

American novelist. *Time* magazine sent a photographer to take a portrait to head its review, and the *Saturday Review of Literature* had Richter's picture on its cover. After the first six months, sales were his best ever, 22,000 copies. But Richter remained uninterested in the novel's reception. He was pleased that he had made several years' living from its various sales, but when Paul Reynolds wrote to complain about critics who were not, to his mind, taking *The Lady* seriously enough, Richter replied bemusedly in his journal: "I didn't tell him that I had no illusions that it was serious."[17] *The Lady* was not *The Mountain on the Desert*, which had sold exactly twenty-six copies during the first six months of 1957. Several years would pass before Richter decided that he had underestimated a novel that was more infused with his principles than he had understood. "Could this be why it has brought me so much financial support in my older years?" he asked himself.[18]

The added income allowed Richter to indulge in one largess, the gift of pulpit furniture to St. John's Lutheran Church in Pine Grove—a pulpit, a lectern, two minister's chairs, and an altar, at a cost totaling more than $1,200—given in memory of his grandfather Elias S. Henry. When the furniture arrived, Richter reluctantly attended the dedication ceremony, telling himself that, much as he dreaded the discomfort he would feel with so much attention directed toward him, he knew he would "hate himself afterward" if he did not attend.[19] But when Reverend Benner asked him to join the church, he declined. For the remainder of his life he would attend occasional services in St. John's, but he would not let himself be numbered among its community of believers.[20]

In June Richter started the second half of his novel. Throughout the summer he would take afternoon walks, often driving out to Swopes Valley for the company of Richard Wheeler. When Vene returned during the summer, she brought with her the working draft of her novel about Watch Hill and also the unhappy subject of Harry Roskolenko. Early in the year Vene had assured her parents that she had no interest in marrying her traveling companion when he returned from his scooter trip, but once Roskolenko was back in New York his name began to appear again in letters, and during the summer she asked her parents to invite him to visit. By then Richter and Harvey had heard enough about the poet to have decided he was not an appropriate husband for their daughter. Harvey even refused to allow Roskolenko in her house.[21] Eventually Harvey relented and Harry Roskolenko visited Pine Grove, but the subject of Vene's suitor remained a difficult one until Richter and Harvey convinced themselves that their daughter would not marry the New York poet.

TWO

By late fall, with Richter approaching completion of his novel's first draft, the family's primary concern was not Vene's suitor but a bronchial cough that kept Harvey in bed and Vene returning intermittently from New York to nurse her. When Harvey's cough finally abated in January, Richter was eager to get her to warmer weather. When inquiries to Banning, California, brought news of a house for rent, Richter decided to spend the remainder of the winter in the town where he had plotted and drafted the early chapters of *The Trees*.

Rather than subject Harvey to the long drive across country, they traveled by train to California, intending to rent a car there. When rental fees seemed exorbitant, Richter shopped for a modest used car, a Ford or Chevrolet, but ended up finding another Cadillac, a 1955 yellow Fleetwood with air-conditioning and power steering. The dealer agreed to sell the car for $2,600, what Richter had paid for the 1950 gray Cadillac at home in Pine Grove, yet Richter had considerable work to do persuading himself that the car was not "a better car than we should have," as he chastised himself in his journal.[22] The Cadillac was used, after all, and though a more expensive model than their gray Cadillac and with more features, it cost the same amount of money. There were practical advantages, he told himself. The air-conditioning would be good for Harvey, and the power steering would allow him to drive with more comfort. But the car was still something of an embarrassment: it was a Cadillac and a top-of-the-line Cadillac at that. And it was an eye-catching yellow. When it came time to take possession of the house they had rented in Banning for three months, Richter sent Harvey on first in a taxi. He and the Cadillac would wait at the hotel until Harvey called to say that the owners had departed in their old, small car.[23]

At the end of January, Richter wrote Vene that he and Harvey were both faring well in the dry air of Banning. Harvey's bronchitis had disappeared almost on arrival. Each morning he worked on "The Gifts," rewriting his chapters at a small table in the breakfast alcove, with windows looking out on Mount San Jacinto. Afternoons were taken up with errands and with reading Finegan's *Light from the Ancient Past*, which provoked Richter's interest with its discussions of early sources for Biblical tales. Preparing himself for the first novel he would write directly from the experiences of his childhood, he was reading aloud to Harvey selected passages from Proust. When Reynolds's quarterly royalty report came in, his earnings were surprisingly high, delaying even further the time when he would have to write strictly for money. But despite all the good news Richter was nonetheless wary, reminding himself in his journal that his last stay in Banning had started well and ended with an abrupt departure.[24]

And soon something was going wrong. Although Richter's letters to his daughter and to others continued to be upbeat, accenting the positive, journal entries to himself began to suggest a different state of mind. Early in February Richter recorded the first "blues" since arriving in Banning. Several days later he reported a night spent awake with his erratic heart. On February 20 he recorded his decision to "PUT NOVEL AWAY INDEFINITELY," intending not to write at all while in California, "except a few, and short letters," reassuring himself that "we have income, thank God, for three years beyond this." After another night trying to calm a racing heart, Richter asked Harvey to lock the manuscript away until they returned to Pennsylvania.

Later Richter scrawled out in large letters a warning note to himself and attached it to the first March entry of his 1958 journal: "Do not Read the A/C [account] from March to Sept." Compared to his journal writing from other springs and summers, these entries appear for the most part unremarkable—the usual lists of vitamins taken, descriptions of drives with Harvey, trips to Palm Springs and to Los Angeles. Later he would record the drive back to Pennsylvania and the daily matters of life in Pine Grove, interspersing these entries with reflective passages on such issues as his propensity, when finishing a novel, to overwork himself because the end seemed so near. Richter wrote about several major disappointments having to do with "The Gifts," but he recorded these in his journal in the same manner and tone as he typically recorded setbacks. There appears nothing so troubling in those entries that he would need later to warn himself away from them, except a number of brief descriptions of his battle with insomnia.

What, then, had happened? It was the return of the irrational nighttime anguish he had suffered as a child, the condition that had twice forced him back to his parents' home to recuperate, the same condition that led to his nervous exhaustion in Florida in 1942.[25] Awakened from sleep by a palpitating heart, Richter would experience what he called an "ugly feeling," a "terrific mental anguish" he could not control, culminating in exaggerated worries and fear about sleeping itself, fear that he would not, if he allowed himself to sleep, ever wake up.[26] Although his nighttime anxieties did not escalate into the nervous prostration he experienced earlier, for the next months he lived in dread of the "night fears." When putting his manuscript away had little result, Richter attempted another tactic: he and Harvey packed up their belongings and informed the real estate rental agent that they might have to leave on short notice. With everything packed and ready to be loaded into the car, Richter could reassure himself in the night that he was not trapped in Banning until the lease expired. Any morning he chose they could turn in the house keys and drive off.[27] For several weeks the stratagem seemed to work, allowing Richter to congratulate himself on March 17 that he had succeeded in at least beginning the third month of their rental. A week later he and Harvey were on their way to Pennsylvania. When the night fears continued in Pennsylvania, he decided that their source was not simply the hard work of finishing the novel, but the novel's subject itself, which made him intensely aware of all the suffering in the world. For Richter the antidote to this distress had always been to assert his belief in the survival of the soul, and for most of his life that belief had sufficed. As he completed his prayer novel, how-ever, Richter found himself experiencing what he termed in one journal entry "a growing belief of extinction."[28] One especially difficult night he cried out to himself repeatedly "I believe in God." During the day he tried asserting "I am not afraid—will not be discouraged," but as evening came on he had to admit to himself that he was "afraid for the night."[29]

On May 8 Richter mailed his new book to Paul Reynolds. Evidently he remained uneasy about the novel, and his letter to Reynolds displayed more than his usual diffidence in promoting his own work. Having read somewhere that Ernest Hemingway had put manuscripts of finished books into a bank vault, to be published when he needed money, Richter suggested to Reynolds that, with sufficient income for another three years already in the bank and awaiting him from Knopf, he might do the same with "The Gifts."[30] In his letter to Alfred Knopf, Richter was unwilling to call the typescript a completed novel, com-menting that "there may still be work to be done on the book version." What he wanted from his publisher was Knopf's candid reaction: "You have been generous in the past in the kind things you have said about those of my books that you liked and outspoken in your opinion of one or two that you didn't think much of. If the present novel falls into the latter class, I hope you will take pains to be frank in your expressed feelings."[31]

The night Richter mailed the typescript to Reynolds he whistled as he washed dishes. It was his one night every two years to whistle, he told Harvey, the night after mailing a novel to his agent. That humor was typical of the public Richter, as opposed to the private one who continued sporadically to suffer night fears throughout the spring and summer. When the University of New Mexico offered an honorary degree, Richter gladly accepted, writing Matt Pearce to ask the protocol on clothing to be worn under an academic gown in the summer heat of Albuquerque. With a new, dark mohair suit from Brooks Brothers, Richter set out by train for Albuquerque, and from his journal summaries evidently enjoyed the occasion of the award and his visits with friends in New Mexico.

During these months when Richter was writing the journal entries he later warned himself not to read, the public Richter showed few signs of special duress. His letters were models of the voice he had perfected—poised, controlled, deferential but quietly assertive and self-assured. These same qualities are evident in a rare radio interview Richter acquiesced to have taped in his home shortly after receiving the honorary degree from the University of New Mexico. In the ten-minute tape one can hear Richter's tenor, comfortably modulated, answering the reporter's questions about his literary apprenticeship, writers who had influenced him, his methods of composition, and about his novel *The Light in the Forest*, the movie version of which was soon to be released. Throughout, Richter responded in a deft balance of good humor and seriousness, speaking thoughtfully in the hesitations and variations of rhythm characterizing conversational speech. Asked about his themes, Richter took the opportunity to mention *The Mountain on the Desert*, saying that some of its ideas informed all of his books.[32] Driving away from Maple Street, the reporter must have been pleased by the careful attention Richter had given to him. From their conversation, he could not have guessed that Richter had just received crushingly bad news from his publisher.

Paul Reynolds, the first reader of "The Gifts," was as usual complimentary and optimistic; he liked the book and was sure it would sell to the *Post*. In this prediction he was wrong: though Erd Brandt and Ben Hibbs had received an outline of the novel's plot and had approved its subject for their magazine, when the retyped copy was submitted to the *Post* Ben Hibbs decided against it, calling it "a novel of frustration." He much preferred, he told Paul Reynolds, Richter's stories about strong people.[33] The rejection came a week before Richter's trip to Albuquerque; his publisher's reaction would arrive soon after his return. A Paul Reynolds letter meant to forewarn Richter of Knopf's opinion, alerting Richter that his publisher "did not like 'The Gifts' at all" and would be writing him "pretty fiercely" about it, actually arrived the same day as Knopf's letter.[34] Although Richter read Reynolds's warning first, his agent's letter could not have prepared him for just how fiercely his publisher felt about his new novel. In part Knopf's letter read:

> This is one of the most painful letters I have ever had to write. . . . It is my considered opinion that you would be most unwise to publish ["The Gifts"]. I do not expect to convince you of the soundness of my judgment,

17.   Portrait of Conrad Richter by Elliot Erwitt, 1950s.

but I do ask you to believe that it is in no way related to the underlying belief in which the book was written—religious, mystical, philosophical, what-you-will. . . . Conrad, my dear friend, it is simply an outrageously bad novel—badly conceived and poorly executed. Entirely apart from the subjective background to which I referred above, it is, as a story, crude and completely unconvincing. I couldn't possibly . . . put my name on this book, much less attempt to do [for] it what you would regard as a minimum of justice.

I realize I am risking a friendship which I value and have always valued very deeply by writing you thus frankly. But I cannot do less. I know from long experience how extremely rare it is for a writer when he fails, as I think you have in this instance failed, to get the truth as they see it, from the best of friends. So I can only hope that you will forgive me.[35]

As Knopf certainly knew and had discussed with Paul Reynolds, he was risking more than his friendship with Richter; his rejection would probably push Richter into a contract with a competing publisher.[36] But when Reynolds wrote to reassure Richter that he could "make a contract with a first-class publisher for this book very quickly," Richter wrote back asking his agent to delay any action at all. As rough as his publisher's language had been in the first paragraph, Richter chose to recall the conciliatory words of the second, commenting to his agent that, after all, Knopf "wrote me rather decently, I think." Before deciding what to do next, Richter wanted to hear all Reynolds knew about reactions to the book by Knopf's staff, by the *Post's*, and by any other editors who might have seen it. And what, he wondered, were the possibilities of offering "The Gifts" to another publisher under a pseudonym?[37]

The same Friday Richter drafted a letter to Knopf to say that he had not expected Knopf to like "The Gifts," but though the publisher's letter was no surprise, "it was sad to get it all the same." As for the novel, he had not decided what to do with it and guessed it should be returned to Reynolds. Four days later, on June 25, Richter retyped the letter to Knopf, rewriting the final paragraph to acknowledge his own acceptance of the novel's failure: "Perhaps a man has to expect certain casualties in life, and it may be that a writer is entitled to one occasionally. In this case the trouble was not the idea but the way I took to work it out for a popular magazine. As a book, I could and should have done it more subtly and convincingly. I still could, but it would take complete rewriting from another viewpoint, and I'm not sure that it's worth that. Even though it may have a market value somewhere, I think I should lay it aside and forget it." Over the weekend Harvey and Vene had read "The Gifts" in its entirety, which they had not previously done. Pressed, they both admitted that they found the book uninteresting. It was Vene's suggestion that the novel needed to be told by a first-person narrator, rather than the storyteller's limited omniscience Richter had chosen, thereby creating more ambiguity and mystery about the young woman's motives and actions.[38] Accepting his daughter's criticism, Richter wrote to his agent to say that he had decided to keep "The Gifts" as a kind of bank deposit, something he could retrieve, rewrite, and publish whenever he needed the money.[39]

In spite of Richter's tempered replies, the failure of his novel was exacting a painful toll on its author. Just before writing to Knopf Richter suffered through the worst bout of night fears he had encountered that spring. On the day he wrote with such composure to Knopf about having to expect "certain casualties in life," Richter described his feelings more baldly in his journal: it was a "bitter disappointment and acid corrosion of the soul" to have "The Gifts" called "crude," to have his publisher declare he would not put his name on the novel. But as had so often happened in the past, Richter soon turned the disappointment into directed action for his next project. For a number of years his complaint on any failure had been that he no longer had the energy that had gotten him through the depression years in Albuquerque. At sixty-seven, confronted with the utter failure of a book that was important to him, he once again found that energy. On June 30, less than a week after writing his publisher and his agent that he was putting "The Gifts" away indefinitely, Richter spent his morning planning the novel he had given the unappealing working title of "Death and Life." Richter's story idea had no definite plot, only a subject and perhaps a mood—a re-creation of life as Richter had experienced it in turn-of-the-century Pine Grove. It seems especially remarkable that, at a time of such duress, assaulted by nights of sleeplessness and his despair at the failure of "The Gifts," Richter would take up a novel that was, in effect, doubly experimental. Although he had already outlined plot for a serial that he was sure would sell to the *Post*, a companion novel to *The Light in the Forest*, he chose to put aside that all but certain success. Instead he would attempt a novel for which he did not have a story, a novel written directly from his life experiences. In addition, he planned to make his new novel, the first of his family trilogy, one that combined his life with his theories.

On July 4, Independence Day, pacing the floor and puzzling over his story difficulties, Richter hit upon a plot device that would allow him to re-create the Pine Grove of his childhood and capture as well his own sense of the loss for that world, a feeling that had begun soon after the death of his mother and had been intensified by the death of his father in 1941. As in "Dr. Hanray's Second Chance," he would have his protagonist magically reenter his childhood world, but as an adult, an outsider unrecognized and suspiciously regarded by the people who would have been most welcoming to him as a boy. Excited by what he saw as the idea's many possibilities, Richter quickly developed them, creating an aging and ill artist who returns to the Pennsylvania valley of his childhood and there finds himself transported into his hometown on a summer's evening in 1899, over fifty years earlier. By July 9 Richter had found his title, *The Waters of Kronos*, and was well into his plotting. When Vene returned for the summer to complete her own novel, Richter talked over his story with her. It was her idea to have a boatman transport the writer across a Styx-like river to Unionville; it was Richter's modification to have John Donner brought into the town in a coal wagon, the horses rutching down the steep hill into the valley where Unionville lay beside the Kronos River.[40]

That summer Richter spent his mornings sitting at his desk in the dining room, planning and drafting the early chapters of his family novel. Remembering his difficulties finishing "The Gifts," he kept a promise to himself not to be satisfied with drafts but to polish each chapter until it was finished copy, sparing himself the difficult rewriting that had taxed him all spring and was then taxing his daughter Vene, upstairs tapping away at her typewriter, revising the last chapters of *The Human Shore*. Although she occasionally came down from her room to talk to her father about her difficulties, she strictly kept to her decision not to show him any of the actual writing. Listening to his daughter's accounts of seemingly intractable problems, Richter watched with secret pride as Vene returned to her typewriter to work out her own solutions.

Although Richter wrote regularly about Vene's activities that summer in Pine Grove, Richter made virtually no comments about the progress of her novel or even his conversations with her about writing. When Vene submitted her novel to Paul Reynolds, Richter recorded the agent's enthusiastic prediction of a great popular success, but he added no response of his own. The next day he noted, again without comment of his own, Harvey's excited raves as she read her daughter's novel.[41] After the book had been accepted by Little, Brown—the first publishing house to consider it—and Reynolds had sold the English rights for 250 pounds—more than Richter had ever received for one of his books—Richter finally let loose in his journal some of the feeling he had not yet put on paper: perhaps, he wrote, Vene's success would be the end of his; once she was able to provide for her mother and herself, that would take from him a primary pressure to write, which had always been the need to care for his family. If he were no longer needed to support them, that could well damage his own "will to survive and accomplish and provide."[42]

But such thoughts were momentary, the kind of conversation Richter had with himself when his energy was low, and there is no evidence that Richter was returning reluctantly each morning to his desk. For the first time ever Richter was portraying himself in words, choosing the name John Donner because "Johnny" sounded so close to "Connie."[43] Like Conrad Richter, John Donner is a successful writer, modest about his own accomplishments and embarrassed by fame. Having arrived at the end of his life, John Donner has returned home one last time to visit the graves of his parents, reburied in a new cemetery above the dammed waters of the Kronos River, waters that have engulfed the valley of his childhood, covering over the red-roofed houses and quiet, gas-lit streets of his hometown of Unionville. With him John Donner carries a photograph of his mother and two brothers, the photograph Conrad Richter himself had taken at the age of ten, prized all his life, and still kept in a black frame on his writing desk. In it his mother sits with her two younger sons, smiling calmly as her eldest son prepares to take her picture. For John Donner the photograph opens up once again his great bereavement, his loss of a life he could never return to. Behind his mother and brothers is the closed door to the kitchen, under which light streams. His mind struggles to open that door, but he knows it can never be opened, he can never again step into that light and warmth.

John Donner turns away from the new graveyard to walk the remains of an old road leading, he had been told, to the shore of the artificial lake. Before the water comes into sight, he encounters a rough wagon, laden with anthracite, creaking down the road from above. Reluctantly its driver accepts John Donner as a passenger, and the two descend together into the valley, further and further down until John Donner is certain they must have passed the water's edge, down the "Long Stretch" where he had sledded as a boy, down into the town of Unionville as it was in 1899, where the Kronos River still slips along quietly within its banks. He has only to step down from the wagon to walk the streets, to enter the stores and perhaps the homes of his childhood, to speak again to his relatives and childhood friends, even to his father and his mother.

Throughout the summer and early fall Richter kept almost exactly to his schedule of a chapter a month, complete except for minor final revisions. By the end of September he had finished the third chapter, in which John Donner meets and talks briefly with his father, Harry Donner, only to find the storekeeper too preoccupied with family matters to attend to an apparently confused old man. Briefly Richter considered abandoning his decision to write each chapter to final form, instead writing first drafts of all the remaining chapters. While one of Richter's reasons for doing so was that he could then dictate revisions to a secretary, speeding the process, his second suggests that his racing heart and fears at night were still with him. If he rushed through the novel quickly, he thought, at least a first draft would be done—"in case I am unable to do more for any reason and someone else can fix it up."[44] Evidently the "someone else" he had in mind was Vene, who just three days later would depart for New York to deliver her novel to Paul Reynolds.

By October 13, his sixty-eighth birthday, Richter was creating in chapter 4 an extended portrait of his Aunt Lizzie Irwin as Aunt Jess, who turns away the old John Donner for his insinuations about her nephew Johnny and her sister, Johnny's mother. In December Richter would complete the fifth chapter, in which Donner is refused entrance into his own home by his mother's maid and spends the night on the covered bridge over the Kronos River. Although Richter had regularly prevailed over his nighttime anxieties for the past two months, they were still a looming presence. Just before Christmas Richter suffered through a night with his heart racing but succeeded in routing his fear; and on Christmas night he again fought off an onset of the "ugly feeling" and finally slept.

On the morning of January 25, 1959, Richter awoke from an especially sound night's sleep. Gathering his thoughts in the chill of a winter bedroom, he was carried back into a childhood memory of calling out to his mother on cold mornings, asking her to wrap him in his blanket and carry him down into the warmth of the kitchen. It was an especially happy memory, anticipating the coming of his mother, and it was emblematic of an emotional core energizing Richter's novel, which concludes with John Donner waiting for his mother to come and smile upon him, to give him renewed life by recognizing him as one of her own. Richter's journal entry about this memory led him to another, suggesting how much pleasure he experienced when he was healthy and his writing was going well. At such times, he wrote, it was "a great joy to get awake after a good sleep and know I can put my strength to work today, to add more to my book, to get more done, to feel the end closer, and a new book beyond that."[45]

Richter would fill *The Waters of Kronos* with memories from his childhood, the sounds of conversation filtering out into the night from porches where people rocked in the cool air, the damp of mossy brick sidewalks. But for all the richly evocative detail, the faithful descriptions of friends and relatives—which Richter took delight in remembering and recording—Richter's Unionville is not simply a nostalgic re-creation of Pine Grove in 1899. John Donner's longed-for past has become retrievable, but at a price: the old writer carries with him into Unionville his foreknowledge of the terrible things time will bring to the people he passes on the streets—unhappy lives, desperate acts, whole families lost to disease, and finally the dammed-up waters of the Kronos River slowly rising to cover the town.

Himself a night walker of Pine Grove's streets, Richter would occasionally return to his desk to record the aura of sadness he felt especially at that time of day. For him that feeling was more than just the difference between his personal sense of the "shabby" Pine Grove of the present and the "nobly rich" town of his memories. It was also, he would write, a "burden and sadness of mortality close around me." It was a "profound bitter sorrow," associated with the spirits of those no longer living, "rising in air in evening and night especially from cemeteries and moldy graves and all those tragic words like 'asleep' and 'fallen asleep,' persons or souls caught up by those powerful sadnesses as if by a great inescapable wave, perhaps foully done or forgotten." And especially for him that sorrow came from his own "close association with environs from which Mother and Dad and most of the rest are gone . . . and those who still remain are like old reeds soon to be laid by the wind." Walking Pine Grove's streets took him back into happy and yet painful memories: "It is all so near, the houses where they lived, the streets they walked, the churches they went to and now they lie in where we must follow."[46] After a visit from his brother Joe spurred more memories, Richter found himself lamenting the gulf between his remembering mind and the experiences themselves: "They were all inside of me, far away, and I couldn't go back. [I] never had the feeling of time being one way as today. I felt that we were on the end of a screw turning us along."[47]

Walking Unionville's streets, John Donner feels Conrad Richter's intense pleasure in reexcited memory and his intense despair that, close as he has come to his childhood, he cannot reach across and become a part of it. After failing to make his real self known to his father and his favorite aunt, John Donner focuses his hopes on his mother, Valeria Donner; if he can just talk to her he is certain she will know him. At his grandfather's funeral John Donner sees his mother only at a distance, her face covered by a black veil. At the funeral dinner afterward her countenance is hidden behind others at the table. As the novel ends Donner is lying ill in the other half of the double house where he had lived as a child, listening to his family across the common wall. There he awaits the coming of his mother, who has promised to visit him.

When the spring royalty report arrived from Paul Reynolds, Richter was surprised to find an unexpected $5,000 from the Reader's Digest Book Club's edition of *The Lady* and good hardback sales, especially for *The Light in the Forest*. And in March he received, without warning, notice that the National Institute of Arts and Letters had chosen him for an award of $1,500, free of any obligation except to receive the award in person. All together this added income bought more writing time for Richter. By Vene's birthday, March 13, Richter was working on an outline of chapter 8, the final chapter, including in it John Donner's great discovery about the feelings of dread he had always associated with his father, a discovery Richter meant as a rebuff to Freud's theory of the natural antagonism of the son for the father. In this last, climactic chapter John Donner confronts the specter from his dreams and discovers that what he has always feared is not the spirit of his father but the haunting image of his own aging self, a vision of his life slipping ever onward toward death. Struggling up from bed to face the terrible presence surrounding him, John Donner discovers through the gloom his own reflection in the bureau mirror—"his hair cruelly thin, the skull revealed, the coarsened smear of a face, the confusion of features once so indubitably his own, now run together as if returning to primordial chaos."[48] Here was his dark oppressor; it was not his father. In his last hours Donner believes that he has found a truth: "It was the great deception practiced by man on himself and his fellows, the legend of hate against the father so the son need not face the real and ultimate abomination . . . his older self to come, a self marked with the inescapable dissolution and decay of his youth."[49]

On March 22, 1959, Harvey confessed that a red, swollen spot had appeared under her right arm and that what had at first been only a slight itching had become a burning pain. Richter suspected the condition had something to do with his wife's tuberculosis, but he also worried that the swelling might be the first signs of a malignant tumor. Thereafter his afternoons would often be taken up with Harvey's illness, driving to see specialists to discuss Harvey's symptoms (Harvey would not go with him), writing letters to others in search of a diagnosis and a treatment that Harvey could be prevailed upon to accept. His daughter was also on his mind, with her novel due to be published at the beginning of June. Paul Reynolds had been wrong when he predicted a book club sale and a magazine sale, and Richter worried about his daughter's reaction if, after having been led to expect so much by her agent and her publisher, her novel did not sell at least modestly well.[50]

When the first bound copies of The Human Shore arrived, Vene finally gave her novel to her father. He read it immediately, first with the impatient rush with which he characteristically read everything, then again more slowly, savoring its unfolding story. Richter had little to say in his journal about his daughter's first book, other than that he could have been more enthusiastic if she had chosen a stronger woman character for her protagonist.[51] His letter to Vene began by assuring her that, like Reynolds and her mother, he had found her novel "impressive" and ended by calling it "really excellent" and "beautifully done." As one novelist to another, Richter congratulated his daughter on the deliberate, measured pace of her narrative, making the story "real, emotional, and effective." His own artistic imagination having repeatedly been catalyzed by stories of lost and orphaned children, it is not surprising that for Richter the children who unknowingly sail off into a coming hurricane "made the suspense in the storm very poignant and hard to bear."[52] If after reading the novel Richter suspected Harvey to be the model for Nona Reardon, he did not voice his suspicion. If he sensed in Nona's teenage affair any intentional similarity to his abiding worry that in Harvey's past there had been an earlier, more intense love than hers for him, he kept his thought to himself. He did not express his disapproval of the novel's scenes of sexual intimacy—he would not have needed to. Nor did he admit to his daughter his suspicion that it had been Harvey's worry over those passages that had made her sick.[53]

On June 6, 1959, Vene's novel came out to excellent reviews but garnered only modest sales, demonstrating that she was her father's daughter. As it became apparent that the novel would not become a best-seller, Richter was disappointed for his daughter, and he offered encouragement and help as she attempted to start another. But there was some measure of relief in the novel's slim sales; later Richter told Vene that had her novel become the popular book it was predicted to be, the contrast of her quick success with his many years of struggle would have been just too much for him. He did not think he would have been able to write again.[54] In 1965 Richter would recall how he had felt that spring, in the weeks before the publication of *The Human Shore*, when Vene's career appeared to have been so favorably launched: "There wasn't the slightest envy in the feeling. I still wished her all the good fortune possible. There was only the realization that in one leap she had outdistanced me and I was left a has been, a defeated old man."[55]

By Independence Day, when Vene returned home to visit, Richter was ready to read his novel to his wife and daughter. He did so beginning in mid-afternoon, pausing between five and six o'clock for a light supper. The next morning he would record their reactions in his journal, as always emphasizing how the novel had affected them emotionally. Both had been enthusiastic, he wrote, and afterwards Vene said that she had been moved to tears most of the way. He himself had also been moved while reading, but he worried that the novel did not have the all-important aftereffect, that their feelings for the story did not carry over to a second day. He ended the journal entry with a comment he would repeat in a letter to Knopf. *The Trees* had been published in 1940, *The Town* in 1950, and they were the novels that had gotten the most public attention and honors. Perhaps it was a good omen for *The Waters of Kronos* that it was to come out in 1960.[56]

Writing to Paul Reynolds, Richter sounded a less optimistic tone. Warning his agent that the novel was "too dark," he instructed Reynolds not even to submit the book to the *Post,* and to "show" it to Knopf, rather than formally submitting it for consideration, allowing Knopf to return it without actually announcing a negative decision. When Knopf's letter arrived on July 22, Richter opened the single sheet of stationery just far enough to be able to read the last sentence. That sentence suggested that the news was not bad, and Richter opened the letter to read from the beginning. "Rest easy," his publisher wrote. "I like *The Waters of Kronos* very much indeed."[57]

The *Post* did not concur, however, when Paul Reynolds finally prevailed on Richter to allow him to submit it to Erd Brandt. "I just can't see a serial in it," Brandt wrote, adding, "I had two other unofficial readings and we all agree that taken in one reading it is a splendid tour de force that would be lost in installments."[58] After the *Atlantic* also turned down serial rights for the book, Richter decided again that his novel was "too dark" and promised himself that the second volume of the family trilogy would be brighter. Late in September when Richter began working on "Dad's book," as he occasionally referred to the project he had previously entitled "The Good People" and would soon be calling "The Man of Kronos," he was determined not to repeat his mistake. *The Waters of Kronos* had been too full of his own anguish for all that had passed away and could never be recovered. Later he would scold himself for succumbing to weakness and confession in the novel, just the traits he had cautioned himself against in his personal life, believing they caused others to think less of him.[59]

After a summer of family discussions about Vene's future, she decided to return to New York University to complete her Ph.D., though it meant putting off work on her second novel and returning to New York without any guarantee of a teaching appointment. But on her second day back in New York Vene happened to meet an English department official on a bus and was offered on the spot the chance to teach two writing courses for twice what she had earned as a teaching fellow. For Richter such meetings were never a matter of chance; fate was taking a hand in guiding his daughter into teaching. But that did not mean, of course, that one should not work to make the most of such advantages. The day Richter heard about Vene's offer he wrote to remind her to "dress well and with dignity" when teaching and attending all other university affairs.[60]

When typescripts arrived from Reynolds, Richter shared a copy of his new novel with his brother Joe, asking him to point out any inaccuracies in the description of the town and its people. When Joe suggested that Trap Irwin might be offended by the comment that nice girls would not ice-skate with him, Richter deleted the line. Trap himself was apparently unconcerned by his portrayal as a rascal; he did comment that, the characters being so directly based on real people, it was a wonder some of them did not haunt Richter.[61] But what actually haunted Richter, as he would write in his journal, were not the inhabitants of Pine Grove's past but the image looking back at John Donner from the mirror. After a dinner meeting in Hershey, Knopf once again sent Richter snapshots he had taken, pictures in which Richter saw himself "an aged, thin, ailing old man."[62] To Knopf, Richter would write lightly of the pictures, declaring them "clear and candid, very candid, perhaps too candid. What I need, I think, is a flattery camera, one that looks at the world and its denizens, including me, with rose colored lenses."[63] Living through nights of heart palpitations and sleeplessness, ever watchful of Harvey's apparently deteriorating health, what he saw, and what was affecting him most deeply, was "the spectacle of those around me in the town and elsewhere steadfastly decaying to their ignoble end."[64] Even in the miraculous world of *The Waters of Kronos*, John Donner can only witness the life of his childhood, he cannot relive it. For he is old: time has swept over Unionville, the deluge has come; the waters have buried his town beneath its depths, leaving John Donner with the vision of himself decaying. That, after all, is the demon John Donner confronts in the novel's climax, the demon of the self in old age that life promises everyone who does not meet some swifter end. For Richter the only hope against this slow dissolution was the survival of the soul, and that is what John Donner longs for as he awaits his mother's coming, knowing that outside a dark stranger has already arrived to carry him back to where he has come from: "She had promised him yesterday that he would see her 'tomorrow' and she had never told him a falsehood yet."[65]

The ending would puzzle readers, beginning with Alfred Knopf, and to those who asked, Richter gave essentially the same reply: that at the novel's ending John Donner is "about to die, that the cemetery guard who called for him is the legendary 'dark man,' that the 'machine' referred to was the unknown mechanism that brought him into life and which carries him on to continued life or oblivion, and that the last line or two referred to the belief of his mother in Christian survival."[66] The last lines also referred to Conrad Richter's own vexed belief in survival. Decades after he had first posed the question, Richter was still asking, "Does my mother love me after she is dead?"[67] His reply in *The Waters of Kronos* is hopeful but hardly convincing. While working on the last revision of the last chapter of his novel, Richter had spent part of an afternoon reading an article that argued against the survival of souls. That night he was unable to sleep, kept awake by night fears, and the next day's journal entry would acknowledge that often he was unable to believe that there was even a fifty-fifty chance for survival.[68] On another June night several years earlier, Richter had dreamed that his mother was locked inside a house and would not let anyone in. Through the window he could see her "looking dull and unwilling." He called out, "Mother, it's Connie." Unlocking the door she seemed to recognize her son for an instant, but then "her mood returned."[69]

THREE

When winter came Richter and Harvey again decided against leaving for a warmer climate. Having begun the actual writing of his new novel, "The Man of Kronos," in late October, Richter had accumulated a growing manuscript of several chapters by the end of December. Then early in the new year Richter grew uneasy about Harvey. Although she protested that she was feeling fine, several times Richter mentioned in his journal that he suspected something to be wrong. Finally Harvey admitted to him that the reddish, swollen spot from the previous year had returned, accompanied this time by severe pain and stiffness in her side and back. Perhaps the condition was brought on by exposure to winter weather, Richter worried, and he regretted that he had not taken his fragile wife on a cruise as she had always wanted, to the Bahamas or perhaps Hawaii. He had $22,000 in the bank, he told himself, and he had "no reason not to spend it on travel."[70] But once Harvey was again suffering her mysterious illness, all he could do was begin another round of letter writing to specialists, describing his wife's condition and adding the complication of her lifelong reluctance to take any drug at all. When Richter himself suffered severe pains in his chest, he stopped work on his novel and put aside his journal as well, abandoning the journal from mid-February until late March and his novel until early April.

On the night of April 1, Harvey's swollen area finally opened and began to drain a yellowish liquid, which the local doctor suspected to be "hot" with tuberculosis bacilli. Fluid in her chest cavity around her collapsed lung had finally burrowed through an old incision from her pneumolysis operations. Laboratory tests proved negative for tuberculosis, but for the remainder of that spring and summer Harvey's health overwhelmed all other considerations for Richter, including the publication of *The Waters of Kronos*, Alfred Knopf's sale of his publishing house to Random House, and the slow progress of the second novel of his family trilogy. With Harvey bedridden most of the time, their housekeeper Edna Miller became their cook as well.

Paul Reynolds guessed that the merger of Knopf with Random House would work to Richter's advantage, as Random House had a superior sales staff.[71] But the first months after the publication of *The Waters of Kronos* brought once again a collection of admiring reviews and modest sales. And once again Richter found himself blaming Knopf but also himself, speculating that his book might have upset modern readers with his revelation that Freud had misunderstood the antagonism of the son for the father. A second—and more personal—reason for the novel's failure, he thought, intertwined his lifelong struggle to "contain" himself when with others and to "contain" himself from exhibiting the same weakness in his writing: the "fault" of his novel, he wrote to Vene, was its "revelation or confession of personal things that came as a weakness to certain readers." For the second volume of his family trilogy he intended to "scrupulously avoid any conscious personal revelation or confession that would give a sense of weakness."[72]

When Harvey's health improved sufficiently to allow her to make visits to friends, Richter began to plan for a winter away from Pennsylvania's cold and damp. By late November he had completed fourteen chapters of the second novel of the Kronos trilogy and was promising himself to let the chapters lie fallow until spring. Just before Christmas Richter packed up the yellow Cadillac and set out for Florida, stopping first in Gainesville and then driving on into the warmer weather of Bradenton, near Sarasota, there to relax until spring. Although sales of *The Waters of Kronos* had been disappointing, he and Harvey had at least three years' income still available, with more to come with the completion of the second book of the trilogy. And "The Gifts" was in Paul Reynolds's safe, which he could take out and revise whenever he wished.

On January 20, 1961, Richter and Harvey set out from Bradenton to Arcadia, taking advantage of the cool afternoon for a drive through pleasant farm scenery. Along the way Harvey was in high spirits. She could not remember when she had been so happy, she told her husband. In fact she was having one of her bubbling sensations, an experience that had often preceded good news.[73] Ten days later, sorting through the day's mail, Richter found a letter from the National Institute of Arts and Letters, informing him that he had been elected to membership in the institute. Glenway Wescott's archly formal letter was an invitation to join. "It floored me for a time," Richter wrote in his journal.[74] Not only did he have decidedly mixed feeling about such elitist organizations, but Wescott's letter mentioned a ceremonial dinner in May at which he would receive "a diploma, of all things."[75] Richter vividly remembered a similar ceremonial a year and a half earlier, when he had stumbled on the steps while going to the podium to receive the award of $1,500 that the institute had given him. The affair was a dinner, with all the members of the institute, together with those of the American Academy of Arts and Letters (which was, Richter summarized for Vene, "a little snootier," having "what it considers more famous names")[76] sitting on display on stage above the invited guests. It was certainly not his kind of affair, but having accepted an institute grant he could not very well decline to join. And as he wrote Vene, he did not want to disappoint Harvey, who was pleased that her "bubbling" had again predicted an honor, or slight Wescott, who had spoken well of *The Waters of Kronos*. And besides, he admitted to his daughter, "while I worry about joining I would probably worry more over rejecting them."[77]

The news Harvey's special feeling had predicted was immediately followed by a blow; the day after Wescott's letter arrived Harvey admitted that she was again having pains in the right side of her chest. This time the swelling and pain came so quickly that Harvey astonished her husband by agreeing to be hospitalized to have the abscess lanced. She even agreed to consider taking drugs if the drainage tested positive for tuberculosis. Perhaps she had accepted the medical treatment so readily, Richter speculated in his journal, because she believed the recurrence began after she had become chilled during a Christian Science service in an air-conditioned room.[78]

Once Harvena was released from the hospital, Richter suffered something he ambiguously reported as "an attack of some kind," which turned out to be a persistent case of diarrhea. Worrying about what would happen to his wife if he became too ill to care for her, he accepted a doctor's prescription for diphenoxylate/atropine and drove Harvey back to Pennsylvania. When they arrived home in Pine Grove on February 24 it was still winter in Pennsylvania, but they were in their own home, close to family and friends and a family doctor who knew Harvey's special needs. Two days after their arrival, Richter felt his wife secure enough in her home to turn his thoughts to other, less weighty matters. That afternoon he wrote to Brooks Brothers to complain that the Lot 239 XL pajamas he had bought for years had, in their latest ordering, been inexplicably altered, no longer allowing "luxurious freedom in bed." Although he was certainly serious in his complaint, Richter's final paragraph suggested that things were going well enough at home to allow for at least a little levity: "I don't know who is responsible for such minute, non-Brooksian penny pinching of material at the expense of a customer's comfort and sleep, but extend curses to him. I can imagine the seventh hell and torment Dante would have consigned him to, had Dante worn pajamas."[79]

Then some unexpected news arrived which Harvey could also attribute to her bubbly sensation. Alfred Knopf telephoned—itself an unusual event—to tell his author that Richter had won the National Book Award for *The Waters of Kronos*. As good as this news was, it also meant that Richter would have to appear at the awards ceremony, perhaps would even have to speak, a thought that would have been almost paralyzing. Richter could at least be grateful that the ceremony came quickly. Knopf called on March 9; the ceremony was scheduled for March 14. Harvey was as eager to attend as her husband dreaded the prospect, if only her health let her. But it would not. When it came time to drive to New York, Harvey was in so much pain that she did not even travel to Vene's apartment to be close to the day's affairs.

At the photo session where he joined the year's other winners, William Shirer for history and Randall Jarrell for poetry, Richter tried to put down the copy of his book, which all three had been asked to hold in front of them. It was politely but insistently given back to him. That evening at the awards ceremony Randall Jarrell was the first to speak, followed by William Shirer. Seated in an anteroom, Richter listened as one of Jarrell's attempts at humor fell flat, then another drew modest laughter. When Richter's turn came, Alfred Knopf went to receive Richter's award and to speak for him. To be sure his shy writer actually attended, his publisher had volunteered to read the acceptance speech. Knopf began with a remark from Koussevitzky, who once after speaking nine words had said he would rather have conducted nine symphonies.[80] When the laughter abated, Knopf read Richter's brief address:

> I'm not speaking in person today because my ancestors prevented me. My father was a preacher. My grandfather was a preacher. My uncle and great uncles were preachers. They spoke in public constantly and used up all the talent in the blood stream so that when I came along, unfortunately there wasn't any left. But I'm grateful that they didn't all write, or I'd have been left in a worse way. As it was, two of them did write, rather prolifically, and that's what makes writing so slow and difficult for me. I simply manage to get enough done to get by.
>
> So when anyone tells me he wants to write, I say to him—first pick your ancestors carefully. The farther from an author, the better. Miners are fine. Stonecutters are still better. So are farmers and stockmen. Their innocence of literary creation leaves plenty of good oxygen in the blood stream. Even ancestors who indulged in a little reading are suspect. Now booksellers are very acceptable. But beware of novelists, poets, and book reviewers.
>
> Of course, there's always hope. In my case I still marvel at and envy the ease with which as a young newspaperman I used to knock out two or three columns a day. Reading some of them now, I wince a little.

Lately it seems that the harder and more painful my writing, the better it stands up next morning. This toughening process which our pioneer ancestors knew so well—this hardship into gain—what Shakespeare called benefit of ill—gives me more hope for my country today and for man. It's one of the themes of my Ohio trilogy and of some of my other novels.

Thank you.

A Country of Strangers

ONE

Conrad Richter spent the morning after the National Book Awards doing errands in New York, taking a bus uptown to pick out two small oriental carpets for Harvey, then downtown to Fourteenth Street to find an AM/FM radio for Vene. While uptown he stopped at Alfred's office to collect his rubbers, left the day before, and a photograph Alfred Knopf had taken of him—perhaps the first—about twenty years earlier. Richter was surprised and pleased by the snapshot. In it his hair was thick and dark, his face composed, sturdy, resolute. It was, he wrote Knopf, just the sort of portrait he would have liked for a dust jacket, a picture projecting quiet authorial confidence. But he no longer looked like the man in the photograph, his face grown slightly gaunt, his hair thin and gray.

Late that afternoon Richter slipped away from Vene's Washington Square apartment. With two heavy bags to carry, he spent the extra money to take a taxi to Penn Station, then hired a porter to get his bags onto the train to Lancaster. Only after the train was rolling smoothly into the countryside did he release himself from the "bracing up" he relied upon to get him through such occasions as the awards ceremony. When he stepped off the train "the country air tasted priceless." It was good to have the "ordeal" behind him.[1] But he had given himself too long a day, ending with a drive in the dark from Lancaster and then, after a light supper with Harvey, the task of carrying in and emptying the suitcases. It had all overtired him. At two in the morning he awoke "in considerable discomfort," fearing that he would be ill. In his next journal entry he admonished himself to be more considerate of his aging body; seventy years old, he still had three important novels to write and the second volume of his family trilogy to finish. If he was going to complete these, he had to be careful of his health.

Always alert to the reactions of his Pennsylvania Dutch neighbors, Richter was pleased by the cheerful compliments that greeted him as he walked daily up Tulpehocken Street, touched by the friendly waves from across an intersection and the sly digs mixed among the jokes and stories in the barber shop, where the older townspeople teased each other in "the dialect," Pennsylvania Dutch. He was proud enough of these gestures to mention them in his next letter to Knopf, deflecting any sense of self-promotion by posing his remarks as a bemused observation about his neighbors: "Townspeople have been unusually cordial. They take any honor I chance to get as a compliment to the town and themselves."[2] The remark was strikingly similar to one he had made ten years earlier, after the announcement of his Pulitzer Prize; but in the decade between the awards his neighbors had come to a better understanding of the novelist living among them. This time there was no talk of a celebratory dinner.

After his bad night's sleep, Richter spent the next morning at his desk in the dining room, preparing to write the last section of his sequel to *The Waters of Kronos*. In the afternoon he took up the delicate assignment of writing to Mrs. Doolittle, Harvey's Christian Science practitioner and, for special circumstances, his own, explaining to her Harvey's hospitalization in Florida and the lancing of the reddish lump under her right arm. At the close of his letter Richter asked Mrs. Doolittle to stop working for him, since the awards ceremony was over, and to send a bill. He had suffered "an attack of some kind" during the night, he admitted, which was "probably a reaction from the last few days' strain" but by morning he was feeling better. As for Harvey, Richter temporized: "She had some work done for her [by a Christian Science practitioner] in Florida and so far this year has not been sick as she was last year . . . and for the present feels content to let well enough be."[3] But letting well enough alone was not to be possible; the same day Richter wrote to Mrs. Doolittle, the surgeon who had treated Harvey in Florida was writing to tell his patient some disturbing news: laboratory tests confirmed that tuberculosis bacilli were again active in her chest. Under extreme pressure from her husband, Harvey unhappily began taking several drugs to bring the illness into remission. She adamantly refused, however, antibiotics of any sort or any drug that had to be injected, and so she could not be talked into the treatment of choice, streptomycin by injection, three times a week.

Several times that spring Richter wrote to Alfred Knopf and Paul Reynolds, urging Knopf to take advantage of the National Book Award to push his books, and Reynolds to push Knopf. Although Reynolds had commented that the National Book Award brought more added sales than the Pulitzer, Richter saw no effort by Knopf to promote his novel, despite his prodding. At the end of April Richter fired off his heaviest weapon, contrasting Alfred's inaction after the award to that of his son, Alfred, Jr., whose departure from Knopf to become a founding partner in Atheneum had left his father smarting; in publishing circles it was widely speculated that his son Pat's defection was the real reason Knopf had agreed to sell his firm to Bennett Cerf's Random House.[4] Atheneum was the publisher of Randall Jarrell, that year's winner of the National Book Award for poetry, and Richter called Alfred's attention to how aggressively Jarrell's book was being publicized.[5] Expecting an angry reply from Alfred, he did not get one. But neither did he get more advertising from his publisher.

Richter did acknowledge that he himself had never been helpful when it came to promoting his books, declining radio and television interviews and even refusing to let the Knopf staff arrange book signings in New York bookstores. And he regretted deeply that his shyness kept him from putting himself forward when there were opportunities to be among prominent writers. Perhaps to demonstrate that he, too, was willing to make an effort, he stiffened himself to attend that year's dinner by the National Institute of Arts and Letters, ordering a new suit for the occasion and making a date to meet his agent for lunch beforehand. But when Alfred Knopf, who thought the organization self-important and the dinner a chore to attend, made the evening trek uptown as a gesture to his author, Richter was not to be found. "Something came up," Richter wrote evasively to apologize to Reynolds for canceling the luncheon.[6] What "came up" Harvey disclosed in a letter to Vene. When his new suit arrived a few days before the dinner, Richter decided it was too dark, all wrong for such an occasion. He could not wear it, and he would not go to the dinner.[7]

As had happened the previous year, with warming weather the drainage from Harvey's pleural cavity gradually diminished. Richter of course hoped that this meant that his wife, through her drug therapy, her Christian Science, and a regimen of vitamins and a high protein diet was overcoming again the disease that had almost killed her in Albuquerque. By mid-May Harvey was well enough to be treated to a dinner at Mrs. Yocum's, who at eighty-five still cooked for boarders as she had for Harvey and Vene in 1919. Richter and Harvey dressed for the occasion, but modestly, taking care not to appear too "high hat," as social pretension was derisively labeled in Pine Grove. Richter wore a gray striped sport jacket and gray slacks, rather than his more usual suit. Although occasionally he could be seen around town with an open collar, when he took Harvey out he always put on a tie. Harvey chose a suit of her favorite blue, and Richter was pleased to see that she once again filled it out, and that her cheeks had regained their rosy hue.

Richter was especially fond of Mrs. Yocum's milk tarts; occasionally when he had not been to one of her dinners for a while, Mrs. Yocum would have a plate of them delivered to him at his home. That particular afternoon in May, the tarts were up to Mrs. Yocum's high standard and the dinner conversation as delightfully rollicking as Harvey, kept from any excitement for weeks, could wish. Richter also was swept up in the fun, writing about it at length to Vene.[8] For Decoration Day, May 30, Harvey seemed well enough to participate in most of the day's activities. With Vene at home after her semester at New York University, Richter allowed Harvey to invite Fred and Emily to stay overnight. But he insisted that she stay at home and rest when he, Vene, Fred, and Emily drove to the cemetery to tend the family graves. Joe and Edna met them at the grave site, as did Joe's youngest son Bill, his wife Rita, and their two girls, Diane and Deborah. Because Bill and his family lived next door to Joe in Reading, Richter had seen more of them than he had the families of Joe's older children, or those of Fred's boys, Frederick and Eduard, both raising families of their own.

Writing in his journal after the day's festivities, Richter commented that Decoration Day 1961 had turned out to be the best of any he remembered. Days when all three brothers could be together were increasingly important to Richter as he and his brothers aged. Earlier that year he had answered a student's inquiry about his life and its relation to his fiction with a long reply. About his

18. Conrad and Harvena Richter in Pine Grove, *circa* 1965.

brothers Joe and Fred, Richter wrote "we had plenty of fights as boys but they are my best friends now."[9] And so they were, as he described them with disarming simplicity and candor; so too was Stanley Achenbach, Harvey's younger brother, who had become, since their return to live in Pine Grove, an almost daily presence in his life and Harvey's. Although in earlier years he had found family gatherings a burden, Richter had come to experience them differently. He no longer dreaded such events for days in advance, and afterwards his comments in his journal were less likely to be complaints about lost time than descriptions of moments he had enjoyed. Later that summer he made a point of taking his brother Joe to see the cemetery plots he bought for himself and Harvey, not as close to those of his parents as he would have liked, but not very far away.[10]

It was the grandchildren of Richter's brother Joe who saw him at his best. With Vene still unmarried and his own chance to be a grandfather fading away, he often sought out children and especially the young daughters of his nephew Bill. When Diane and Deborah visited, Richter would take them off for an hour or more, leaving their parents and grandparents to talk with Harvey. If the weather was fair, they would go outdoors to discover with Uncle Connie what they could about the flowers and trees and birds around them. If the weather was rainy or cold, he would lead them to his desk in the dining room, showing them editions of his books in exotic foreign languages. Once Richter returned from his desk with a copy of *Tacey Cromwell* to give to Diane and Debbie. Before Rita Richter could gather herself to say that her daughters were too young for a book about a reformed bawdy house madam, Richter slid the paperback into her hands. It was a Persian edition, printed in the elegant arcs and indecipherable squiggles of Arabic.[11]

Around town the children all knew him, and as often as not called him Connie. When the local newspaper referred to him once as "Pine Grove's leading citizen," Richter visited the editor to ask that he never repeat the expression. The older children knew Richter as the writer of the novel they had read in school, *The Light in the Forest*, and many more had seen the Disney film made from Richter's novel. They saw him walking to the post office and on other errands around the small town stretched along two main streets, and on warm spring afternoons he could sometimes be seen at high school baseball games, sitting high up on the wooden bleachers. They recognized at a distance the tweed jacket with patches on the elbow and baggy dress pants he habitually wore, even to ice-skate on the old canal.[12] Often he walked in the early evening, as dusk settled into night, strolling along with his hands behind his back. Perhaps he would be on his way to see Augusta Filbert, or, if his route chanced to take him by the home of Lawrence Hoy, the organist for St. John's Lutheran, Richter would look in to see if Hoy was busy with a piano lesson. If Hoy was still with a pupil, Richter would wave through the window; if Hoy had finished lessons for the evening, Richter would stop in for a visit.

Stories about Richter made their way through the different social groups of the community. After the new post office was built, they heard that he had stopped delivery of mail to his home, preferring the brief walk each day to pick up his mail. A local dentist spread the tale about Richter becoming angry over the background music in the dental office, insisting that it be turned off while he was there. Many knew he wore thin slices of adhesive tape on the fingers of his left hand, and thought they knew why. It was to keep from biting his nails, Richter had himself told them, which was almost the truth. The finger taping had actually begun decades earlier, in Albuquerque, just after Arthur Achenbach's death from an infection in his nose that developed into blood poisoning. Since that time Richter had tried to train himself to keep his hands away from his nose, including intermittent periods when he taped the fingertips of his left hand. He renewed this practice when he decided that there must be some connection between slight infections in his nose and his ongoing troubles with his prostate, a supposition for which he had no medical authority. A widely repeated story about Richter's peculiar notions came from his especially unusual request at the bank. When cashing a check he always asked the teller for uncirculated bills. Finally Charlie Hikes, a bank vice president and family friend, asked him why he insisted on new bills. Richter replied that it was to keep from carrying germs into his home, where they might infect Harvey.

With his friends Richter was not reticent about his political views, which were conservative. Believing as he did that individual hardship was necessary for spiritual growth and that the evolutionary journey must be taken alone, he saw much more harm than good in social programs meant to help whole classes of people. Friends like Richard Wheeler chose to avoid political discussions with Richter, though Julia Hikes, the novelist who wrote as Julia Truitt Yenni, could not resist an argument any more than Richter could. In such disputes Richter was far more concerned with the idea of right government than with the practical reality of programs proposed by either political party, and though he conscientiously read a daily newspaper he was seldom as fully engaged by the international events or national politics he read there as he was by local and immediately personal concerns—the cutting of shade trees, the contamination of a mountain spring where he went for water, the smoldering fires at the city dump. Only the more catastrophic or dramatic of world events would be recorded in worrying journal entries, and these too were spurred by personal concerns. It was primarily Richter's anxiety about a nuclear attack on New York, where Vene lived, that prompted occasional journal entries on the Korean conflict during the Eisenhower administration. When John F. Kennedy became the Democratic Party's nominee for president in 1960, Richter like many other Americans worried about the consequence of electing a Catholic to the White House, but he worried more about trusting the office to too young a man. He was so concerned that Kennedy was insufficiently seasoned to lead the free world that shortly after Kennedy's election, Richter wrote to the new president urging him to be stalwart against foreign aggressors: "Our founding fathers pledged their lives and fortunes, and you must pledge ours. A cowardly nation incurs only contempt trying to buy respect from its fellow nations with money and retreat. A brave man or nation requires neither."[13]

Early in July 1962 Richter completed the first draft of his fictional biography of his father. He had promised Harvey that he would take a vacation from writing once he finished the first draft, but four days later he was again at his typewriter, and in just two months he finished revising the second novel of his family trilogy. In spite of two long periods when Harvey's abscesses kept him from writing, he completed his chronicle of his father's ministry, half again as long as *The Waters of Kronos*, in just about his usual two years. The accomplishment was all the more remarkable in that Richter seldom extended his morning writing sessions, even when his writing was going well. When he attempted to work for longer periods, the additional close work of reading and writing put a strain on his eyes and, he thought, his heart, bringing on episodes of his heart behaving erratically. These occurred primarily at night, while he was lying down, robbing him of sleep and leaving him, the next day, restless and fretful of the onset of another series of "gyrations," as he had come to call his heart's fluttering and palpitations. During this period he developed a mannerism that his wife and daughter soon learned to recognize, Richter holding his left wrist lightly with the fingers of his right hand, checking his pulse. He did this habitually, stopping on the landing of a flight of stairs or pausing on a walk to the post office or to Augusta Filbert's. Harvey and Vene both protested that he was only increasing his anxiety and risking more gyrations by repeatedly checking on his heart, but to no avail.

When he visited doctors on his own behalf, their diagnoses repeated what doctors had been telling him for years: there was no evidence of heart disease; his irregularly beating heart was caused by nerves. They prescribed drugs to lessen his nervous tension, but these drugs brought on side effects that interfered with his writing.[14] Thorazine left Richter drowsy the next morning; chlordiazepoxide, when taken in sufficient dosage to stop the gyrations, resulted in dizziness that lasted for days. He had no better success with probanthine or the various quinine derivatives. Phenobarbitol had no noticeable effect, nor did hydrozyzine; procainamide helped occasionally, but only briefly. Antacids had no effect. The tranquilizers thioridazine and reserpine, though of some help with the gyrations, gave Richter a day of agitated nerves. He could not write while taking such drugs, and so he would not take them. Although he experimented intermittently with all the drugs doctors prescribed, he relied primarily on his own regimen of vitamins, healthful foods, and restricted hours of writing and reading. Once when having an especially difficult time sleeping, he wrote to J. I. Rodale, publisher of *Prevention Magazine*, suggesting that Rodale market an alarm clock with a slow, sleep-inducing tick.[15]

Throughout the two years when he was writing his version of his father's life, Richter recorded little in his journal about the actual process, seldom noting more than the completion of a chapter. Daily entries about the "hard going," worries about false starts and unsolvable plot difficulties did not occur, not even during the months in Florida in winter 1960–61 when his daily writing sessions yielded only a single slim chapter. Nor did he record his annoyance at distractions, as he had done so often in the past. Only once during Vene's month-long visit to Pine Grove in June 1961 was he provoked into the petulant shorthand typical of other times when Vene returned home: "IT JUST DOESN'T GO with everything going on here, V[ene] dawdling and discussing at breakfast, H[arvey] staying up when she should be resting, people phoning, Fred's [family] coming. I must have peace, rest, change, quiet; can't work, am nearly at end of my rope."[16] Otherwise, from the record of the journal, Richter seems to have succeeded as never before in keeping the daily vicissitudes in perspective. He was simply no longer subject to worries that he was unable to complete a novel, that he had gone dry. However badly a day's writing went, the unsolved problems only delayed his ultimate success; they no longer seemed ill omens.

Separately he kept a special devotional book, small enough to carry with him, in which he inscribed quotations he took from Christian Science literature, the Bible, and other sources. Inside its maroon plastic cover he placed a snapshot of himself from the thirties, a visual counterpart to his various exhortations to "brace up" and his habitual and long-standing charge to present himself as— indeed to be—more amiable, more approachable, more in touch with other people. It was the photograph of himself below which he had written "Smile, damn you, smile."

Through Harvey's bouts with abscesses Richter devoted at least part of each day's journal entry to her, commenting on how she slept at night, how well she had eaten, what vitamins she had taken, and whether she had rested sufficiently during the day. Often he merely speculated about her health; after all their years together he still could not count on Harvey's telling him truly how she felt. Good days were cause for elation. At the end of October 1960, Erd and Jeppy Brandt stopped by to visit so that Brandt could pick up a typescript of the new novel to consider for the *Saturday Evening Post*. In his journal Richter observed first that the Brandts had come on the thirtieth, perhaps a warning that the *Post* would turn his novel down. (Richter had learned to be wary of the number thirty during his days working on newspapers, where "30" was used as an editorial mark to designate the termination of a news story.) Speculating that Erd might be unhappy about his impending retirement, Richter described his old friend as looking "a little dull, as if he had taken a sleeping pill the night before, or perhaps some barbiturate." Jeppy, though, "looked fine," and Harvey "looked the best of all . . . rosy cheeked, plump faced, happy." In another paragraph Richter amplified his thoughts about his wife: "So good to come home last evening from walk and call for a few minutes on A[ugusta] old and withered and complaining and see H[arvey] standing in her cap and pajamas ready for bed on the porch, cheerful, smiling, rosy-cheeked, compact. Felt lucky to have her."[17] After Harvey's first bout with abscesses, he admonished himself in his journal to remember Harvey's special value to him and to his daughter: "She is the spark that keeps V[ene] and me going, writing. When she is ill or unhappy, we are desolate. Her spirit is what fires us, makes us content." But they must remember that she had, after all, her own needs: "her spirit must be kept up, fed. Frost or heat will blight it."[18] At times he worried guiltily that her abscesses were caused by compounding the restrictions of her life as an invalid with those placed on her as a writer's spouse. Harvey needed to be encouraged, not criticized, he told himself,[19] though dealing with her in her varying degrees of illness and health took forbearance he could not muster when he discovered her doing self-destructive things against all good advice: "The better H[arvey] is," he complained, "the more she must be held down."[20]

Caught in his conflicting feelings and often afraid that he might lose her, his emotional composure was at times more than a little frayed. "Something must be done about my wife," he began his call for help to Dr. Henry C. Jernigan, the tuberculosis specialist from New Mexico.[21] And to Dr. Hawley H. Seiler, the Florida surgeon who had lanced the abscess in 1961, Richter ended a letter asking for advice by admitting that he himself felt "imprisoned, trapped, frustrated" by Harvey's illness, unable to work at all, even to read proofs from his novel, desperately in need of help.[22] During the fourth year of struggling with the abscesses, Richter wrote a remarkable letter to his daughter, admitting that Harvey's depression had him upset and worried for her survival. Drawing on Cornillier's descriptions of astral life in *The Survival of the Soul* and on his own theory of spiritual development, he assessed his wife's condition:

> Mother frightened me today, so lifeless and discouraged. It took a great deal to get her to feel she is not useless or no account but is really the stout heart that has kept us going all these years, made a home for us and the conditions under which both of us produced creative work. Our work sustains us but she has nothing. . . . I have a notion you and I will find her soul far above ours. She might have even chosen the humble part she has played. And the suffering she has had, the years of it and her rising above it, would refine the astral self far further. What she has gone through would submerge you and me, and she has always up to

now done it cheerfully and with rare courage. Her instincts and intimations are signs of a higher self. But we must restore her mortal belief in herself, her usefulness and worth, or we won't have her long.[23]

A month later, in May 1963, writing in his journal, he admitted to worries he could not explain even to Vene. On this occasion it was Richter rather than his wife who was despondent, a feeling brought on by a minor difference of opinion that had escalated into shouting and bitter words. The result was, for Richter, another meditation based on his speculations about the causal relation between fortune, good and ill, and the actions of spirits from the astral—Cornillier's "those that be." The entry ends with a revealing expression of his lifelong anxiety about being "forsaken and alone," separated from loved ones: "I suspect H[arvey] has given me strength from her stout being, mortal or immortal, and support, and once she is on her own, freed from this partnership which those who be seem to have engendered, she will go free in her own orbit with little interest in mine or ours."[24]

Would Harvey love him after she was gone? Would he lose his wife into her own sphere where her spirit would no longer have any interest in him? The worry echoes Richter's anguished question just before the death of his father. Did his mother still love him, he then asked. And his reply: "Nobody knows." On Christmas Day 1962 he had recorded another version of this question. The sight of migratory robins, newly arrived from the north to Bradenton, Florida, led him to reflect on his impending flight from this world to the next: "'I am going to migrate, too,' I told the robins on the wires this morning on my walk. 'I am going farther than you. Whether anyone will be there, I don't know, but I hope so.'"

Two weeks earlier, Richter had answered the letter of a reader from Ohio, Hattie Chesney, who had written an eerily perceptive commentary on *The Waters of Kronos*. It was a great book, Chesney said, one that would be read for centuries. But it had given her nightmares. *The Waters of Kronos* had within it a "stark horror," the sensations of "pain stripped naked." Here was a reader able to understand the novel's conclusion: as Chesney wrote, "There was no doubt— you left none—that the man in the book was yourself and that you had come hunting into the past of your boyhood for assurance that the future was not oblivion."[25] Richter replied openly to Chesney, acknowledging the book's painfulness to him as well, a sadness brought on by his fear that all earthly love is only temporary. Will we wake into the next life, he asked, to discover ourselves not as we have seemed in this? Perhaps we will discover "that only the affinities of the spirit or real self within us persist, that those who cared so much for us in the flesh may now be uninterested in us or prevented by conditions to live with us even after they themselves have passed over, and unable to bestow the visible affection that they did in the past."[26] The idea of losing into eternity the love of his mother and the love of his wife was for Richter utterly haunting. After death could his mother still care for him? Could Harvey? If Harvey was, as he suspected, a higher spirit than he, would she be too far beyond him for communication in the astral? Once free from life would Harvey choose to be free from him as well? These anxieties lurked behind Richter's thoughts about death, and his unease found its symbolic expression in his memory of the look on his father's face in death. Was it a sign, an intimation that, on his first vision of an afterlife, John Absalom Richter had been bitterly disappointed?

T W O

Although the added publicity for *The Waters of Kronos* brought on by the National Book Award resulted in no additional sales for Richter (the sum of its sales for the first six months of 1961 had been exactly 298, Richter remarked acidly to Paul Reynolds),[27] the award did bring a flurry of invitations to speak and offers from colleges and universities to teach a seminar or spend a semester as a writer-in-residence. To each of these Richter gave essentially the same reply: he could not accept the kind invitation, for he was a late bloomer who found himself, at an age when others settle into a more leisurely life, with several important books yet to write. "There is too much to do and too little time to do it in,"[28] he wrote to each. During one week in June, Richter opened his post office box to find letters from two graduate students, Clifford Edwards from the University of Michigan and Marvin LaHood from Notre Dame, both declaring plans to write doctoral dissertations about Richter's fiction and asking his help. Later the same week Richter opened a letter from a professor in Texas, Edwin Gaston, who wrote to ask Richter to come speak at Stephen F. Austin State College. When Richter declined, Gaston wrote again to say that he had been commissioned by Twayne Publishers to write a biographical and critical work about Richter and asked if he could come to Pine Grove for an interview.[29] The letters from all three were deferential and academic, and to each Richter responded conscientiously but cautiously, agreeing to provide what help he could. Such scholarly interest was a register of his growing reputation and could be a factor in further raising it, he understood, and he encouraged all three, if mildly. The letters that such people wrote, and the questions they asked, were not ones that particularly spurred his interest, and he was unsure how his answers to their questions would be received. Before mailing his replies, Richter read them to both Harvey and Vene. When a question seemed to him opaquely academic, he would rely on his daughter's expertise as a literary critic. Vene would explain the questions to her father, jot down his replies, then type up answers for him.

The most persistent of the questioners was Clifford Edwards, perhaps because Richter, recognizing that Edwards took seriously his theories of human evolution through energy deprivation, actively encouraged him. Although he acquiesced to interviews with Gaston and LaHood, Richter repeatedly urged Edwards to visit and entered into a two-year correspondence with the graduate student, asking questions as well as answering them. When toward the end of that time Edwards wrote to say that his graduation had been delayed for a year, his dissertation committee wanting him to work further on his thesis, Richter felt the blow personally, worrying that his encouragement had in the end interfered with Edwards rather than helped him.[30]

Richter spent half a day preparing for Edwin Gaston's visit on August 23, 1962, only to be disappointed when Gaston seemed to consider the visit a courtesy call rather than a working session. To illustrate his writing method Richter showed Gaston his notebooks, but only briefly—Gaston's questions in person being no more engaging than those he had sent by mail, and primarily bibliographical. Richter found Marvin LaHood easier to talk to when he visited in summer 1963, though he was made uncomfortable by the young scholar's eager enthusiasm. Reluctantly Richter allowed the Notre Dame graduate student to leave behind his article on Richter's writing, intending to have Harvey and perhaps Vene read and comment on it. But after LaHood's article was misplaced in Harvey's pile of reading material and neglected for over two months, Richter then felt obliged to read and comment himself. Returning the article with apologies for keeping it so long, Richter was as kind as honesty would allow him to be: "We found much of interest but my wife felt that my stories and books are not quite made over the same last. My own feeling is that what I write about escapes most critics. It is not material rewards for physical hardship but something more."[31]

Richter saved for his journal his thoughts about what it was that critics missed: "They all misunderstand me. I write simply about people I admire, principally those who have the vision to accept their life and its hardships as something given to grapple with and try to overcome for both temporary and permanent benefit."[32] The permanent benefit Richter refers to is of course spiritual, part of the process of psychic evolution he had theorized in *Human Vibration* and *The Mountain on the Desert*. Richter characters like Sayward and Doña Ellen accept their hardships as things life has given them to bear, as do Colonel Brewton and Tacey Cromwell; the result is a raised consciousness, a vision that sustains them and, at times, even some lucky few around them. Harry Donner, Richter's fictional representation of his father, has that same vision. There would be, however, one significant difference between *A Simple Honorable Man* and Richter's earlier novels. In his novel about his father's life, Richter asked more openly than before just why so much unhappiness was visited on such seemingly good people. Why were men like his father, good men dedicated to their God, left to toil in the wilderness, with little acknowledgment of their accomplishment or worth? And why, so often, did their efforts encounter bedeviling circumstances, as if some power chose deliberately to thwart their good intentions? These were questions Richter asked about his own most important work, *The Mountain on the Desert*, which had been all but ignored by readers, and about his inability to earn enough from his novels to allow him to write further about his energy theories. Was the fictional Harry Donner's reward for his life of faith and good works to come in an afterlife? What, then, of the real John Absalom Richter's bitter mouth in death, so vexing to Conrad Richter?

And what of Lottie Richter's long years of humiliating poverty? What reward would there be for that? Near the novel's end, Richter allows his fictional representation of his mother to reflect on her life as a minister's wife. Valeria Donner is dying, and like Sayward Wheeler in her final days, she prefers the memories of friends now dead to the people of her husband's ministry, who were not her people but his. Her final thought in the chapter is her hope that at her funeral Hal will use his special gift for prayer to convey to God her fervent wish—that her loved ones on earth will remain loved ones in an afterlife: "And if it is possible, may we be kept in communion in death as in life until reunited by the river."[33]

After Valeria Donner's death, Harry Donner has no doubt about her place in heaven; his faith is whole. There would be one flicker of worry in his own last days, and it would concern the "communion in death" for which he had prayed. Visiting Valeria's grave with his son Johnny, Harry stops to watch a flock of migrating birds fly up into the sky and wing off to the south. A few strays are left behind, flitting from bush to bush, feeling the pull of the long journey but not yet ready to depart. About these stragglers Harry Donner says half to himself, "You'd wonder how they'd ever catch up to the rest." Hearing these words,

John Donner turns to see on his father's face a surprising look, "a wry expression at the mouth, an expression the son was not to understand until years later he felt it on himself in the same cemetery at seventy."[34]

In *A Simple Honorable Man*, seventy-one-year-old Conrad Richter did not pursue the memory of his father's bitter mouth in death; instead, he chose as the source of the son's quest another characteristic of John Richter, one he was notorious for, groaning loudly in his sleep. In the novel's final chapter, John Donner revisits the various churches of his father's ministry, pondering the meaning of the apparent misery his father experienced in sleep. At a small country church he encounters an old organ tuner, painstakingly tuning each key. When he has finished, the tuner tests out his work by playing Bach: he always played Bach, he explains to John Donner, because Bach "groans a little but he never stops praising God."[35] When the tuner plays again, Donner sits listening to the prayer of thanksgiving pouring forth, a profligacy of beauty issuing out of the church to dissipate into the air, unheard, unacknowledged. John Donner's reflection on this experience closes the novel: "He thought, all this improvidence of praise for God and good will toward men, lavished, wasted, on an obscure log church in an obscure mountain valley, poured out through the open door on stony fields, worn rail fences and a poor yellow dirt road that led to the small weathered barns and smaller unpainted houses of obscure unremarkable men." Once again Richter had written an ending that vexed readers. When asked to explain, Richter would reply that he intended "to show by contrast of Johnny's point of view what Harry Donner had accomplished in his life." Although he could have added to his ending an explanatory clause—that "Christ's disciples and those he labored among were for the most part obscure unremarkable men"—such explanations would be "too obvious" and he had hoped that "Harry Donner's life would have stood untouched above any such thoughts of his son."[36]

Through most of the first draft, Richter's working title for his second volume of his family trilogy had been "The Man of Kronos," a title he abandoned after talking with a book reviewer from Chicago at the National Book Award ceremony. Speculating on *The Waters of Kronos*'s slow sales in Chicago, the reviewer suggested that the alien sound of "kronos" had put buyers off—that and the book's gloomy dust jacket. Searching for a title that would attract rather than repel, Richter finally settled on *A Simple Honorable Man*, modifying a declaration James Joyce had made in a letter to Norah, an assertion Richter liked well enough to choose as his novel's epigraph: "I have enormous belief in the power of a simple honorable soul." But as important as sales were to Richter, they were not his overriding concern. When Knopf's sales staff expressed doubts about marketing a book with that title and suggested "Parson Donner" as one they could more enthusiastically promote, Richter declined. It demeaned his father's life work, he thought. His brother Joe agreed. If Fred had thoughts about a title, his older brother did not record them. But Fred did protest at being depicted in the novel as a secretary for a pottery company, and his wife Emily disliked being named "Martha." Both these details could be, and were, changed, but on the title Richter was adamant. The title would be *A Simple Honorable Man*, with no comma separating the two all-important adjectives.

A month before the official publication day of *A Simple Honorable Man*, *Life* magazine sent staff writer Jane Alexander and photographer Carl Mydans to Pine Grove to prepare a feature on Richter. At Mydans's request, Richter led the *Life* writer and photographer on a walking tour of Pine Grove, then drove them out into the anthracite country surrounding Richter's hometown, stopping at an abandoned coal breaker, a mining patch, and the home of the alleged Molly Maguire, Paddy Dolan. Along the way Mydans snapped several hundred photographs of Richter, using Pine Grove streets and the Pennsylvania countryside for background. Richter was taken with Mydans, admiring the ease with which the photographer overcame the reluctance of people to be photographed. Yet after Alexander and Mydans had departed, Richter found himself worrying that *Life* might choose to emphasize the economic depression of the area, embarrassing the community. When Richter wrote Mydans to express his concern, Mydans replied quickly. He intended no such result, Mydans wrote, and to illustrate what he had in mind he sent a portrait of Richter that for technical reasons could not be used. In it Richter lounges against one of the shade trees on Tulpehocken Street, arms crossed, smiling generously beneath the downturned brim of his favorite hat. It would be a picture Richter could take pleasure in, with no need to remonstrate with himself for seeming too stern, unfriendly, unlikable. Rather, he seems the man his neighbors would almost always describe him to be: modest, somewhat shy but nonetheless self-assured—a man at ease, comfortably in place in his community.

Time magazine also sent a photographer for a portrait to accompany the magazine's review of *A Simple Honorable Man*. A "colorless" man, his portrait of Richter turned out, to Richter's mind, as bland as the man who had come to photograph him. Richter had better luck with John Hutchins, book critic for the *New York Herald Tribune*, who visited on April 13, 1962. Hutchins announced openly that his purpose in writing a background piece on Richter was to attract more readers to Richter's novels. True to his word, his article in the *Tribune* book section on April 22 was a rave for Richter's fiction in general, as was Coleman Rosenberger's accompanying review of *A Simple Honorable Man*, which called attention to Richter's creation of a country parson as "an enormously revealing portrait, and one of great psychological validity," in a novel "studded with insights."[37] With a single exception, other reviewers were equally kind, passing over the novel's lax narrative structure and emphasizing Richter's success in writing a psychologically convincing and entertaining novel about a simple and a good man. In his review in the *Boston Herald*, Edward Wagenknecht went so far as to suggest that "it may even be that simple honorable men are due for a renascence."[38] But despite the good reviews, the new novel sold only slightly better than *The Waters of Kronos*: 22,000 copies, of which 6,000 were to a cut-rate book club, for which Richter received only ten cents a copy. Such sales seemed a final comment upon his father's years of toil with little recognition. "Dad's life was always unlucky," Richter wrote in his journal.[39]

Richter continued to tell himself that he had three important books to write, but he was too uneasy about his depleting savings to attempt any of these. *A Simple Honorable Man* had taken two years to write; when it had not sold to a book club or as a serial in the *Post* he knew he would not make two years' income from it. Well before the actual publication of *A Simple Honorable Man* he was spending his mornings planning a novel set in Clark's Valley and based on characters he remembered from his years at Pine Tree Farm. From former neighbors in Clark's Valley Richter had heard that Esther Minsker, the daughter of one of Harvey's maids at Pine Tree Farm, had inherited $9,000 and a farm from a man who believed her to be his daughter. With this as his kernel Richter began plotting a story he would first call "The Three Grandfathers," then simply *The Grandfathers*, in which two families dispute which has the right to claim Chariter Murdock, the child of an unmarried woman, as one of its own. Richter intended his story to be another portrait of a strong-willed woman, calm in the face of confusion. In this novel, however, the upsets and alarms would be comic, for Richter a delightful change. Writing the novel would give him the pleasure of re-creating the special expressiveness of the backcountry people whose speech had been the model for his Ohio trilogy, and it would allow him to draw on his many reminiscences of Clark's Valley, including the antics of the families who served as models for Chariter's.

Richter worked on this novel through the summer and fall, gathering incidents and plotting out a course of narration. With so many memories of Clark's Valley fresh in his mind, in November he accepted an offer to write an article for *Country Beautiful*, "Valley from the Past," a remembrance of the years at Pine Tree Farm. When the article was finished and mailed just before the end of November, Richter packed up and carried with him to Florida a substantial manuscript for his Clark's Valley novel. There the writing went so well that Richter broke his winter pattern of reduced work and set himself an ambitious goal of three pages each morning, a goal he accomplished often enough so that by late spring 1963, back in Pine Grove, Richter was revising his completed first draft, working especially to capture the lyricism of untutored native speech. That spring Harvey suffered through her fourth year of trouble with abscesses, but by the end of April she was sufficiently recovered for Richter to note in his journal that Harvey was "her old, busy, industrious, improving self."[40] On June 1 Richter had a completed version of his novel to read to his wife and daughter. From its opening introduction of Grandpap, "Ant" Dib, Uncle Heb, and Chariter Murdock, the story announces itself as a lighthearted tale, a novel of comic incidents, leisurely pursuing its twin plots. In the first, the young Chariter, just old enough to be thinking of marriage, is curious to discover who her father might have been—a secret her mother has kept from her. In the second, Chariter must deal with her disappointment when she discovers that the man she plans to marry has other ideas, conniving to cohabit with her rather than marry her. Herself born out of wedlock and surrounded by siblings and cousins who were also the offspring of illegitimate relationships, Chariter has set for herself a different standard. While the story might be comic, its heroine has the qualities of all Richter's heroines. Chariter knows intuitively exactly what is right for her. She might fail to achieve it, but she will never be diverted to another, a lesser goal.

Reading the novel to Harvey and Vene took five hours, including a break for dinner and pauses for criticism: there was too much talk about grandfathers, his wife and daughter thought. And too many colloquialisms. Early chapters were "too sweet," and others "not natural." But though Harvey and Vene agreed with Richter that the story was light, without much of an idea, nonetheless Richter was encouraged; they had often interrupted his reading with their laughter. By September 7 Richter had his typescript ready to mail to Reynolds, with a letter asking for his thoughts about selling it first as a magazine serial or even a play. When Richter inferred from Reynolds's reply that his agent had little hope for the novel, Reynolds once again had to protest. "You are wrong about a lack of enthusiasm for *The Grandfathers*," he replied. "I just write bad letters." There was no misinterpreting Alfred Knopf's reaction to the new novel when his letter arrived. Knopf announced he was "absolutely delighted" with Richter's first comic novel. Calling the tooth-pulling scene "one of the great comic episodes of our time," he predicted that it would be anthologized separately.[41]

Glad for the compliments, Richter nonetheless was more interested in sales predictions. He was also concerned about the reaction of his former neighbors in Clark's Valley and uneasy enough about the possibility of lawsuits to ask Knopf to consult his legal department. Although he had set his novel among the hills of western Maryland and had changed names and all distinguishing personal characteristics and family circumstances, some of the events of the novel were based on actual occurrences in Clark's Valley. And for Richter there was another concern: some of the people of Clark's Valley might have their feelings hurt. Richter did not want any of his former neighbors to think he was ridiculing them. Far from it: "We loved them all," he wrote, "the drunken and rascals alike, for they were very nice to us."[42]

Waiting for the galley proof for *The Grandfathers* and undecided what book to write next, Richter took up the article he had agreed in May to write on Pine Grove for a book on small towns, *A Vanishing America*. Part of the enticement to write this article had been the list of contributors, which included Hodding Carter, William O. Douglas, and A. B. Guthrie; another was the book's title, an open invitation to Richter to return to a favorite lament, the loss in modern generations of creativity, individuality, and old-fashioned vigor. But after spending, sporadically, October, November, and much of December crafting "Individualists Under the Shade Trees," Richter found himself admitting that he was not a writer of facts and opinions but of feelings and people.[43] His forte was not the jeremiad, not even the gentle one. It was almost the middle of January 1964 before Richter completed the article on Pine Grove. By then he had been in Florida for over a month, settled into a guest house at Riviera Beach. Much of that time Richter had been feeling "greatly discouraged" because of his nervous heart, and the unexpected death of a friend from Pine Grove, Pete Henninger, left him thinking about life's end, the winding down of the body and mind into final extinction.

What made the experience especially trying for Richter were the long, empty days when his heart would not let him work. "This nuisance of dying," his December 10 entry had begun, describing the end of life as a mundane exasperation, comparing it to particular experiences he had especially dreaded but been forced to endure—"like going to church, driving the freeway to L.A. and 3000 miles home, and attending the National Book Award." On December 20 he complained: "I can't bury myself in my work as I always have." Later that day he added to this lament an acknowledgment that more emotional baggage was attached to death than he had earlier understood. "It isn't the dying. It's the feelings and emotions and elaborate nervous system that has built fears into us that make it bad. Without them, we would subside into death as easily as a fallen raindrop into the ground."

After finishing "Individualists Under the Shade Trees" Richter spent little time writing during the remaining weeks in Florida, though he did continue to make notes for the third novel of his family trilogy. Once back in Pine Grove, Richter began the process of turning the notes into a novel about his life, despite the heart troubles that continued to plague his nights. When the first copies of *The Grandfathers* arrived, no letter from Alfred Knopf was included, to Richter a bad sign. Nor did he like the picture of himself on the dust jacket, too mild and glum. But after an hour leafing unhappily through his new novel, Richter rebounded as he often did; if the book was not to be a success, at least he could still write another—just as long as he was "given health."[44] Shortly thereafter, Richter decided to put away the third part of his family trilogy. Instead he would take the advice he had himself given to another would-be writer, a correspondent of several years, John Jones. He would do a novel with a single large subject, as he had done with *The Sea of Grass*, *The Trees*, and the novel that continued to bring in the most income in royalties, *The Light in the Forest*.

On April 11, 1964, Richter wrote his daughter to say he was looking forward to her next visit so they could talk over what he would write next. Three days later Richter's journal entry records that he had made up his mind to write a story with a broad American historical theme, something legendary, a chronicle of the land or people as he had done with *The Sea of Grass* and the Ohio trilogy. Richter's thought was to take up again the plight of a white child who has been raised by American Indians. This time he would tell the story of a young woman who is forced to leave her Indian husband and return with her child to the settlement from which she had been taken. The loss of her Indian heritage, and the subsequent loss as well of her white identity and lawful right to property, connected in Richter's mind to the Indians' collective loss of their land. The novel would be a companion piece, not a sequel, to *The Light in the Forest*, though Richter intended to introduce the character of True Son into his new novel. Richter had regularly received letters from adolescents and adults alike, asking what had become of the young man who at book's end was unable to return to his Indian family, unwilling to return to his white. In the new novel Richter planned to have True Son appear briefly, answering the question about True Son's later life as he had responded to reader's questions about Sulie, the child lost in the wilderness of *The Trees*, by reintroducing her briefly in the final novel of that trilogy, *The Town*.

The week Richter began his new novel he noted in his journal that Vene had passed her doctoral orals. That same week he recorded that Harvey had startled him by reporting a pain in her right side, the advent, apparently, of a fifth year of problems with an abscess in her pleural cavity. Writing in his journal, Richter summarized how deeply worrying the looming illness seemed: "The whole long painful course of suffering stood before me in my mind and seemed insurmountable now with my heart condition."[45] In spite of his upset over Harvey's possible abscess, Richter spent most mornings at his desk, even after nights when he had been kept awake by his jumping, pulsing heart. Early in May he was at work on the second chapter of "The Lost Land," well enough satisfied with the draft to write humorously to Vene that after a morning writing the novel his letter to her sounded like an Indian speaking.[46] Apparently there would not be a fifth year of dealing with an abscess, the pain in Harvey's right side gradually dissipating, and once Richter had switched from the story of his own life to the story of Stone Girl's, his heart, while still irregular, at least allowed him to write mornings. But then on May 30 he suffered through the worst night of "fibrillations" he had yet experienced.

THREE

His daily writing limited severely by his erratic heart, Richter made the surprising choice to interrupt the story of Stone Girl and accept two additional writing tasks, both commissioned articles and both rather special circumstances. That he accepted the first was more easily understandable: it was to write an introduction to a Time-Life educational edition of *The Sea of Grass*, an opportunity for Richter to explain his sources for Lutie Brewton and by doing so to answer indirectly the charge that his plot and character were derived from Willa Cather's *A Lost Lady*.[47] The second choice was more problematic, an essay commissioned by a new magazine, *Sky*, sponsored by *American Heritage* magazine. Flattered by the request to be an initial contributor, Richter agreed to allow its editor, David McCullough, to visit him in Pine Grove to talk about possible topics. When he arrived at one o'clock on July 9, David McCullough turned out to be younger than Richter expected, about thirty, tall and poised and with a young man's easy charm. Quickly Richter settled into a comfortable conversation with his visitor, McCullough telling stories and Richter responding in kind, the two laughing together. At McCullough's request Richter gave him a tour of the town, the churches, the Mansion House that had once been the Conrad home, the lake, the canal. McCullough asked questions about everything and was obviously interested in Richter himself. Back at 11 Maple Street, Harvey served their visitor shoofly pie and ice cream.

McCullough drank his coffee black, Richter noted in his journal, adding that he had to rest after the young editor's departure, fighting off the heart pulsing, which had begun during their talk. Richter was unusually taken with his visitor and pleased to be offered the opportunity, if he wished, to write several articles. McCullough was "a very personable young fellow," Richter wrote to his daughter. In his journal he added that McCullough reminded him of himself at the same age.[48] In just over a week he was at work on an article on trees for *Sky*, putting his Indian novel aside while he wrote it; and before the middle of August his personal essay was ready to read to Harvey and Vene, then type and send to Reynolds.

That fall Vene took up her thesis proposal, for Richter another cause for worry about his daughter. After her adviser, Leon Edel, had approved it with glowing praise, Vene sent it to her father. Pleased and reassured by his daughter's proposal, Richter found himself encouraged that someday his daughter might take up his energy theories. "Your thesis was brilliant and brilliantly said," he wrote. "If I still believed as I once did that certain minor powers were trying to get through an understanding of the mechanism of thought to me, I would now have a suspicion that they had given me up and were grooming you to carry on someday. . . . For the first time I can see that you would be able to present them in a far more intellectual way than I who am only the simple and concrete workman rather than the architect."[49] To Vene her father's reply may have seemed a curious thought, and perhaps a disturbing one. Well accustomed to her father's modesty, she would not have been surprised by his description of himself as a simple workman. But Vene may have been struck by the "if I still believed" with which Richter chose to introduce the subject of his energy theories. Was he seriously doubting the importance of what he had written and of what he still planned to write? Was this more of the candor that had occasionally led him to admit that he was only 80 percent sure of the survival of the soul? Or was this a tactic, suggesting to his daughter that, as his own life came to an end, he hoped to pass on to her responsibility for explaining his theories? Certainly that thought was in his mind. When he proposed it more explicitly to Vene, she reacted sharply: her father's theories were a burden she did not intend to let him place on her.[50]

When Richter departed for Florida on December 10, he carried a draft of "The Lost Land" with all but the last chapter written and his plot complete. Stone

Girl's tale begins when her husband attempts to hide her far from the "Yengues," a journey that takes her and her child to the western shore of Lake Erie, then north to Lake Ontario, and finally back into the white settlements along the Susquehanna. There she is rejected twice by her father and her sister, who are unable to understand her behavior and even misinterpret the actions she takes to save her sister's life. Those actions cost Stone Girl the life of her own child. At novel's end Stone Girl's husband is dead, killed in a raid, and her child is dead, murdered by warring Indians. Without husband or child and cast out by her white father and sister, she has no choice but to depart with True Son for the land of the Tuscaroras, two orphans escaping far to the west of white civilization.

It was mid-March 1965 before Richter finished a draft of the companion novel. A problem had been, he wrote Vene, to keep himself from "getting infected" by clichéd television and film treatments of Indians.[51] Once he was satisfied that he had found an appropriate ending, Richter was ready to return to Pennsylvania and there begin to rewrite. In this draft he was especially concerned to create a tone and a mood to prepare for the novel's emotional climax, Stone Girl pausing to look behind her before turning forever from the family that has denied and rejected her. Richter found a useful correspondence in a collection of verse translations of Old English poetry. To Vene he wrote that the most famous of these alliterative poems, "The Wanderer," had become an inspiration to his revision and had even led him to compose a similar song for Stone Girl. "Some lines came to me and I spent part of the morning setting down something which may do when properly worked up,"[52] he wrote matter-of-factly. Those lines would grow into the poem with which Richter closed his novel, an imitation of the haunting lament of his model. Soon Richter dropped "The Lost Land" as a title for his novel and replaced it with his poem's title, "I Am the Wanderer." Later Vene would suggest a title from the poem's second and last lines:

> I am the wanderer. I am the exile,
> Banished to live in a country of strangers,
> Scanning their faces. None are familiar.
> Where are my fathers? Where are my people?
> They are no more. Their lands have been taken,
> Their graves are defiled, by barbarians rifled.
> Often at daybreak, often at twilight,
> Often in dreams rise the bitter longings
> For faces of brothers, for songs of their triumph,
> For sight of their village with blue smoke curling.

Rises no more the sun on their lodges.
Rises no moon to the sound of the love lute,
The heart is a shell, the limbs are the turtle,
The blood crawls slow like brown swamp water.
Only the heart like the wind never ceases,
Calling old names, the names of companions.
There is no answer. Sorrow walks with me.
Grief goes before me. No one comes after.
I am the exile. I am the wanderer,
Destined to die in a country of strangers.[53]

Curiously, Richter did not like A Country of Strangers as a title; he thought it would mislead possible buyers into thinking the book was a dreary story about loneliness in a foreign land. Of course that was just what Richter himself found so moving in the lament of "The Wanderer," and it was that emotion he attempted to weave into the texture of his novel. Rewriting A Country of Strangers, Richter found himself dwelling on Stone Girl's loss of her two families, both Indian and white. The image of Stone Girl setting off into the wilderness provided an emotional correspondent to Richter's own unhappiness as he thought about an eternity without his own family, as he thought about awakening from death to find himself alone.

In April Paul Reynolds wrote to say that there was serious interest in buying the movie rights to The Lady, teasing Richter with the possibility of a $25,000 windfall. The same week a flicker somehow got caught in the kitchen chimney. Richter worried that the struggles of the trapped bird were an omen. In May David McCullough returned. Sky having folded before its first publication, McCullough was once again editing for American Heritage and eager to write an article on Richter. On Friday, May 14, David McCullough arrived just before nine o'clock in the evening and remained until well after eleven. The next day Richter took him on another tour of the town, stopping to see the shoe repairman who talked while keeping an astonishing number of tacks poised between his lips, then to a grocery store where McCullough could hear people speaking Pennsylvania Dutch. Richter would introduce McCullough to the diminutive, doll-like Augusta Filbert, and to Dick Wheeler at his cabin in Swopes Valley. Later in the day Richter drove McCullough through the coal country, stopping again at the patch house of Paddy Doran. After a light evening meal back at 11 Maple Street, the two men shared the chore of doing the dishes. McCullough announced he intended to attend St. John's Church services the next morning, thinking Richter would offer to go with him, but Richter declined to go and gave no explanation for his refusal. On Sunday McCullough returned for a late lunch. Harvey had a loaf of homemade bread and a box of freshly cut lilies of the valley waiting for him.[54]

Just days after McCullough's visit a letter from Reynolds arrived, saying the movie deal for *The Lady* had fallen through, a disappointment that seemed to Richter another sign of his declining fortune and stature. Added to this failure was the folding of *Sky* and Reynolds's inability to sell elsewhere the article Richter had written, and also the unexpectedly small sale of *A Vanishing America*—only 7,000 copies, not enough to cover the $500 advance. These unhappy events led Richter to write a despondent journal entry, wondering if his next disappointment would be McCullough's losing interest in writing an article on him. But at seventy-four Richter was still able to turn such disappointments into a kind of bitter tonic: "I found the old strength in disappointment, neglect and failure," he wrote; and with that strength he promised himself not to falter but to undertake "what was left to me, hard work and God."[55]

In June came word of Alfred Knopf's heart attack, which would have been a jolt at any time for Richter, but it was especially startling at that moment. In a letter written just days before being hospitalized, Knopf had urged his author to accept a compromise proposal for two new editions that the author and publisher had been fighting over for at least three years. In August 1962 Richter had made what would be his last visit to his publisher's office in New York City, there lobbying Knopf to issue a special children's edition of *The Light in the Forest*. Richter was convinced that an edition with slightly larger type and illustrations would have a large sale without reducing the number of adult copies still being sold annually, primarily to libraries. Knopf disagreed, and his unwillingness to consider the juvenile edition fueled an angry outburst from the author. He was glad Knopf was not president of the United States, Richter exclaimed; if he were he'd behave like a South American dictator. That sally was the first skirmish in the battle over several years between the two headstrong men. Later in the meeting Knopf, ever the camera buff, attempted to take pictures of Richter. "Not when I'm angry, Alfred," Richter snapped at his publisher, and Knopf put the camera away.[56]

For his part, Knopf had his own idea for increasing Richter's sales and reputation, and he would try on several occasions to persuade Richter to agree to a single-volume edition of the three Ohio novels. But though Knopf offered an entirely new edition, handsomely printed and bound, the publishing costs, Knopf insisted, meant Richter would have to accept a lower royalty rate. To Richter's mind, the reduced rate, coupled with the loss of sales of the individual novels—which brought him yearly an average of $1,750—meant that whatever prestige came with the new edition would be paid for in lost royalties. He refused to accept, and there the issue remained, neither man being able to move the other, until late April 1965 when Knopf reopened the discussion with a new proposal, promising the juvenile edition if Richter would agree to the single-volume trilogy.

The rub for Richter was that once again Knopf was offering reduced royalty rates, and hard bargaining by both Reynolds and Richter led to only minor concessions from Knopf. Finally Reynolds wrote to say he was certain Knopf would not make a better offer; indeed, under his arrangement with Random House, Knopf was probably unable to.[57] Harvey urged Richter to accept, adding that her Christian Science practitioner had advised Richter to accept what had been offered. But still Richter hesitated until he received a final letter from Knopf saying that the contracts were "the absolute best" he could do and introducing a new line of thought, which would have caught immediately all of Richter's attention. "After all," he wrote, "neither of us is going to live forever, and I am determined that we should be committed to the trilogy in one volume as well as the juvenile illustrated edition of *The Light in the Forest* without further delay. I don't mean to sound ominous, but only to recognize the facts of life."[58] On June 16 Richter wrote to Knopf to accept, then to Vene to say he had acquiesced "more to end the suspense and arguments than anything else." The next day Alfred Knopf was hospitalized with a heart attack. Although Blanche Knopf would write reassuringly that Alfred was experiencing only "a little angina," Knopf remained hospitalized for a month. When he was able to write himself, Richter's publisher would confide that "just about the last thing" he had done before being taken to the hospital was the paperwork for the two editions.[59]

Alfred Knopf's sudden illness would of necessity have led Richter, still suffering regularly from his own heart's erratic behavior, to think again of help from doctors. A letter in August, one of several Richter sent to a new group of heart specialists, suggests just how difficult many of his nights had become:

> My irregularities have become very serious to me since palpitations with tremors in lower left abdomen and insides of the legs have set in whenever I lie down. If I can get on my feet quickly enough, they often soon subside but if I am too slow or have fallen asleep beforehand, they persist, grow worse with nausea and last from two to four hours, sometimes longer. During their duration it is almost impossible to lie down for then

the gyrations and tremors become really violent. However, once the siege is over, I have been able to lie down freely without taking further care. It's as if some change in the chemistry of the blood organs, such as the transfer of oxygen to needy parts, has been accomplished. . . . I try nightly to stop [the gyrations] by rising but getting up quickly six or eight times is pretty discouraging and the chances are it will catch me before that. If I am able to put off the threats by change of breathing and other devices for an hour or so, I am usually able to stay down for the rest of the night.[60]

Richter did not explain the "other devices," but the primary one was, at the onset of the palpitations, to wake Harvey and have her ride with him as he drove for an hour or more through the dark countryside surrounding Pine Grove, waiting for the gyrations to subside.

In late July Richter read his novel, still under the title "I Am the Wanderer," to Harvey and Vene. After one more revision, he was ready to send copies to Paul Wallace, a historian of early Pennsylvania, and to Walter Edmonds, author of *Drums Along the Mohawk* and other novels Richter admired for their historical accuracy, asking for their criticism. As with *The Light in the Forest,* Richter was determined to present fairly both sides of the conflict, with no idealizing of Indian life. On October 4 Richter had a typescript ready to mail—just before the onset of activities associated with his seventy-fifth birthday.

In effect the attempts to celebrate this milestone birthday had already begun, with substantial evidence that, despite Richter's worries to the contrary, many others were paying attention to his life. In March, shortly before returning to Pine Grove from Florida, Richter had found a biography of André Maurois in the Bradenton library. The night he finished reading it Richter found himself feeling "inexpressibly sad" at the contrast of his own life with Maurois's: "How many well known people he knew. How easily he moved among them. How few have I ever known or even seen and how awkwardly and boorishly I [behave] among them, gauche, tongue tied, unpolished. What poor judgments I show."[61] But however attractive the French novelist's life might have seemed from the distance of a biography, when Richter himself was presented with opportunities to play the literary lion, his judgment unerringly led him immediately to withdraw. As regularly as invitations arrived to meetings of P.E.N. and the National Institute of Arts and Letters, he turned them down. Within the previous few months he had declined invitations to speak at Columbia and Harvard Universities, he had put off again the yearly request from Ted Morrison to participate in the Bread Loaf summer writing seminars, and he had written a polite but firm refusal to Paul Engle's invitation to come to Iowa University as a writer-in-residence.[62] During the spring and summer he had received as well two invitations to dine with Governor William Scranton at the governor's mansion in Harrisburg. After declining both, Richter was surprised to receive Scranton's congratulatory telegram on October 12, the day before his birthday. Then came word of a special resolution passed by the state legislature, citing him for his life's accomplishments. As for his actual birthday, Richter celebrated it as he always had when at home in Pine Grove. Joe and Edna came to visit, bringing with them a birthday cake.

One especially unhappy event occurred shortly after Richter's birthday: the death of Augusta Filbert. Always frail, Augusta seldom left her bed during her last months, and often when Richter visited that fall he would simply sit by her bedside while she slept. On October 27 Augusta Filbert was hospitalized, and on October 30 she died. "Another 30," Richter noted in his journal. With Augusta's death an era had ended. To Vene, who had often joined her father on visits to the sharp-tongued vestige from an earlier way of life, he would say that the last of the aristocrats was gone.[63] In her days in the hospital Augusta had not recognized Richter.

She had, however, remembered her friend in her will. Richter would get the joke, but he was not pleased by it, when he discovered that the puckish old aristocrat had bequeathed to him a large, dreary engraving from her attic, a gift from his great-uncle Victor Conrad to Augusta's parents on their wedding. Augusta hated it, and she knew that Richter would hate it as well.

In the same letter that Richter wrote to Vene to describe Augusta's funeral ceremony, he announced that Temple University had invited him to receive an honorary degree at its February commencement. Pleased by the offer and happy to accept, Richter nonetheless griped that having to return by train from Florida for the ceremony meant that the honorary degree would cost him $200. Soon two more invitations to receive honorary degrees would arrive, the first from Lebanon Valley College, a short drive from Pine Grove, and the second from Lafayette College, in Pennsylvania's Lehigh Valley. In writing his acceptance letters, Richter made clear that he would be happy to attend and to be recognized, but that he would not speak, not even briefly. When Lebanon Valley asked what Richter would like to have included in the citation, Richter simply declined to answer.[64]

With the submission of *A Country of Strangers*, Richter experienced a brief relief from the internal urge to write each day, and with that relief had come a lessening of nighttime heart fibrillations. But soon the pressure to write was building, and soon his heart would react again. Ahead of him lay the chore of proofreading all three novels of his trilogy and writing an introduction for the combined edition. And ahead of him, still, was the third and final novel of his family trilogy, the novel based on his life and his energy theories. But he was not yet ready to take up that novel, which his heart had forced him to put aside each time he had attempted to write it.

With the trees on the hillsides almost bare of leaves, Richter was ready to go south to Florida, looking forward to the warm days ahead of him, "relaxed with the door and windows open and nothing to do but answer an occasional letter."[65] He had expected to leave for Florida early in December, but one delay led to another and finally Harvey's severe cold kept them at home until after Christmas. In November Alfred Knopf wrote to thank Richter for dedicating the new novel to him, and soon thereafter the publisher wrote again to ask that Richter inscribe all Knopf's personal copies of his novels. Others were having the same thought, friends stopping by 11 Maple Street to ask that he sign their copies of his books. This, too, could be attributed to the publicity of his seventy-fifth birthday, Richter remarked to Vene, concluding wryly that people were rushing "to get books signed while the signing is good, and I'm still around."[66]

At 6:30 A.M. on December 27, Edna Miller arrived to help pack the car, and an hour later Richter and Harvey were off. That day they covered 422 miles, Harvey wrote to Vene from a Howard Johnson's Motor Lodge—not because there was any reason to hurry, but simply because Vene's father had not changed at all with age: "At seventy-five Daddy still must pass all cars."[67]

River to the Sea

ONE

Looking back at the end of the year, Conrad Richter would remember 1966 as one with especially good memories: "1966 was the top for me," he wrote to Matt Pearce, his friend from the University of New Mexico.[1] During that year three books had been published: in May, *A Country of Strangers*, accompanied by excellent reviews; in September, the single-volume edition of his Ohio trilogy, for which he had chosen the title *The Awakening Land;* and in November, the juvenile edition of *The Light in the Forest.* There had been as well three honorary degrees, the first at Temple University's winter graduation ceremony, then in June, on successive days, at Lafayette College and Lebanon Valley College.

In late June Richter finally began to write the first chapter of his book about his own life. The spur to begin the actual writing was Richter's discovery of a title—"River to the Sea"—which came to him as he awakened one morning.[2] Months earlier, just back from Florida and not yet settled into his working routine, he had come to a surprising conclusion. On the same day that Richter drove to Pottsville to have an electrocardiogram, he wrote to Vene his latest thoughts about completing the story of his own life and also the "fate book" he had tentatively entitled "The Angry Saint" and a third book to explain his theories. "It came to me the other night," he wrote, "that I was almost 76 years old and I had better take the three books I have planned to do and put them into one if I can, the last vol[ume] of the trilogy."[3] However unrealistic this undertaking, after a month of planning and note-taking Richter would repeat the idea to Vene, still voicing his optimism that he could combine the three into a single book.

Perhaps a reason for Richter's continuing confidence was that the material from his second and third books was to come in later chapters. Plotting the novel's opening chapters, Richter found his first difficulty to be narrating the "curse" of his life, his nervous troubles. To write convincingly about what he still thought of as nervous breakdowns, he had to recall the episodes so intensely that it was as if he were undergoing the suffering once again.[4] When his heart's fibrillations worsened, he blamed the strain from writing about his own nervous condition. Before the end of July he had resorted to a ploy he had used at other times when his heart was frightening him; he asked Harvey to hide his manuscript in a place where he could not find it.[5] By summer's end he had a name for his heart condition, a diagnosis by a new specialist, Dr. Wilton R. Glenny. Richter's "gyrations" were paroxysmal atrial fibrillations, a condition confirmed by electrocardiogram when his heart began to fibrillate while Richter was in the doctor's office.[6] The drug Dr. Glenny prescribed, quinadine glutamate, offered relief from his heart's erratic behavior, but shortly after starting the treatment Richter began to experience spasms of angina, which he attributed to the new drug.

Unable to write and having difficulty with eye strain when he attempted to read for more than short periods, Richter found the summer days tediously long. To make matters worse, summer 1966 was "the most persistently hot" Richter could remember, making him feel more housebound than ever before.[7] Although he still looked forward to walks in the countryside, his opportunities were diminished by the summer's heat and his battle with his heart, and by the encroachment of new houses along his favorite routes. Even on Bird's Hill a house intruded where Richter had for years walked in solitude, its windows seeming to glare at him suspiciously. The only place he did not feel uncomfortably watched was Swopes Valley, where the residents were used to seeing Richter and Dick Wheeler strolling along, walking sticks in hand.[8] Often the afternoon heat limited Richter's outing to a drive with Harvey, the two of them remaining inside the air-conditioned Cadillac. For diversion Richter turned to his collection of classical music, choosing his favorite Chopin études or one of his record albums of Mozart's quartets. At times he was reduced to watching afternoon television programs, passing the hours until morning, when he could return to his desk in the dining room. And even that writing was jeopardized by his heart.

To Harvey, Richter complained that, without the daily work of writing to look forward to, his life felt meaningless.[9] To escape the intense strain of writing "River to the Sea," Richter decided to turn temporarily to something far from his nervous affliction and his quarrel with God. He would write a book for children. From the Lutheran minister's wife Richter had heard the story of John Brommer, a Pine Grove resident who as a boy had set out to discover for himself the truth of a Pennsylvania Dutch legend. Each year on July 2, the tale went, Mary the mother of Jesus carried her baby over Blue Mountain. That July 2 John Brommer hid out on the mountain, waiting to see Mary pass by on the road.[10]

Richter chose September 17, the day before the official publication date for *The Awakening Land*, to begin a vacation trip to New England. First he and Harvey would visit Vene at the MacDowell Writers Colony in New Hampshire; then they would drive on to Acadia National Park in Maine. On the second morning of their trip Harvey insisted on buying a Sunday *New York Times*, containing a review of Richter's Ohio trilogy. But neither looked at the book review section; the paper remained in the car's trunk until finally, in Maine, Harvey slipped into a conversation that she had read the review and that it was excellent. The general tenor of the review could not have been a surprise, for weeks earlier the reviewer, William Rogers, had written to say that his purpose for the review was to persuade more people to read Richter's novels.[11] In the daily *New York Times* review, Orville Prescott declared that the trilogy was "a masterpiece which will be read into the next century." Writing in *Life* magazine, Isaac Bashevis Singer seconded the judgment, proclaiming *The Awakening Land* "a great novel in any literature."[12]

By the time he was assured of *The Awakening Land's* critical success, Richter was well into writing *Over the Blue Mountain*. That writing went so easily, with no apparent strain on his heart, that he and Harvey chose to stay on in Acadia National Park while he finished his first draft, about 7,500 words. Rewriting, Richter was confident of completing and submitting the book to Knopf before departing for Florida. Richter's plan for the winter of 1966–67 was to remain in Pine Grove until after Thanksgiving, hoping to spend the holiday with Vene. But when Harvey began to cough and Richter suffered through a bad night with his heart, he wrote his daughter that they could not stay after all.

On November 26 Richter and Harvey drove away from 11 Maple Street, arriving three days later in Bradenton. Within twenty-four hours there was "trouble," the word Richter still used occasionally in his journal to mark an argument with Harvey. In Bradenton, Richter was surprised and upset when Harvey told him that her cough in the days before their departure had been caused by her dreading their return to a cabin. She wanted to find a house to rent. But to Richter a house meant a much larger expense and, just as important, more work for Harvey and worry for him. "I am destroyed by her wanting things that I can't furnish," Richter wrote in exasperation, then finished his journal with an apt summing sentence: "Poor day, but what else can you expect from the 30th?"[13]

For most of December Richter found little in Florida to comment favorably on in his journal. After several especially bad nights of fibrillations, Richter called Vene to ask for her reassurance that, if need be, she could join them on short notice. On December 25 Richter recorded a cold, dreary Christmas, with no tree and no presents. Evidently Harvey was still making her husband miserable: "She has always got what she wanted by being ill," he wrote angrily, "but she won't tell me what she wants except a better house here and I can find none." Before the end of the year, Richter did succeed in finding a house to rent, in the old section of Bradenton, surrounded by Spanish moss and live oaks, just one house away from the Manatee River. In his most upbeat letter of the month, Richter described the house to Vene, adding that he was eager to have her join them.[14] Perhaps the improvement in Richter's mood was brought on as well by a change in his writing project. Putting aside the notebook on his own life, he took up the notebook full of epigrammatic quotes from Augusta Filbert, planning a novel based loosely on Miss Augusta's last years in Pine Grove. In his first letter telling Vene about the book, Richter again urged her to come to Bradenton for a vacation; the house was old and a bit dark but comfortable, and her room had an enclosed porch with windows that opened on three sides.[15]

Not until the beginning of March was Vene free to join her parents in Bradenton. By then Richter was ready to share his ideas for *The Aristocrat*, a novel about the end of an era, the last days of the last of the Victorians.[16] Even more than *The Grandfathers*, it was to be a plot of anecdotes, relying for its sustaining interest on the trenchant opinions of Alexandra Morley, who holds forth against the encroachments of the modern world. Some of the novel's incidents were taken directly from events well known to Richter. For example, when Lawrence Hoy received a letter from the heirs of Mary Boyer, insisting he return the antique chest Mary Boyer had given to him, Richter had offered to hide the chest in his attic. In the novel it is Alexandra Morley who advises a young Sunday school superintendent to ignore a lawyer's threatening letter and to bring the piece of furniture to her for safekeeping. Instilling life to such anecdotes were the pithy and often tart quips of Miss Alexandra, her comments on the world of her childhood and early adulthood, on the practices of the current residents of the town, and on the striking difference between the two. The novel would offer Richter's last portrait of a stronghearted woman.

For their return trip to Pennsylvania, Richter and Harvey chose to take the train. Stanley Achenbach and his wife came to Florida for a vacation of their own, staying on in the house beside the Manatee River and then drove Richter's 1960 Cadillac home. Whether it was Harvey's health or his own that led Richter to this expediency, Richter did not record. His only comment, to Paul Reynolds, was that "Harvey felt we shouldn't make the long drive this time."[17] But journal entries reveal that his heart remained a daily worry, and back in Pine Grove he continued to have problems with a fibrillating heart and then with angina. Except for his rides with Harvey, Richter spent his afternoons listlessly watching daytime television programs, listening to his albums of Chopin and Mozart, and waiting for the morning, when he would have the luxury of an hour or two's work.[18] When the angina and threats of heart gyrations would allow, he gave himself the pleasure of walking the streets as darkness settled upon Pine Grove. These walks were shorter than in years past, and slower, Richter pausing often to check his pulse. With Augusta Filbert no longer expecting his visits at her home on Tulpehocken Street, habitually he walked by Aunt Lizzie's house at the corner of Mifflin and Morris Streets, where he had been born.[19]

In late April Richter wrote to Alfred Knopf about *The Aristocrat*, admitting to his publisher that his angina was interfering with his writing. Knopf's reply on May 8 barely acknowledged Richter's information about his new novel before delivering to his friend some tough advice:

> If you have the slightest suggestion of angina pain, no internist or any other practitioner will be worth a damn to you. You have to go to the best cardiologist you know. And no monkey business. If nitro-glycerine

doesn't give you immediate relief, you will probably need, as I did, a month in a hospital, and then another month of slow and delightful convalescence at home. I had no angina pains once I was in the hospital, but severe and recurring angina before that made it quite clear I was having a coronary. If you behave, it will be, at your age perhaps the best thing that ever happened to you. If you don't . . . [ellipsis Knopf's].

On Decoration Day, May 30, Joe and his family visited, bringing with him his granddaughter Debbie Richter, who had grown taller and "less shy but enough to make her likable."[20] It was a good day, with no hint of angina to spoil the trip to the cemetery or the picnic at the lake. Then came word that Henry "Trap" Irwin had died in White Fish, Montana. The thought that he was now the oldest of the cousins living brought to Richter a renewed sense of urgency. "You better get a draft of this book done as soon as you can," he admonished himself.[21] In this frame of mind Richter decided to take what remained unused of Augusta Filbert's epigrammatic commentaries on modern life and put them together as addenda to the novel, rather than to write additional narrative chapters.

When he had completed typing out the addenda, Richter again allowed himself a September vacation into New England. This time he planned to drive Harvey to Watch Hill, visiting the seashore resort that had served as the setting of Vene's novel, *The Human Shore*. Afterwards they took the ferry to Martha's Vineyard, thinking to return the visits of the young writer and editor he had encouraged, David McCullough. Although he was looking forward to visiting the writer and meeting his family, Richter did not write or call in advance, and so when he telephoned from the island he did not know if McCullough was at home. McCullough's wife Rosalee answered the phone. Yes, her husband was on the island, but he was taking a walk at that moment. Yes, he would be available for a visit later. Would the caller leave his name? "Just tell him it's a friend who wants to stop by," the anonymous voice said, thereby allowing Richter and Harvey their pleasure in surprising a friend.[22]

T W O

Richter and Harvey arrived back in Pine Grove in time to receive the first copies of *Over the Blue Mountain*. Richter had ordered fifty copies, planning to give these to children who visited that fall. On October 13, Richter's seventy-seventh birthday, Joe Richter and his family came to Pine Grove, bringing a cake. That evening Vene called from New York. Having successfully defended her dissertation, she was sailing to Greece the next day, rewarding herself with a vacation on Mykenos and perhaps a winter in Italy. Two days later Fred and Emily arrived; with them were Eduard and his wife Beverly and their two children. Richter thought that young Billy, seven, looked like Trap Irwin as a boy. And Karen, eight, had "a beautiful Irish face" and the "presence and calm" to win over her great-uncle immediately.[23] A frequent visitor that month was John Brommer, bringing young relatives to hear from the writer himself that yes, John Brommer had been the model for Henner in *Over the Blue Mountain*. Richter signed copies for them all. During two nights of trick-or-treating at Halloween, more than one hundred costumed children knocked on the door of 11 Maple Street. As they came to the door, Richter and Harvey would invite them in and have them sign a register. One young boy wrote only his first name. When Richter asked him to write his last name too, he turned to his older brother and asked, "What's my other name?" Later Richter told the story to the boy's father in the hardware store, to general laughter. When the laughter subsided, the father was ready with a reply. On the second night of trick-or-treating, his young son had said to him, "Let's go back to that rich man's house." Asked why he thought Mr. Richter was rich, the boy replied that he gave everybody two pieces of candy.[24]

Just after Halloween Richter drove to Pottsville to have the typescript of *The Aristocrat* photoduplicated. After mailing the original to Paul Reynolds, he wrote to Knopf to alert his publisher that the novel was on its way. In his reply Alfred Knopf pressed Richter to visit him in New York. Richter needed to meet the new staff, who would be the "important people who will have to do with you when I am not around," the publisher wrote.[25] But Richter was not to be enticed. Nor could Paul Reynolds persuade him to meet a producer who appeared ready to meet Richter's price of $100,000 for the film rights to *The Awakening Land*.[26] In spite of his ever-present worry about money for his and Harvey's future, Richter was unwilling to undergo the stress of such meetings. Richter did allow Wesley Stout, a former general editor for the *Saturday Evening Post*, to visit to discuss an article for the *Reader's Digest*. But Richter acquiesced less because of the $5,000 offered for the article than because of Richter's memory that, when the *Post* was considering serializing *The Sea of Grass*, it had been Wesley Stout who had championed the novel when others had been less sure. In addition, an article for the *Digest* required no visits to main offices to meet new people. Richter could write at his own pace, as his health allowed, which in the late fall of 1967 continued to be a factor.

Just a week after his seventy-seventh birthday, Richter used his journal entry to explore the curious nature of health, especially his own vicissitudes. That day he had experienced only one small occasion of heart fibrillation—a "gyette"— and throughout the day he had had better energy and less shortness of breath than at any time in recent months. But that improvement only opened the pathways for other feelings, which carried him back to the blackest times of the depression. "One is never free," he began his entry, and at a later point continued this thought: "The false and blind cries of freedom sadden and provoke me, knowing that we are not free and can never be free, that what we are born with determines our life. . . . We do what we are and what we are powers beyond our grasp have made us."27

By the middle of November Richter was ready for Florida, though reluctant to drive such a distance himself. When he could find nobody to drive his Cadillac south for him, he set out with Harvey on November 21, along the way stopping twice for the night. When Vene wrote from Greece to hope that at least they had found a good restaurant for Thanksgiving dinner, her father replied good humoredly, telling a tale on himself: "You ask about our Thanksgiving dinner, hoping we had a good one which makes Mother laugh. We ate ours in the car driving through northern Florida, Mother feeding me from the remnants of three days of lunch she packed before we left."28 All things considered, Richter had reason to be in better spirits than he had been the previous December. His new novel was in the hands of his publisher, and his daughter had completed her dissertation and had been encouraged by her adviser to publish it. Vene was celebrating with a vacation in Greece, and he was treating himself to a Florida regimen of open windows and doors and hours sitting in the sunshine, talking to any neighboring vacationers who happened to catch his interest.

When Vene returned from Greece, Harvey wrote to her expressing feelings for herself and Richter: "it is a comfort to know you are home, and New York now, after Europe, seems close to Florida."29 They had always relied on her nearness, made real to them by her regular letters, but increasingly Richter's comfort in Vene's proximity was becoming something more of a dependency: he needed to know that his daughter was close enough to come quickly, should either he or Harvey need her help. Any letter from Vene was treated as a family event, and it would be read more than once, usually out loud by one to the other. When a letter from Vene was found in a batch of letters, it was the first to be read—at times immediately. Sitting inside the Cadillac in the parking lot of the Bradenton post office, with heat rising in waves from the macadam surrounding them, Harvey would open the envelope and read aloud the latest news from their daughter.30

Working each morning, Richter wrote and rewrote "My Friends, the Trees" for the *Reader's Digest*. Afternoons he attended to the various letters having to do with contract rights for *The Aristocrat*, sent by Paul Reynolds and by the people Knopf had implored him to come to meet. All in all, Richter was pleased by the tone of the letters from the new people at Knopf; they seemed optimistic and ambitious for his novel, people who would push his novels hard, the aggressive salespeople he had always wanted at Knopf. In February 1968, when Harvey developed what would be called the "bronchial version" of the flu, Richter began to feel the need of his daughter's help in Florida. In March Vene joined them and remained into April, then accompanied her parents by train back to Pennsylvania. For the second year, Richter chose not to drive his own car back. This time Fred and Emily Richter came to vacation with friends in Florida and then drive the car back to Pine Grove.

In Pine Grove, Harvey continued to suffer from her cough and Richter from his nighttime fibrillations. His eyes were also a problem, straining easily, and when he went out even for brief walks he was interrupted by the sharp pains of angina. Richter continued to search for relief for his ailments, experimenting with various combinations of vitamins and foods. Each morning he returned to his desk in the dining room, but he accomplished little new writing. Part of his morning would be spent reading proofs for *The Aristocrat* and, as best he could, keeping up with his correspondence. It had been months since he had accomplished any real writing on "River to the Sea."

At times during spring 1968 Richter was overwhelmed with despondency: his heart would not let him work, his book about his own life lay unfinished, and Harvey continued to suffer from a deep bronchial cough. On Easter Sunday Richter's anguish over Harvey's health led to an angry journal entry. "Evil Easter," it began, and continued with Richter's description of his attempts to pray for Harvey's recovery. Those efforts at healing intercessions had brought no relief, he complained; only when he was worried to despair did she seem to improve. "This final realization shook me," he wrote. But only temporarily; he "refused to accept such a foul truth."[31]

On April 22 Richter resumed work on "River to the Sea," correcting the first chapter, the only one written, and starting the second. After bad nights with his heart, he would put the manuscript aside, then be unable to keep himself away from it for more than a day or two. On May 18 Richter recorded in his journal that he had again put his novel away, apparently an act intended to test the "powers that be": "If I am meant to do the 3rd vol[ume] of the trilogy my health will be better," he told himself. Two days later he returned to the last volume of

19. Conrad Richter poses before his desk and bookshelves in the dining room of 11 Maple Street, *circa* 1968.

his family trilogy, but on May 24, after another bad night, he was forced to stop. "It's apparent the powers that be don't wish enough for me to write it," he concluded his journal entry. Then early in June Richter returned to work on the novel, which he had begun to call "The Search for Meaning," writing two pages of chapter 4 only to put the typescript back into the safe once again.

In spite of his exasperation and anger over his health and Harvey's, Richter tried to keep up with his correspondence. After his visit to David McCullough on the Vineyard, Richter kept up a steady correspondence with the young writer. When he returned from Florida, Richter sorted through the boxes of second- and third-class mail searching for McCullough's first book, *The Johnstown Flood*, and immediately began to read it. On Easter, the same day Richter wrote a journal entry railing at the powers that be, he wrote to McCullough to express his pleasure at the book's success. When he discovered that McCullough did not have a literary agent, Richter wrote to Paul Reynolds, urging him to contact McCullough and offer his services.[32] In June, when Vene wrote that her ex-fiancé and traveling companion Harry Roskolenko had fallen on difficult times, Richter put aside his personal dislike for Roskolenko and wrote Glenway Wescott, the secretary of the National Institute of Arts and Letters, to ask the institute's help. The result was a $500 grant to Roskolenko.[33]

That summer Vene was in residence at another writers colony, the Wurlitzer Foundation near Taos, New Mexico. Her letters from the high desert carried news to her parents of a growing relationship with another writer, playwrite and novelist, Bill Weber. After Vene wrote of her plans to go to California to meet Weber's family, Richter found himself worrying about his daughter's entanglement with a man who had been married twice. But by late July Richter's worries were focused on Harvey who, having never recovered from the bronchial cough of the previous winter, had fallen into one of her depressions. One afternoon when Harvey asked that they not go far on their drive, she admitted, in response to Richter's questions, that she was suffering daily from headaches and was so worn down by her cough and her health in general that the day before she had prayed to be taken by God. "Another 30th," Richter noted disconsolately in his journal.

In August came the first word about *The Aristocrat*, a *Publisher's Weekly* review so good that Richter suspected Knopf had somehow gotten a member of his staff to write it. Again Richter attempted to work on "The Search for Meaning," relying on all his stratagems to make himself well enough to work. In addition to vitamins E and C and niacin, he was regularly taking several prescription drugs, primarily ones to reduce his nervous tension and allow him to sleep. Many nights he would sleep fitfully, rising to wander through the dark house, shifting from bed to bed to find cooler air or to escape the hum of the air conditioner from across the street. Mornings he read his journals from the Pine Tree Farm years, gleaning entries to include almost verbatim in "The Search for Meaning." Still to be written were the stories of leaving their valley friends for the mountains of Saranac, New York, and then the high desert of Albuquerque, New Mexico. Ahead of him were his foolishness in the stock market and Harvey's near death and her request that, though she would have to be buried in New Mexico, she be buried with buckets of earth from Pine Tree Farm. Ahead of him were the long years of writing stories that sold for pennies a word or did not sell at all.

One August event offered a day's respite from the pattern of his life, the wedding of his favorite niece, Diane Richter, on August 17. The Saturday of the wedding was hot and sultry, the afternoon full of the sound of locusts. Diane's parents, Bill and Rita Richter, did not expect Richter and Harvey to attend the evening wedding, knowing Uncle Connie disliked crowds and celebrations and that he would be uneasy about driving home so late at night. They had cautioned Diane not to be disappointed if her great-aunt and -uncle did not attend. But for Richter there had not been any question that, health allowing, both he and Harvey would attend the wedding of the spirited girl they had watched grow into a vivacious young woman, although they would have to sit inside the church in the evening heat, where the still air barely flickered the flames of the candles set in each window. Richter and Harvey sat in the back pew, where they could see into the vestibule and watch the final preparations of the bride and her parents.

After the ceremony Bill Richter asked the newlyweds to shorten their traditional drive through town, both because of the oppressive heat in the church social room, where the reception was held, and out of concern for Richter's drive home in the dark. To everyone's surprise, Richter stayed on well into the reception, enjoying himself despite being a center of attention, smiling and shaking hands with people who knew of the famous writer and wanted to meet him. When Richter did prepare to depart, his nephew Bill came to say, "You made us very happy. We thought you wouldn't come." Walking his brother to his car, Joe Richter echoed the sentiment, thanking Richter and Harvey for coming and saying, "You've made our day." Perhaps to his own surprise as well as that of his closest relatives, he had spent the time in obvious enjoyment.

On the way home, Richter told Harvey that he had never before been treated like a literary lion. Certainly he had never before felt like a lion and never before accepted the attention as his due. But this had not been a dinner of the National Institute of Arts and Letters or a reception for the National Book Award. At

Diane's wedding he was surrounded by his own people, relatives and others who had no need to flatter him falsely. He had happily attended the wedding of a favorite relative, and, for one of the very few times in his life, he had found himself comfortable in the special attention that was paid to him. The next morning he wrote a long journal entry, recapitulating his pleasure. Two weeks later he rewrote the entry into more polished prose, perhaps to send to Vene. The only hint of a concern was for Diane herself, who looked, her fond uncle thought, pale and thin. But he himself had felt fine, going all evening without any threat of a gyration. And though he did not arrive back in Pine Grove until 11:30, he had driven home "without trouble or tiredness."[34]

THREE

In late September Vene departed from Wurlitzer to visit Bill Weber in California. At home in Pine Grove her father worried about her being so far away while he was struggling through difficult days. Letters arrived in Los Angeles, warning Vene that she might have to come back to Pine Grove with little notice. There were as well regular phone calls, reports on her father's health, which Vene was not altogether sure were not simply an expression of her father's unhappiness over her possible marriage to Weber.[35]

In Pine Grove Richter was finding his daily life increasingly more difficult to accept. Every time he attempted to lie down, his heart began jumping and racing, and if he did not get up immediately, he risked the hours he would have to endure before his heart returned to its normal pattern. Just after his birthday Richter asked Vene to come home from Los Angeles. On October 19, he drove through fog and rain to Lancaster to meet Vene's train. If he asked her about Bill Weber, he did not record it in his journal, which had become almost entirely an account of his heart's fibrillations and angina and his own attempts to make his heart improve. He must certainly have been relieved to have his daughter at home, and Vene's return gave Richter something to look forward to. Vene had asked her father to explain his theories of psycho-energetics to her in a personal seminar.[36] Such an event would have been a happy and perhaps energizing occasion for Richter, preparing his daughter to carry on his most important work, but apparently he never felt well enough to begin.

On October 24 Richter reported in his journal a new, ominous symptom, something he did not tell Harvey or Vene. He was having trouble on the stairs, blacking out momentarily, and when undressing he was seeing dark flashes before his eyes. On October 25 he felt so unsteady on his feet that he did not attend Pine Grove's Halloween parade, an event he had never missed when he was in Pine Grove. In his October 27 journal entry Richter mentioned that he talked by phone with Helen Frankel, a Christian Science practitioner, asking her to suspend her efforts after that day. He did not say why.

On the morning of October 28 Richter wrote his last journal entry, recording a change in his heart's behavior:

> Terribly irregular heart most of night. Uncomfortable, some pain in upper chest with it. I remember had irregularity like this some years ago. It seemed to let up a good deal after taking a double [vitamin] E during night but was back again when I awoke at 6.
>
> Possible causes: Helen stopping work but I asked her to work last evening. Ate one of Arlene's rich fresh small buns for supper. The social doings of afternoon.

When the fibrillations and pain continued all day and into the evening, Dr. Marshall ordered his patient to the hospital for an electrocardiogram. At about nine o'clock that night Richter got the 1960 Cadillac from the garage and drove himself to Pottsville. Vene rode with him. Driving the dark country roads to Pottsville, he admitted to his daughter that he was no longer sure of a primary tenet of his theories, that personal suffering was a means to higher personal evolution. As he spoke, however, Vene understood how her father's words were to be taken: they registered the dissipation of faith he had always suffered when his energy was low.

At the hospital, Richter was rushed to the intensive care unit. Soon thereafter Vene was given his clothes to take home, a procedure usual enough in hospitals but upsetting nonetheless to her, and to Harvey when Vene returned home. The following day, when the fibrillations seemed to have been brought under control, Harvey and Vene implored Dr. Marshall to place him in a private room, where he could feel more comfortable. Dr. Marshall promised he would the following day, provided that his patient had a quiet night. But late that evening Richter's heart began to race, and the hospital staff could not bring it under control. For some reason the hospital called Harvey's brother Stanley, and so Stanley Achenbach and his wife Emma came to 11 Maple Street, ringing the doorbell just before dawn to deliver the news. Connie's heart had begun to fibrillate wildly, and then it had stopped. In the early hours of October 30, Conrad Richter died.

Harvena Richter knew with certainty Conrad Richter's wishes concerning his burial. He wanted a simple funeral service at his own home, and he wanted only family members present. Harvey and Vene carried out his wishes exactly, inviting only their closest relatives. Paul Reynolds, his agent for almost thirty years, was discouraged from attending. So too was the publisher of all his novels, Alfred Knopf. Even Edna Miller, Richter and Harvey's housekeeper and cook for many years, was denied her request to come before the ceremony to pay her last respects. The service was presided over by Lyman Achenbach, Harvey's brother. The music was provided by a relative, though a distant one: Anna Siegel, whose grandmother had been an Achenbach, accompanied herself on Vene's piano and sang "How Firm a Foundation." Richter's coffin was mahogany, the simplest, least expensive one available.

Harvey chose the casket to fulfill another of Richter's desires for his interment, that he be allowed to return naturally to the earth. Although she had not read her husband's journal entry for December 20, 1963, she would not have been surprised by what he had written: once he had gotten through the "nuisance of dying" he expected "to subside into death as easily as a fallen raindrop into the ground."[37] He did not want his body to be buried in an expensive coffin, and he did not want his coffin placed in a concrete vault. Reluctantly the cemetery committee of St. John's Lutheran Church agreed, instructing that the coffin's packing box, a light wooden crate, be placed in the ground to receive Richter's coffin.[38]

No cars were on the street, and no townspeople were on the sidewalk when the funeral procession traveled the short distance from Maple Street to Cemetery Hill. Richter's grave was on a gentle slope facing southeast, one of five plots he had bought in 1960. A few steps to the left are the white granite stones marking the graves of his mother and his father. In time Vene would have a headstone prepared to match those of his parents: a simple rectangle, the granite polished on all sides to a smooth surface. Carved into the stone beneath his name were two lines Conrad Richter had himself written for his grave:

> Little grasses, I have come among you
> Little grasses, you are taller now than I.

Acknowledgments

From his first attempts to write stories for magazines, Conrad Richter filed away all the correspondence having to do with his writing. In separate files he kept the letters he received from friends, relatives, and fellow writers, and from about 1920 on he kept copies of almost every letter he wrote. This correspondence has been an invaluable resource, a window into Richter as others saw him and as he preferred to present himself to the world. For a perspective on Richter's private life and most private thoughts, I have had the good fortune of access to Richter's personal journals, begun in 1925 and, with few interruptions, filled with end-of-day entries until his death in 1968. Here Richter recorded the activities of ordinary life—vitamins taken; errands run; conversations with his banker, or barber, or a passing child—and also his own most interior thoughts about his health and his wife's, about the day's writing, about his expectations for his most recent novel or story, about his worries that he was losing the gift that made his writing special to readers, and therefore salable. And if all this were not enough for a biographer interested in the story of a writer writing, Richter further obliged by keeping an assortment of notebooks, some for novels planned or in progress, others full of kernels for possible novels, still others with demonstration plots and formulas for successful stories. In separate notebooks he kept his personal thesaurus for the language of historical periods: long lists of words appropriate to particular settings or characters. Happily, selections from all these are available in Harvena Richter's *Writing to Survive: The Private Notebooks of Conrad Richter* (University of New Mexico Press, 1988).

My first debt to acknowledge is to Harvena Richter, Conrad Richter's daughter, who allowed me to read all her father's papers and granted permission to quote as needed from all his published and unpublished work. During my visits to her home, Ms. Richter generously offered me many opportunities to prod her memory about particular times, places, events, and about her own and her mother's unusual participation in Richter's story-writing process. A scholar herself, Harvena Richter offered me the enormous benefit of her own insights into her father's work and life without asking that I accept them as my own. For all her help and encouragement, and for her many gifts of hospitality, I am deeply grateful.

Several of the people who have provided me firsthand testimory about Conrad Richter and his family are no longer living. Richter's brother Frederick Richter and his wife Emily welcomed me into their home in Syracuse, New York, answering all my questions and sharing their personal collection of Conrad Richter memorabilia, including a number of letters. Matthew and Helen Pearce were helpful with their memories of Albuquerque during the Great Depression and of the Richters' social circle. Margretta Gundel recounted to me the kindness of Conrad and Harvey Richter following the death of her husband, and she painted for me a vivid picture of Richter as his Pine Grove neighbors saw him. William Richter, Richter's nephew, told me a number of family stories. Mary and Stuart Filbert added their recollections of Pine Grove social life. I regret that I am not able to tender again my thanks in person to all these.

Of the many others who have answered inquiries and otherwise helped me to make this biography as complete, reliable, and readable as possible, the following deserve a special thanks for their assistance. Lawrence Hoy and Richard Wheeler offered accounts of Pine Grove life and their friendships with Richter and were especially helpful; others who supplemented their views were Herbert Barr, Kathleen Bross, and Margery Mattox. Rita Richter helpfully added to the memories of her husband Bill. Richter's nephews Frederick and Eduard, and Ed's wife Beverly, were generous hosts, sharing stories of visits with Uncle Connie and Aunt Harvey. Evalyn Strickler contributed a special perspective on Harvey Richter. David McCullough shared his notes from interviews with Richter, and he and his wife Rosalee added their recollections of visiting Pine Grove and of the Richters' visit to their home. Mary Trost and her son David provided me a delightful tour of Pine Tree Farm. Reverend Wayne Matthias-Long helped solve a puzzle about John Richter's ministry in Reading, as did J. T. Herber a question about Richter's grave.

Tom Golden, Melissa Lennon, and Mary Seaman were indefatigable and resourceful research assistants; Susanna Boyleston, Richard Everett, and Ronald Robbins demonstrated impressive skills as reference librarians, answering my many inquiries. The staffs of the libraries of Boston University, the University of New Mexico, the Pennsylvania State University, Princeton University, and Williamsport Area Community College have been helpful. The late Charles

Mann, director of the Rare Book Room at The Pennsylvania State University, provided me with expert assistance as I read the Richter papers collected there.

I owe a special debt to colleagues at Lafayette College and elsewhere who have read and commented on chapters or larger sections of my book: Deborah Byrd, Patricia Donahue, Arthur Ford, Hamlin Hill, James Lusardi, Charles Molesworth, Peter White, and James Woolley. Mary Beckman read a late version of the complete manuscript and offered valuable suggestions. And at the point when a too-long manuscript needed to be pruned and pointed, Donald Miller provided a careful reading and expert advice. I am grateful to him and to all the readers and editors who generously helped me keep to the path through the forest.

I am also indebted to Lafayette College and its Committee on Advanced Study and Research for ongoing support. Former president David Ellis and former provost Sarah Blanshei were especially helpful, sometimes in creative ways, as have been Provost June Schlueter and Associate Provost Jeff Bader. I am also grateful to the National Endowment for the Humanities for a grant which furthered my research.

For permission to quote passages from *The Sea of Grass, A Simple Honorable Man, The Trees,* and *The Waters of Kronos,* I am grateful to Harvena Richter and to Alfred A. Knopf, a Division of Random House, Inc. For permission to quote from the letters of Alfred A. Knopf and Blanche Knopf to Conrad Richter, I thank Alfred A. Knopf, Jr. For permission to quote from the letters of Paul R. Reynolds and Paul R. Reynolds, Jr., to Conrad Richter, I thank Mary Robbins Reynolds, Jane Swain, and Rebecca Wells.

Throughout the publication process, the staff of Penn State Press has been efficient and generous with its time. I am especially appreciative of the help of Shannon Pennefeather and Cherene Holland, and for the deft touch of Eliza Childs in copyediting my book.

And, finally, I am thankful for the support and encouragement of Jean, Kate, and Ted, who kept their patience and sense of humor through a long, long process.

Notes

SOURCES FOR UNPUBLISHED DOCUMENTS

With the exception of several manuscripts that Conrad Richter donated to libraries and a very few letters to and from relatives and friends that I did not find in Richter's files, the written record of Richter's life was made available to me at the home of his daughter, Harvena Richter, in Albuquerque, New Mexico. These documents included Richter's journals and writing notebooks, his correspondence, his financial records, his personal collection of family memorabilia, and such miscellaneous compilations as his Health file and his "Record of Dreams, Signs, Etc." Manuscripts that Richter donated to libraries and files that have been donated subsequent to my reading of them are to be found in the following places:

American Academy of Arts and Letters: manuscript of *The Light in the Forest*.

Mugar Library, Boston University: manuscripts of *The Mountain on the Desert* and *A Simple Honorable Man*.

Paterno Library, The Pennsylvania State University: manuscripts of nine novels and many short stories; an unpublished novel, "The Gifts"; writing notebooks; published articles; family letters, 1911–14; unpublished early writing; miscellaneous correspondence.

Firestone Library, Princeton University: Richter's correspondence with Alfred A. Knopf, Paul R. Reynolds, and Paul R. Reynolds, Jr.; correspondence with George Horace Lorimer and Erdman Brandt of the *Saturday Evening Post*; correspondence with his daughter Harvena Richter; manuscript of *The Town*; correspondence with writers and notable people; correspondence with readers; writing notebooks.

University of California at Los Angeles Library: manuscript of *Tacey Cromwell*.

Toppan Library, University of Wyoming: manuscripts of *The Lady*; manuscripts of ten western stories; financial records.

INTRODUCTION

1. "I think I have"; "Even Faulkner": J, March 9, 1961.
2. telephone conversation with Alfred Knopf: J, March 9, 1961.
3. Richter at the National Book Award ceremony: J, March 16, 1961.
4. "The boy didn't know": RTS, 1–2.
5. "a little pile": CR to HAR, May 1, 1918; "desperate penury": J, March 24, 1928.
6. three C's: Health file, undated sheet entitled "MY FAILURE CONTACTS WITH PEOPLE"; also repeatedly in J.
7. Richter meets a reporter: interview with Frederick D. Richter and Eduard C. Richter, September 21, 1991.
8. "I am a little overwhelmed": J, August 1, 1936.
9. "the guts and integrity": J, September 23, 1936.
10. "just amazed with you": J, September 23, 1936; "the most sought after": CR to PRR, December 7, 1936.
11. "the best fiction": CR to AK, October 14, 1936.
12. fable of writing career; "The first better story": CR to AK, October 14, 1936.
13. "When people ask me": CR to Frank Gruber, November 12, 1955.
14. "I told Adams": J, September 7, 1936.
15. watering lawn: J, May 1, 1950.
16. "I tell people about the book": J, March 16, 1961; salutation "Dear Master": I. B. Singer to CR, May 1, 1965; also March 6, 1968, in which Singer himself reports on his attempts to promote Richter's novels: "Wherever I go I keep on telling people that there lives a great talent amidst us."
17. "we only make toast": interview with William Richter, September 18, 1992.

CHAPTER 1. PINE GROVE

1. Sources for "Pine Grove": interviews with FR, May 13, 1982, and June 18, 1982; interviews with HR, conducted over the period 1982–99; Henry Irwin to CR, May 26, 1941; "Reminiscences of Henry Irwin"; "Memories of My Home Town," uncompleted MS in several versions by CR, fictionalizing the reminiscences of Henry Irwin; "Observations and Happenings in the Seventies, Before, and After," a

fourteen-part reminiscence by JAR, ca. 1938 (see esp. chap. 2, "About Yours Truly"); *SHM, WK,* RTS; *History of Schuylkill County* (New York: W. W. Munsell, 1881); Capt. J. W. Barr, *Biographical Notes of Pine Grove, 1841–1916* (Pine Grove: Anderson & Reber, 1916); "St. Peter's Lutheran Church, 125th Anniversary" (church history); "Accounting of John A. Richter, Administrator for the estate of Elias S. Henry"; Rev. P. C. Croll, "Rev. Elias S. Henry," *Lutheran Observer,* May 14, 1897; "Pa-Pa," unpub. CR MS, 8 pp.; "Frederick Conrad, Esq. of Worcester Township," *Norristown Daily Herald,* May 14, 1889; "The Life and Times of Frederick Conrad," *Norristown Daily Herald,* May 15, 1889; "Family Tree: Richter-Henry Families"; CR to Jean Henry, February 13, 1949; CR to L. B. Sloan, editor, *National Cyclopedia of American Biography,* May 23, 1951; Walter Hanneman to CR, March 13, 1953; CR to Walter Hanneman, March 30, 1953.

2. running away to the West: CR, "Who's Who—and Why," *SEP,* July 13, 1935, 30.

3. "the menace that spoiled": J, February 13, 1927.

4. "So it's pleasure": Henry Irwin to CR, May 26, 1941.

5. Elias S. Henry's service: Rev. P. C. Croll.

6. "I had to work": JAR reminiscence, "Observations and Happenings in the Seventies, Before, and After," chap. 8.

7. "Never was a baby": CHR to CR, October 13, 1918.

8. Lottie's vision: HR, FR, CR to John Jones, June 12, 1955.

9. peeing contest: FR.

10. Lottie gifted with an extra sense: FR.

11. "painful separation": J, August 18, 1927.

12. Guild night: J, August 19, 1928.

13. "beautiful modulated voice": Pearl Schaller to CR, August 28, 1966.

14. "He would walk one step": RTS, 2.

15. "I don't want patience": J, June 13, 1966.

16. "Only three grains": HR.

17. not telling mother: CR to Leicester Foulk Kent, December 3, 1932.

18. "For years it had stood": *WK,* 27–28.

CHAPTER 2. A BOY'S WILL

1. Sources for "A Boy's Will": interviews with FR; interviews with HR; RTS; *SHM, WK,* "Nerve Energy and Its Management" (unpub. MS); Elizabeth Clark Tyler Miller to CR, thirty-nine letters and six telegrams, October 19, 1911, to October 21, 1913; Nathaniel Barbehenn and W. H. Carney, letters reminiscing about Susquehanna University and Selinsgrove; James H. Sexton to CR, reminiscences about newspaper reporting together, June 2, 1912, December 9, 1912, August 8, 1913; "Sheridan" to CR, November 23, 1912; CR to Nathaniel Berkabile, W. H. Bruce Carney, Lawrence Henry Gibson, Harding Lemay, Pearl Schaller, Mary Thurber, and "Dr. Woods," sharing reminiscences; Anthropomorphic Charts, December 3, 1902, March 10, 1905, September 7, 1905; letters of reply from writers and prominent people declining CR's requests for a job as private secretary; CR to the Literary Bureau, four letters; the Literary Bureau to CR, six letters.

2. Selinsgrove home: FR.

3. meals in Selinsgrove: CR to Nathaniel C. Barbehenn, February 14, 1944; peaches: W. H. Bruce Carney to CR, May 7, 1947.

4. bullying schoolmaster: Richter's representation of the problem in *A Simple Honorable Man* was close enough to his memory that he worried about being sued by the teacher, who was still alive in 1962. See CR to Harding Lemay, February 2, 1962.

5. boyhood reading: FR, HR; Harvena Richter, *Writing to Survive* (Albuquerque: University of New Mexico Press, 1986), 213.

6. railroad trestle: FR.

7. "desperate penury": J, March 24, 1928.

8. memories of Selinsgrove: FR; undated letter, FR to CHR: "We were too little and didn't understand but it's wonderful when you think how poor we were and yet how respectfully and decent we lived and were brought up. . . . You and Dad gave us everything."

9. Family's tradition of the ministry: CR to Dr. Hugh Black, December 20, 1922: "I had some time escaping the pulpit. . . . I was made to feel I was going back on my own."

10. Tremont: George Wheeler, "Early Days of Tremont and Donaldson," *West Schuylkill Express and Pine Grove Herald*, n.d.

11. "the feeling of another world": CR to Erdman Brandt, December 4, 1936.

12. feelings for parents: J, June 28, 1948.

13. "what the Church did": J, May 21, 1931.

14. Blackwood Breaker: J, September 30, 1927.

15. Fred's visit: FR; "oases of lifegiving greenery": unpub. article written for Library Week in Pennsylvania, 1964, beginning "When I was a boy, there was no public library in town."

16. fascination with mountains: HR.

17. Farmers and Citizens Bank: CR to "Dr. Wood," May 29, 1953.

18. Bernarr McFadden: *Dictionary of American Biography*, supp. 5 (New York: Scribner's, 1951–55), 452–54.

19. feelings leaving the theater: J, October 8, 1960.

20. emotions on reading: J, August 2, 1945, and July 16, 1964.

21. "Conrad iss a liar": HR.

22. "those Richter boys": Charles Berger to CR, n.d.; also, Joseph Richter to CR, n.d., *circa* 1951.

23. "didn't understand": "Conrad Richter, Short Story Writer, Follows Inclinations Revealed as Montgomery Lad," *Williamsport Sun*, April 8, 1924.

24. "the new minister's son": Pearl Schaller to CR, August 28, 1966.

25. "If you care": Robert W. Chambers to CR, October 4, 1910.

26. articles on newspapermen: unpub. article for Library Week in Pennsylvania, 1964, beginning "When I was a boy there was no public library in town."

27. "undertakers": J. L. Berkebile, managing editor, *Johnstown Journal*, October 9, 1910.

28. "Nowhere": quoted in HR, *Writing to Survive*, 14; CR's introduction to journalism: CR to Mary Thurber, March 4, 1954; also CR to "Mrs. Cooper," November 14, 1954, which contains another version of Richter's first submission as a reporter.

29. "The story": CR to Mary Thurber, March 4, 1954.

30. "the short story": J. R. Wright to CR, December 27, 1910.

31. "refuses to give up": Jack London to CR, January 21, 1911.

32. possible job as housekeeper: Upton Sinclair to CR, January 24, 1911.

33. trip abroad: CR to Harding Lemay, March 31, 1952. In this letter CR remembers that he wrote to "more than a dozen well known and successful authors."

34. "I heartily wish": William Dean Howells to CR, March 3, 1911.

35. "Three Little Outcasts from Paradise": the Literary Bureau to CR, April 6, 1912; "The Secret of Health" and "The First Case": May 22, 1911.

36. "no vacancy": Ernest Thompson Seton to CR, May 23, 1911.

37. "already had two": Gifford Pinchot to CR, June 3, 1911.

38. "The only advice": Richard Harding Davis to CR, April 4, [1911].

39. "Look Before You Leap": Vitograph Company to CR, June 13, 1911.

40. information about job: Mrs. E. C. T. Miller to CR, October 29, 1911.

41. "Well I've gone and done it": CR to "Dear Everybody," May 18, 1912. I have corrected typographical errors in this letter.

42. "a man's man": CR to CHR, December 13, 1912.

43. CR buys stock: CR to family, October 21, 1912.

44. rejection by *St. Nicholas Magazine*: November 30, 1912; by the *Woman's Home Companion*: December 28, 1912.

45. unhappiness in Cleveland: CR to family, December 25, 1912.

46. "The Bravest Little Soul": Robert Hobart Davis to CR, July 19, 1913.

47. Pennsylvania Dutch: CR to Johanna Kenngott Klein, March 3, 1957.

48. "The Sister of Rudd": *Cavalier* to CR, October 14, 1913; "James Stacey": *Adventure* to CR, October 22, 1913; *Smart Set* to CR, November 17, 1913.

49. "Ebenezer Straint, deacon": *BNK,* 1.

50. "It was a steep and sandy Allegheny road": *BNK,* 13.

51. "with sincere interest": *Harper's Magazine* to CR, October 23, 1913.

52. "The Old Debt": *BNK,* 70–85.

53. Otto's birthday party: Elizabeth C. T. Miller to CR, October 21, 1913.

54. "the fears": RTS, 5; this fictional account of Richter's experience is confirmed by his biographical testimony in "Nerve Energy: Its Management," 1–8.

55. "Something can't be nothing": RTS, 6.

56. "merely a nervous one": Jacques Loeb to CR, January 8, 1914.

57. "Ideas without acts": Dr. Dubois to CR, March 29, 1913.

58. "No brain surgeon": Richard C. Cabot to CR, January 3, 1914.

59. "just friends": My reading of the relationship of CR and Johanna Kenngott is inferred from three letters from her to CR, based upon sentences like the following: "I will try to be for you a good friend, only a friend, a sister as you say"; and "And if it is over, all over, then I am no coward, Conrad Richter, I'll go my own way, not sad but perhaps stronger and my soul has a beautiful memory more,— and nobody can take that away from me."

60. departure from Cleveland: Among members of the Richter family is a story that Richter was fired or quit in Cleveland when the gossip his employer worried about finally surfaced in a newspaper's social column as a reference to a young man living under the same roof with a prominent single woman. If such an item appeared, it might well have been damaging enough to cause Mrs. Miller to abandon a comfortable and needed arrangement to care for her sons. There is no corroborating evidence in Richter's journal or correspondence (including subsequent correspondence with Mrs. E. C. T. Miller) to support this version, however, and there is Richter's own testimony that his job in Cleveland ended in emotional collapse. Of course such gossip would have been a convenient reason to release an employee who had become a burden.

CHAPTER 3. EARLY MARRIAGE

1. Sources for "Early Marriage": interviews with FR; interviews with HR; CR to HAR, eighty-three letters, August 18, 1914, to September 26, 1919; Mulford B. Foster to CR, fifteen letters, December 10, 1915, to March 7, 1918; A. L. Kimball, I.M.P., Cora Paget, and numerous other agents and editors for magazines to CR, January 1914 to March 1921; "Experience" summary of CR's employment with the Handy Book Company, ca. 1930.

2. recommendations: Wesley Everett, February 2, 1914; C. C. Latus, managing editor of *Public Opinion*, Pittsburgh, February 5, 1914; H. D. Hoover, February 16, 1914; Willis B. Hale, February 17, 1914; H. H. Hower, February 19, 1914; Charles T. Aikens, February 20, 1914; W. R. Cadweiler, February 24, 1914.

3. "a hell of a good fellow": Wesley Everett to Peter Taylor, February 12, 1914.

4. "We have to send back": W. A. Frost to CR, February 28, 1914.

5. "Your work is unusually good": A. L. Kimball to CR, March 3, 1914.

6. "P.S. 'Reader' is the word": Isabel M. Paterson to CR, March 10, 1914.

7. "Never mind": Isabel M. Paterson to CR, March 28, 1914.

8. "I don't like this story": Isabel M. Paterson to CR, April 2, 1914.

9. "We are glad": A. L. Kimball to CR, April 11, 1914.

10. "I have read": Isabel M. Paterson to CR, April 14, 1914.

11. "Never mind the trouble": Isabel M. Paterson to CR, April 14, 1914.

12. "Mrs. Wharton's Secretary": Robert Hobart Davis to CR, April 15, 1914.

13. "Let me warn you": Isabel M. Paterson to CR, April 25, 1914. Richter would never meet I.M.P., nor would she, during this correspondence, reveal the name behind the initials. In 1917 Richter guessed her identity on seeing a story of hers. In reply to his letter, Isabel M. Paterson confirmed that she had been the I.M.P. from *Hearst's Magazine*. In 1916 she published the first of several novels; from 1922 to 1949 her weekly column "Turns with a Bookworm" appeared in the *New York Herald Tribune*. There she delivered her provocative opinions in a disarmingly humorous way, including occasional—and to Richter distressing—comments on Richter's books.

14. "What are you thinking of": FR, HR; RTS, 11.

15. "We're coming": FR

16. "dared the crowd": CR to HAR, August 18, 1915; more summary of the first days with HR: CR to HAR, August 19, 1914.

17. "Half laughing": CR to HAR, August 19, 1914.

18. "Only your '14 love": CR to HAR, September 2, 1914.

19. "if nothing turns up": CR to HAR, August 25, 1914.

20. "pal, comrade, big brother": CR to HAR, August 24, 1914.

21. "We'd better not have children": CR to HAR, August 24, 1914.

22. Harvey's misgivings and Richter's response: J, October 17, 1943.

23. "no one could help": CR to HAR, October 9, 1914.

24. "Connie has a nice girl": CR to HAR, October 19, 1914.

25. "start up alone": CR to HAR, November 19, 1914.

26. "You and I dearest": CR to HAR, November 14, 1914.

27. "The Passing of Tombstone Mike": the Vitograph Company to CR, August 18, 1914.

28. Two movie scenarios sold: "The Seesaw" (Biograph Company to CR, October 8, 1914); "The Double Cross" (the Vitograph Company to CR, October 14, 1914).

29. "The Tangle of Lace": *Women's Stories* to CR, October 23, 1914.

30. "But dearest, I believe you are right": CR to HAR, n.d., ca. November 15, 1914.

31. writing in mid-December: CR to HAR, December 16, 1914.

32. "handle almost anything": fair copy of letter, on stationery of the Cleveland Athletic Club, dated February, 1915.

33. "Then she needs": HR, *Writing to Survive* (Albuquerque: University of New Mexico Press, 1986), 20.

34. "Tell me," "it won't be a secret," "I believe": CR to HAR, March 30, 1915.

35. first apartment: FR, HR; location: J, March 23, 1925.

36. manager of Handy Book Company: "Experience" (summary of business experience, for prospective employers, ca. 1930).

37. Mrs. Kimball eager to help: A. L. Kimball to CR, May 12, 1915.

38. "almost impossible": PRR to CR, July 22, 1915.

39. "a chance, though": Cora Paget to CR, October 5, 1915.

40. "afraid to tell": CR, "The King of Cold Spring," 1 (unpub. article).

41. "done splendidly": Cora Paget to CR, February 7, 1916.

42. "to butt in": Harold Paget to CR, February 8, 1916.

43. Harvey disguises her pregnancy: HR, FR.

44. Harvey's mother visits: HR.

45. "inclined to be long-winded": Cora Paget to CR, May 17, 1917.

46. estimate of sales: Cora Paget to CR, December 12, 1917, and December 17, 1917.

47. "Didn't he write": CR to HAR, May 1, 1918.

48. Joseph and the coat of many colors: HR.

49. "Joey's cough": CR to parents, n.d., ca. July 10, 1918.

50. "He gives to his sweetheart": CR to HAR, January 10, 1915.

51. Harvey does not meet Richter at door; marriage a battleground: HR.
52. "This week-end business": CR to HR, May 1, 1918.
53. "getting my nerve back": CR to HAR, May 1, 1918.
54. "Oh, Darling": CR to HAR, July 22, 1918.
55. movies: CR to HAR, May 9, 1918; CR to HAR, July 7, 1918.
56. Mary Pickford: CR to HAR, May 14, 1918.
57. "You've got to get right": CR to HAR, May 6, 1918.
58. "Darling, sweetheart": CR to HAR, May 6, 1918.
59. "Sweetheart when I see these movies": CR to HAR, May 9, 1918.
60. troubles at Cold Spring: HR.
61. "double tongued": CR to HAR, July 16, 1916.
62. "unpleasantly surprised," "Kindly do not repeat": CR to Mulford Foster, July 16, 1918.
63. "Sweetheart—I wish": CR to HAR, July 17, 1918.
64. neglecting Vene: CR to HAR, August 17, 1918.
65. hospitalized at birthday: J, August 18, 1949; CHR to CR, October 13, 1918.
66. "Smokehouse" was submitted under the title "The Peopled Wilderness," "You're Too Contwisted Satisfied, Jim Ted" under the title "Bad Luck Is Good Luck."

CHAPTER 4. PINE TREE FARM

Conrad Richter's journal, beginning in 1925 and continuing until his death in 1968, is for this and each succeeding chapter the primary source for information concerning Richter's inner life and often for the details of his writing, his health, and his day-to-day activities. As in earlier chapters, important incidents are noted separately, as are all quotations from the journals, the correspondence, and the writing notebooks.

1. Harvena overextends herself: J, June 24, 1954; symptoms follow flu: HR, FR.
2. "I don't like to tell": HR.
3. Public Health Service pamphlets: see, e.g., "Getting Well; Some Things Worth Knowing About Tuberculosis" (Washington: Government Printing Office, 1922).
4. tuberculosis therapy at Saranac Lake: Philip Gallos, *Cure Cottages of Lake Saranac* (Saranac Lake, N.Y.: Historic Saranac Lake, 1985).
5. "trying to get Harvey": CR to James Manning, December 19, 1925.
6. "the prettiest backwoods valley": J, March 23, 1923.
7. illnesses: HR, FR, Thomas Hinds to CR, January 5, 1923.
8. "If I had the con": CR to HAR, March 23, 1923.
9. "hippopotamus of a dog": J, October 31, 1926.
10. "the most haunted": CR, "Valley from the Past," *Country Beautiful* (April 1963), 10.
11. "something grayish": HR; "a light passing from room to room" and "two bobbing yellow lights": "Valley from the Past," 10–11; for another description of following the will-o'-the-wisps, see Harvena Richter's poem, "Swamp Light," *South Dakota Review* (summer 1993), 28.
12. little to show: J, June 5, 1926.
13. "I want to take you": CR to HAR, March 23, 1925.
14. "What will they do": J, October 20, 1926.
15. "'I sat down'": J, December 27, 1927.
16. CHR's hypochondria: J, December 10, 1961. In this entry CR speculates that his mother's hypochondria was a result of an especially active imagination—and that his own imagination was inherited from her. An equally strong case may be made that CR's own obsessive worry about his own health—and Harvey's—was acquired from Charlotte Richter.
17. "I have always said": "Seven Sales-Writing Principles," 46.
18. low opinion of books published: J, July 12, 1927.

19. "There's been a lot of ink": CR to Willard Hawkins, October 31, 1922.

20. recommends Christian Science: J, July 17, 1927.

21. "I am not afraid": CR to Steward Edward White, January 15, 1926.

22. hears Bertrand Russell: J, October 19, 1927.

23. completed a manuscript: CR to A. L. Kimball, March 7, 1923.

24. "Dear Mr. Rockefeller": CR to Rockefeller Institute, October 10, 1923.

25. *Human Vibration:* My discussion of Richter's energy theories is based on *HV*, and on *Principles in Bio-Physics,* "Nerve Energy: Its Management," and Richter's correspondence with interested readers. For a more extended discussion of Richter's theories, one Richter himself generally approved of, see "Richter's Theories of Psycho-Energics: A Restatement of Evolutionary Naturalism," in Clifford D. Edwards, *Conrad Richter's Ohio Trilogy* (The Hague: Mouton, 1970), chap. 2. By far the most comprehensive treatment of CR's theories is to be found in Harvena Richter, "The Golden Fountains," an as yet unpublished explanation and elaboration of CR's thought.

26. "plan of life": *HV,* 41–42.

27. "raising an individual's": *HV,* 51.

28. "commanded vibration" explained: *HV,* 51–55; "where before we were indifferent": *HV,* 55.

29. sympathy as "the mark of evolutionary progress": *HV,* 96.

30. "'simply the characteristics'": *HV,* 159.

31. "association considerably above the average": *HV,* 141.

32. "may be below the average": *HV,* 141–42.

33. "vague phenomena": CR to Rockefeller Institute, October 10, 1923.

34. "The only fact or truth": *HV,* 18.

35. "we can do what we wish": *HV,* 131.

36. "even God": *HV,* 22.

37. Fred's job: in an undated letter ca. 1928 FR acknowledges that CR wrote the letter that "got me my job and my Ford and my house."

38. John Richter purchasing a car: CR to JAR and CHR, September 13, 1924.

39. "ghastly bright and fair": J, October 8, 1926.

40. new doctor's advice: interview with Frederick D. Richter and Eduard C. Richter, September 21, 1991.

41. "lacked the human touch": CR to HR, September 13, 1948.

42. letter to *Woman's Home Companion:* CR to Gertrude Lane, editor, October 9, 1924.

43. "zero hour": J, June 12, 1933.

44. "incredulously" and "And yet": CR to Albert S. Crockett, November 18, 1924. Richter's first letter to Crockett has not survived; Crockett's letter of response, November 12, 1924, notes that it was dated October 31, 1924. Crockett's *Revelations to Louise* was published in 1920 in New York by Frederick A. Stokes Co.

45. Pierre-Emile Cornillier, *The Survival of the Soul and Its Evolution After Death* (New York: E. P. Dutton, 1921).

46. "correct a certain feebleness": Cornillier, 192.

47. skepticism of scientists: CR to Joseph Collins, April 17, 1926.

48. "lay off art": CR to Curtis Brown, June 14, 1922; CR is quoting from Carl Clausen to CR, February 12, 1922.

49. Clausen on editors: Carl Clausen to CR, March 3, 1922.

50. "only to furnish": CR to William Breck, January 15, 1924.

51. "knocked him out": CR to William Breck, March 6, 1924.

52. "good, solid, middle-class": William Breck to CR, March 10, 1924.

53. writing stories to accommodate: CR to Merle Crowell, March 28, 1924.

54. "a powerful and original": Isabel M. Paterson in the *New York Tribune,* January 6, 1924.

55. feeling superior to *American Magazine:* J, May 10, 1926.

56. "publishing and fiction": J, June 27, 1926.

57. "profitmaker": J, September 25, 1925.
58. butcher: J, March 13, 1926.
59. "That part of me": J, February 8, 1926.
60. "more hocum": CR to William Breck, November 10, 1926.

CHAPTER 5. NEW MEXICO

1. "A new issue": J, July 12, 1927.
2. "Don't let Vene": Elizabeth Henry to HAR, May 14, 1922.
3. "something serious" and "If sending Vene": J, October 28, 1926.
4. winter in Harrisburg proposed: J, November 2, 1926.
5. tuberculosis no further advanced: J, January 14, 1927.
6. "a few books": J, October 11, 1927.
7. "when one has": J, June 15, 1927.
8. "a dead level" and "This much": J, November 27, 1927.
9. "come sooner": J, August 26, 1927.
10. "a labor of love": CR to Bill Breck, September 5, 1927.
11. "The three chief interests": J, June 2, 1927.
12. "Tonight I received": J, March 18, 1927.
13. "I dare not": J, June 13, 1927.
14. "a decided change": CR to HAR, January 11, 1928.
15. "a flapper air" and "The city seems": CR to HAR, January 11, 1927.
16. "like a butcher's icebox": J, February 1, 1928.
17. "They have ease": J, January 30, 1928.
18. "I hope it poisons": J, August 5, 1928.
19. artificiality of Saranac Lake: J, July 27, 1928; superiority of Clark's Valley: J, August 17, 1928.
20. "An examination": CR to Donald McCormick, August 22, 1928.
21. "For weeks": J, August 28, 1928.
22. footsteps of mother: J, August 19, 1928.
23. blue light at Saranac Lake: J, August 20, 1928.
24. 2,500 chasing the cure: Jake Spidle, *Doctors of Medicine in New Mexico* (Albuquerque: University of New Mexico Press, 1986).
25. homesickness: CR to Donald McCormick, October 5, 1928.
26. "stories": J, December 6, 1928.
27. "I cannot be reconciled": J, February 2, 1929.
28. "a life drab": J, February 26, 1929.
29. "any sympathy": Erdman Brandt to CR, August 2, 1929.
30. sparring with John Gardner: John Gardner to HR, November 1, 1972. Both enjoyed the repartee so much that after Johnny Gardner returned to Colorado the two continued their disagreements in a correspondence—much of it about Richter's theories and Gardner's religion—until Richter's death in 1968.
31. "I was alive": J, October 9, 1929.
32. reaction to market crash: J, September 23, 1948.
33. Harvey's ordeal, Vene frightened and crying: HR; J, December 26, 1929.
34. Dr. Peters giving up on Harvey: "When, after three operations on the chest, her doctor, one of the best in the world, gave her up, I put her into the only hands left—my own." CR to Charles S. Kettering, December 14, 1933.
35. sun lamp as therapy: HR.
36. "asked gravely": "Depression Journal," unpub. article, n.d., p. 1.
37. "deep inner loneliness": J, January 19, 1930; melancholy: February 19, 1930.

38. "the loveliest spring": J, April 5, 1930.
39. "sallow, sad": undated notes in "Breakdown file," on sheet beginning "Bad Crisis 1617, July 1941."
40. soil from Pine Tree Farm: CR to S. Omar Barker, February 16, 1931.
41. "written into the streets": J, June 22, 1930; also "What You Have Now," undated sheet from Health file, c. 1940.
42. Sander's advice: Sydney A. Sanders to CR: September 26, 1930.
43. financial situation: J, August 8 and 10, 1930.
44. "Shall I sacrifice": CR to George A. Kaseman, October 9, 1930.
45. "I will do anything": CR to Marguerite Harper, October 21, 1930.
46. Harvey names pallbearers: J, December 12, 1930.
47. "get in a minimum": CR to Marguerite Harper, March 5, 1931.
48. "We're flat": CR to Marguerite Harper, December 10, 1931.

CHAPTER 6. EARLY AMERICANA

1. $10,000 in debt: CR to Marguerite Harper, February 16, 1932.
2. refusal to consider bankruptcy: FR; also CR to JAR, May 10, 1934.
3. Vene giving no answer: HR.
4. Richter at home: HR.
5. Harvey reclining on a sofa: interview with Matthew Pearce, August 8, 1984.
6. family outings on the desert: HR.
7. coaching himself: e.g., J, June 24, 1932, describing his "remorse" after visits to Paul Everman, the Dalbeys, and others, for staying too long, talking too much, and misspeaking.
8. not being excessively grateful: HR; entry in "Personal Notebook."
9. Harvey's setback caused by worry: CR to Marguerite Harper, February 16, 1932.
10. rather have a beefsteak: J, March 26, 1932.
11. "forgotten by God": J, November 2, 1961.
12. a new way of introducing his ideas: CR to Joseph Collins, May 26, 1930.
13. "A Book for Your Life Work": CR, undated notes.
14. "catastrophe" and "unconscious pilgrimage": CR to Joseph Collins, May 26, 1930.
15. forced to mountain cabin: CR to Marguerite Harper, March 31, 1932.
16. "sea of grass": J, August 22, 1931; also, CR, "Introduction," *The Sea of Grass* (New York: Time-Life Books, 1965), xvi.
17. "the yeast of living": CR, "Introduction," *Sea of Grass*, xvii.
18. Stanford Street house unlucky: J, April 5, 1932; CR to JAR, April 3, 1932.
19. not telling Vene: HR; Harvena Richter would eventually be told by her mother, after her father's death.
20. "I've got to get": CR to Marguerite Harper, June 2, 1932.
21. Alma's promise: HR.
22. "rich who have fattened" and "I have been hard hit": CR to Enrique Blanco, April 4, 1933.
23. missing New Mexico: CR to Paul Everman, April 23, 1933.
24. "heavy, hopeless": J, June 12, 1933.
25. proposes himself as tutor: CR to George St. Clair, November 3, 1933.
26. clothing list: J, November 7, 1933; trouble writing pulps: CR to PRR, December 14, 1933.
27. "At least": J, November 23, 1933.
28. "California beckons": J, December 3, 1933.
29. *"Blue Again"*: J, December 13, 1933.
30. "Black, yet Happy": J, December 15, 1933.
31. voice breaking at bank: J, December 19, 1933.
32. "if we both": PRR to CR, December 19,1933.

33. "a poor effort": J, January 4, 1934.
34. "a failure": Record of Dreams, Signs, etc., January 5, 1934.
35. "not tired so much" and "I was somewhere far from Albuquerque": J, January 10, 1934.
36. "very blue," etc.: J, January 16, 1934.
37. "When I was finished": J, January 19, 1934.
38. "Both enthusiastic": J, January 28, 1934.
39. "I could think": J, January 30, 1934.
40. "almost ran away:" PRRjr to CR, January 29, 1934.
41. "most real story": J, February 2, 1934.
42. "old eternal fear" to "keeping things to myself": J, February 3, 1934.
43. "moved her more": J, February 6, 1934.
44. "What I Believe": J, February 6, 1934.
45. "A Bargain with God": J, February 11, 1934.

CHAPTER 7. THE SEA OF GRASS

1. "Nothing else": J, November 22, 1934.
2. "Nancy Belle felt": "Early Marriage," EA, 306.
3. "How could you": Dona Saye to CR, n.d.
4. friendship with Sadie Garduño: HR.
5. relationship with Sadie Garduño: HR.
6. Sadie Garduño as model for Lutie: CR, "Introduction," The Sea of Grass (New York: Time-Life Books, 1965), xix.
7. "Reputations are built": PRRjr to CR, July 20, 1934.
8. "a big gamble": PRR to CR, August 22, 1934.
9. "That's the way": PRR to CR, July 6, 1934.
10. worries about sorority: J, September 22, 1934.
11. Vene moves to Kappa house: J October 30, 1934.
12. "too thin": J, November 5, 1934.
13. "high hat": J, November 5, 1934.
14. "the best I have seen": J, December 7, 1934.
15. articles on loss of vitality: "That Early American Quality," Atlantic, September 1950, 26–30; "Individualists Under the Shade Trees," in A Vanishing America: The Life and Times of the Small Town, ed. Thomas C. Wheeler (New York: Holt, Rinehart, and Winston, 1964), 34–42.
16. "thinning, declining" and "My father was not so severe": "That Early American Quality," 28.
17. "trite and unconvincing": Julian Johnson to CR, January 11, 1935.
18. story with an epic sweep: J, December 15, 1936.
19. despondent after mailing "Smoke Over the Prairie": J, March 19, 1935.
20. personal statement wanted: PRR to CR, April 18, 1935; CR reaction: J, April 22, 1935.
21. "there is a kind of blur": J, June 24, 1935.
22. "Sometimes I think": J, June 24, 1935.
23. "never raise your voice": excerpts from undated lists and personal notes in Health file.
24. "he had to add": J, July 20, 1935.
25. "something to help": J, July 7, 1935.
26. "The only way": CR to Carl Taylor, September 24, 1935.
27. "no place to work": CR to John Gardner, September 24, 1935.
28. "whenever I went over": CR to Ruth Laughlin Alexander, June 22, 1937.
29. "write the story": CR to Ruth Laughlin Alexander, June 22, 1937.
30. "frantic," etc.: J, October 1, 1935.
31. "taking Vene out of school": J, September 27, 1935.

32. "incident of doling out" and "The sub-ideas for it flowered": J, October 2, 1935.
33. "a man will do": CR to Carl Taylor, October 31, 1935.
34. "most decidedly": AK to CR, October 24, 1935.
35. "Due Albuquerque": AK to CR, October 31, 1935.
36. "a big stout German": CR to FR and Emily Richter, December 1, 1935.
37. conversation with Knopf: J, November 1, 1935.
38. putting off writing a novel: CR to AK, December 21, 1935.
39. Ed Sargent: J, August 8, 1932; "his dramatic entrance": CR, "Introduction," *Sea of Grass*, xx.
40. "Not a little": CR, "Introduction," *Sea of Grass*, xix.
41. "To Willa Cather": CR to Ruth Laughlin Alexander, June 22, 1937.
42. woman never returned: Zoe Ferguson to CR, October 7, 1934.
43. Carl Taylor's death: J, February 5, 1936.
44. choosing "The Sea of Grass" as title: J, March 1, 1936.
45. "was plainly bluffing": J, March 8, 1936.
46. "Mr. Lorimer writes": PRRjr to CR, March 21, 1936.
47. "Have you noticed": *SG*, 149.
48. serial may do *Post* harm: J, June 12, 1936.
49. color from St. Vincent's: CR to Thomas J. Kennedy, December 5, 1936.
50. abstaining from sex: J, March 12, 1939.
51. "to try blurring": CR to PRR, July 8, 1936.
52. not wanting to embarrass G. H. Lorimer: CR to PRRjr, July 25, 1936.
53. "Have smelling salts": CR to FR, July 13, 1936.

CHAPTER 8. SOMETHING FOR MYSELF

1. "I am more sure": AK to CR, July 21, 1936.
2. Reynolds writes that Knopf is pleased: PRR to CR, August 21, 1936.
3. "you have staked": CR to AK, August 29, 1936.
4. Harvey and Vene on Richter's corrections to galleys: J, August 3, 1936.
5. "several changes": CR to AK, August 31, 1936.
6. Interview at MGM: CR to HAR, September 8, 1936.
7. "a modest four-month contract": CR to HAR, September 9, 1936.
8. "I felt that": CR to AK, September 21, 1936.
9. "I should be willing": J, September 11, 1936.
10. repaying all debts: CR to Gregory Achenbach, October 20, 1936; CR to FR, October 11, 1936;
FR.
11. refusing lower interest rate: FR.
12. meeting with Considine: J, October 5, 1936.
13. asking Vene to play the piano: J, October 1, 1936.
14. typing two copies: J, October 26, 1936.
15. feeling at studio: J, October 28, 1936.
16. "one of the highest": J, October 13, 1936.
17. Considine telephone call: J, October 29, 1936.
18. "tremendously interested": J, November 13, 1936.
19. Richter considered "tops": J, November 24, 1936.
20. "Benefits Forgot" as best script: J, December 4, 1936.
21. "cursing the stupidity": J, December 13, 1936.
22. "the lack of energy": J, December 24, 1936.
23. Considine suggests another writer: J, December 15, 1936.
24. "I told him": J, January 6, 1937.

25. "Shall be very glad": CR to FR, March 8, 1937.
26. "Chiefly I feel sorry": J, February 9, 1937.
27. "wait for the remainder": CR to PRR, February 12, 1937.
28. "golden chords running down": CR to John Jones, June 12, 1953.
29. *The Sea of Grass* on best-seller lists: CR to FR, March 8, 1937.
30. "I am glad" and "I have no respect": J, April 6, 1937.
31. "matured into a determination": J, April 5, 1937.
32. "I felt that I wanted": J, April 26, 1937.
33. "If only we had a sign": J, May 1, 1937.
34. blood in handkerchief: J, May 1, 1937.
35. "the place is bound": CR to AK, June 13, 1937.
36. "I've sat down": CR to Wesley W. Stout, June 15, 1937.
37. "disappoint your audience": Wesley W. Stout to CR, August 19, 1937.
38. reason for rewriting "The Rawhide Knot": J, August 20, 1937.
39. throws fork at Harvey: the only record of this event occurs in a journal entry years later, January 16, 1955, which places the occurrence at Dauphin but does not provide a date.
40. "I am convinced": J, August 25, 1937.
41. Wesley Stout on Richter's market: J, August 27, 1937.
42. trip to New York: J, September 12, 1937.
43. "and make no more": J, September 12, 1937.
44. uses of Hollywood money: J, November 1, 1937.
45. staying on in Hollywood: J, October 23, 1937 and November 1, 1937.
46. Lorimer's death, Dalton Trumbo incident: J, October 23, 1937.
47. "When I am away" and "If I want to write": J, November 1, 1937.
48. upset by changes in "Benefits Forgot": J, November 13, 1937.
49. meeting with Knopf; telegram; Richter's speculation: J, November 13, 1937.
50. meeting with Stromberg; "All in all": J, November 18, 1937.
51. "useless": J, November 18, 1937; "nervous and worthless" and "like a cheap cad": J, November 23, 1937.
52. "It is very funny": J, November 20, 1937.
53. "to think and feel": J, November 23, 1937.
54. "shamed"; needing a story more real: undated notes entitled "Four Way Conference of NORTHWEST PASSAGE."
55. meeting with Stromberg: J, December 6, 1937.
56. "The first thing": J, December 6, 1937.
57. "a little stunned"; "with John Minsker shouting": J, November 20, 1937.
58. comparison to Steinbeck: J, November 22, 1937.
59. "I must be simpler": J, November 22, 1937.
60. "I am convinced": J, December 14, 1937.
61. "well enough to do": Edwin H. Knopf to CR, January 7, 1938.
62. "I am terrifically ashamed": J, January 23, 1938.
63. new plans for his novel: J, February 9, 1938.
64. "I am not excited"; signs portending success: J, February 13, 1938.
65. writing "Bread"; "Of course it is very rough": J, February 15, 1938.
66. worries of failure: J, March 10, 1938.
67. "was moving chiefly": CR to Erdman Brandt, May 10, 1938.
68. carries briefcase into theater: J, October 23, 1967.
69. putting off operation: J, March 11, 1939.
70. "at a bad age": CR to HR, February 12, 1939.
71. worries about money: J, March 12, 1939; HAR to HR, March 12, 1939.
72. "would not yield"; "natural occurrences": J, January 7, 1939.

73. "real things": J, March 21, 1939.
74. deflating Stout: J, February 13, 1939; CR to Gerald D. Adams, March 13, 1939.
75. not enough interest for trilogy: CR to AK, May 21, 1939.
76. unlikely to interest Hollywood: CR to PRR, July 1, 1939.
77. Adams not to encourage MGM: CR to Gerald D. Adams, March 13, 1939; no part for Gary Cooper: CR to Edwin H. Knopf, April 19, 1939.
78. novel ordinary: CR to FR, April 19, 1939.
79. remorse and promises after Harvey's attack: Health file, undated sheet beginning WARNING OF YOUR GREATEST CRISIS AHEAD.
80. "black wave of nerve weakness": J, May 11, 1939.
81. "necessary drive of story": Erdman Brandt to CR, July 11, 1939.
82. signs warning of rejections: J, July 16, 1939.
83. contract offer: Gerald D. Adams to CR, July 28, 1939; Blanche Knopf's telegram: July 30, 1939.
84. "enormously enthusiastic": Blanche Knopf to CR, August 4, 1939.
85. "fine offer": J, September 18, 1939.
86. *The Trees* not for sale: CR to Gerald R. Adams, November 7, 1939.

CHAPTER 9. NOMADS

1. "a peculiarly bitter look": CR to HAR, January 20 and 22, 1940; also CR to John Jones, September 9, 1960.
2. bitter look: references to his bitter mouth after he was prepared for burial would appear in J as late as January 11, 1964.
3. "A peculiar thing": CR to HAR, January 20, 1940.
4. "read this again": undated sheet, entitled "Standing Death."
5. "Does my mother": J, January 7, 1940.
6. music painful to hear: J, February 19, 1940.
7. visiting psychics: Richter records a first session in J, February 2, 1940; J mentions follow throughout the year, including Richter's description of visiting an obviously fake palmist (J, September 24, 1940).
8. Eeland on Cornillier: L. E. Eeland to CR, June 7, 1940; also Dutton, Inc. to CR, July 24, 1940.
9. "I am Pennsylvania Dutch": CR to Emile Cornillier, November 27, 1940. It is surprising that Richter here referred to himself as Pennsylvania Dutch, a group he associated with qualities he did not admire—stubbornness, clannishness, narrow-mindedness, and coldness of demeanor—and a group he habitually declined to accept as his own. (The Conrads had made a distinction Richter himself continued, distinguishing people of German extraction from the Palatines, who spoke a German dialect that would become known in America as Pennsylvania Dutch.) In his introductory letter to L. E. Eeland Richter had been careful to separate himself from Pennsylvania Germans, writing that despite his "German-sounding name," his "people" had been English, French, and Scotch-Irish, as well as German. It is perhaps a reasonable inference that Richter, anticipating German censorship of mail arriving in France, guessed that announcing his Pennsylvania Dutch heritage might increase his chances of having the letter actually delivered to Cornillier.
10. "My last two novels": CR to L. E. Eeland, July 26, 1940.
11. letters to Cornillier: November 5, 1944; written in CR's hand on his copy of this letter is: "Wrote again June 16, 1946 and asked whoever received the letter to reply."
12. refuses $25,000 for film rights: J, March 21, 1940; CR to AK, May 2, 1940.
13. "just sweeps everything": AK to CR, April 12, 1940.
14. "I hold Knopf's": J, February 8, 1940.
15. "I think you must reckon": AK to CR, April 12, 1940.

16. "I think you are all wrong": AK to CR, May 10, 1940.

17. "a grand and important work": Blanche Knopf to CR, June 6, 1940.

18. "If I am really": CR to Blanche Knopf, May 31, 1940.

19. "America's incredible indifference": response to questionnaire from Charles Lee, literary editor of the *Philadelphia Record*, with cover letter dated August 20, 1943. One protest letter does survive, from CR to James L. Fly, chairman of the Federal Communications Commission, with a copy to the National Broadcasting System, expressing his outrage at a radio broadcast, a "free speech forum," which was "packed with Nazi, Fascist, and Communist sympathizers," May 5, 1941.

20. God not allow Nazis into heaven: J, March 29, 1940.

21. "A wave of frightful consequences": CR to Johnny Gardner, June 5, 1940.

22. "[Knopf] carries a little Leica": CR to Agnes Morley Cleaveland, May 4, 1947.

23. "had been a frost": CR to FR, August 27, 1940.

24. reaction to *Our Southwest*: J, September 28, 1940.

25. Hollywood powers could not be trusted: J, January 21, 1938; "the field is a tricky one": CR to HR, October 1, 1940.

26. date of original letter: J, October 26, 1940. Richter's fountain pen ran out of ink as he signed the November 26 letter, an event he recorded in his list of possible signs from the astral.

27. "What a cad": CR to AK, January 21, 1941.

28. Vene's explanation of trial period at Saks: HR to CR, March 21, 1941.

29. major issue of *Tacey Cromwell*: CR to AK, August 4, 1942.

30. "Her face hardens": J, February 10, 1941.

31. "hard, bitter, unforgiving," "Will you walk": loose sheet in "Health notes" file, entitled "This Must Be Kept in Front and Studied Daily, ESPECIALLY WHEN THINGS ARE GOOD, or You Are a Lost Soul in Hell."

32. ferocious fight: HR to David Johnson, December 1, 1995.

33. *The Trees* misses the Pulitzer Prize: J, June 8, 1941.

34. "Say nothing to anyone": CR to HR, March 30, 1941.

35. "I thought I felt": CR to HR, June 4, 1941.

36. "so bad [that] it seemed": J, December 3, 1941.

37. Richter's nervous collapse: there are two specific J acknowledgments: in a May 29, 1949, summary of "ill fortunes," CR lists "my hernia; my gland trouble; my breakdown in Tucson; my heart trouble at Pine Grove"; in a August 14, 1949 comment on "Cycles of My Life," Richter mentions his "breakdown in Tucson," comparing it to those in Pittsburgh and Cleveland. Surviving CR and HAR letters to HR are remarkably circumspect about CR's health during this period, but an Easter 1942 letter from HAR to HR ("Daddy might not be equal to the strain of a city like New York yet") verifies that HR had been informed about her father's condition, as does a June 8, 1942, letter from HAR to HR commenting that CR was still not sufficiently recovered in strength to take long walks. On March 11, four days after CR attempted to return to his writing, HAR wrote to HR that she had talked CR into buying a fishing rod to get him to spend more time relaxing out-of-doors.

38. "my feelings against Jews": loose sheet entitled "Trouble about Book with Knopf was not only because of lack of publicity."

39. "to recognize American authors": Karl J. Holzknecht to CR, March 2, 1942.

40. worrying about attending award ceremony: HAR to HR, April 1, 1942.

41. telegrams not sent: J, March 2, 1942.

42. "wonderful time in N.Y.": J, May 26, 1942.

43. "practical, not puritanical": Edward Weeks to CR, May 18, 1942.

44. "very difficult": PRRjr to CR, June 18, 1942.

45. *Post* still interested in Richter: Ben Hibbs to CR, May 15, 1942; sale of serial: PRRjr to CR, September 9, 1942.

46. "I'm a believer": CR to FR July 26, 1953.

47. pep talk to Fred, sun lamp: FR.

48. living in Pine Grove and New York: between 1942 and 1946, CR and HAR made extended stays in New York nine times, Pine Grove ten; they also made a number of shorter trips to New York for visits with HR.

49. "Knopf values you": PRRjr to CR, June 5, 1941.

CHAPTER 10. NOTHING BUT CHRISTMAS

1. series of blunders: J, July 25, 1943; December 16, 1945.

2. Richter finances: according to PRR account statements for the period, CR's average annual income from royalties and sales, 1941–44, was more than $6,300.

3. anticipation of return to Sayward's story: even Joseph Richter, ever forthright, praised *Tacey Cromwell* but then commented that it did not compare to *The Trees*, his brother's "masterpiece": JR to CR, ca. November 15, 1942.

4. synopsis for MGM: PRRjr to CR, July 28, 1943; CR to PRRjr, August 20, 1943.

5. Hunt Stromberg interested in *Tacey Cromwell*: PRRjr to CR, September 23, 1943; Stanwyck reported to refuse: J, October 9, 1943.

6. Harvey's opposition to writing chapters as stories: J, October 2, 1943.

7. "It was not a native talent": J, October 2, 1943.

8. "Mother used to tell": J, October 26, 1943.

9. "She just looks": J, November 29, 1943.

10. "had worked too hard": J, January 15, 1943.

11. pleased with *The Trees*: J, January 10, 1944.

12. Pine Grove ugly: J, January 23, 1944.

13. "There is humor": J, March 30, 1943; not storytellers: J, March 24, 1943.

14. "The light was gone," "It is not just the person": J, February 22, 1944; "At the feel": J, February 23, 1944.

15. Harvey leaving: J, March 19, 1944.

16. Stanley's advice: J, March 13, 1944.

17. Harvey not returning to Pine Grove: HAR to CR, May 1, 1944.

18. drives to New York: J, May 5, 1944.

19. "That's how life was": TR, 302.

20. "I kicked at the bed," P.E.N. dinner: J, November 15, 1944.

21. "I wish you would tell": CR to AK, April 19, 1945.

22. "magnificent": Blanche Knopf to CR, May 18, 1945.

23. Harvena's journal: fifty-six pages, with more than eighty handwritten entries, dated 1937 to 1962.

24. "Harvey and 'The Nettle Patch'": J, January 28, 1946.

25. "a bit beneath": J, January 10, 1944.

26. "half Christian Science": CR to HR, June 6, 1943.

27. "support of people who loved you": J, May 1, 1945.

28. "high silk hat": CR to Robert M. Yoder, September 1, 1946.

29. "The artist in me": J, August 2, 1945.

30. allows Reynolds to submit *The Fields* to competition: PRRjr to CR, May 16, 1945. "ghost of a chance": CR to PRRjr, May 22, 1945.

31. reaction to atom bomb: FR to CR, July 29, 1950.

32. "I wanted to write": J, October 28, 1945.

33. "the arrangement of all": J, November 2, 1945.

34. sale of *Always Young and Fair* to the *Post*, ice cream sodas: J, November 28, 1945.

35. "as much as we": CR to PRRjr, November 30, 1945.

36. "poor cracker colony": J, December 2, 1945; advice to Vene: CR to HR, November 26, 1945.

37. dissatisfied with plot: J, December 16, 1945.

38. Reynolds on *Always Young and Fair*: PRRjr to CR, July 28, 1947.

39. telephone number: J, April 29, 1946.

40. atmosphere of Hess house: CR to HR, May 10, 1946; J, April 2, 1947.

41. "a season of preparation": J, June 21, 1946.

42. too comfortable in Pine Grove: J, July 27, 1946.

43. faults of *The Fields*: J, May 17, 1946, July 15, 1946.

44. Sutherland article: CR to HR, May 10, 1946.

45. Harvard, Bread Loaf invitations: CR to HR, May 10, 1946: Theodore Morrison to CR, May 15, 1946.

46. Iowa inquiry: Emily Morrison (of Knopf's) relaying information from Paul Engel, August 22, 1946.

47. "should it happen": CR to Theodore Morrison, June 3, 1946.

48. at Bread Loaf: J, August 19 and 22, 1946; "a futile gesture": J, September 24, 1946; on the inebriation of the singers: CR to T. A. Buhl, September 24, 1950.

49. "too slight and tenuous": J, October 5, 1946.

50. Reynolds report: November 11, 1946; Knopf letter: November 13, 1946.

51. description of departure: CR to HR, November 19, 1946.

52. "everything western": HAR to HR, ca. November 22, 1946; "more gorgeous every minute": HAR to HR, November 26, 1946.

53. Thanksgiving in the Manzanos: J, November 28, 1946; HAR to HR, November 27, 1946.

54. "It is very difficult": CR to AK, November 24, 1946.

55. seeing *The Sea of Grass*: J, June 19, 1947.

56. "What am I to turn": J, April 16, 1947.

57. wishing for a Pulitzer Prize: J, May 5, 1947.

58. announcement of Ohioana award: Florence R. Head to AK, March 27, 1947.

59. acceptance: CR to Florence R. Head, March 29, 1947; influence on writing: J, March 28, 1947.

60. change in Ohioana Library Association award: J, October 7, 1947.

61. "I lost my dignity": J, October 11, 1947.

62. suitor lying: J, December 31, 1947.

63. "I feel evil": J, October 29, 1949.

64. Vene not marrying: J, January 4, 1946.

65. "What do Knopf and Reynolds matter": J, October 14, 1947.

66. "could handle herself": J, June 17, 1948.

67. "Tonight after more trouble": J, September 4, 1948.

68. finances while writing *The Town*: "Paul R. Reynolds and Son, Statements of Earnings"; J, December 19, 1948: "Shocked at how poor we are," listing expenses of $619 for October, $717 for November, leading to agreement between CR and HAR to buy no Christmas gifts for each other (J, December 25, 1948).

69. "Camp Junco": HAR to HR, January 24, 1949.

70. "Queer": CR to HR, May 14, 1950.

71. Chancey's angel has been his mother: Richter's source for this incident, recorded in a Richter's writing notebooks, dates back to 1938 or 1939. When a bookstore clerk told Richter that a man praising his work had bought a copy to send abroad, Richter asked to what country. When the clerk replied Germany, the light flashed: "Then I knew. It was Dad. Taken down like Chancey. Then is when I got the Chancey episode."

72. "this is it": AK to CR, September 9, 1949.

73. Reynolds's estimate of *The Town*: PRRjr to CR, September 8, 1949; "You just don't realize": PRRjr to CR, November 30, 1949.

74. "idea story": PRRjr to CR, December 13, 1949; also December 14, 1949.
75. "as fine as anything": Ben Hibbs to CR, December 14, 1949.
76. "Perhaps when you": *SEP,* June 10, 1950, 22.
77. "Now as I came": CR to Ralph Knight, December 28, 1949.
78. "If only I could go in": J, June 4, 1947.
79. "My mother": J, November 11, 1944.
80. "Only work counts": J, November 24, 1938.
81. "That week went quick": J, January 15, 1944.
82. "My work is all": J, October 26, 1943; "All that matters": J, October 14, 1947.

CHAPTER 11. PUTTING AWAY TOYS AND PAWNS

1. more spiritual book: J, January 22, 1950.
2. books which were "a must to write": maroon notebook 1 (September 1949), 51.
3. "glum, shabby": J, January 18, 1950.
4. looking old: J, January 16, 1950.
5. "Don't unpack": HAR to HR, January 13,1950.
6. Pine Grove a haven: J, February 2, 1950.
7. Harvey's assessment of early drafts: J, April 1, 1950.
8. "heartbroken": AK to CR, May 24, 1950; "I haven't, alas": AK to CR, July 10, 1950.
9. mediating between Darwinism and Mary Baker Eddy: J, June 2, 1954.
10. "I am only dimly beginning to see": CR to Douglas Matthews, September 12 1944.
11. drive to Socorro; "I have not been too well": CR to HR, June 3, 1950.
12. "We live in the most": CR to Charles Warfel, September 11, 1950.
13. "Should the need arrive": CR to PRRjr, July 3, 1950.
14. Harvey's response to six chapters: J, July 22, 1950.
15. Vene sells story to the *Post:* J, September 22, 1950; HR; the story was published by the *Post* as "Freighter's Feud" on June 16, 1951.
16. "homeless wanderers, as usual": CR to Anna Boyer, September 11, 1950.
17. reasons for not staying in Mexico: CR to HR, October 16, 1950, and October 31, 1950.
18. letter describing 11 Maple Street: Stanley Achenbach to CR and HAR, November 11, 1950.
19. house a good buy: J, December 17, 1950.
20. "Shawnee Raid": *SEP,* January 19, 1952.
21. "Lately I have felt": CR to PRRjr, April 14, 1951.
22. "Hate is the raw" and "Love is only": typescript of MD1, 146.
23. characteristics of higher self: typescript of MD1, 159.
24. "In theory we grow": typescript of MD1, 161.
25. "perfectly willing to publish": AK to PRRjr, May 4, 1951.
26. "I have received more letters": CR to Eve Kroeger, May 21, 1951.
27. letter from Korea: Sgt. Norman L. Clements to CR, May 8, 1951; gave the most pleasure: CR to Eva Kroeger, May 21, 1951.
28. dream of Lottie Richter: J, May 12, 1951.
29. Pulitzer Prize as encouragement: J, May 7, 1951.
30. "[Harvey's ambition] astonished": J, May 14, 1951.
31. Vene criticizes *The Mountain on the Desert:* J, May 28, 1951.
32. Harvey and Vene's criticisms take away confidence: J, October 1, 1951.
33. restless in Pine Grove: J, August 14, 1951.
34. Harvey's worries over house: J, September 2, 1951.
35. "Sad over Vene": J, September 28, 1951; visit to Joe's: J, September 2, 1951.

36. Vene must take Jack Haggerty out of house: HR.

37. long struggle to affirm his relationship: in a letter to Helen M. Madsen, June 18, 1967, Richter acknowledged the connection in his own mind between the mythic search for the father and the search for God: "the general experience of man from time immemorial is his eternal search for his real father. Is it his parent or God?"

38. heart palpitations caused by worry: J, June 20, 1952.

39. "You old bubbly": J, June 24, 1952.

40. "Fortunately, the *Post*": CR to AK, June 25, 1952.

41. "I haven't seen": HAR to HR, June 29, 1952.

42. Fred and Emily's visit: CR to HR, July 4, 1952; also FR.

43. changes to respond to Vene's criticism: J, July 16, 1952.

44. reasons for choosing title: J, July 29, 1952.

45. "actually weaken": AK to CR, September 22, 1952.

46. "interesting sermon": Erdman Brandt to CR, December 16, 1952.

47. "beloved": J, January 16, 1953.

48. recurrence of ache in chest: J, January 19, 1953.

49. not meant to finish: J, January 25, 1953.

50. "buried in the Ozarks": CR to AK, May 17, 1953.

51. "more impressive, commanding and oriental": J, May 31, 1953.

52. selling movie rights to Walt Disney: J, May 31, 1953.

53. "seemed grand": J, June 5, 1953.

54. "like most humorists": J, September 2, 1953.

55. buying used Cadillac: J, July 24, 1953, and J, September 3, 1953.

56. "come home with a car": CR to FR, July 26, 1953.

57. failing his mother, father, and Jack Haggerty: J, January 22, 1954.

58. impressions of Florida sojourn: J, March 7, 1954.

59. "Why am I so often": J, March 23, 1954; "aura of sadness," J, March 24, 1954.

60. Vene keeps novel to herself: HR; also J, November 21, 1954.

61. Harvey and Vene criticize *MD*: J, July 11, 1954.

62. "I have written a dud": J, August 8, 1954.

63. Reynolds's comments on *MD*: PRRjr to CR, August 20, 1954.

64. "I will shortly be sending": AK to CR, September 20, 1954.

65. comparison to William James: J, September 18, 1954.

66. "The writer of such journals": J, September 23, 1954.

67. "Strangely [the journals]": J, October 10, 1954.

68. article better than hoped: J, September 29, 1954.

69. declining reputation, loss of ability to work long hours: J, December 20, 1954.

70. Harry Warfel's claims, Richter's response: CR to HR, March 6, 1955.

71. attends Frost lecture: J, March 14, 1955.

72. "As is his custom": J, March 20, 1955.

73. leaving success to God: CR to HR, September 21, 1954.

74. reaction on reading *The Mountain on the Desert*: J, May 8, 1955.

75. no review copies sent out: AK to CR, May 27, 1955; William Cole to CR, May 27, 1955.

76. disbelieves Cole explanation: J, May 27, 1954; CR to PRRjr, June 1, 1954.

77. "I had thought that my work": J, May 25, 1955.

78. "looking more sharp and clean": J, May 31, 1955.

79. "If the book is true": J, May 17, 1954.

80. sales distribution: Suzanne M. Stewart to CR, September 8, 1955.

81. on craft of storytelling: J, August 2, 1955.

82. attempts to sell 11 Maple Street: J, August 30, 1955.

CHAPTER 12. THE CLOSED DOOR

1. grateful for several years' income: J, June 6, 1956.
2. description of Harry Roskolenko: HR to CR and HAR, February 9,1956.
3. "If I can only": J, April 26, 1956.
4. clipping notices of sailing dates: HAR to HR, May 14, 1956.
5. "Interested—not to say": HAR to HR, June 8, 1956.
6. worries about murder and white slavery: such worries were not without reason. Bandits were known to prey on travelers along Iranian roads, and when Vene arrived in Teheran she was told that the daughter of the Swedish ambassador and her American boyfriend had disappeared in Afghanistan.
7. "You will probably smile": CR to John G. Gardner, April 5, 1957.
8. wants portable record player: CR to HR, March 4, 1956.
9. breaking in to HR's apartment: J, August 25, 1956; HR.
10. invitation to join the Western Writers of America: Frank Gruber to CR, August 1, 1955.
11. Gruber's $50,000 movie deal: Frank Gruber to CR, September 10,1955.
12. Gruber's method in studio conferences: Frank Gruber to CR, September 3, 1955.
13. promotional material: AK to CR, November 19, 1956.
14. "like a cheap western": J, November 23, 1956; "The clash is not": CR to AK, November 27, 1956.
15. "there is so much writing": J, January 18, 1967.
16. limiting work on "The Gifts": J, April 11, 1957.
17. Reynolds complains about reviews: PRRjr to CR, May 18, 1957; CR response: J, May 19, 1957.
18. "Could this be why": J, March 28, 1959.
19. reluctantly attends dedication: J, July 7, 1957.
20. refuses church membership: J, April 4, 1957.
21. Trouble over Harry Roskolenko: J, July 31, 1957; J, August 1, 1957.
22. "a better car": J, January 17, 1958.
23. description of car; waiting in hotel for house owners to leave: J, January 17, 1958.
24. recalls first stay in Banning: J, January 24, 1958.
25. nighttime anguish: Richter himself made the connection with his childhood fears: J, June 25, 1958: "troubled by fear that hit me stronger than any time. Reminded me of original onset when a boy."
26. fears will not wake up: J, April 10, 1958.
27. packing for quick departure: HAR to HR, March 10, 1958.
28. awareness of suffering: J, April 10, 1958.
29. "I believe in God": J, April 26, 1956.
30. proposing delay of publication of "The Gifts": CR to PRRjr, May 8, 1958.
31. "You have been generous": CR to AK, May 16, 1958.
32. radio interview: CR and Henry Homan of WLBR, Lebanon, Pennsylvania, June 25, 1958.
33. *Post* rejects "The Gifts": PRRjr to CR, May 26, 1958; reasons for rejection: PRRjr to CR, June 23, 1958.
34. Reynolds warns about Knopf: PRRjr to CR, June 19, 1958.
35. "This is one of the most painful letters": AK to CR, June 18, 1958.
36. Knopf risking loss of Richter: PRRjr to CR, June 23, 1958.
37. "make a contract with a first-class publisher": PRRjr to CR, June 19, 1958; "wrote me rather decently": CR to PRRjr, June 21, 1958.
38. novel uninteresting: J, June 24, 1958.
39. instructions to Reynolds: CR to PRRjr, June 2, 1958.
40. Vene suggests a boatman: J, August 17, 1958.
41. predictions about Vene's novel: J, September 10, 1958; also, HR; Harvey's response on reading Vene's novel: J, September 11, 1958.
42. thinks Vene's writing success may interfere with his writing: J, November 2, 1958.
43. "Johnny" close to "Connie": CR to John Gardner, March 15, 1960.

44. "in case I am unable": J, September 6, 1958.
45. "a great joy to get awake": J, January 25, 1959.
46. contrast of Pine Grove to memories of it: J, March 14, 1954; "burden and sadness of mortality": J, April 11, 1954; "profound bitter sorrow" . . . "rising in air": J, September 4, 1955; "the close association with environs": J, March 24, 1954.
47. "They were all inside of me": J, May 27, 1951.
48. "his hair cruelly thin": WK, 160.
49. "It was the great deception": WK, 161.
50. worries about Vene's book: J, May 9, 1959.
51. reaction to The Human Shore: J, May 14, 1959.
52. letter to Vene about The Human Shore: CR to HR, May 2, 1959.
53. suspicion about Harvey's illness: J, February 18, 1959.
54. admits his relief at Vene's book sales: HR.
55. "There wasn't the slightest envy": J, June 6, 1965.
56. year of publication perhaps a good omen: CR to AK, July 24, 1959.
57. "Rest easy": AK to CR, July 21, 1959.
58. "I just can't see": Erdman Brandt to PRRjr, August 17, 1959.
59. criticizing weakness in The Waters of Kronos: J, December 7, 1960.
60. "dress well and with dignity": CR to HR, September 22, 1959.
61. characters might haunt Richter: CR to HR, December 8, 1960.
62. snapshots taken: J, July 17, 1959.
63. "clear and candid": CR to AK, July 24, 1959.
64. "the spectacle of those around me": J, July 17, 1959.
65. "She had promised him": WK, 176.
66. "about to die": CR to Matthew and Helen Pearce, April 17, 1960; CR to Dayton Kohler, April 17, 1960.
67. "Does my mother love me": J, January 7, 1940.
68. loss of belief in survival: J, June 1, 1959.
69. dream of his mother: J, June 8, 1950.
70. "no reason not to spend": J, January 27, 1960.
71. Knopf merger with Random House an advantage: PRRjr to CR, March 6, 1961.
72. "revelation or confession": J, December 7, 1960; "scrupulously avoid any conscious personal revelation": CR to HR, December 8, 1960.
73. Harvey has bubbly sensation: J, January 20, 1961.
74. invitation to join National Institute of Arts and Letters: Glenway Wescott to CR, January 25, 1961; "It floored me": J, January 30, 1961.
75. "a diploma": J, January 30, 1961.
76. "a little snootier": CR to HR, February 15, 1961.
77. "while I worry": CR to HR, February 4, 1961.
78. Harvey's hospitalization: J, February 1, 5, 7, 8, 13, 1961; CR to H. C. Jernigan, February 2, 1961; CR to HR, February 12 and 15, 1961.
79. "I don't know who": CR to Brooks Brothers, February 26, 1961.
80. National Book Award festivities: J, March 16, 1961.

CHAPTER 13. A COUNTRY OF STRANGERS

1. reaction to photograph and "the country air": CR to AK, March 18, 1961.
2. "Townspeople": CR to AK, March 18, 1961.
3. "had an attack" and "she had some work": CR to Mrs. Doolittle, March 16, 1961.
4. Knopf sells to Random House: New York Times, April 17, 1960, p. 1.

5. Atheneum publicizing Jarrell's book: CR to AK, April 19, 1961.

6. "Something came up": CR to PRRjr, April 1, 1961.

7. absence from dinner: HAR to HR, April 8, 1961.

8. Dinner at Mrs. Yocum's: CR to HR, May 13, 1961.

9. "we had plenty of fights": CR to S. N. King, Jr., January 27, 1961.

10. shows Joseph Richter cemetery plots: J, July 26,1961.

11. Arabic edition of *Tacey Cromwell*: Rita Richter.

12. Richter as seen by inhabitants of Pine Grove: conversations with Margretta Gundel, Lawrence Hoy, Margery Mattox, Rita Richter, William Richter, Richard Wheeler.

13. "Our founding fathers pledged": CR to John F. Kennedy, October 9, 1961.

14. summary of drugs taken for nerves, heart fibrillations: CR to Dr. Emmanuel Richter, June 14, 1964; CR to Dr. Harvey Ewing, August 5, 1964.

15. alarm clock with slow tick: CR to J. I. Rodale, August 8, 1964.

16. "IT JUST DOESN'T GO": J, June 16, 1961.

17. "Erd seemed a little dull" and "So good to come home": J, October 30, 1961.

18. "She is the spark": J, September 16, 1960.

19. Harvey needing encouragement: J, September 15, 1960.

20. "The better H[arvey] is": J, June 16, 1961.

21. "Something must be done": CR to Henry C. Jernigan, February 15, 1962.

22. "imprisoned, trapped": CR to Hawley H. Seiler, January 16, 1962.

23. "Mother frightened me": CR to HR, April 20, 1963.

24. "The mystery of deep blues": J, May 26, 1963.

25. "stark horror": Hattie Chesney to CR, December 2, 1962.

26. "that only the affinities": CR to Hattie Chesney, December 13, 1962.

27. WK sells 298 copies: CR to PRRjr, ca. September 10, 1961.

28. "There is too much to do": CR to Robert Kocher, Coe College, July 5, 1961.

29. letters from scholars: Clifford Edwards to CR, June 19, 1961; Marvin LaHood to CR, June 22, 1961; Edwin Gaston to CR, June 23, 1961.

30. worries about interfering: CR to Clifford Edwards, April 10, 1962.

31. "We found much": CR to Marvin LaHood, November 10, 1963.

32. "They all misunderstand me": J, November 9, 1963.

33. "And if it is possible": *SHM*, 281.

34. "a wry expression": *SHM*, 291.

35. "he groans a little": *SHM*, 310.

36. "to show by contrast": CR to Joyce Tilden, October 11, 1964.

37. Hutchins and Rosenberger reviews: "Books," *New York Herald Tribune*, p. 3.

38. Wagenknecht review: April 22, 1962.

39. "Dad's life was always": J, May 21, 1962.

40. "her old, busy, industrious": J, April 26, 1963.

41. "absolutely delighted": AK to CR, September 25, 1963.

42. "We loved them all": CR to Harding LeMay: September 29, 1963. Richter's worries would be alleviated just after the publication of GR when a member of a family prominently represented in the novel visited and "unabashedly" regaled Harvey and Richter with much racier tales than any he had put in his novel.

43. not writer of facts: J, October 23, 1963.

44. reaction to *The Grandfathers*: J, March 25, 1964.

45. Vene passes orals: J, April 16, 1964; "The whole long painful course": J, April 19, 1964.

46. letter sounding like an Indian speaking: CR to HR, May 7, 1964.

47. purpose of Time-Life introduction: CR to PRRjr, May 22, 1965.

48. "a very personable young fellow": CR to HR, July 13, 1964; impressions of McCullough: J, July 9, 1964.

49. "Your thesis was brilliant": CR to HR, November 14, 1964.

50. Vene's reaction to the passing of the torch: HR; later Vene would change her mind; at the time of Richter's death she and her father were planning "a seminar in psycho-energics."

51. becoming infected by television clichés: CR to HR, March 13, 1965.

52. "Some lines came to me": CR to HR, May 2, 1965.

53. "I Am the Wanderer": CS, 168.

54. David McCullough's visit to Pine Grove: J, May 16, 1965; interview with David McCullough, April 26, 1986.

55. "I found the old strength": J, May 20, 1965.

56. "Not when I'm angry": CR to PRRjr, August 25, 1962.

57. Knopf unable to make better offer: PRRjr to CR, June 11, 1965.

58. "the absolute best": AK to CR, June 11, 1965.

59. "just about the last thing": AK to CR, July 9, 1965.

60. "My irregularities have become very serious": CR to D. Van Dellen, August 19, 1965.

61. "inexpressibly sad": J, March 5, 1965.

62. invitations to speak and be writer-in-residence: HAR to HR, May 21, 1965.

63. Augusta Filbert the last aristocrat: CR to HR, November 4, 1965.

64. honorary degree offer from Temple University: CR to HR, November 4, 1965; declines to offer information to Lebanon Valley College: CR to Frederick Miller, president, Lebanon Valley College, December 11, 1965.

65. "relaxed with the door and windows open": CR to HR, November 30, 1965.

66. "to get books signed": CR to HR, November 30, 1965.

67. "At seventy-five Daddy still must pass": HAR to HR, December 30, 1965.

CHAPTER 14. RIVER TO THE SEA

1. "1966 was the top": CR to Matthew Pearce, December 26, 1966.

2. awakens with title "River to the Sea": J, June 17, 1966.

3. "It came to me": CR to HR, April 19, 1966.

4. recalling episodes brings on suffering: J, June 27, 1966.

5. asks Harvey to hide MS: CR to HR, July 21, 1966.

6. heart problem diagnosed: J, August 3, 1966; this diagnosis was reconfirmed in Glenny's report dated July 10, 1968, which includes a medical history and summary comments: "Patient is extremely anxious regarding his condition," and "he requires a great deal of reassurance and should not delay his yearly examination."

7. "most persistently hot summer": CR to HR, July 27, 1966.

8. description of walks: CR to HR, April 19, 1966.

9. life meaningless without writing: J, August 3, 1966.

10. story of John Brommer: CR to HR, July 16, 1966.

11. purpose of Rogers's review: William G. Rogers to CR, August 10, 1966.

12. "a masterpiece which will be read": *New York Times*, October 26, 1966; "a great novel in any literature": *Life*, September 30, 1966, 17.

13. "Poor day, but what else": J, November 30, 1966.

14. description of house in Bradenton: CR to HR, December 30, 1966.

15. first description of "The Death of the Aristocrat": CR to HR, January 19, 1967; description of Vene's room: CR to HR, January 2, 1967.

16. Augusta the last of the Victorians: CR remark to Mary Filbert, following Augusta Filbert's funeral: interview with Mary and Stuart Filbert, September 18, 1992.

17. "Harvey felt that we shouldn't": CR to PRRjr, April 14, 1967.

18. restrictions due to health: especially J, June 21, 1967.

19. walks by Aunt Lizzie's house: J, July 12, 1967; Richter was born in the front bedroom of the smaller half of double house: CR to HR, October 25, 1964.

20. "less shy but enough": CR to HR, May 30, 1967.

21. "You better get a draft": J, July 13, 1967.

22. visit to Martha's Vineyard: J, September 20, 1967; "Just tell him it's a friend": interview with David and Rosalee McCullough, April 26, 1986.

23. description of Billy and Karen Richter: J, October 15, 1967.

24. one hundred Halloween visitors: CR to HR, November 1, 1967; "Let's go back to that rich man's house": CR to HR, November 19, 1967.

25. Knopf urges to meet new staff: AK to CR, November 20, 1967.

26. will not meet producer: CR to PRRjr, November 28, 1967.

27. "One is never free": J, October 21, 1967.

28. "You ask about our Thanksgiving": CR to HR, December 5, 1967.

29. "it is a comfort to know": HAR to HR, postscript to CR to HR, January 2, 1968.

30. reading Vene's letter in post office parking lot: CR to HR, February 22, 1968.

31. "Evil Easter": J, April 14, 1968.

32. recommends David McCullough: CR to PRRjr, July 14, 1968.

33. asks help for Harry Roskolenko: CR to Glenway Wescott, June 21, 1968.

34. Diane Richter's wedding: J, August 18, 1968. Also, a revision dated September 5, 1968.

35. motives in telephoning Vene: HR.

36. Vene requests a seminar: HR.

37. "to subside into death": J, December 20, 1963.

38. packing box placed inside grave: interview with Lawrence Hoy, June 9, 1997; HR.

Index

Peter Burke, *The Fortunes of the* Courtier: *The European Reception of Castiglione's Cortegiano*

James M. Hutchisson, *The Rise of Sinclair Lewis, 1920–1930*

Julie Bates Dock, ed., *Charlotte Perkins Gilman's "The Yellow Wall-paper" and the History of Its Publication and Reception: A Critical Edition and Documentary Casebook*

John Williams, ed., *Imaging the Early Medieval Bible*

James G. Nelson, *Publisher to the Decadents: Leonard Smithers in the Careers of Beardsley, Wilde, Dowson*

Ezra Greenspan, *George Palmer Putnam: Representative American Publisher*

Pamela Selwyn, *Everyday Life in the German Book Trade: Friedrich Nicolai as Bookseller and Publisher in the Age of Enlightenment*

David R. Johnson, *Conrad Richter: A Writer's Life*

PENN STATE REPRINTS IN BOOK HISTORY
James L. W. West III and Samuel S. Vaughan, Editors

Roger Burlingame, *Of Making Many Books: A Hundred Years of Reading, Writing, and Publishing*